Ultimate Splunk for Cybersecurity

Practical Strategies for SIEM Using Splunk's Enterprise Security (ES) for Threat Detection, Forensic Investigation, and Cloud Security

Jit Sinha

www.orangeava.com

First published: January 2024

Published by: Orange Education Pvt Ltd, AVA™

Address: 9, Daryaganj, Delhi, 110002

ISBN: 978-81-96815-02-8

www.orangeava.com

Dedicated To

My son, Caesar Sinha,

My mother, Smriti Das Sinha,

My aunt, Dipa Das,

And my wife, Saptapadi Sen Sinha

whose love, guidance, and support have shaped my journey and inspired every page

About the Author

Jit is a distinguished IT professional with an impressive 12 years of experience in the technology sector. He is currently serving in a leading multinational IT company. His expertise as a certified Solution Architect in renowned platforms like Splunk, AWS, Azure, and Google Cloud has positioned him as an authority in designing and implementing advanced IT solutions for clients across various industries, including banking, telecommunications, and healthcare.

His deep involvement in these sectors has provided him with a rich understanding of diverse business needs. Within the banking industry, Jit has developed security-centric solutions adhering to rigorous compliance standards. His contributions to the telecommunications sector have centered on establishing scalable and resilient IT infrastructures vital for robust communication networks. In healthcare, his emphasis has been on safeguarding sensitive data while enhancing the efficiency of IT systems.

His professional journey is marked by a strong passion for cybersecurity and data analytics. Recognized as an expert in utilizing Splunk for security operations and threat detection, he has significantly contributed to enhancing cybersecurity measures in complex IT environments. His recent foray into the realm of generative AI reflects his commitment to staying at the forefront of technological advancements. By exploring generative AI applications in cybersecurity and data analysis, Jit is pioneering in integrating cutting-edge technology with traditional IT practices to offer innovative solutions.

His interests extend beyond technical prowess to mythology, geopolitics, and storytelling. His storytelling skills, in particular, enable him to communicate complex concepts in an engaging and understandable way, adding a unique flair to his professional and training endeavors.

Jit's passion for knowledge extends beyond his work. He is an avid participant in training programs, workshops, and public speaking engagements. As a Udemy trainer, Jit recently developed a course on generative AI, sharing his insights and expertise on this groundbreaking technology. This course reflects his dedication to educating others and staying at the forefront of technological advancements. His ability to demystify complex technical concepts and present them in an accessible manner has made him a sought-after speaker and trainer. Through these platforms, he shares his insights and experiences, contributing to the growth and development of professionals in the IT industry.

About the Technical Reviewer

Aditya Mukherjee is a Global Information Security Leader with over 15 years of industry experience in spearheading security, technology, and business transformation initiatives across diverse environments. His expertise includes design, strategy planning, road mapping, and implementation. Aditya has consistently pioneered operational streamlining and service creation to enhance delivery and adhere to regulatory requirements. Additionally, he possesses deep consulting experience in briefing boards and risk committees about the organization's cybersecurity posture, maturity, and roadmap.

Aditya holds various cybersecurity certifications, such as SANS, C|CISO, CRISC, and CISM, and has been a Member of the NCDRC Technical Committee. He has also published three books on InfoSec and has been featured in over 20 articles in leading publications. Aditya has actively contributed to course content design for EC|Council Code Red and C|CISO, and has reviewed several books for Packt Publishing and Peerlyst.

Aditya has spoken at over 200 speaking engagements and has numerous prestigious industry awards to his name, including being featured in Forbes - India's 50 Best Technology Leaders, India's Best CXOs and Leaders at WhitePage Leadership Conclave, and Business Leadership Award at the Indian Achievers' Award.

Acknowledgements

As I pen down the final words of this book, I am filled with immense gratitude towards those who have been instrumental in its creation.

First and foremost, I extend my heartfelt thanks to my family, who played a pivotal role in the creation of this book. To my son, Caesar Sinha, born just a year ago as I embarked on this journey, his arrival not only marked the beginning of a new life but also the commencement of this literary endeavor. His youthful curiosity and joy have been a constant source of inspiration. To my mother, Smriti Das Sinha, for her mental fortitude and the values she instilled in me, guiding my path through challenging and uncertain times. Special gratitude goes to my Aunt, Dipa Das, for her unwavering support and wise counsel, offering a steadfast presence throughout this process. Lastly, my wife, Saptapadi Sen Sinha, whose endless encouragement has been a sustaining force throughout this journey.

I am deeply grateful to one of my colleagues and mentors in the industry, whose insights and experiences have enriched the content of this book. Their willingness to share knowledge and provide feedback has been invaluable.

Special thanks go to the Orange AVA team, whose dedication and hard work behind the scenes have been crucial in bringing this project to fruition. Their commitment to excellence has been a driving force throughout this journey.

I would also like to acknowledge the contributions of the editorial and publishing team. Their expertise and attention to detail have been instrumental in refining and polishing this work to its final form.

To the readers and the broader community of cybersecurity enthusiasts and professionals, your eagerness to learn and evolve continues to inspire authors like myself to share knowledge and experiences. This book is a product of our shared commitment to advancing the field of cybersecurity.

Finally, I extend my gratitude to anyone who has directly or indirectly influenced the creation of this book. Your collective wisdom and support have served as a guiding light.

Thank you all for being a part of this journey.

Preface

In the rapidly evolving world of digital security, "*Mastering Splunk for Cybersecurity*" serves as a comprehensive guide, bridging the gap between theoretical knowledge and the practical applications of Splunk in the field of cybersecurity.

Chapter 1: *Introduction to Splunk and Cybersecurity* sets the stage for our exploration, outlining the importance of Splunk as a tool in the cybersecurity landscape and its relevance in the current digital era.

Chapter 2: *Overview of Splunk Architecture* delves into the structural aspects of Splunk, providing a detailed understanding of its framework and components, essential for grasping its full potential.

Chapter 3: *Configuring Inputs and Data Sources* focuses on the initial steps necessary for integrating various data sources into Splunk, a fundamental process for effective data analysis.

Chapter 4: *Data Ingestion and Normalization* discusses the techniques and importance of processing and standardizing data within Splunk to ensure accuracy and relevance in security analysis.

Chapter 5: *Understanding* SIEM explores the concept of Security Information and Event Management, emphasizing its critical role in modern cybersecurity strategies and how Splunk enhances these systems.

Chapter 6: *Splunk Enterprise Security* (ES) introduces readers to Splunk's dedicated security platform, highlighting its capabilities in enhancing organizational cybersecurity measures.

Chapter 7: *Security Intelligence* covers the strategic use of Splunk in gathering and analyzing security intelligence to proactively identify and mitigate potential threats.

Chapter 8: *Forensic Investigation of Security Domains* examines how Splunk can be utilized for in-depth forensic analysis, aiding in investigating and understanding security incidents.

Chapter 9: *Splunk Integration with Other Security Tools* emphasizes the importance of integrating Splunk with a variety of other security tools, enhancing its functionality and scope in cybersecurity ecosystems.

Chapter 10: *Splunk for Compliance and Regulatory Requirements* discusses how Splunk aids organizations in adhering to compliance standards and managing regulatory challenges, a critical aspect in the current security landscape.

Chapter 11: *Security Orchestration, Automation, and Response* (SOAR) *with Splunk* highlights the role of Splunk in automating and streamlining security operations, enhancing the efficiency and effectiveness of response strategies.

Chapter 12: *Cloud Security with Splunk* addresses the unique challenges of securing cloud-based environments and how Splunk can be effectively leveraged in these scenarios.

Chapter 13: *DevOps and Security Operations* explores the integration of Splunk within the DevOps framework, demonstrating its impact on aligning security operations with software development processes.

Chapter 14: *Best Practices for Splunk in Cybersecurity* shares expert tips and practices to maximize the effectiveness and efficiency of using Splunk in cybersecurity applications.

Chapter 15: *Conclusion and Summary* concludes the book by summarizing the key insights and contemplating the future role of Splunk in the ever-changing world of cybersecurity.

This book is designed as a thorough guide for anyone looking to harness the power of Splunk in their cybersecurity endeavors, whether you are just beginning your journey or seeking to deepen your existing expertise.

Get a Free eBook

We hope you are enjoying your recently purchased book! Your feedback is incredibly valuable to us, and to all other readers looking for great books.

If you found this book helpful or enjoyable, we would truly appreciate it, if you could take a moment to leave a short review with a 5 star rating on Amazon. It helps us grow, and lets other readers discover our books.

As a thank you, we would love to send you a free digital copy of this book, and a **30%** discount code on your next cart value on our official websites:

www.orangeava.com

www.orangeava.in (For Indian Subcontinent)

☑ **Here's how:**

Leave a review for the book on Amazon.

Take a screenshot of your review, and send an email to **info@orangeava.com** (it can be just the confirmation screen).

Once, we receive your screenshot, we will send you the digital file, within 24 hours.

Thank you so much for your support – it means a lot to us!

Downloading the code bundles and colored images

Please follow the links or scan the QR codes to download the
Code Bundles and Images of the book:

https://github.com/ava-orange-education/Ultimate-Splunk-for-Cybersecurity

The code bundles and images of the book are also hosted on
https://rebrand.ly/2fadf7

In case there's an update to the code, it will be updated on the existing GitHub repository.

Errata

We take immense pride in our work at **Orange Education Pvt Ltd,** and follow best practices to ensure the accuracy of our content to provide an indulging reading experience to our subscribers. Our readers are our mirrors, and we use their inputs to reflect and improve upon human errors, if any, that may have occurred during the publishing processes involved. To let us maintain the quality and help us reach out to any readers who might be having difficulties due to any unforeseen errors, please write to us at :

errata@orangeava.com

Your support, suggestions, and feedback are highly appreciated.

DID YOU KNOW

Did you know that Orange Education Pvt Ltd offers eBook versions of every book published, with PDF and ePub files available? You can upgrade to the eBook version at **www.orangeava.com** and as a print book customer, you are entitled to a discount on the eBook copy. Get in touch with us at: **info@orangeava.com** for more details.

At **www.orangeava.com**, you can also read a collection of free technical articles, sign up for a range of free newsletters, and receive exclusive discounts and offers on AVA™ Books and eBooks.

PIRACY

If you come across any illegal copies of our works in any form on the internet, we would be grateful if you would provide us with the location address or website name. Please contact us at **info@orangeava.com** with a link to the material.

ARE YOU INTERESTED IN AUTHORING WITH US?

If there is a topic that you have expertise in, and you are interested in either writing or contributing to a book, please write to us at **business@orangeava.com**. We are on a journey to help developers and tech professionals to gain insights on the present technological advancements and innovations happening across the globe and build a community that believes Knowledge is best acquired by sharing and learning with others. Please reach out to us to learn what our audience demands and how you can be part of this educational reform. We also welcome ideas from tech experts and help them build learning and development content for their domains.

REVIEWS

Please leave a review. Once you have read and used this book, why not leave a review on the site that you purchased it from? Potential readers can then see and use your unbiased opinion to make purchase decisions. We at Orange Education would love to know what you think about our products, and our authors can learn from your feedback. Thank you!

For more information about Orange Education, please visit **www.orangeava.com**.

Table of Contents

CHAPTER 1

Introduction to Splunk and Cybersecurity

Introduction

This chapter provides readers with a foundational understanding of Splunk and its role in cybersecurity. It begins with an overview of Splunk and its capabilities, highlighting its ability to collect, analyze, and act on large volumes of data from various sources. It also introduces the concept of cybersecurity and the diverse types of cyber threats that organizations face.

The chapter explains how Splunk can help organizations address these threats through threat detection, incident response, and compliance. Additionally, the chapter discusses Splunk's search and analytics capabilities, real-time alerting, and compliance features.

Overall, by the end of this chapter, readers will have a solid understanding of Splunk and its potential applications in cybersecurity.

Structure

In this chapter, we will cover the following topics:

- Overview of Splunk
  - Defining Splunk
  - Splunk Ecosystem

- Search and Analytics
  - Search Capabilities
  - Visualization
- Real-time Alerting
  - Advanced Features
- Introduction to Cybersecurity
  - Types of cyber threats
  - Common cybersecurity frameworks and methodologies
  - Importance of cybersecurity in today's digital world
- Role of Splunk in Cybersecurity
  - Log management and event correlation with Splunk
  - Accelerating incident response and investigation
- Use Cases for Splunk in Cybersecurity
- Points to Remember

Overview of Splunk

This section provides an introduction to the software platform, including its capabilities and use cases. It also explores the Splunk ecosystem, including its apps, add-ons, and partners.

Defining Splunk

Splunk is a powerful platform for searching, analyzing, and visualizing large amounts of machine-generated data. Founded in 2003, Splunk has grown to become an industry leader in providing software solutions for organizations to gain valuable insights and operational intelligence from their data. This helps businesses across various industries make informed decisions and optimize their operations.

Machine-generated data refers to any digital information generated by devices, applications, or systems. This includes log files, sensor data, application performance monitoring (APM) data, and many more. Since organizations continue to rely heavily on digital systems, the volume of machine-generated data increases exponentially. Traditional data management and analysis tools often struggle to keep up with this data growth, leading to a need for specialized solutions like Splunk.

At its core, Splunk is a data-to-everything platform that enables users to collect, index, search, analyze, and visualize data in real-time. It provides a versatile and user-friendly interface for querying and exploring data, making it accessible even to users with less technical exposure. Splunk's flexibility allows it to ingest a wide variety of data formats, making it suitable for organizations with diverse data sources.

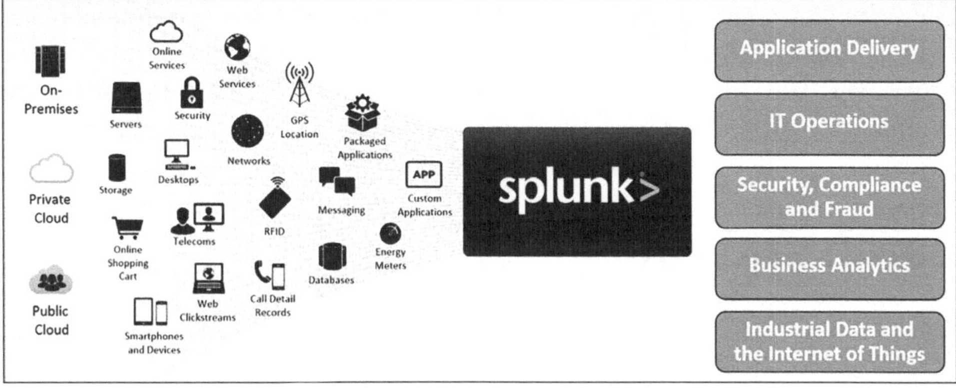

***Figure 1.1**: Overview of Splunk*

Splunk Ecosystem

Splunk supports a rich ecosystem of apps and add-ons, which extend its functionality and integrate with other tools and platforms. This makes it easy for organizations to adapt Splunk to their specific needs and customize it for their unique use cases. Some popular apps and add-ons include:

- **Splunk App for Enterprise Security:** This app provides a comprehensive security information and event management (SIEM) solution, with pre-built dashboards, visualizations, and searches for detecting and responding to security threats.
- **Splunk App for AWS:** This app helps organizations monitor and manage their Amazon Web Services (AWS) infrastructure, providing insights into usage patterns, cost optimization, and security.
- **Splunk Add-on for Microsoft Office 365:** This add-on enables organizations to monitor and analyze their Office 365 environment, tracking user activity, security events, and performance metrics.

In addition to its robust functionality, Splunk has a strong community of users and developers who contribute to its ongoing development and share knowledge and resources. The Splunk community organizes events such as Splunk.conf and Splunk Live!, where users can learn about the latest features, best practices, and use cases. Additionally, numerous online forums, blogs, and resources are available to help users get the most out of their Splunk deployment.

In summary, Splunk is a versatile and powerful platform that provides organizations with a comprehensive solution for managing and analyzing their machine-generated data. Its ability to ingest, process, and visualize large volumes of data in real-time, combined with its rich ecosystem of apps and add-ons, makes it an indispensable tool for businesses seeking valuable insights and maintaining a strong security posture. By leveraging the capabilities of Splunk, organizations can make informed decisions, optimize operations, and provide better protection to their digital assets against the ever-evolving threat landscape.

Search and Analytics

Search and Analytics encompass advanced search capabilities for efficient data retrieval and visualizations for insightful data representation, enabling users to make data-driven decisions.

Search Capabilities

One of the most powerful features of Splunk is its search and analytics capabilities, which provide users with the ability to quickly and effectively explore, analyze, and visualize large volumes of machine-generated data. The platform's search processing language (SPL) allows users to create complex queries that can be used to filter, transform, and aggregate data, enabling organizations to gain actionable insights into their operational and security environments.

Splunk's search functionality is designed to manage large-scale data processing, capable of ingesting and indexing millions of events per second. This makes it an ideal solution for organizations with extensive data streams that need to be monitored, analyzed, and visualized in real-time. Splunk's search engine can be used to perform a wide range of tasks, including:

- **Filtering and transforming data**: Users can create SPL queries that filter out irrelevant data, extract useful information, and transform data into a more manageable format for analysis.
- **Aggregating data**: Splunk's search capabilities can be used to aggregate data by various criteria, such as time, source, or specific field values, making it easier to identify trends and patterns in the data.

- **Statistical analysis**: Splunk's SPL includes statistical functions that can be used to perform calculations and generate statistical summaries of the data, such as averages, sums, and counts.
- **Machine learning and advanced analytics**: Splunk's analytics capabilities can be extended with the Machine Learning Toolkit, which provides a range of pre-built machine learning algorithms and custom functions for advanced data analysis.

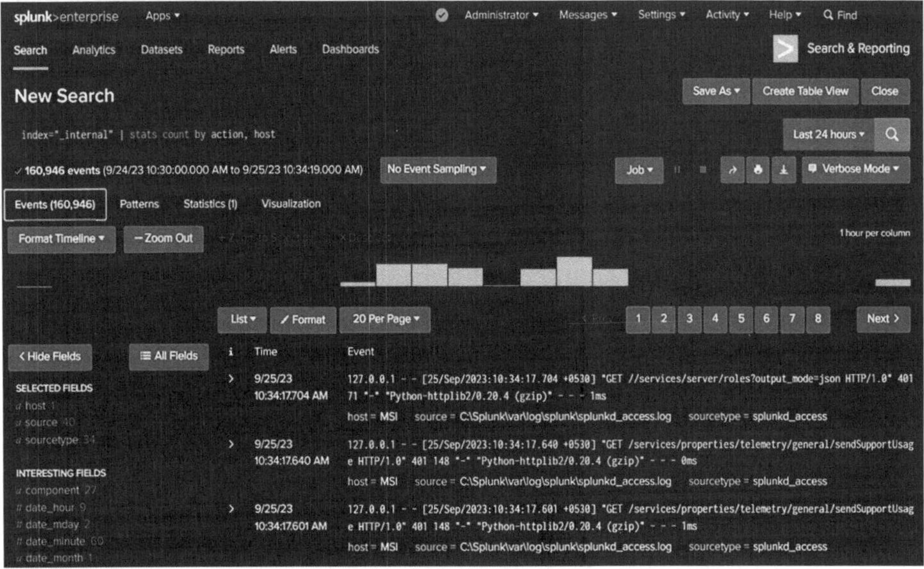

***Figure 1.2**: Splunk Search*

Visualizations

Splunk's analytics capabilities are not limited to search queries; the platform also includes a wide range of visualization tools that can be used to create custom dashboards and reports. These visualizations can help organizations better understand their data by presenting it in a more accessible and understandable format. Some of the most popular visualization types in Splunk include:

- **Time series charts:** These charts display data over time, making it easy to identify trends and patterns in the data.
- **Bar charts and column charts:** These visualizations are useful for comparing data across different categories or groups.
- **Pie charts**: Pie charts are an effective way to visualize the distribution of data across various categories.

- **Maps and geospatial visualizations:** Splunk can integrate with geospatial data to create interactive maps and other location-based visualizations.
- **Custom visualizations:** Users can create their custom visualizations using Splunk's built-in visualization editor or by leveraging third-party visualization libraries.

These visualizations can be combined and arranged on custom dashboards, providing users with a comprehensive, at-a-glance view of their data. Dashboards can be shared easily with other team members, enabling collaboration, and promoting data-driven decision-making across the organization.

In conclusion, Splunk's search and analytics capabilities are a powerful and versatile tool for organizations seeking insights into their data and aiming to make data-driven decisions. With its powerful search processing language, advanced analytics features, and robust visualization tools, Splunk provides users with the ability to explore, analyze, and visualize their data in ways that were previously unimaginable. In the context of cybersecurity, these capabilities are particularly valuable, enabling organizations to proactively detect and respond to potential threats, streamline incident investigations, and maintain a strong security posture.

Real-time Alerting

Real-time alerting is a key feature of Splunk that allows organizations to proactively monitor their environment for potential threats, anomalies, and critical events. By leveraging Splunk's powerful search and analytics capabilities, users can create alerts based on specific criteria or patterns in the data, ensuring that relevant stakeholders are notified immediately when an important event occurs.

Splunk's real-time alerting functionality is built on its powerful search processing language (SPL) and can be configured to monitor various types of data, including log files, network traffic, application performance metrics, and security events. This flexibility makes it an ideal solution for organizations looking to stay ahead of potential issues and respond quickly to incidents.

Creating alerts in Splunk involves defining a search query and specifying alert conditions, such as the frequency of the event or the presence of specific keywords or values. Users can also configure alert settings, including the triggering mechanism (for example, real-time or scheduled), alert severity (for example, low, medium, or high), and notification method (for example, email, SMS, or custom webhook).

Advanced Features

In addition to basic alert configuration, Splunk offers several advanced features that enhance its real-time alerting capabilities, as follows:

- **Throttling**: This feature allows users to control the frequency of alerts by setting a minimum time interval between alert notifications. This can help prevent alert fatigue by ensuring that stakeholders are not overwhelmed with notifications for the same issue.
- **Alert suppression**: Users can configure alerts to be temporarily suppressed during specific time windows or under certain conditions. This is useful for avoiding false positives and reducing the number of irrelevant alerts.
- **Correlation searches**: Splunk's Enterprise Security (ES) application offers a more sophisticated approach to real-time alerting through the use of correlation searches. These searches are designed to identify complex patterns and relationships in the data, enabling users to detect multi-stage attacks and other advanced threats.
- **Adaptive Response Framework**: The Adaptive Response Framework (ARF) in Splunk Enterprise Security enables users to automate and streamline their response to alerts. With ARF, users can configure automated actions, such as blocking an IP address or disabling a user account, to be triggered when specific alert conditions are met.

In conclusion, real-time alerting with Splunk is a powerful tool for organizations looking to proactively monitor and respond to critical events and potential threats in their environment. By leveraging Splunk's powerful search and analytics capabilities, users can create alerts based on specific criteria or patterns in the data, ensuring that relevant stakeholders are notified immediately when an important event occurs. In the context of cybersecurity, this functionality is essential for enabling organizations to detect and respond to potential threats in a timely and effective manner.

Introducing Cybersecurity

This section highlights the critical role of cybersecurity in the digital era, explores various cyber threats, and presents common frameworks and methodologies for safeguarding digital assets and maintaining a secure online environment.

Importance of cybersecurity in today's digital world

Cybersecurity is the practice of protecting digital assets, including computers, servers, networks, and data, from unauthorized access, theft, damage, or disruption. As the world becomes increasingly connected and reliant on digital systems, the importance of effective cybersecurity measures cannot be overstated. In this digital age, organizations of all sizes and industries face a wide range of cyber threats, which can result in significant financial losses, reputational damage, and even physical harm.

One of the primary reasons cybersecurity has become a pressing concern is the rapid growth of the internet and the proliferation of connected devices. The number of internet users has increased exponentially in the past two decades, and the Internet of Things (IoT) has introduced billions of additional devices to the digital landscape. This growth has created a vast attack surface for cybercriminals, making the protection of digital assets more challenging than ever (see *Figure* 1.3).

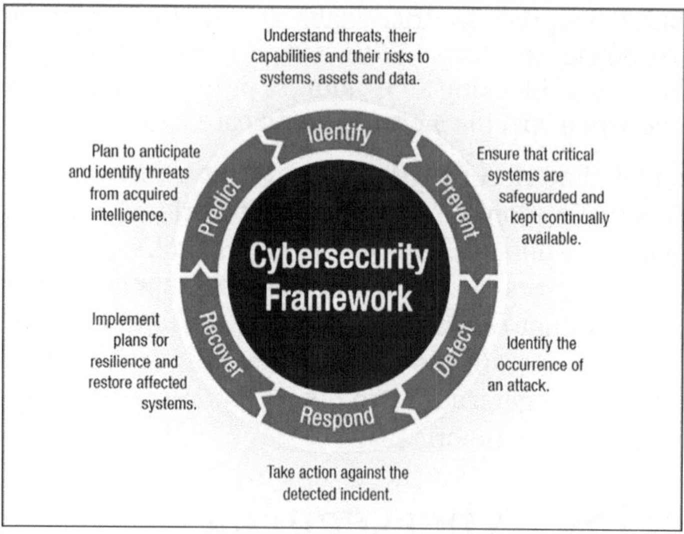

Figure 1.3: *Introduction to Cybersecurity*

Types of cyber threats

Cyber threats come in various forms, and understanding the diverse types of attacks is essential for developing effective defense strategies. Some common types of cyber threats include:

- **Malware**: Malicious software designed to infiltrate or damage computer systems. Examples include viruses, worms, ransomware, and Trojans.
- **Phishing**: A type of social engineering attack where cybercriminals attempt to trick users into revealing sensitive information, such as login credentials or financial data, by posing as a trustworthy entity.
- **Distributed Denial of Service (DDoS) attacks**: A form of attack where multiple systems are used to overwhelm a targeted system, causing it to crash or become unavailable to users.
- **Insider threats**: Attacks perpetrated by individuals within an organization who have authorized access to sensitive data or systems.

To protect against these and other cyber threats, organizations need to adopt a comprehensive, multi-layered approach to cybersecurity. This typically involves implementing a combination of technical, administrative, and physical controls designed to prevent, detect, and respond to potential cyber-attacks. Some key elements of a robust cybersecurity strategy include:

- **Risk assessment**: Identifying and prioritizing potential threats, vulnerabilities, and risks to an organization's digital assets. This process helps organizations allocate resources effectively and focus on the most critical areas of concern.
- **Access control**: Implementing policies and mechanisms to restrict unauthorized access to sensitive data and systems. This may include user authentication, role-based access control, and network segmentation.
- **Encryption**: Protecting the confidentiality of sensitive data by converting it into an unreadable format that can only be decrypted by authorized users with the appropriate key.
- **Intrusion detection and prevention systems (IDPS):** Monitoring network traffic for signs of malicious activity and automatically blocking or alerting security teams to potential threats.
- **Security awareness training**: Educating employees on cybersecurity best practices, common threats, and their role in protecting the organization's digital assets.
- **Incident response planning**: Developing and maintaining a formal process for identifying, containing, and recovering from security incidents.

Common cybersecurity frameworks and methodologies

In addition to adhering to established frameworks and standards, organizations must also comply with various cybersecurity regulations and laws that govern data protection and privacy. These regulations differ across countries and industries but generally aim to ensure the confidentiality, integrity, and availability of sensitive data. Some notable cybersecurity regulations include:

- **General Data Protection Regulation (GDPR):** A comprehensive data protection law that applies to all organizations operating within the European Union (EU) or processing the personal data of EU residents. GDPR mandates strict data protection measures and grants individuals greater control over their data.
- **Health Insurance Portability and Accountability Act (HIPAA):** A US law that establishes privacy and security standards for the protection of health-related information. Organizations in the healthcare industry must comply with HIPAA to safeguard the privacy of patient data.
- **California Consumer Privacy Act (CCPA):** A state-level data privacy law in the United States that grants California residents specific rights regarding their personal information, such as the right to know what data is collected and the right to request deletion of their data.

Organizations can also turn to various cybersecurity technologies and tools to bolster their defenses against cyber threats. Some of these technologies include:

- **Endpoint protection platforms (EPP):** Comprehensive security solutions that protect endpoints, such as laptops, desktops, and mobile devices, from several types of malwares, exploits, and other cyber threats.
- **Security information and event management (SIEM) systems**: Tools that collect, analyze, and correlate security event data from multiple sources to identify and respond to potential security incidents in real-time.
- **Firewalls**: Network security devices that monitor incoming and outgoing network traffic and permit or block data packets based on a set of predefined security rules.
- **Virtual private networks (VPNs):** Secure communication channels that encrypt data transmitted between a user's device and a private network, ensuring confidentiality and integrity of the data.

In conclusion, cybersecurity is an essential aspect of modern business operations, given the increasing reliance on digital systems and the ever-evolving threat landscape. By understanding several types of cyber threats and implementing a multi-layered approach to cybersecurity, organizations can better protect their digital assets and minimize the risk of cyber-attacks. Adherence to industry standards, regulatory compliance, and the use of cutting-edge cybersecurity technologies, all contribute to building a robust cybersecurity posture, ensuring the safety and resilience of an organization's digital infrastructure.

Role of Splunk in Cybersecurity

Splunk plays a vital role in the cybersecurity landscape by providing organizations with the tools and capabilities necessary to monitor, detect, and respond to potential threats in real-time (see *Figure* 1.4).

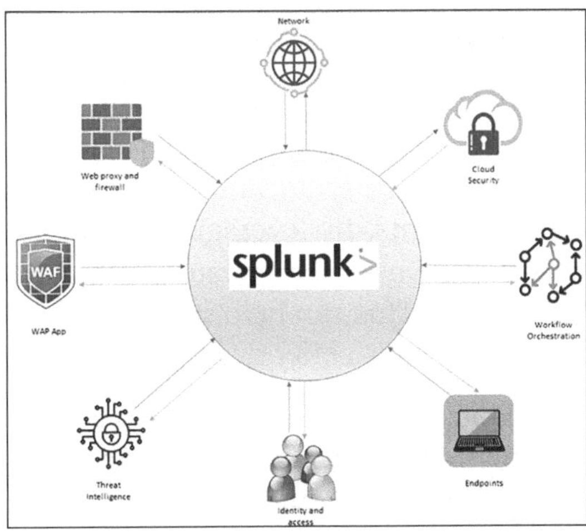

Figure 1.4: *Role of Splunk in Cybersecurity*

Now, let's explain how Splunk helps organizations detect, analyze, and respond to threats

As a data-to-everything platform, Splunk specializes in collecting, analyzing, and visualizing machine-generated data, which is invaluable for organizations seeking to identify and mitigate cybersecurity risks. This data may include log files, network traffic, application performance metrics, and many more. By leveraging the power of Splunk, security teams can gain actionable insights into their security posture and make data-driven decisions to protect their digital assets.

Log management and event correlation with Splunk

One of the primary functions of Splunk in cybersecurity is log management and analysis. Log files generated by various devices, applications, and systems contain a wealth of information that can help security teams identify potential threats, investigate incidents, and uncover patterns indicative of malicious activity. Splunk can ingest and process large volumes of log data, making it easy for security analysts to search, filter, and analyze this information to detect anomalies and potential security incidents.

In addition to log management, Splunk also excels in the domain of security information and event management (SIEM). SIEM systems collect and analyze security event data from multiple sources. It then correlates events to identify potential threats and provide real-time alerts to security teams. Splunk's Enterprise Security (ES) application is a comprehensive SIEM solution that delivers pre-built dashboards, visualizations, and correlation searches for detecting and responding to security threats.

Another crucial aspect of Splunk's role in cybersecurity is its ability to support advanced analytics and machine learning techniques. These capabilities allow organizations to proactively identify and mitigate potential risks before they escalate into significant incidents. By leveraging machine learning algorithms, Splunk can analyze vast amounts of data and detect patterns that may be indicative of malicious activity. This can help security teams uncover previously unknown threats and respond more effectively to evolving attack vectors.

Splunk's flexibility and adaptability make it an ideal platform for integrating with other security tools and platforms. This enables organizations to create a unified security ecosystem, where data from multiple sources can be ingested, analyzed, and correlated to provide a comprehensive view of the security landscape. Some popular integrations include:

- **Network security tools:** Splunk can integrate with firewalls, intrusion detection and prevention systems (IDPS), and other network security devices to monitor and analyze network traffic for signs of malicious activity.
- **Endpoint security solutions:** By integrating with endpoint protection platforms (EPP) and other endpoint security tools, Splunk can help organizations detect and respond to threats targeting their devices and systems.
- **Threat intelligence feeds:** Splunk can ingest data from external threat intelligence sources, allowing organizations to enhance their threat detection and response capabilities with up-to-date information on emerging threats and attack indicators.

Accelerating incident response and investigation

Beyond its core functionality, Splunk also supports Security Orchestration, Automation, and Response (SOAR) capabilities, which streamline and automate various aspects of the security incident response process. By integrating with

SOAR platforms or leveraging built-in automation features, organizations can improve their response times, reduce manual workloads, and minimize the risk of human error in the incident response process.

Some of the ways Splunk contributes to SOAR include:

- **Automated threat detection and response**: Splunk can automatically trigger alerts or initiate predefined response actions when specific threat indicators or patterns are detected, reducing the time it takes to respond to potential security incidents.
- **Workflow automation**: Splunk can automate various security processes and workflows, such as creating tickets for security incidents, updating threat intelligence feeds, or initiating vulnerability scans, to improve efficiency and reduce manual workloads.
- **Incident management and collaboration**: Splunk can serve as a central hub for incident management, providing security teams with a unified view of all relevant information and facilitating collaboration among team members. This enables organizations to streamline their incident response process and ensure that all necessary steps are taken to contain, investigate, and remediate potential threats.

Splunk's capabilities also extend to cloud security, making it an invaluable tool for organizations with cloud-based infrastructure and services. By integrating with various cloud service providers and platforms, Splunk can help organizations monitor and manage their cloud environments, providing insights into usage patterns, cost optimization, and security.

In conclusion, Splunk plays a critical role in modern cybersecurity by providing organizations with the tools and capabilities necessary to monitor, detect, and respond to potential threats in real-time. Its ability to ingest, process, and visualize large volumes of machine-generated data, combined with its robust ecosystem of apps and integrations, makes it an indispensable tool for organizations looking to strengthen their cybersecurity posture. By leveraging the capabilities of Splunk, security teams can gain actionable insights into their security environment and take initiative-taking measures to protect their digital assets.

Use Cases for Splunk in Cybersecurity

Splunk's powerful data processing, search, and analytics capabilities make it an ideal platform for organizations looking to strengthen their cybersecurity posture. By ingesting and analyzing data from various sources, Splunk can provide valuable insights into an organization's security environment and enable proactive threat detection and response. In this section, we will discuss some common use cases for Splunk in cybersecurity.

Threat Hunting

Threat hunting is the process of proactively searching for potential threats and malicious activity within an organization's network, rather than waiting for alerts to be triggered. Splunk can be used to facilitate threat hunting by enabling security analysts to search through vast amounts of data and identify potential indicators of compromise (IOCs) or anomalous behavior. By leveraging Splunk's powerful search and analytics capabilities, security teams can quickly sift through large volumes of log data, network traffic, and other security events to identify potential threats and initiate a response.

Incident Investigation and Response

When a security incident occurs, it is essential for organizations to quickly determine the root cause, scope, and impact of the event to respond effectively. Splunk can play a critical role in this process by providing a centralized platform for gathering and analyzing data related to the incident. Security analysts can use Splunk's search capabilities to query and filter data from various sources, enabling them to identify the affected systems, users, and data, as well as the attacker's tactics, techniques, and procedures (TTPs). Splunk's visualization and dashboard features can also be used to create custom incident response workflows, streamlining the investigation process and facilitating collaboration among team members.

Anomaly Detection and Behavior Analytics

Splunk's advanced analytics capabilities, including the Machine Learning Toolkit, can be used to build models that detect unusual patterns or deviations from normal behavior, which may indicate potential security threats. For example, organizations can use Splunk to monitor user behavior and identify anomalies, such as unusual login times, failed login attempts, or unexpected file access patterns. By leveraging machine learning algorithms and statistical models, security teams can quickly identify and respond to potential insider threats or compromised accounts.

Network Security Monitoring

Splunk can be used to ingest and analyze network traffic data, providing organizations with valuable insights into the security of their network environment. By monitoring network traffic for unusual patterns, suspicious activity, or known IOCs, security teams can proactively detect and respond to potential threats, such as malware infections, data exfiltration, or distributed denial of service (DDoS) attacks. Splunk's integration with network security tools, such as intrusion detection systems (IDS) and firewalls, further enhances its capabilities in this area.

Vulnerability Management and Risk Assessment

Organizations can use Splunk to monitor and manage their vulnerability data, helping to identify and prioritize risks in their environment. By ingesting data from vulnerability scanners, asset management systems, and other security tools, Splunk can provide a comprehensive view of an organization's risk landscape. Security teams can use Splunk's search and analytics capabilities to identify high-risk vulnerabilities, track remediation efforts, and monitor the effectiveness of their vulnerability management program.

Compliance Monitoring and Reporting

Splunk's powerful search and analytics features can be used to generate compliance reports, helping organizations demonstrate adherence to various regulatory requirements and standards, such as the General Data Protection Regulation (GDPR), the Health Insurance Portability and Accountability Act (HIPAA), or the Payment Card Industry Data Security Standard (PCI DSS). By creating searches and visualizations that highlight key compliance metrics, organizations can easily monitor and maintain their compliance posture.

Security Orchestration, Automation, and Response (SOAR)

Splunk's integration with security orchestration, automation, and response (SOAR) platforms enables organizations to streamline their security operations and automate routine tasks. By ingesting data from various security tools and systems, Splunk can act as a central hub for security event information and facilitate automated responses to potential threats. Using the Adaptive Response Framework (ARF) in Splunk Enterprise Security or integrating with third-party SOAR solutions, security teams can create automated playbooks and workflows to respond to specific alert conditions or incidents, such as blocking an IP address, disabling a user account, or updating firewall rules. This not only reduces the manual workload for security analysts but also helps organizations respond more quickly to potential threats.

Cloud Security Monitoring

As organizations increasingly adopt cloud services and infrastructure, maintaining visibility and control over their cloud security posture becomes critical. Splunk can ingest and analyze data from various cloud platforms, such as Amazon Web Services (AWS), Microsoft Azure, and Google Cloud Platform (GCP), enabling organizations to monitor their cloud environments for potential security threats and compliance issues. By leveraging Splunk's powerful search and analytics capabilities, security teams can quickly identify misconfigurations, unauthorized access, or other security risks associated with their cloud infrastructure.

Conclusion

Splunk's powerful data processing, search, and analytics capabilities make it an ideal platform for organizations looking to strengthen their cybersecurity posture. Through a wide range of use cases, including threat hunting, incident investigation, anomaly detection, network security monitoring, vulnerability management, compliance monitoring, and security orchestration, Splunk enables organizations to gain valuable insights into their security environment and proactively detect and respond to potential threats. By leveraging Splunk's capabilities in these areas, organizations can improve their overall security posture and provide better protection of their critical assets and data.

After gaining a solid understanding of Splunk and its applications in cybersecurity, the next chapter will delve into the intricacies of Splunk architecture, providing insights into its components and how they work together to deliver powerful, real-time analytics.

Points to Remember

- **Overview of Splunk**: Splunk is a powerful platform for searching, analyzing, and visualizing machine-generated data. It helps organizations to gain insights from their data and make informed decisions, especially in the context of cybersecurity.
- **Introduction to Cybersecurity**: Cybersecurity is the practice of protecting digital assets, such as networks, computers, and data, from unauthorized access, theft, or damage. It involves implementing various security measures, including technology, processes, and policies, to safeguard against cyber threats.
- **The Role of Splunk in Cybersecurity**: Splunk plays a crucial role in cybersecurity by helping organizations identify, investigate, and respond to security threats. It can aggregate data from various sources, correlate events, detect anomalies, and provide real-time alerts to aid in threat detection and response.

- **Search and Analytics**: Splunk's powerful search and analytics capabilities enable users to process large volumes of data, create complex queries, and generate valuable insights. Understanding the basics of Splunk's search processing language (SPL) is essential for efficient data analysis and threat detection.
- **Real-time Alerting**: Splunk's real-time alerting feature allows organizations to be notified of potential security threats as they occur. This enables security teams to react quickly and minimize the impact of cyber incidents.
- **Use Cases for Splunk in Cybersecurity**: Splunk is versatile and can be used in various cybersecurity use cases, such as threat detection, incident investigation, security monitoring, compliance reporting, and more. Understanding these use cases can help you effectively utilize Splunk to address specific cybersecurity challenges.

By keeping these important concepts in mind while working on this chapter, you will establish a strong foundation in Splunk and cybersecurity. This knowledge will be vital as you progress through the book and explore more advanced topics and techniques related to leveraging Splunk for cybersecurity purposes.

References

1. Yerukala, M. (2023) Figure 1.1: Overview of Splunk. MindMajix. https://cdn.mindmajix.com/blog/images/splunk-01_04.png
2. World, I. (2017). Figure 1.3: Introduction to Cybersecurity. Twitter. https://pbs.twimg.com/media/DNAM4fcUQAAGMKg.jpg

CHAPTER 2

Overview of Splunk Architecture

Introduction

This chapter examines various aspects of Splunk, such as its architecture, essential components, and capabilities. The chapter begins with an architectural overview of Splunk, concentrating on its distributed, scalable, and fault-tolerant nature. Components, including data sources, Universal Forwarders, Heavy Forwarders, Indexers, and Search Heads, are discussed, along with optional elements such as Deployment Server, Cluster Master, and License Master.

This chapter explains the functions of these essential components and their interplay in data collection, processing, and analysis. It explores the Search Processing Language (SPL), which enables users to construct complex search queries by combining commands and functions for data analysis and visualization.

Finally, the chapter concludes with a discussion of indexing strategies, highlighting the significance of efficiently managing and storing data. In addition, it discusses Splunk deployment best practices and the numerous deployment options available to meet varying organizational requirements.

Structure

In this chapter, we will cover the following topics:

- Overview of Splunk architecture
- Understanding the key components of Splunk
- Search Processing Language (SPL)
    - Advanced SPL commands and examples
    - More advanced SPL commands and examples
- Indexing data and strategies
    - Data parsing and event processing
    - Data storage and indexes
    - Components of an index
    - Configuring indexing in Splunk
    - Index management and performance considerations
    - Indexing strategy
- Scalability and high availability
- Splunk deployment options
    - Best practices for Splunk deployment
    - Search optimization techniques
    - Security best practices in Splunk deployment
    - Splunk health check and maintenance

Overview of Splunk Architecture

Splunk's architecture is optimized for ingesting, processing, and analyzing large volumes of real-time data. Multiple components, including forwarders, indexers, and search heads, collaborate to acquire, store, and analyze data. These components can be deployed in various configurations to satisfy the specific performance, scalability, and high availability requirements of an organization.

Splunk's architecture is composed of the following three principal layers:

- **Data Input Layer:** This layer collects data from various sources and forwards it to the indexing layer. Forwarders are agents that can be deployed on servers, network devices, and other data sources.
- **Indexing Layer:** This layer is tasked with receiving, processing, and storing data from the data input layer. It consists predominantly of

indexers, which perform data compression, indexing, and storage to facilitate quick and efficient searching.

- **Search Layer:** This layer processes search queries, analyzes data, and generates visualizations and reports. It consists primarily of search nodes, which serve as the primary user interface for interacting with Splunk.

Each of these layers can be scaled independently to meet the data volume, query performance, and user traffic requirements of an organization.

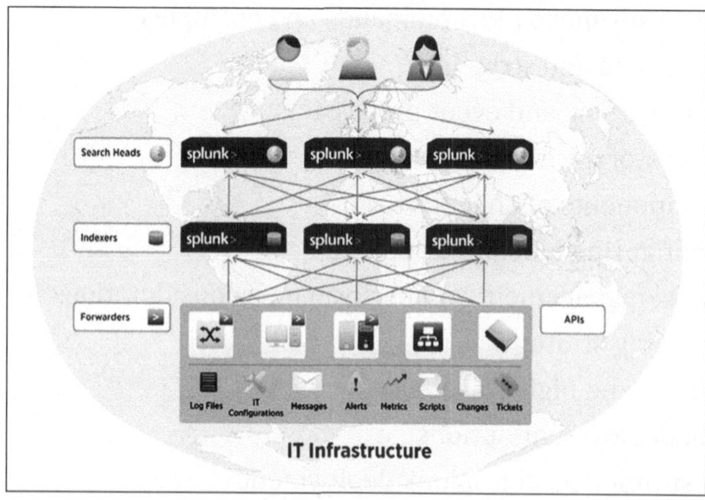

***Figure 2.1**: Splunk Components Overview (source: Kalakota, R. (2012): https://practicalanalytics.wordpress.com/2012/03/26/machine-data-analytics-splunk/)*

Understanding the Key Components of Splunk

By understanding the key components of Splunk, you can gain a greater understanding of how they work together to provide insightful analytics. Here, we discuss some of Splunk's primary components:

- **Data Sources:** These are the systems and devices that generate machine data, including logs, events, and metrics. Servers, network devices, applications, and IoT devices are examples.
- **Universal Forwarder:** Universal Forwarders are lightweight data collection agents that are deployed on data sources such as servers, network devices, and other IT systems. They collect and transmit to a Splunk indexer log data, system metrics, and other machine-generated data for processing and storage.

- **Heavy Forwarders:** These agents acquire data and perform pre-processing, such as filtering, parsing, and field extractions, before forwarding it to indexers. Heavy Forwarders are beneficial when advanced data processing is required or when the volume of data sent to indexers must be reduced.

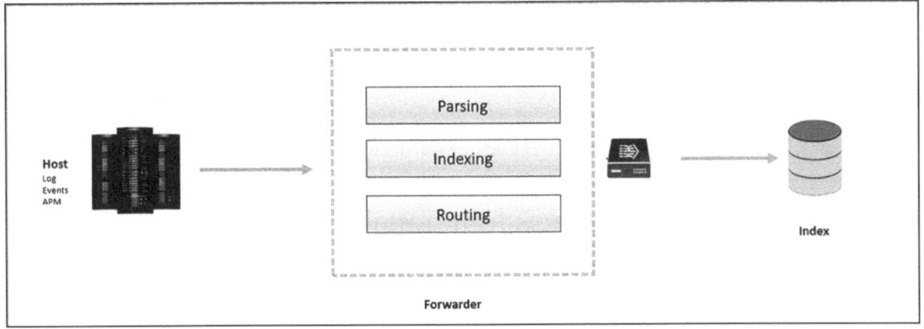

Figure 2.2: *Splunk Forwarder*

- **Indexer:** The indexer is the fundamental component of Splunk that receives, processes, and stores the data collected by forwarders. Indexers extract fields from incoming data, organize them into indexes, and make them accessible for searching and analysis.
- **Search Head:** A search head is the user interface for Splunk, allowing users to construct and execute searches, reports, dashboards, and alerts. Search managers are accountable for coordinating search requests, processing search results, and generating visual representations.
- **Deployment Server:** The deployment server is an optional component that facilitates the configuration and deployment of Splunk components, including forwarders and indexers. It automates the distribution of configuration files and applications, ensuring that every component has the most recent settings and decreasing administrative burden.
- **Cluster Master:** The cluster master is responsible for administering and coordinating the activities of indexer cluster members in a clustered Splunk environment. It ensures that data is replicated correctly across indexers, monitors the health of cluster members, and initiates recovery procedures in the event of failure.
- **License Master:** The license master is responsible for managing Splunk licenses and ensuring the organization adheres to its licensed data ingestion limits. It monitors license usage across all Splunk components and can notify administrators if the data ingestion limit has been reached or is close to being reached.
- **Knowledge Objects:** Knowledge objects in Splunk are reusable components that help define and organize data, making it simpler for

users to search, analyze, and visualize data. Fields, field extractions, event types, identifiers, and lookups are a few examples of knowledge objects.

- **Apps and Add-ons:** Splunk offers a broad variety of apps and add-ons that extend the platform's functionality and provide pre-built configurations, dashboards, and integrations for particular use cases or data sources. Splunk App for Enterprise Security, Splunk IT Service Intelligence, and numerous add-ons for integrating with third-party tools and services are a few examples.
- **Captain:** The Splunk Captain is a crucial component in a Splunk Search Head Cluster, managing and coordinating the activities of the cluster members to ensure seamless functionality and high availability. It acts as a leader within the cluster, overseeing the distribution of configuration bundles, managing member nodes, and maintaining uniformity across search heads

By understanding the main Splunk components and their roles in data collection, processing, and analysis, you can better leverage the platform's capabilities to improve your organization's security and operational efficiency and gain valuable insights.

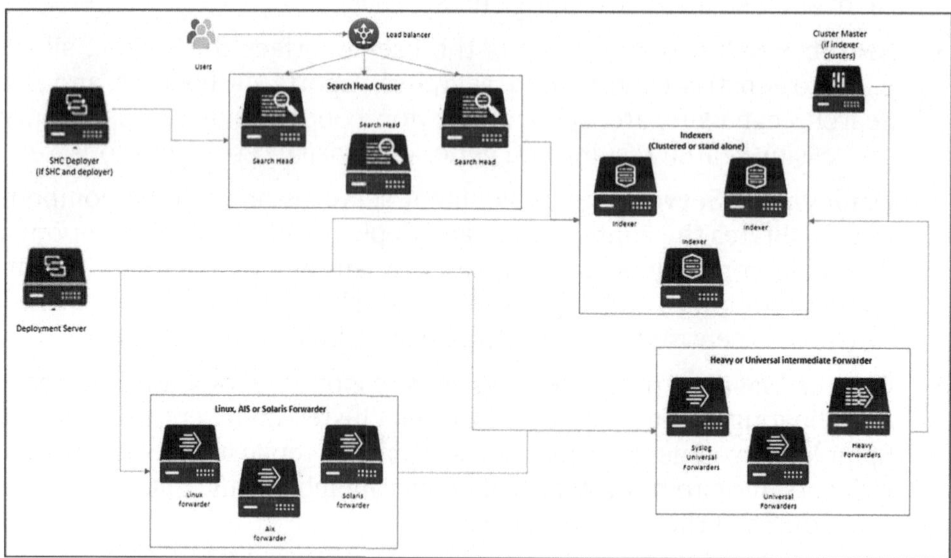

Figure 2.3: *Splunk Architecture*

Search Processing Language (SPL)

Splunk utilizes Search Processing Language (SPL) to search, analyze, and visualize data. SPL permits users to construct sophisticated search queries to extract valuable insights from indexed data. The strength of SPL is derived from its extensive collection of commands and functions, which can be combined to conduct a vast array of data manipulation and analysis tasks.

An SPL query consists of a series of commands, each of which is followed by a set of parameters and options.

Note: The SPL queries provided in this section are formulated to be generic and illustrative. They do not specify any index, to allow for broader applicability. If you wish to experiment with these examples, you may adapt them to your specific use case; for instance, by using **`index=_internal`** or any other index suitable to your environment.

Here are examples of fundamental SPL queries:

- **`Simple search query`**: error

This query looks for events that contain the term **`error`**.

- **`Using the search command`**: search error

As the search command is implied when not explicitly specified, this query is identical to the previous example.

- **`Combining multiple search terms`**: error OR warning

This query looks for events that contain either the word **`error`** or **`warning`**.

Here are some common SPL commands and examples of how to use them in search queries.

Typically, commands are executed in a pipeline, where the output of one command becomes the input for the subsequent command. This pipelining feature permits users to construct complex inquiries by chaining multiple commands and transformations.

- **`stats`**: The stats command is used to generate summary statistics for the events returned by a search query.

  Example: `error | stats count`

  This query counts the number of events containing the word **`error.`**

- **`timechart:`** The timechart command is used to create time-based charts and visualizations.

  Example: `error | timechart count`

  This query creates a time-based chart showing the number of events containing the word **`error`** over time.

- `top`: The top command is used to display the most frequent values of a field.

  Example: `error | top user`

  This query shows the top users associated with events containing the word **`error`.**

- `table`: The table command is used to create a table with specified fields.

  Example: `error | table user, action, _time`

  This query creates a table with the user, action, and timestamp fields for events containing the word **`error`.**

- `eval`: The eval command is used to create or modify fields using expressions.

  Example: `error | eval duration = endTime - startTime | table user, action, duration`

  This query calculates the duration of each event by subtracting the **`startTime`** field from the **`endTime`** field and displays the results in a table.

- `join`: The join command is used to combine the results of two or more search queries based on a common field.

  Example: `search error | join user [search warning]`

  This query returns events containing the word **`error`**. It also includes associated events with the word **`warning`** based on the common **`user`** field.

Advanced SPL commands and examples

In addition to the previously discussed basic SPL commands, Splunk also supports more advanced commands that enable users to conduct complex data manipulation and analysis tasks. Here are some sophisticated examples of SPL commands:

- `transaction`: The transaction command is utilized to group events that share a common attribute, such as a session ID or user ID.

  Example: `search error | transaction user`

  This query organizes error-containing events by user and treats each user's events as a separate transaction.

- `rex`: Using regular expressions, the rex command is used to extract elements from event data using the rex command.

  Example: `error | rex "user=(?<user>[^ ]+)"`

  This query extracts the **`user`** field from events containing the word **`error`** using the regular expression provided.

- `lookup`: The lookup command is used to add attributes from an external lookup table to event data.

  Example: `error | lookup user_info user OUTPUT email`

  This query adds the **`email`** field from the **`user_info`** lookup table to events that contain the word **`error`**, based on the common **`user`** field.

- **`spath`**: The spath command is utilized to extract fields from structured data formats such as JSON and XML.

  Example: `search error | spath input=raw_output path=results.user`

  This query extracts the **`user`** field from JSON or XML data in the **`raw_output`** field of events that contain the word **`error`.**

- **`multikv`**: The **`multikv`** command extracts fields from multi-value fields, such as those found in log files with multiple key-value pairs.

  Example: `search error | multikv fields user, action`

  This query retrieves the **`user`** and **`action`** fields from **`error`**-containing events with multiple-value fields.

- **`streamstats`**: The **`streamstats`** command calculates summary statistics for streaming events, enabling users to analyze trends and changes over time.

  Example: `search error | streamstats count by user`

  This query calculates a running count of events containing the word **`error`** for each user.

More Advanced SPL Commands and Examples

As you continue to explore SPL, you will encounter additional commands that further expand the range of data analysis and manipulation tasks you can perform. Here are some more advanced SPL commands with examples:

- **`dedup`**: The **`dedup`** command is used to remove duplicate events based on one or more fields.

Example: `search error | dedup user`

This query removes duplicate events containing the word **`error`** based on the unique **`user`** field.

- **`sort`**: The sort command is used to sort events based on one or more fields, either in ascending or descending order.

  Example: `search error | sort - count`

  This query sorts events containing the word **`error`** in descending order based on the **`count`** field.

- **`mvexpand`**: The **`mvexpand`** command is used to expand multi-value fields into separate events.

  Example: `search error | mvexpand user`

  This query expands the multi-value **`user`** field from events containing the word **`error`** into separate events.

- **`fillnull`**: The **`fillnull`** command is used to replace null or missing values in fields with a default value.

  Example: `search error | fillnull value=”unknown” user`

  This query replaces null or missing values in the **`user`** field of events containing the word **`error`** with the default value **`unknown`**.

- **`fieldformat`**: The **`fieldformat`** command is used to change the display format of a field without modifying the underlying data.

  Example: `search error | fieldformat user=”User: “+user`

  This query changes the display format of the **`user`** field in events containing the word **`error`** by adding the prefix **`User:`**

As you become more proficient with SPL, you can leverage these advanced commands to create custom searches, analytics, and visualizations that address the unique needs of your organization. With a comprehensive understanding of SPL, you can unlock the full potential of the Splunk platform and transform raw data into actionable insights.

Indexing Data and Strategies

Splunk's indexing functionality enables efficient data browsing, analysis, and visualization. Indexing entails ingesting unstructured data, transforming it into a structured format, and preserving it in a manner that facilitates quick and efficient retrieval. This document explains how Splunk indexes data, including data parsing, event processing, and data storage.

Data Parsing and Event Processing

When Splunk receives unprocessed data, it first parses the information. This method consists of the following steps:

- **Breaking raw data into individual events:** Splunk divides raw data into discrete events, which are the fundamental data elements that can be searched, analyzed, and visualized.
- **Timestamp extraction:** Splunk identifies and extracts the timestamp associated with each event, which is essential for time-based searching and analysis.
- **Field extraction:** Splunk mechanically extracts key-value pairs, also known as fields, from the event data. These fields enable users to explore and analyze particular data characteristics.
- **Event processing:** Splunk performs additional processing on events, such as line separation, event separation, and character set encoding.

Data Storage and Indexes

After events are parsed and processed, Splunk archives them in indexes. An index is a collection of events structured to enable efficient searching and retrieval, organized by time. Splunk can have multiple indexes, each dedicated to particular data types or use cases. You can designate custom indexes or use the default **main** index when configuring Splunk.

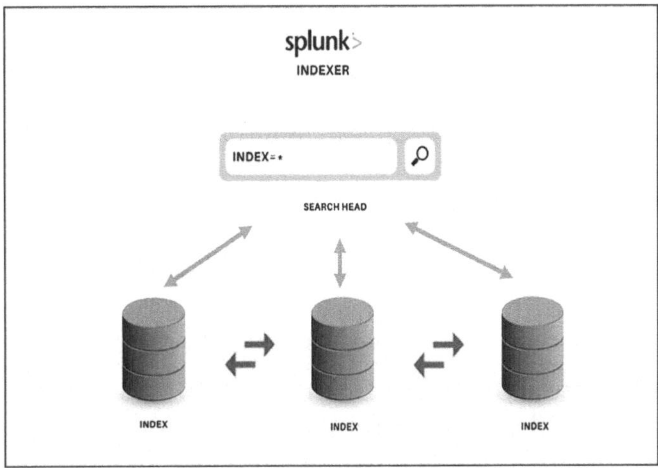

Figure 2.4: *Indexing in Splunk*

Components of an Index

The components of an index are as follows:

- **Buckets:** Each index is organized into containers, which are directories containing events for particular time intervals. Throughout their lifetime, buckets pass through several stages: hot, warm, cold, and frozen. Warm buckets are read-only and no longer being updated, cold buckets are read-only and were rolled from warm due to age or size, and frozen buckets are either deleted or archived.

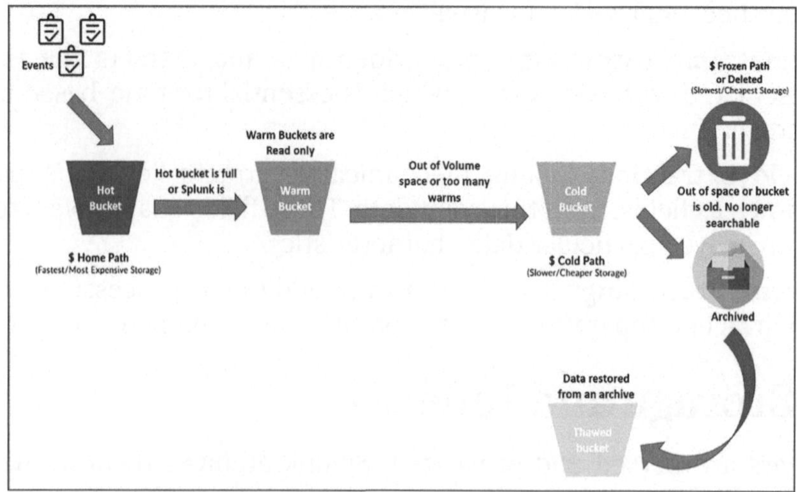

Figure 2.5: *Index buckets in Splunk*

- **Raw data:** The index compresses and stores raw data as it was initially ingested. This ensures that the original data is always accessible and can be reprocessed if necessary.
- **Index files:** These files contain metadata and other information required for efficient data searching. Examples of index files include time series index (TSIDX) files, which contain pointers to events in the raw data files, and bloom filter files, which facilitate faster searches by excluding events that do not match the search criteria.

Configuring Indexing in Splunk

Typically, configuring indexing in Splunk entails the following tasks:

- **Creating custom indexes:** Define custom indexes to enhance data organization and search performance. Each index must serve a distinct function, such as storing data for a particular application or team.

- **Setting index properties:** Set index properties such as the maximum index size, the time range for each container, and the data retention policy. These parameters can assist in managing storage needs and ensuring that data is retained for an adequate period.
- **Configuring data inputs:** Define data inputs and indicate to which index the data should be sent. Configuring inputs is possible via Universal Forwarders, Heavy Forwarders, or the Splunk Web interface.
- **Assigning permissions for an index:** Control index access by assigning permissions to particular users and responsibilities.

Index Management and Performance Considerations

Managing indexes and optimizing performance are essential aspects of working with Splunk. Here are some best practices and recommendations for index management and search performance optimization:

- **Plan yourindexes:** Plan your indexing strategy before deploying Splunk by considering the data types that will be ingested, the data retention requirements, and the anticipated search traffic. Developing a well-structured index plan can facilitate the optimization of storage and search performance.
- **Monitor index growth:** Monitor the development of your indexes regularly to ensure that they do not exceed their storage limits or hinder search performance. Splunk offers a variety of monitoring tools and dashboards to trace index usage and expansion.
- **Optimize searches:** Use specific index and field names in your search queries to minimize the quantity of data that must be processed when designing searches. This can help increase search performance and reduce Splunk deployment load.
- **Use summary indexing:** Summary indexing is a technique that pre-aggregates data so that it can be retrieved more quickly during queries. By establishing summary indexes for frequently used searches or dashboards, search performance can be enhanced by reducing the amount of data that must be processed during each search.
- **Archive old data:** When data in your indexes reaches the end of its useful existence, consider archiving it in order to reduce storage costs and enhance search performance. Splunk can be configured to archive data to a distinct storage system or delete it when it reaches a certain age or size.

By adhering to these best practices and recommendations, you can ensure that your Splunk deployment remains efficient and performs well as your organization's data grows and its requirements change. Proper index management and performance tuning are essential for optimizing your Splunk investment and ensuring that your team can analyze and visualize your data swiftly and easily.

Indexing Strategy

Splunk provides several configurable strategies to optimize search performance, manage data retention, and ensure data availability through effective handling of indexed data:

- **Data Partitioning**: Indexed data can be organized based on various criteria, such as data source, data type, or department. This enables enhanced search performance and more effective management of data retention policies. It's important to note that it is the data that is partitioned, not the indexes themselves.
- **Data Clustering**: Splunk can be configured to cluster indexed data to ensure data redundancy, high availability, and improved search performance. In such a configuration, data is replicated across multiple indexers to secure its availability in the event of hardware failures or other disruptions. Again, it is the data that is clustered, not the indexes.
- **Data Tiering**: Different storage tiers (hot, warm, cold, and frozen) can be assigned to indexed data based on its age, optimizing both storage costs and search performance. Cold and frozen data are stored in slower, less expensive storage for long-term retention, while hot and warm data are stored in faster storage, enabling optimal search performance.

These strategies are not inherent default settings but are configurable options designed to optimize the management and performance of indexed data. They emphasize the optimization and configuration of the data within the indexes, rather than the indexes themselves.

Scalability and High Availability

Scalability and high availability are essential features of all enterprise-grade software, particularly data analytics platforms such as Splunk. A scalable system can accommodate growing data volumes, user counts, and search burdens, while high availability ensures that the system remains operational and accessible despite component and network failures. In this exposition, we will discuss how Splunk's architecture and various features address scalability and high availability.

- **Scalability:** The distributed architecture of Splunk is designed to scale both horizontally and vertically to accommodate expanding data volumes, user counts, and search loads.
- **Horizontal Scaling:** Splunk can be scaled out horizontally by adding more instances of specific components, such as Indexers or Search Heads, to manage larger data volumes or increased search requirements. This is referred to as horizontal scaling, and it can be accomplished by deploying additional instances and distributing data and search traffic across them. This methodology enables Splunk to scale nearly linearly as the number of instances increases.
- **Vertical Scaling:** Splunk can also be scaled vertically by increasing the available resources to individual components, such as memory, CPU, and storage. This is referred to as vertical scaling, and it can help improve the efficacy of existing instances as well as accommodate larger data volumes and search loads.
- **High Availability:** Splunk achieves high availability by implementing redundancy and failover mechanisms to keep the system operational in the event of component failures or network issues.
- **Indexer Clustering:** Splunk supports indexer clustering, which enables the creation of a group of indexers that replicate data among themselves. This replication ensures that multiple duplicates of the data are available so that if one indexer fails, the remaining indexers can continue to fulfill search requests. By distributing the search load across cluster members, indexer clustering also enhances search performance.
- **Search head clustering:** Splunk also supports search head clustering, a feature that enables the creation of a group of search heads that service search requests collaboratively. By distributing the search load and providing redundancy, search head clustering enhances both search performance and availability. If one search head in a cluster fails, the remaining search heads can continue to service queries.
- **Load balancing and failover:** Splunk can be configured to interact with load balancers to distribute traffic across multiple instances of a component, such as indexers or search heads. This ensures that no single instance becomes a bottleneck or single point of failure, thereby enhancing performance and availability.

By incorporating scalability and high availability features, Splunk ensures that its platform can expand to meet the requirements of organizations of all sizes, while also providing the reliability and resilience required for mission-critical applications. This combination of scalability and high availability makes Splunk a popular option for businesses that require a robust and flexible data analytics platform.

Splunk Deployment Options

Splunk provides a variety of deployment options, each of which is tailored to distinct organizational requirements, infrastructure specifications, and scalability concerns. Understanding these options will allow you to select the most suitable one for your particular use case. Here are Splunk's primary deployment options:

- **Single-instance deployment**

All Splunk components (data inputs, indexing, and querying) are hosted by a single machine in a single-instance deployment, which is the simplest deployment option. This option is appropriate for small-scale environments or testing, where the volume of data is comparatively low and the number of users accessing the system is limited.

Advantages

- Simpler installation and management
- Reduced hardware and infrastructure needs

Disadvantages

- Limited scalability and performance
- Single point of failure – all Splunk functionality is lost if the instance fails.

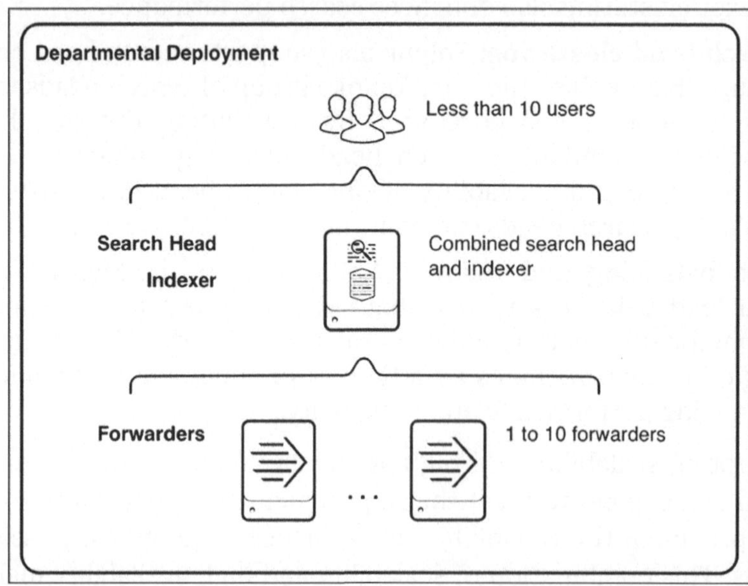

***Figure 2.6**: Splunk Single-instance deployment (source: Splunk Inc., (2022): https://docs.splunk.com/Documentation/Splunk/9.0.4/Deploy/Singleindexer)*

- **Distributed deployment**

Distributing Splunk components across multiple machines increases scalability, performance, and defect tolerance in a distributed deployment. In a distributed architecture, forwarders, indexers, and search heads can exist as discrete instances, allowing each component to be scaled independently as needed. Distributed deployments are appropriate for medium- to large-scale environments with greater data volumes and user demands.

Advantages

- Enhanced scalability and performance
- Enhanced fault tolerance and high availability via clustering and data replication

Disadvantages

- More difficult setup and management
- Higher hardware and infrastructure requirements

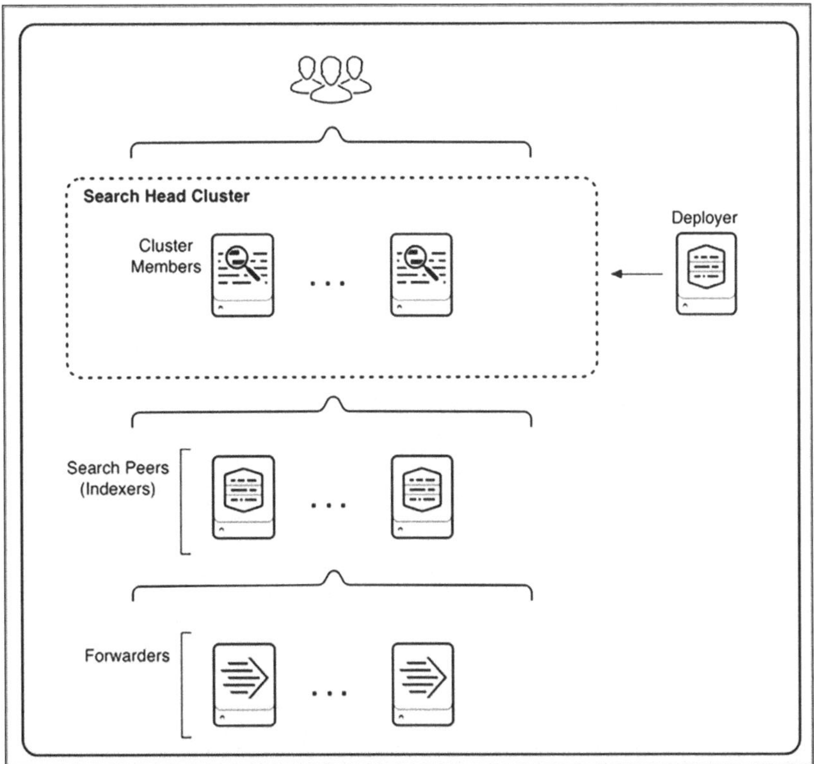

***Figure 2.7**: Splunk Distributed deployment (source: Splunk Inc., (2022): https://docs.splunk.com/Documentation/Splunk/9.0.4/Deploy/SHCwithindexers)*

- **Splunk Cloud**

Splunk Cloud is a fully managed, cloud-based deployment option that provides all the features and capabilities of an on-premises Splunk Enterprise deployment without requiring the management of the underlying infrastructure. Splunk Cloud is appropriate for businesses that prefer not to invest in on-premises infrastructure and wish to take advantage of the Cloud's flexibility and scalability.

Advantages

- No need to manage hardware or infrastructure
- Quick and simple deployment and scalability
- Cloud infrastructure offers high availability and dependability

Disadvantages

- Ongoing subscription costs
- Potential data security and compliance concerns, depending on the organization's specific needs

Hybrid Deployment

A hybrid deployment combines on-premises and cloud-based Splunk instances, enabling organizations to utilize both deployment options based on their unique requirements. For instance, a hybrid deployment may employ on-premises indexers for the storage of sensitive data and cloud-based search engines for remote users or external data sources.

Advantages

- Ability to select the optimal deployment method for particular use cases
- Combines the advantages of on-premises and cloud deployments

Disadvantages

- Potentially higher costs due to the combination of infrastructure and subscription costs

Your organization's size, data volume, user needs, budget, and infrastructure preferences will determine which Splunk deployment option is most suitable. By understanding the benefits and drawbacks of each option, you can make an informed decision that best meets the requirements of your organization.

Best Practices for Splunk Deployment

Organizations should adhere to best practices when deploying Splunk to ensure optimal performance, scalability, and high availability. Among the essential best practices are the following:

- **Plan and design architecture:** Develop the architecture according to data volume, user traffic, and performance specifications.
- **Monitor resource utilization:** Regularly monitor CPU, memory, disk, and network usage to identify potential performance issues or bottlenecks. Splunk provides several monitoring tools, including the Monitoring Console and the metrics.log file, which can be used to analyze resource utilization.
- **Analyze search performance:** Utilize the integrated search task inspector to analyze the performance of individual search queries and identify slow or resource-intensive queries. Identify and address the underlying causes of performance issues, such as suboptimal search queries and inadequate hardware resources.
- **Review indexing efficiency:** Monitor the indexing rate and indexing queue to ensure that data is indexed quickly and effectively. Investigate any indexing delays or problems that could affect search performance or data accessibility.
- **Configure alerts:** To proactively identify and resolve potential issues, configure alerts for critical system events and performance metrics, such as high resource utilization, lengthy queries, and indexing failures.
- **Plan for capability and growth:** Assess the capacity of your Splunk environment regularly and plan for future growth by adding or upgrading hardware resources, such as CPU, memory, and storage, as necessary.
- **Data Retention:** Implement data retention policies to control storage costs and comply with regulatory requirements.

Monitoring and troubleshooting Splunk's performance are essential for sustaining a high-performance environment and keeping the system responsive to user demands.

Here, we discuss some recommendations for Splunk performance monitoring and troubleshooting.

Search Optimization Techniques

Splunk's optimal search performance requires the implementation of search optimization techniques. Several of these strategies include:

- **Use selective filtering**: Filter events as early as possible in your search query to reduce the quantity of data that must be processed, thereby enhancing search performance.

- **Limit the time range**: Specify a limited time range for your search to reduce the amount of data that must be searched, which will result in faster search results.
- **Utilize indexed fields**: Utilize indexed fields in your search queries to optimize search performance and take advantage of Splunk's indexing capabilities.
- **Optimize SPL commands**: Select the most efficient SPL commands and functions for your search queries and use them in the proper order to reduce processing latency.
- **Schedule intensive resource searches**: Schedule resource-intensive queries during off-peak hours to reduce their impact on search performance and resource consumption.

Security Best Practices in Splunk Deployment

It is crucial to follow security best practices when deploying and managing Splunk in order to safeguard sensitive data and maintain compliance with regulatory requirements. Among the essential security best practices are the following:

- **Secure communication:** Encrypt communication between Splunk components using SSL/TLS to prevent unauthorized data access.
- Implement role-based access control (RBAC) to restrict user access to sensitive data and functionality based on their assigned roles and responsibilities.
- **Regularly apply patches and upgrades:** Keep your Splunk environment up-to-date with the most recent upgrades and updates to address security flaws and maintain security standards compliance.
- **Audit and monitor Splunk activity:** Review Splunk logs and audit traces on a regular basis to identify and investigate suspicious activity and security incidents.
- **Implement data masking:** Protect user privacy and maintain compliance with data protection regulations by masking or removing sensitive data such as personally identifiable information (PII) or payment card information.

Splunk Health Check and Maintenance

Regular health tests and maintenance can help ensure that your Splunk environment continues to be stable, secure, and performant. Among the most important health check and maintenance duties are the following:

- **Review system logs and internal Splunk logs:** Review system logs and Splunk's internal logs (_internal index) on a regular basis to identify and investigate errors, warnings, and other issues that could impact system stability or performance.
- **Validate configuration files**: Examine and validate Splunk configuration files on a regular basis to ensure they are formatted correctly and do not contain any errors or inconsistencies that could cause problems.
- **Planning for backup and recovery:** Implement a thorough backup and recovery strategy to safeguard your Splunk data and configuration files against loss or corruption. Test your backup and recovery procedures frequently to ensure their efficacy and currency.
- **Test and validate upgrades:** Before applying any upgrades or patches to your Splunk environment, evaluate them in a non-production environment to identify and resolve any potential issues or incompatibilities.
- **Monitor and maintain security:** Regularly review and update security configurations, including access controls, encryption settings, and security policies, to maintain a secure environment and comply with regulatory requirements.

By adhering to these recommendations and best practices, organizations can maintain a healthy, high-performance Splunk environment that supports their cybersecurity and data analytics requirements effectively.

Conclusion

This chapter concludes with a thorough examination of Splunk's architecture, essential components, and functionalities. We have explored the distributed, scalable, and fault-tolerant nature of Splunk and the roles of its various components, including data sources, Universal Forwarders, Heavy Forwarders, Indexers, and Search Heads, as well as optional elements such as Deployment Server, Cluster Master, and License Master. In addition, we have presented the Search Processing Language (SPL) and its capabilities for constructing complex search queries for data analysis and visualization.

We have also addressed the significance of efficient data management and storage via indexing strategies and shared best practices for Splunk deployment, emphasizing the availability of flexible deployment options to meet the varying requirements of organizations. With this foundation in place, you are well-equipped to design and maintain a robust Splunk environment and leverage its potent data analysis and visualization capabilities to drive informed business decisions.

As we transition to the next chapter, *Configuring Inputs and Data Sources*, we will explore various data ingestion techniques, such as files and directories, network events, and more. In addition, we will cover how to configure data inputs and source types, as well as how to manage data parsing and transformation to ensure that your Splunk deployment effectively processes and analyzes data. This knowledge will enable you to maximize Splunk's capabilities and extract valuable insights from your organization's data.

Points to Remember

- **Overview of Splunk Architecture:** Splunk's architecture is modular and consists of several essential components, including forwarders, indexers, and search heads. Understanding the functions of these components and their interactions is essential for effective data processing and analysis.
- **Key components of Splunk**: Familiarize yourself with the primary Splunk components, such as forwarders, indexers, search heads, deployment servers, and license controllers. Each component performs a distinct role in data intake, processing, searching, and administration.
- **Search Processing Language (SPL)**: Splunk uses SPL, a sophisticated search language, to query and manipulate data. You can extract valuable insights from your data and construct complex search queries, visualizations, and alerts by mastering SPL.
- **Indexing Data**: In Splunk, indexing is the process of preserving and organizing data. Effective data storage and retrieval requires an understanding of indexing strategies, index types, and data retention policy management.
- **Indexing Strategies**: Employ the appropriate indexing strategies, including the use of multiple indexes, the establishment of data retention policies, and the consideration of data prioritization. These strategies can optimize your Splunk environment's data storage, management, and retrieval.
- **Scalability and High Availability**: Ensure that your Splunk deployment can accommodate growing data volumes and user requirements. Implement strategies for clustering and data replication to maintain high availability and provide fault tolerance in the event of hardware failures.
- **Splunk Deployment Options**: Familiarize yourself with the different deployment options, such as single-instance deployments, distributed deployments, and cloud deployments. Choose the option that best fits your organization's needs, budget, and infrastructure.

- **Splunk Best Practices for Deployment**: Follow Splunk deployment best practices to optimize performance, security, and maintenance. This encompasses hardware dimensions, capacity planning, monitoring, and routine maintenance.

Chapter 3

Configuring Inputs and Data Sources

Introduction

This chapter explains how to configure Splunk to capture and analyze data from multiple sources. The chapter begins with an overview of the various data sources that Splunk can consume, including logs, events, metrics, and network data.

This chapter describes how to configure inputs in Splunk, including file and directory input configuration, network input configuration, and scripted input configuration. It also explains how to forward data from remote sources to Splunk and how to utilize Splunk's Universal Forwarder.

In addition, the chapter elaborates on Splunk's data source management capabilities, including data input and output settings, as well as the application of source types and tags to classify and organize data. A discussion of data parsing and transformation, including the use of field extractions, event types, and lookups, concludes the chapter.

By the end of this chapter, readers will have a thorough comprehension of how to configure Splunk to collect and analyze data from multiple sources.

Structure

In this chapter, we will cover the following topics:

- Introduction to configuring inputs and data sources
- Types of data sources
- Configuring data inputs
- Understanding data inputs
- Managing data inputs
- Data onboarding

Introduction to configuring inputs and data sources

Splunk is a robust platform for analyzing and visualizing data from a variety of sources, making it crucial for organizations to configure inputs and data sources accurately. Configuring inputs and data sources entails establishing how Splunk transforms data, such as log files, network traffic, and databases, into searchable events. In this section, we will provide an overview of the inputs and data sources configuration process, which enables Splunk to efficiently collect, process, and analyze data.

The processes involved in configuring inputs and data sources in Splunk are as follows:

- **Identifying data sources:** This is the first step in configuring inputs - identifying the data sources you wish to import into Splunk. These sources may include log files, network traffic, databases, and APIs from various systems and applications.
- **Choosing the appropriate input method:** Splunk supports a variety of input methods, including monitoring files and directories, eavesdropping on network ports, and querying databases. Depending on the data source, you must select the appropriate data input method for Splunk.
- **Configuring the input settings:** After identifying the data sources and selecting the input method, you must configure the input settings. This may involve specifying file paths, network ports, or database connection information, as well as any data parsing and transformation parameters that are required.
- **Testing and validating the input configuration**: Following the configuration of the input settings, it is essential to test and validate the

input configuration to ensure that Splunk can successfully ingest and process the data. This may involve examining the indexed data, detecting parsing errors, or confirming field extractions.

- **Monitoring and managing data inputs:** After inputs have been configured and validated, it is crucial to monitor and manage them to ensure that data ingestion continues seamlessly and efficiently. This may include modifying input settings and resolving problems.

  By following these steps, you can configure inputs and data sources in Splunk to effectively acquire and process data from a variety of systems and applications. To maximize Splunk's potent data analysis and visualization capabilities, inputs and data sources must be configured properly. It ensures that the platform can efficiently manage the data, making it searchable and valuable for the analytics requirements of your organization.

In the remainder of this chapter, we will delve deeper into various types of data sources, explore the configuration and management of data inputs, and investigate best practices for data onboarding. This information will assist you in comprehending the process of configuring inputs and data sources in Splunk and equip you with the knowledge required to optimize data ingestion and processing for your particular use cases.

Types of data sources

Splunk is capable of ingesting data from numerous sources (see *Figure 3.1*), which can be broadly classified as follows:

- **Files and directories:** Splunk can monitor local or remote files and directories, such as log files, configuration files, and CSV files, for new or updated data. This is one of the most common types of data sources for Splunk, as many applications and systems generate log files that can provide insightful information about their operation and performance.

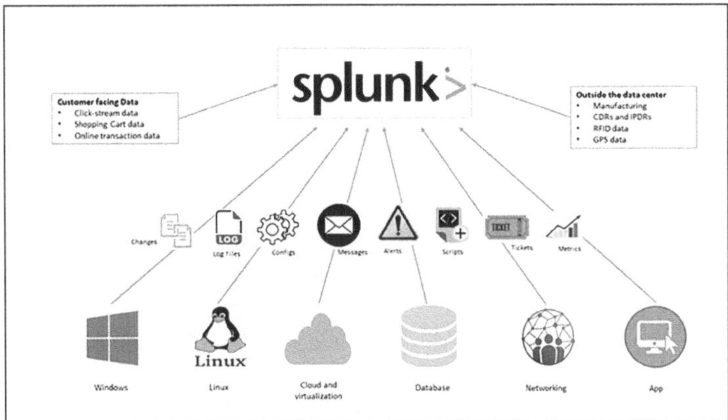

Figure 3.1: *Data sources of Splunk*

- **Network events:** Splunk can capture network events, including Syslog, SNMP traps, and NetFlow data, by monitoring particular network ports. This enables Splunk to receive data from network devices, firewalls, and other systems that transmit network-based events.
- **APIs and web data:** Splunk can connect to APIs and web services to collect data in JSON, XML, and other formats. This permits Splunk to consume data from cloud services, social media platforms, and other applications that expose their data via APIs or web interfaces.
- **Databases:** Splunk can query SQL, NoSQL, and time-series databases to ingest data directly from these sources. This helps accumulate structured data and integrate Splunk with other data analytics platforms.
- **Custom data sources:** Splunk also supports custom data sources that utilize scripts, modular inputs, or other custom input methods. This enables custom integrations with proprietary systems, IoT devices, and other specialized data sources that Splunk may not support out of the box.

Understanding the various types of data sources is essential for configuring inputs in Splunk, as it allows you to determine the input method and settings for each data source. By ingesting data from multiple sources, you can obtain a comprehensive view of the IT infrastructure of your organization and identify patterns, trends, and anomalies that may not be apparent when analyzing data from a single source.

Configuring data inputs

After identifying the data sources that you wish to import into Splunk, you must configure the data inputs. Depending on the sort of data source, Splunk offers a variety of data collection input methods. Here, we'll discuss some common input mechanisms and their configuration.

Configuring data inputs for log files

Suppose you want to onboard Apache web server access logs into Splunk. First, you need to identify the data source - in this case, the Apache access log files, typically located at `/var/log/apache2/access.log`. To configure the data input for these log files, follow these steps:

1. In the Splunk Web interface, navigate to **`Settings`** > **`Data Inputs`** > **`Files & Directories`**.
2. Click **`New Local File & Directory Monitor`**.
3. In the **`File or Directory`** field, enter the path to your Apache access log file. Choose the path where your log file is located. For example, if your log file is named **`access.log`**, you would find and enter the path where it is stored.

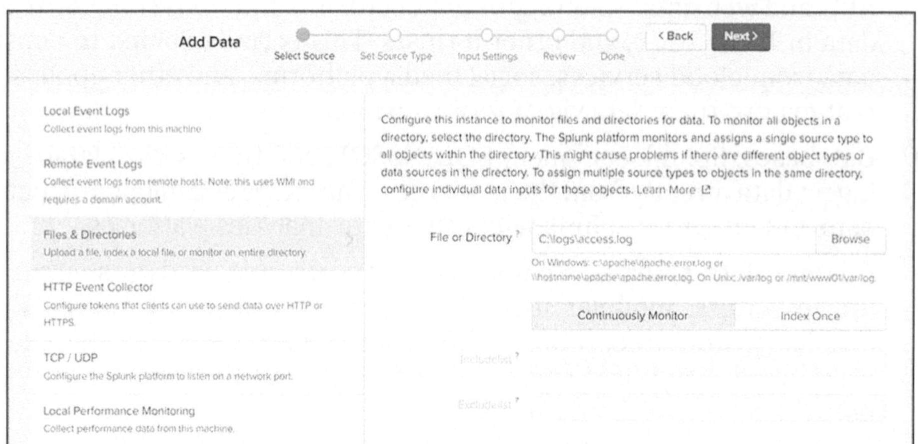

Figure 3.2: *Configuring data inputs for log files*

4. Set the **`Source type`** field to **`apache_access`** (Splunk's predefined source type for Apache access logs).
5. Configure any additional settings as needed, such as indexing options or file rotation policies.
6. Click **`Save`** to create the data input.

Splunk will now monitor the specified log file for new events and ingest them as they are written.

Configuring data inputs for network events

Consider the scenario where you wish to import syslog events from network devices into Splunk. To configure a UDP data input to monitor for incoming syslog messages, perform the following instructions:

1. In the Splunk Web interface, navigate to **`Settings`** > **`Data Inputs`** > "UDP."
2. Click on **`New Local UDP`**.
3. In the **`Port`** field, enter the UDP port number on which Splunk should listen for syslog messages (for example, 514).

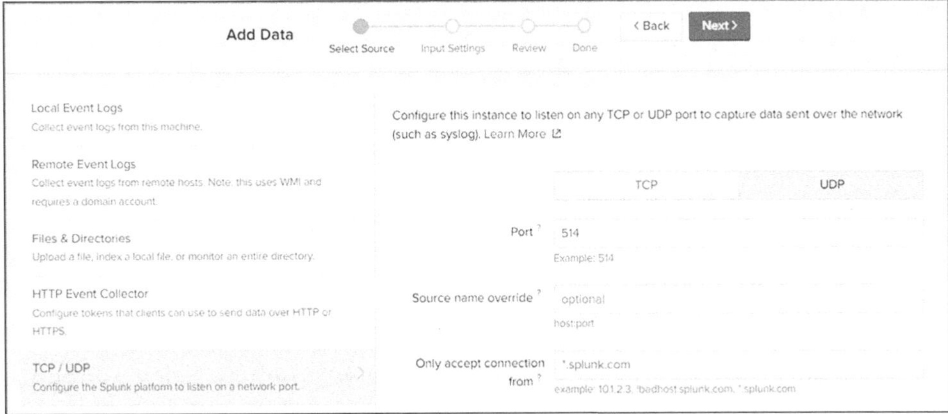

Figure 3.3: *Configuring data inputs for network events*

4. Set the **`Source type`** field to **`syslog`** (Splunk's predefined sourcetype for syslog events).
5. Configure any additional settings as needed, such as IP filtering or event parsing options.
6. Click **`Save`** to create the data input.

Splunk will now monitor the specified UDP port for syslog messages and consume them as events.

Configuring data inputs for APIs

Suppose you wish to retrieve data from a third-party API, such as a threat intelligence feed or the monitoring API of a cloud service. In this scenario, Splunk's HTTP Event Collector (HEC) can be used to consume API data. Perform the following instructions:

1. In the Splunk Web interface, navigate to **`Settings`** > **`Data Inputs`** > **`HTTP Event Collector`**.
2. Click **`New Token`**.
3. Provide a name for the token (for example, **`Threat_Intelligence_Feed`**).

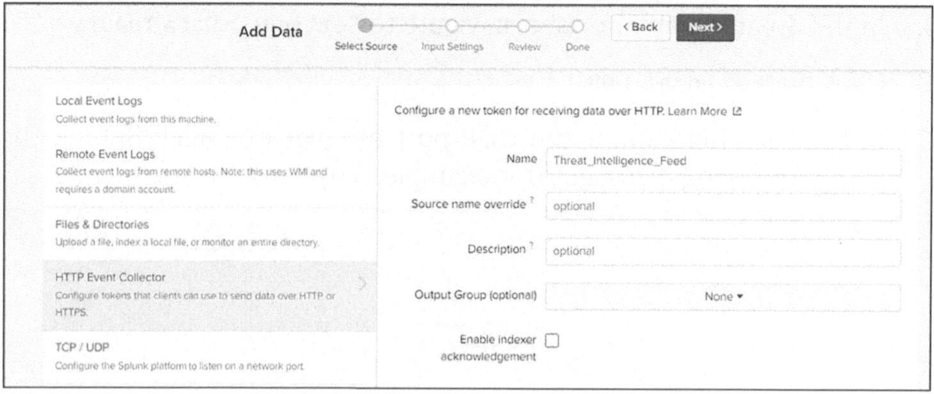

Figure 3.4: *Configuring data inputs for APIs*

4. Set the **`Source type`** field to an appropriate value for the data you are ingesting (for example, "json" for JSON data or "xml" for XML data).
5. Configure any additional settings as needed, such as index assignments or IP filtering.
6. Click **`Save`** to create the HEC token.

Once the token has been generated, it can be used in your API integration script or tool to transmit data to Splunk via HTTP or HTTPS requests.

By configuring data inputs for various data sources, you can ensure that Splunk can efficiently consume and process data, making it accessible for analysis and visualization.

A Few other types of data configuration

Splunk's **DB Connect** app allows you to generate inputs for various databases, including SQL, NoSQL, and time-series databases, and can be used to query databases. To begin, install Splunk DB Connect from Splunkbase, then navigate to **`Apps`** > **`DB Connect`** > **`Data Lab`** > **`Inputs`**. Next, select the relevant database type by clicking **`New Input`** and selecting the appropriate database type. Provide the connection details, specify the query or table, and configure the sourcetype along with any additional settings.

To collect data from custom data sources, you can construct scripts, modular inputs, and other custom input methods. The configuration procedure for custom data sources will vary based on the method employed. For guidance on creating and configuring custom data inputs, consult the Splunk documentation and developer resources (https://dev.splunk.com/enterprise/docs/developapps/manageknowledge/custominputs/).

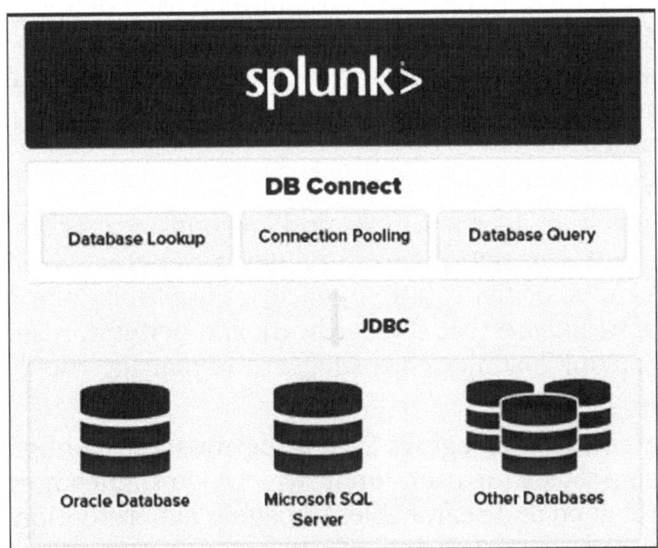

Figure 3.5: *Splunk DB Connect App (Source: Splunk Big Data: a Beginner's Guide - Cloudian. (n.d.). Cloudian. https://cloudian.com/guides/splunk-big-data/splunk-big-data-a-beginners-guide)*

By configuring the appropriate data inputs for each data source, you can ensure that Splunk can efficiently ingest and process the data, making it searchable and valuable for the analytics requirements of your organization.

Understanding and managing data inputs

After configuring data inputs in Splunk, it is crucial to comprehend and administer them for efficient data ingestion and processing. This entails observing the status of the inputs, resolving problems, and optimizing performance. Consider the following factors when managing data inputs:

- **Monitoring data inputs:** Splunk offers multiple monitoring tools for data inputs, including the **`Data Inputs`** page under **`Settings`** and the **`Monitoring Console`** application. These tools can assist you in identifying problems like sluggish data ingestion, missing data, and parsing errors. Reviewing the status of your data inputs regularly enables you to proactively resolve potential issues before they compromise your analytical capabilities.

- **Troubleshooting issues:** When problems arise with data inputs, such as data not being ingested, incorrect parsing, or errors in field extractions, it is essential to identify and rectify the underlying cause. Scrutinizing the input settings, scrutinizing the indexed data, or examining the Splunk logs for errors and warnings may be required during debugging. The Splunk documentation and community resources (https://docs.splunk.com/Documentation/Splunk/9.0.4/Data/Troubleshoottheinputprocess) offer guidance and best practices for troubleshooting typical data input problems.
- **Optimizing performance:** Efficient data ingestion is essential to preserving the performance and responsiveness of your Splunk environment. Consider adjusting input parameters, such as batch size, throttle limits, or file rotation policies, to optimize the performance of data inputs. Ensure that the hardware and network resources allocated to your Splunk instances are adequate to manage the data volume and velocity.
- **Data retention and aging:** Splunk permits the configuration of data retention policies for each input, which determines how long ingested data is retained and searchable. Managing data retention effectively can help you strike a balance between storage requirements and the need for historical data analysis. Review and adjust the data retention parameters for each input to ensure that they comply with the data retention and compliance requirements of your organization.

By understanding and managing data inputs in Splunk, you can ensure that the platform can efficiently capture, process, and analyze data from a variety of sources, thereby meeting your organization's analytical requirements.

Data onboarding

Data integration involves importing new data sources into Splunk, transforming them into searchable events, and ensuring that the data is properly indexed, parsed, and enriched. Data onboarding involves a number of phases, including:

- **Identification of data sources and input configuration:** This involves identifying the data sources you wish to import into Splunk, selecting the appropriate input method, and configuring the input parameters.
- **Data parsing and transformation:** After ingesting the data, Splunk must parse and convert it into a format suitable for indexing and searching. This may involve configuring field extractions, timestamp recognition,

or event breaking settings to ensure the data is parsed and enriched appropriately.

- **Normalization of data:** To enable effective analysis and correlation of data from various sources, it is crucial to normalize the data by employing standard field names and data formats. This may entail the creation of field aliases, lookups, or calculated fields in order to map the ingested data to a standard data model.
- **Data validation and testing:** Before completely integrating new data sources into your Splunk environment, you must validate and test the data onboarding process. This may require a review of the indexed data, a check for parsing errors, or confirmation of field extractions and data normalization.

Custom log file onboarding example

In this section, we will navigate through each step using an example of onboarding a custom application log into Splunk, as well as sample configuration files and log files.

Identification of data sources and input configuration

Suppose you have a custom application log file named "**`app_log.log`**" with the sample content as follows:

```
2022-10-01 12:30:00 INFO: User logged in, UserID: 123
2022-10-01 12:31:15 ERROR: Failed database query, Query: SELECT * FROM users
2022-10-01 12:34:45 WARNING: High memory usage, Memory: 80%
```

To configure the data input for this log file, follow these steps:

1. In the Splunk Web interface, navigate to **`Settings`** > **`Data Inputs`** > **`Files & Directories`**.
2. Click **`New Local File & Directory Monitor`**.
3. In the '**`File or Directory`**' field, enter the path to your application log file. Choose the path where your log file is located. For example, if your log file is named **`app_log.log`**, you would find and enter the path where it is stored.

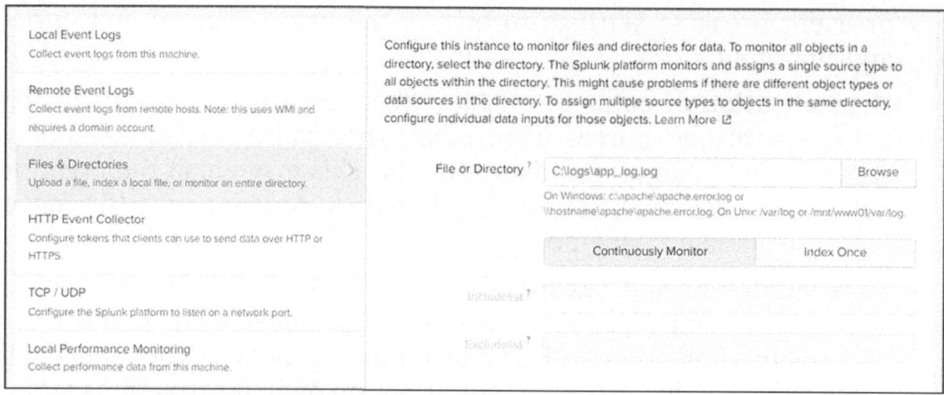

Figure 3.6: *Identification of data sources and input configuration*

4. Set the "**`Source type`**" field to a new custom value, for example, "**`my_app_log`**".
5. Configure any additional settings as needed, such as indexing options or file rotation policies.
6. Click **`Save`** to create the data input.

Parsing and transforming data

You must construct a new sourcetype and define field extractions, event breaking, and data transformations for the custom application log. Create the **`props.conf`** and **`transforms.conf`** files in your application's local directory.

Sample props.conf:

```
[my_app_log]
TIME_FORMAT = %Y-%m-%d %H:%M:%S
MAX_TIMESTAMP_LOOKAHEAD = 19
LINE_BREAKER = ([\r\n]+)
SHOULD_LINEMERGE = false
EXTRACT-loglevel = ^\d{4}-\d{2}-\d{2} \d{2}:\d{2}:\d{2} (?<log-
level>[A-Z]+):
EXTRACT-message = (?<log_message>[A-Z]+): (.+)
```

Sample transforms.conf (optional):

You can include any transformations you require, such as anonymizing user IDs:

```
[anonymize_user_id]
SOURCE_KEY = log_message
REGEX = (UserID: )\d+
FORMAT = $1XXX
DEST_KEY = _raw
```

We have defined the time format, line break, and field extractions for **`loglevel`** and **`log_message`** in **props.conf**. If necessary, custom data transformations can be added to the **transforms.conf** file.

Normalizing data

Normalizing data is essential for ensuring consistency and comparability across multiple data sources. This is typically accomplished using CIM in Splunk. Common Information Model (CIM) provides a standard set of field identifiers and event tags that can be used to normalize data from diverse sources.

For the custom application log, you can either map your data to an existing Splunk data model or construct a custom data model to meet your specific requirements. This entails mapping the extracted log file fields to their corresponding data model fields. As necessary, you can define these mappings in the **props.conf** and **tags.conf** configuration files.

Add the following lines to your **props.conf** file if you want to map the **`loglevel`** field to the **`severity`** field in the **`Web`** data model:

```
[my_app_log]
...
FIELDALIAS-loglevel_to_severity = loglevel AS severity
```

Similarly, you can define event tags in **tags.conf** file to categorize your events:

```
[eventtype=my_app_log_errors]
search = sourcetype=my_app_log loglevel=ERROR

[my_app_log]
my_app_log_errors = enabled
```

We will explain **Normalized data** in detail in *Chapter* 4, *"Data Ingestion and Normalization"*.

Validating and testing the onboarding process

Prior to thoroughly integrating the onboarded data into your Splunk environment, it is necessary to validate and test the data onboarding process to ensure that the data is correctly ingested, parsed, and normalized.

You can use Splunk's **`Search`** application to confirm that events from the custom application log are being accurately ingested and that extracted fields correspond to your expectations. In addition, you can use the **`Data Model Audit`** dashboard in the **`Common Information Model`** application to verify that the data is mapped accurately to the selected data model.

If any issues are discovered during validation and testing, you can modify your configuration files and data input settings as necessary, and then retest until the data onboarding process is operating as expected.

By incorporating field extractions, event types, and lookups, we can improve the data integration process for our custom application log. These techniques will help provide additional context and enrich the data that Splunk receives.

Field extractions

Using the props.conf file, we have already extracted the **`loglevel`** and **`log_message`** fields from the previous example. To provide additional context, let's extract the **`UserID`** and **`Query`** fields as well.

The following field extractions should be added to the **props.conf** file:

```
[my_app_log]

...

EXTRACT-user_id = UserID:\s(?<UserID>\d+)

EXTRACT-db_query = Query:\s(?<Query>[^,]+)
```

Now, the **`UserID`** and **`Query`** fields will also be extracted from the log events.

Event types

Splunk's data search and analysis are facilitated by event types, which categorize events based on specific criteria. Using the sample log data, we can construct event types for user login events, failed database queries, and warnings for excessive memory consumption.

Update the **eventtypes.conf** file with the following definitions for event types:

```
[user_login]
search = sourcetype=my_app_log log_message="User logged in"

[failed_db_query]
search = sourcetype=my_app_log log_message="Failed database query"

[high_memory_usage]
search = sourcetype=my_app_log log_message="High memory usage"
```

Now, you can use these event types to easily filter events by category in your searches.

Lookups

Lookups are used to enrich data by incorporating fields from external sources. In this example, let's suppose we have a CSV file named **user_info.csv** containing user information with the columns `UserID`, `Username`, and `Department`:

```
UserID,Username,Department
123,jdoe,IT
124,asmith,HR
125,jbrown,Finance
```

We can use a lookup to add `Username` and `Department` information to log events based on the `UserID` field.

Navigate to `Settings` > `Lookups` > `Lookup table files` > `Add new` to upload the CSV file to Splunk. Select the CSV file and specify the desired destination app and file name.

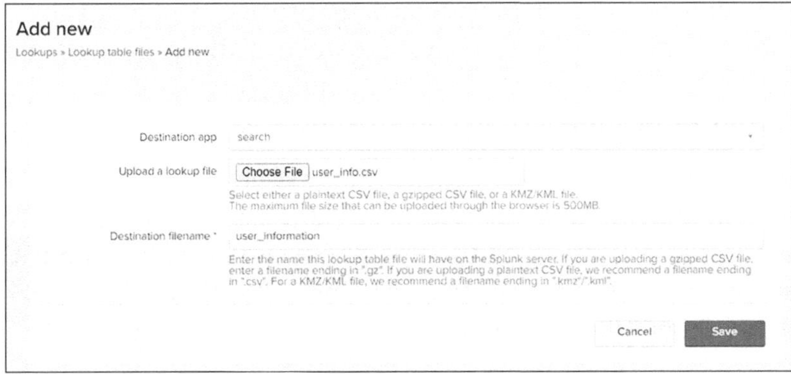

Figure 3.7: *Lookup table files configuration*

Alternately, the query can be defined in the **transforms.conf** file:

```
[user_info_lookup]
filename = user_info.csv
```

Then, define the lookup in the **props.conf** file:

```
[my_app_log]
...
LOOKUP-user_info = user_info_lookup UserID OUTPUT Username Department
```

Now, based on the **`UserID`** field, the log events will be enriched with **`Username`** and **`Department`** information, providing additional context for analysis.

Having implemented field extractions, event types, and lookups, you can now use the enriched data to create more sophisticated Splunk searches, visualizations, and alerts. Here are some examples of how you can search using the newly created event types and query data:

- Count the number of user login events by department:

```
eventtype=user_login | stats count by Department
```

- Identify the most common failed database queries:

```
eventtype=failed_db_query | stats count by Query | sort -count
```

- Find high memory usage events and display the username and department associated with the user who was logged in during that time:

```
eventtype=high_memory_usage | table _time, UserID, Username, Department, log_message
```

These examples illustrate how field extractions, event types, and lookups can considerably enhance the data onboarding process in Splunk by supplying richer context and more precise event categorization. By employing these techniques, you can obtain a deeper understanding of your data and strengthen your cybersecurity posture.

Please note that the SPL queries provided in this chapter are formulated to be generic and illustrative. They do not specify any particular index, allowing for broader applicability. If you wish to experiment with these examples, you may adapt them to your specific use case, for instance, by using **index= `<your_index>`** or any other index that is suitable to your environment.

Example of data onboarding via scripted input:

Scripted inputs are a powerful technique for ingesting data into Splunk through the use of custom scripts. They become particularly useful when you need to collect data from an API, perform data manipulation or transformation, or collect data from a source not supported by Splunk's built-in data inputs.

Consider an example of importing **`OpenWeatherMap`** API data into Splunk.

First, obtain an API key for **`OpenWeatherMap`** by registering for a free account at https://home.openweathermap.org/users/sign_up.

Next, create a Python script (for example, **weather_data.py**) that retrieves weather data from the **`OpenWeatherMap`** API:

```
import requests
import json
import sys
import os

api_key = "YOUR_API_KEY"
city_name = "San Francisco"
base_url = f"http://api.openweathermap.org/data/2.5/weather?q=
{city_name}&appid={api_key}"

response = requests.get(base_url)
data = response.json()

if data["cod"] != "404":
    weather_data = {
        "city": data["name"],
        "country": data["sys"]["country"],
        "temperature": data["main"]["temp"],
        "humidity": data["main"]["humidity"],
        "pressure": data["main"]["pressure"],
        "weather": data["weather"][0]["description"],
    }
```

```
    print(json.dumps(weather_data))
else:
    print("City not found.")
```

Replace "**YOUR_API_KEY**" with your actual API key obtained from **OpenWeatherMap**.

Make the script executable by running the following command:

```
chmod +x weather_data.py
```

Now, create a new scripted input in Splunk to run the **weather_data.py** script by following these steps:

1. In the Splunk Web interface, navigate to **Settings** > **Data inputs**.
2. Click **Scripts** > **New Local Script**.
3. Set the **Name** field to **weather_data.py** and the **Source name override** field to **weather_data**.

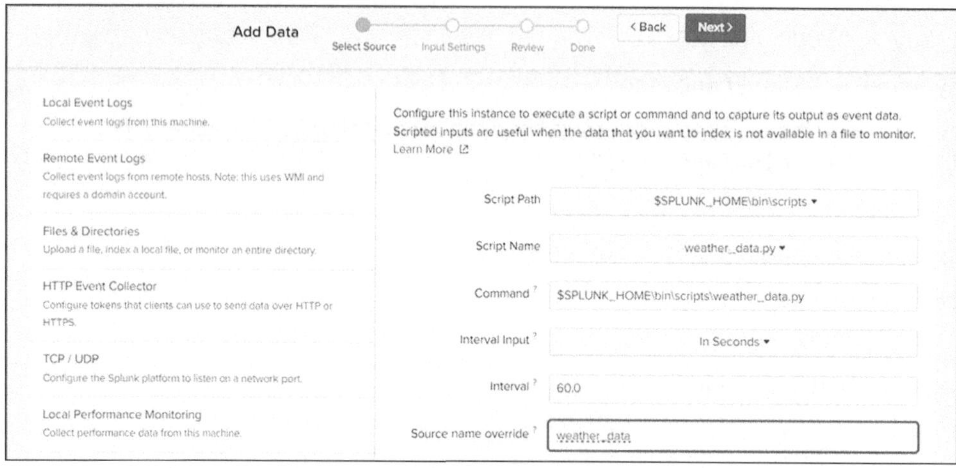

Figure 3.8: *Lookup table files configuration*

4. In the **Script** field, provide the full path to your desired Python script. Please ensure that your script is located in the splunk/bin directory of your Splunk installation. Once placed in the correct directory, navigate through the user interface to locate and select your script. For example, if you have a script named weather_data.py, ensure it is stored in the splunk/bin directory, and then select it from the UI.

5. Set the **Interval** to the desired frequency for running the script (for example, 3600 seconds for hourly updates).
6. Choose the appropriate app context and click **Next**.
7. Review the input settings and click **Submit** to create the scripted input.

Once the scripted input has been configured, the **weather_data.py** script will be executed at the interval specified, and the weather data will be ingested into Splunk. You can now search and analyze meteorological data using the **weather_data** sourcetype in Splunk.

To display the most recent weather information for San Francisco, for instance, you can use the following search query:

```
sourcetype=weather_data | head 1 | table _time, city, country,
temperature, humidity, pressure, weather | city="San Francisco"
```

This example illustrates how to construct a scripted input in Splunk for importing data from an external API. Scripted inputs can be used for a variety of data sources and formats, allowing you to exploit Splunk's complete capacity for data analysis and visualization.

Conclusion

This chapter provided insightful information on the significance of properly configuring and managing data inputs to extract meaningful information from various data sources. Following an introduction to the concept of configuring inputs and data sources, the chapter explored the various categories of data sources. It delved deeper into the complexities of configuring data inputs and comprehending their importance within the data processing pipeline.

The chapter also discussed the significance of effectively managing data inputs, which is crucial for preserving data quality, consistency, and precision. Data onboarding is the first stage in integrating new data sources into the system, ensuring a smooth flow of information and minimizing potential data pipeline bottlenecks.

Now that a solid foundation has been established in configuring inputs and data sources, it is essential to concentrate on the subsequent phases of the data pipeline. Importing data from various sources into the system, and then transforming and normalizing it to ensure consistency and compatibility with other data sets will be the focus of the following chapter.

In the upcoming chapter, you will learn about various data ingestion techniques, their advantages and disadvantages, and how to choose the most appropriate technique for your particular use case. In addition, the chapter will discuss the significance of data normalization in the context of data processing, analysis, and visualization, guiding you on how to effectively normalize data to improve its usability and extract valuable insights.

Points to Remember

- **Identify pertinent data sources**: In the context of cybersecurity, it is crucial to capture data from security devices, systems, and applications, such as firewalls, IDS/IPS, antivirus software, and network devices. This provides extensive visibility into your environment and aids in the identification of potential hazards and vulnerabilities.
- **Use secure communication channels**: When configuring inputs and data sources, ensure that secure communication channels such as encrypted protocols (for example, TLS, SSL) are used to safeguard sensitive data during transmission from unauthorized access or tampering.
- **Correctly configure log and event collection**: Ensure that logs and events from data sources are collected at the appropriate level of granularity to provide useful data for analysis. This includes enabling logging on devices and applications and adjusting logging levels accordingly.
- **Implement data retention policies**: For historical analysis, trend identification, and incident response, it is essential to retain data for a sufficient period. Establish data retention policies that strike a balance between storage needs and the requirement for historical data in cybersecurity investigations.
- **Configure data parsing and normalization**: For effective analysis and correlation of data from diverse sources, it is essential to parse the data into a consistent format. This facilitates the analysis and correlation of events, resulting in a speedier detection and response to threats.
- **Monitor data quality and integrity**: Examine and validate the accuracy and completeness of the collected data regularly. This increases the efficacy of your security measures by ensuring that your cybersecurity tools and processes are functioning with reliable data.
- **Test and validate configurations**: After configuring inputs and data sources, test and validate the configuration to ensure that data is collected, parsed, and normalized appropriately. This assists in identifying

any issues or voids in data collection that could have an effect on your cybersecurity posture.

- **Maintain current data sources and inputs**: Regularly assess and update the configuration of data sources and inputs to adapt to changes in your environment, such as new devices, applications, or system updates. This guarantees continuous visibility into your security landscape.
- **Comprehend compliance requirements**: Be cognizant of any regulatory or industry compliance requirements pertaining to data collection, storage, and analysis. Configure your inputs and data sources accordingly to maintain compliance and meet these requirements.
- **Educate your team**: Ensure that your cybersecurity team is well-versed in configuring and administering data sources and inputs. This allows them to utilize data effectively for threat detection, analysis, and response

Chapter 4
Data Ingestion and Normalization

Introduction

In this chapter, we will examine the process of data ingestion and normalization in Splunk, which is essential for ensuring accurate and consistent analysis of data from multiple sources. From ingesting raw data to transforming it into a structured and normalized format for analysis, we will discuss the various phases of data processing in Splunk.

The chapter will cover important topics such as data parsing, data normalization techniques, the common information model (CIM), and the implementation of data normalization in Splunk. In addition, we will discuss the advantages of data normalization, as well as the difficulties and best practices associated with this procedure.

By the end of this chapter, readers will have a deeper understanding of how data ingestion and normalization operate in Splunk and will be better equipped to use these techniques to improve the cybersecurity posture of their organization.

Structure

In this chapter, we will cover the following topics:

- Overview of data ingestion in Splunk
- Data parsing and processing
- Data normalization
- Data models and common information model (CIM)
- Best practices for data ingestion and normalization

Overview of data ingestion in Splunk

The process of collecting, integrating, and processing raw data from various sources into Splunk for analysis and visualization is known as data ingestion. Data ingestion is crucial in the context of cybersecurity because it enables organizations to consolidate and analyze data from multiple sources, such as logs, network devices, applications, and security tools, to gain insights into their security posture and detect potential threats.

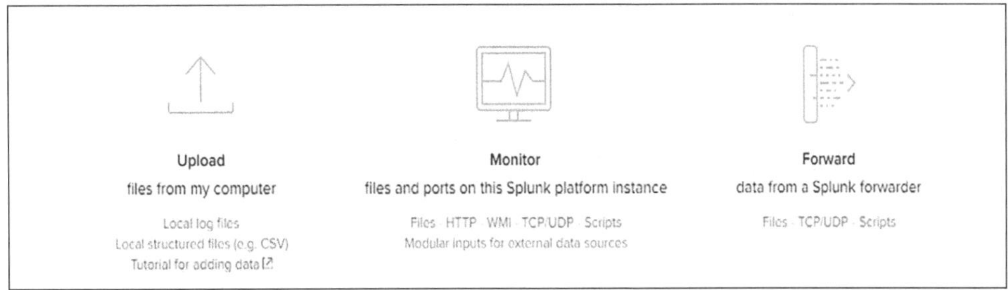

Figure 4.1: *Overview of Data ingestion in Splunk (Source: Splunk Data Ingestion - Javatpoint. (n.d.). www.javatpoint.com. https://www.javatpoint.com/splunk-data-ingestion)*

Splunk supports numerous data sources, such as files, network streams, APIs, and databases. Splunk can receive data in real-time or in bulk, depending on the use case and requirements.

Data Ingestion Process in Splunk

Splunk's data ingestion process includes the following steps:

- **Data Collection**

  Lightweight agents, referred to as forwarders, are used by Splunk to collect data from a variety of sources. These forwarders, which are used on data-generating devices, fall into the following general categories:

  - **Universal Forwarders**: They take in and send raw, unprocessed data directly to Splunk indexers.
  - **Heavy Forwarders**: These forwarders have sophisticated capabilities and can parse, filter, and perform preliminary data processing before sending it to the indexers.

- **Edge Processors**

  Splunk makes use of Edge Processors in the early phases of data ingress, particularly with Heavy Forwarders. These elements are the first in the pipeline for data processing, engaging directly with incoming data and enabling quick alterations or enlargements. The following are typical tasks carried out by edge processors:

- **Timestamping**: Establishes an event's precise timestamp.
- **Annotation**: Adds crucial metadata or extra information to raw data.

- **Ingest Actions**

Ingest Actions are predefined processing rules that can be applied to data as it enters Splunk. Through these steps, Splunk is equipped with the flexibility to carry out real-time data modifications throughout the ingestion stage. Examples include:

- **Data Masking**: To comply with compliance requirements, mask specific patterns, such as hiding credit card information.
- **Data Transformation**: Transform specific data types into a more illuminating format, such as IP addresses into geographic coordinates.

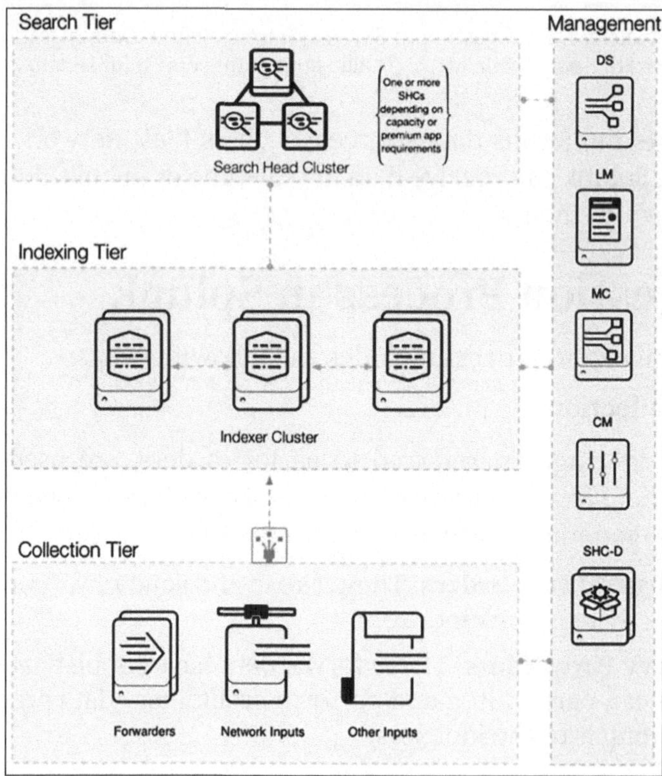

Figure 4.2: *Data ingestion in Splunk (Source: Get Answers from Your Data with Cisco UCS Integrated Infrastructure for Splunk Enterprise. (2023, March 20). Cisco. https://www.cisco.com/c/en/us/products/collateral/servers-unified-computing/ucs-c-series-rack-servers/splunk-eference-architecture-m6-cseries-solution-brief.html)*

- **Data processing**

  After data has been collected, it goes through a succession of processing stages in Splunk, including:

  - **Parsing**: Splunk identifies and extracts relevant fields from the raw data, such as timestamps and key-value pairs. This procedure helps the data become more organized and navigable.
  - **Event breaking**: Splunk divides incoming data into discrete events, which are then stored and indexed for subsequent analysis. This step ensures that Splunk treats each event as a distinct entity.
  - **Field extraction**: Splunk extracts additional fields from events based on predefined or user-defined field extraction rules. This step adds more context and information to the data, making it simpler to analyze and correlate.
- **Indexing**: After processing, the data is stored in an index on Splunk indexers, which manage and store the ingested data. Each index is comprised of a series of containers that represent various stages of the data's lifecycle, ranging from **hot** and **warm** to **cold** and **frozen.** This indexing procedure guarantees the efficient storage and retrieval of data for analysis and search.
- **Search and analysis:** Once the data has been indexed, it becomes accessible for search, analysis, and visualization within Splunk. Splunk's powerful search processing language (SPL) enables users to create complex queries, build dashboards, and generate reports, enabling organizations to obtain data-driven insights and make informed decisions.

Splunk's data ingestion plays a crucial role in enabling organizations to consolidate and analyze data from diverse sources, thereby providing a unified view of the cybersecurity landscape. By grasping the various aspects of data ingestion, you can effectively leverage Splunk's capabilities to improve the security posture of your organization.

Data Parsing and Processing

Data parsing and processing are essential stages in the data ingestion procedure, as they facilitate the transformation of raw, unstructured data into a more organized and searchable format. This ensures that Splunk can analyze and correlate the data effectively.

- **Line breaking**: When data is initially imported into Splunk, it undergoes the line-breaking process. Splunk recognizes the boundaries of individual events by searching for line breaks, which are typically represented in the raw data by newline characters or other delimiters. This procedure ensures that Splunk treats each event as a distinct entity.

Example: Assume that your log file contains the following entries:

```
2022-10-01 12:00:01 [INFO] User logged in: john@example.com
2022-10-01 12:01:15 [ERROR] Failed login attempt: jane@example.com
```

Splunk would recognize the newline at the end of each log entry and use it to separate the events.

- **Timestamp extraction:** Splunk extracts the timestamps from the events following line breaking. Timestamps are indispensable for time-based analysis and event correlation. Splunk can detect and extract timestamps from data automatically, but you can also configure custom timestamp extraction criteria if necessary.

Example: In the aforementioned log entries, Splunk would extract **`2022-10-01 12:00:01`** and **`2022-10-01 12:01:15`** as the timestamps for the respective events.

- **Field extraction:** Splunk extracts additional fields from events based on predefined or user-defined field extraction rules. This step adds more context and information to the data, making it simpler to analyze and correlate.

Continuing with the example of log entries, Splunk could extract the following fields:

```
Log level: INFO and ERROR
Action: User logged in and Failed login attempt
User: john@example.com and jane@example.com
```

- **Event type:** Splunk can categorize events into various types based on their content, structure, or other factors. Event types can facilitate the organization and classification of events, making it simpler to analyze and correlate data from multiple sources.

Example: Splunk could classify the events in our example log entries as **`successful_login`** and **`failed_login`** according to the log level and action fields.

- **Field transformations**: Field transformations are used to extract or modify field values in Splunk utilizing regular expressions or other pattern-matching techniques. These transformations can assist in the cleansing, formatting, and enrichment of data, making it more suitable for analysis and correlation.

Example: Suppose, in the example of log entries, that the email addresses are followed by a unique identifier (UID) in the unprocessed logs, as follows:

```
2022-10-01 12:00:01 [INFO] User logged in: john@example.com|UID:12345
2022-10-01 12:01:15 [ERROR] Failed login attempt: jane@example.
com|UID:67890
```

You could extract the UID as a discrete field using field transformations, allowing you to track user activity based on this unique identifier.

- **Lookups:** Lookups are a method for enriching Splunk event data by mapping field values to additional information recorded in external lookup files or database tables. This can provide additional context for the events and enhance the data analysis process as a whole.

Continuing with the log entries example, you could use a lookup file to map email addresses to usernames, roles, or departments, providing you with a more complete picture of user activities within your organization.

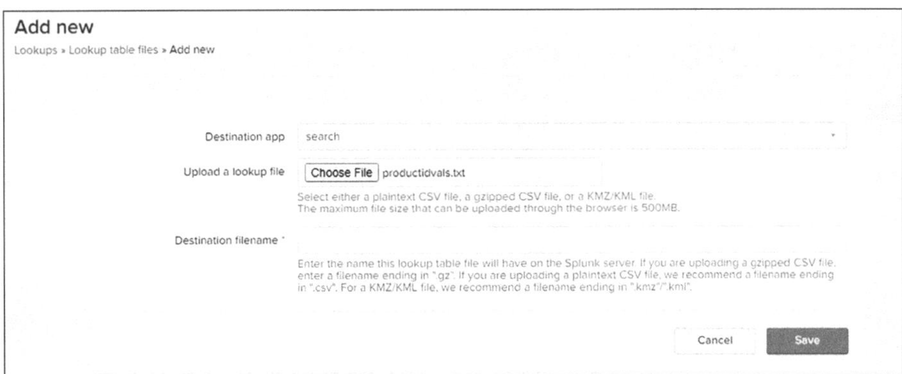

***Figure 4.3**: Lookups in Splunk*

- **Data retention and lifecycle management**: Splunk offers multiple features for managing the lifecycle of ingested data, such as index and data retention policies. By configuring these policies, you can determine the length of time data is retained, when it is archived or deleted, and how it is stored at various phases of its lifecycle.

Example: For compliance purposes, you may be required to retain certain log data for at least one year. By configuring a data retention policy in Splunk, you can automatically transfer data to a cold or frozen state after the required retention period, thereby optimizing storage and ensuring regulatory compliance.

By understanding and utilizing these various aspects of data parsing and processing in Splunk, you can optimize the ingestion process and maximize the analytical and decision-making value of your data. This will ultimately improve the security posture of your organization and enable you to respond more effectively to cybersecurity threats.

Data Normalization

Data normalization is the systematic approach of organizing data in databases to reduce redundancy and improve data integrity. It involves structuring data in a way that dependencies are properly aligned with the primary keys of their tables. The primary goal of data normalization is to eliminate any inconsistencies and anomalies, ensuring that data is stored logically and in its most coherent form.

Data normalization is an essential phase in the data management process, especially in industries like cybersecurity that deal with massive amounts of data. Fundamentally, normalization tries to restructure and "clean" data to increase its organization, effectiveness, and value. Let's explore the methods for data normalization, especially in the context of cybersecurity.

Defining Data Normalization in the Cybersecurity Context

Data normalization and log and event management are frequently used together in the context of cybersecurity. As a result of multiple security tools and software programs frequently reporting logs in different formats, normalization ensures a uniform representation. It makes analysis, threat identification, and incident response more streamlined by transforming different logs into a uniform format.

Here are the steps to achieve data normalization in cybersecurity:

- **Collect a Variety of Logs**: Before normalizing, collect a variety of logs from various systems and devices, including firewalls, IDS/IPS, endpoint solutions, and more.
- **Identify Crucial Information to Retain from Each Record**: Identify the timestamp, source IP, destination IP, port number, and the type of event that must be maintained from each record.
- **Create a Standard Format**: Create a standardized layout that will be applied to all normalized data. This may entail adopting a uniform date and time format, naming objects or systems consistently, and allocating data points in a predetermined order.

- **Conversion Process**: Transform or convert the various log entries into the predetermined format. This could entail rearranging the data points in a given sequence, renaming specific fields, or altering data types.
- **Validation**: Following conversion, validate to make sure the data was accurately changed. Make sure no important data is lost while the normalization process is in progress.

A Real-Life Cybersecurity Example

Think about a business that employs System A and System B, two distinct intrusion detection systems (IDS).

- Logs from System A record events as: **`[Timestamp] [Source IP] -> [Destination IP] [Type of Attack]`**

  Example: **`2023-10-17 12:30:15 192.168.1.1 -> 10.0.0.5 SQL Injection`**
- Logs from System B record events as: **`[Attack Type] detected from [Source IP] targeting [Destination IP] on [Date] at [Time]`**
  Example: **`SQL Injection detected from 192.168.1.1 targeting 10.0.0.5 on 17-Oct-2023 at 12:30:15`**

Both logs can be normalized to convert them to a common format, such as:

`[Date] [Time] [Source IP] [Destination IP] [Attack Type]`

The normalized log would appear as follows: **`17-Oct-2023 12:30:15 192.168.1.1 10.0.0.5`** SQL Injection.

With the logs in this uniform format, a cybersecurity analyst can rapidly and clearly compare and analyze data from both IDS systems, improving the effectiveness of threat detection and response.

How Splunk Can Help to Normalize Data

Data normalization is made simple and effective with Splunk's wide range of tools and features. Splunk helps with data normalization in the following ways:

- **Common information model (CIM)**

In Splunk, the common information model or CIM is a popular data normalization technique. It provides a standard set of field names and event categories for common data sources including network traffic, authentication logs, and system performance metrics. By mapping the fields from various data sources to a standard set of field names and event types, the CIM facilitates consistency and comparability across diverse log sources.

- **Field extraction and field aliases**

Field extraction is a technique used in Splunk to extract specific data elements from raw logs and allocate them to fields. Field aliases are a method for assigning aliases to fields. This may entail the use of regular expressions, delimiters, or other pattern-matching techniques to recognize and extract the desired data. Then, field aliases can be used to map the extracted field names to standardized field names, which further promotes consistency and comparability across various log sources.

- **Lookups**

Lookups are a method for enriching Splunk event data by mapping field values to additional information recorded in external lookup files or database tables. This can provide additional context for the events and enhance the data analysis process as a whole. By utilizing lookups, you can standardize the format of additional data across multiple data sources, which can then be used to generate field names and values that are shared.

- **Data parsing and processing**

Data parsing and processing entails converting unstructured data into structured fields and then processing them to ensure a consistent format. This may involve converting data types, applying field transformations, or utilizing field extractions to extract additional data from raw data.

- **Timestamp and timezone normalization**

In many instances, log data from various sources may contain timestamps in different formats or time zones. Timestamps are normalized by converting them to a standard format, such as UNIX time or ISO 8601, and ensuring that they are consistently expressed in a single time zone, typically Coordinated Universal Time (UTC). This method facilitates event correlation across multiple log sources and time-based analysis.

- **Categorization and labeling**

Categorizing and tagging events based on their characteristics or significance is another data normalization technique. By assigning consistent tags or categories to events, you can facilitate the identification and analysis of particular types of events, regardless of the data source from which they originated. For example, you could identify events associated with authentication, network traffic, or system performance, allowing you to filter or group events based on these categories during analysis.

- **Standardized event taxonomies**

Adopting a standardized event taxonomy, such as the MITRE ATT&CK framework, can help further normalize and contextualize data from various sources. You can create a more consistent and structured view of your security data by mapping events to specific tactics, techniques, and procedures (TTPs) within a well-defined taxonomy. This strategy can facilitate the identification of trends, patterns, and potential hazards across multiple log sources.

- **Data enrichment**

Data enrichment is the process of adding additional context or information to raw data in order to enhance its quality and analytical utility. This can be accomplished using a variety of methods, including the incorporation of threat intelligence feeds, geolocation data, and user and asset information. By augmenting the data, it is possible to standardize the context and enable more precise and exhaustive analysis across multiple data sources.

- **Data pipelines and pre-processing**

Before ingesting data into Splunk or another analysis platform, you can cleanse, transform, and normalize data using data pipelines and pre-processing tools. This may involve the removal of superfluous data, the conversion of data types, or the standardization of field names and values. By pre-processing data, it is possible to ensure that it conforms to a standard format and structure, making it simpler to analyze and correlate events from various sources.

- **Custom apps and add-ons**

In some instances, off-the-shelf data normalization techniques may not be adequate for particular use cases or data sources. In these instances, you can create custom applications or add-ons to normalize data in accordance with your organization's specific needs. These applications and add-ons can be customized to extract, transform, and normalize data from specialized devices, applications, or systems, thereby ensuring that data for analysis is consistent and comparable.

- **Data retention and normalization**

Data retention policies play a crucial role in assuring the normalization of data from various data sources. By standardizing the data retention periods for different data types, you can ensure that data is always accessible for analysis and correlation. This can be crucial when investigating historical trends, identifying patterns, or identifying the fundamental cause of security incidents.

- **Data quality and validation**

Maintaining data quality and validating the data's veracity are essential components of data normalization. Ensuring that your data is clean, accurate, and devoid of duplicates and inconsistencies can aid in enhancing the overall efficacy of your security analysis. Auditing and validating your data sources, field extractions, and normalization rules on a regular basis can aid in identifying and resolving any issues that could affect the consistency and quality of your data.

- **Training and documentation**

To ensure consistent and effective data normalization throughout your organization, you must provide your team with appropriate training and documentation. This includes training on best practices for data onboarding, field extraction, and normalization techniques, along with documentation on your organization's particular data standards, nomenclature conventions, and taxonomy. By investing in training and documentation, you can ensure that your team has the skills necessary to effectively normalize and analyze data from multiple sources.

Benefits of Normalization of Data

- **Efficient Storage**: This improves system performance by reducing data redundancy and freeing up critical storage space.
- **Improved Query Response Time**: Faster query execution and data retrieval are both made possible by the streamlined data.
- **Consistency and Accuracy**: Makes sure that data is kept logically by reducing anomalies and inconsistencies.
- **Improved Data Analysis**: Offers a standardized framework that makes it easier to cross-examine data from diverse sources and analyze it.
- **Promotes Growth**: Supports lead segmentation and other corporate growth goals by ensuring that data is accessible and well-organized.

Issues with Data Normalization

- **Possibility of Slower Queries**: Highly normalized data might occasionally cause queries to respond more slowly, especially when combining huge volumes of information from various tables.
- **Need for Expertise**: A detailed understanding of data structures and normal forms is necessary for proper data normalization. Execution errors can produce major data anomalies.
- **Team Complexity**: Teams may face additional challenges due to the inclusion of codes and numerical values in normalized data tables, which forces them to often consult query tables.

- **Emerging Options**: As NoSQL databases and non-relational systems gain popularity, denormalization is being seen as a potential replacement.

In conclusion, data normalization is a crucial aspect of cybersecurity analysis, as it ensures that data from various sources is consistently formatted and structured for straightforward comparison and correlation. You can enhance the quality and utility of your security data by implementing various data normalization techniques, such as CIM, field extraction, data enrichment, and custom applications. In turn, this will enable your organization to detect, analyze, and respond to potential threats and security incidents more effectively, ultimately enhancing your cybersecurity posture.

Data Models and CIM

In this section, we will discuss data models, which are abstract frameworks for organizing and interpreting data, and the Common Information Model (CIM), a standardized data model that, in the context of Splunk, provides a common language for correlating data from different sources within the logging and IT operations analytics platform.

Data Models

Data models in Splunk are a method for structuring and classifying data from various sources in a meaningful manner. By providing a higher level of abstraction over raw data, they enable users to obtain insights from their data. Data models assist in defining the structure of your data by employing a set of reusable objects, also known as data model objects, which represent various categories of events, transactions, and measurements in your data.

A data model comprises one or more hierarchically organized data model objects. Each object has a set of fields that represent the numerous data properties. These fields may be extracted from the original data, calculated from other fields, or inherited from their parent objects. Data model objects can also be connected via parent-child relationships, enabling users to examine and analyze data at multiple granularity levels.

Imagine you have a variety of toys, including cars, aircraft, and boats. Each object has distinctive characteristics, such as color, size, and composition. Now you need to organize these toys in a way that makes them simple to locate and compare.

Here, data models come into play. A data model is analogous to an organizational blueprint. In our toy example, the data model would assist us in creating toy categories and deciding which attributes, such as color, size, and material, to record.

Consider a large organization that wants to monitor user authentication activities across its vast network. The organization collects logs from Active Directory servers, VPN gateways, and various other applications.

Types of Datasets

- **Event Datasets**: These depict particular categories of events.

  Example: An 'authentication event' is produced each time a user logs in.

- **Search datasets**: These are adaptable and may be created using any type of search, enabling the collection of more intricate data.

  Example: To identify any brute force attacks, the security team might set up a search dataset to collect all unsuccessful login attempts over a 24-hour period.

- **Transaction Datasets**: Over time, these datasets compile collections of connected occurrences.

  Example: Grouping all a user's authentication actions throughout a week to look for any odd behavior.

- **Child Datasets**: These can be further filtered and inherit parent datasets' attributes.

  Example: A child dataset from the larger "authentication event" dataset might only include "failed authentication events."

Distinguishing Between Event and Search Datasets

The degree of complexity is the primary differentiator between event and search datasets. Search datasets allow for complicated search commands, whereas event datasets are simpler and include conditions defining them.

Example: A search dataset can be created to collect VPN logins from a particular geographic area or during non-business hours, whereas an event dataset might catch all VPN login events.

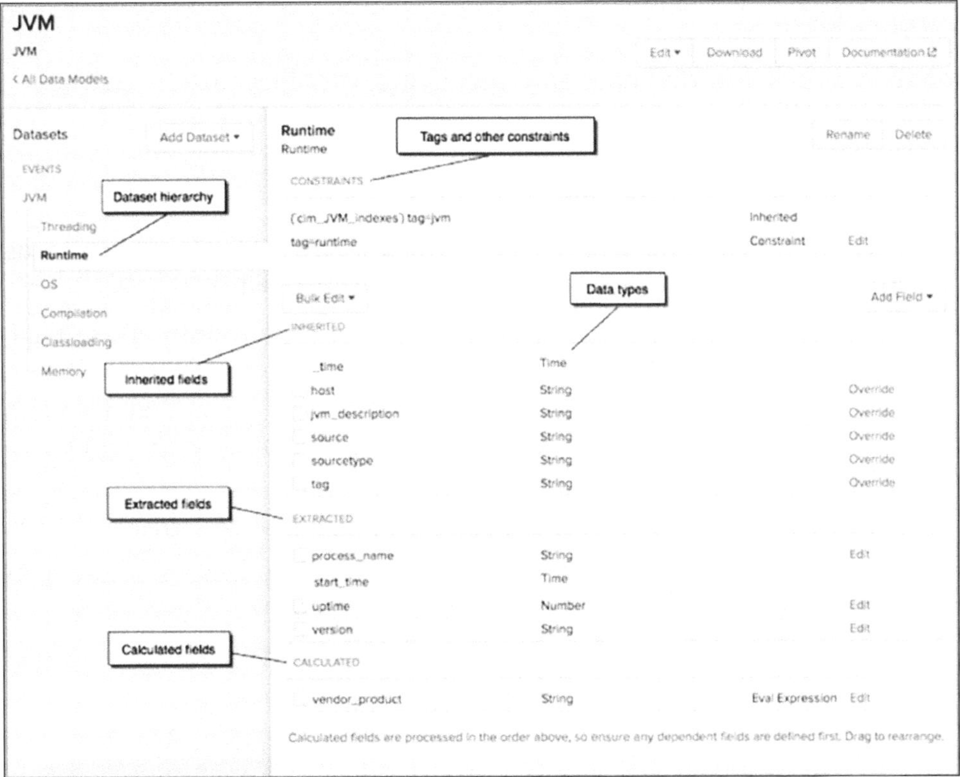

***Figure 4.4**: Common information model (Source: Splunk Documentation. (n.d.). https://docs.splunk.com/Documentation/CIM/5.1.0/User/Howtousethesereferencetables)*

Inherited Fields and Hierarchies

Upon specifying a dataset with restrictions, Splunk will automatically include several fields, such as **`host`**, **`source`**, and **`sourcetype`**. Datasets are standardized and consistent because of this inheritance method.

Constraints from the parent dataset will also be inherited by child datasets, although new constraints can also be applied. The **`AND`** boolean operator links this hierarchical relationship together.

Example: Let's assume that the root dataset for our authentication events includes data on every login that occurs within the company. A child dataset may inherit all of these events but also include a new restriction, such as only recording events that originated from IP addresses that are not corporate. This could help discover potential external threats more rapidly.

Dataset Fields

Several methods for defining and modifying variables inside datasets are provided by Splunk:

- **Auto-Extracted**: These are the fields that Splunk automatically detects and extracts from the data.

  Examples include `username`, `timestamp`, and `authentication_status` in our authentication logs, which may be automatically extracted.

- **Eval Expressions**: These fields are produced when an evaluation expression is applied to an existing field.

  Example: As an illustration, a new field may be added to identify authentication events as `suspicious` if they take place after regular work hours.

- **Lookup**: This method enriches data by using a lookup table.

  Example: A lookup table of known malicious IP addresses could be used to compare IP addresses in authentication records.

- **Regular Expressions**: These fields were created with regex, enabling the extraction of more precise data.

  Example: Extracting specific error codes from logs to see why certain authentication attempts were unsuccessful.

- **Geo IP**: This makes use of Geo IP data to incorporate fields such as latitude, longitude, country, and more.

  Example: Identifying the location of a login attempt to look for potential risks from particular areas.

Application of Cybersecurity in the Real World

Imagine a company that experiences frequent cyberattacks. The company's security staff can create structured datasets to track various aspects of their network using Splunk Data Models:

- **Event Dataset for Login Events**: Keep track of each login event across all servers and applications.
- **Search Dataset for Anomalies**: Look for login attempts made at odd times or from IP addresses that are blocked.
- **Transaction Dataset for User Behavior**: Compile a user's daily actions to look for any outliers from their usual behavior.
- **Child Dataset for External Threats**: Concentrate only on login events coming from unknown IP addresses or from places where the firm doesn't operate

The security team can build a multi-layered surveillance system by intelligently arranging the datasets mentioned above.

Example: If an employee, say John Doe, typically accesses the company's systems between 9 AM and 7 PM from New York, but suddenly there is an authentication attempt at 2 AM from, say, Moscow, this would trigger alerts.

- The transaction dataset can assist in highlighting such unusual behavior patterns.
- The system may detect several failed login attempts coming from an IP range recognized for malicious activity using the child dataset centered on external threats. This can be a sign of a system-level brute-force attack attempt against the company.
- When there is a sudden increase in traffic or authentication attempts from a particular country or region, the Geo IP capabilities might be extremely helpful, especially if the firm has no commercial relationships in that area. This can be a sign of a planned attack or the possible transmission of malware.
- Lookup fields and regular phrases can help quickly identify the precise causes of authentication failures. For instance, if a specific error code connected to password failures surges, it can indicate that a password-cracking effort is still being made.

The organization receives deeper insights into its network activity and can respond to threats more quickly and effectively by utilizing the organized approach of Splunk Data Models. Dashboards that display organized data enable easy monitoring and quicker decision-making. Such qualities are essential in a field like cybersecurity, where every second counts.

Benefits of Splunk Data Models

- **Abstraction and Simplification**: Data models offer a higher level of abstraction, enabling users to browse complicated data without directly interacting with raw data or sophisticated search queries.
- **Reusability**: Reusable items can be created by users and shared and used in a variety of searches, reports, and visualizations.
- **Decreased Query Complexity**: The data analysis process is simplified by eliminating the need to regularly create and manage complex search queries for various use cases.
- **Optimized Performance**: Splunk's ability to accelerate data models with summary indexes and tsidx files provides faster search performance and increases its suitability for large datasets.

- **Rapid Data Access**: Users no longer need to conduct time-consuming searches since accelerated data models enable quick access to and examination of data.
- **Adherence to CIM**: Splunk data models support consistency and seamless integration across various data sources and applications by abiding by the Common Information Model (CIM).
- **Improved Data Visualization**: Because data models are structured, they make for better visualization, which helps users draw insights more naturally.
- **Support for Standardization**: The CIM promotes coherence in data analysis by ensuring that various data sources may be understood and analyzed uniformly.
- **Better Collaboration**: Teams may work together more successfully when using shared and standardized data models since everyone is looking at the data from the same perspective.
- **Scalability**: Data models provide a scalable solution to ensure effective data management and analysis as enterprises expand and data volume rises.

In conclusion, data models in Splunk are a potent method for organizing, structuring, and analyzing data from various sources, which makes it simpler for users to gain insights and generate meaningful reports and visualizations.

Common Information Model

Let's discuss CIM now. Think of CIM as a super-useful guide that helps us standardize the organization of various categories of data, just as we did with our toys earlier. Data in the field of cybersecurity originates from a variety of sources, including computers, network devices, and security tools. Each of these sources has its way of describing things, making it difficult to analyze all the data at once.

The CIM assists in resolving this issue by supplying a standard set of categories and details (called "fields") for organizing data from various sources. By adhering to the CIM, we can ensure that our data is consistently organized, making it much simpler to locate, compare, and analyze.

The CIM enables us to organize data from diverse sources in a consistent and structured manner, similar to how we organize objects based on their characteristics. This makes it simpler for cybersecurity professionals to comprehend the data and protect our computers and networks from malicious actors.

Real-Life Example from the Cybersecurity Area

Now, let's explore the world of cybersecurity. Consider a business that employs an antivirus program and a firewall as its two main security measures.

- The firewall keeps track of and logs network traffic, gathering information about established and attempted connections, including any that might be hazardous or unlawful.
- The antivirus program runs a system scan for the business and records any malware or virus activity that is found.

There is a problem, though. Despite having similar functions, these instruments may utilize various terminologies in their logs. For instance, the antivirus software may refer to an external device's IP address as **`source_ip`**, but the firewall may record it as **`src_ip`** when it attempts to connect. This discrepancy can be confusing for an analyst who is attempting to compare data from both of these logs.

CIM steps in to save the day here. Both **`src_ip`** from the firewall and **`source_ip`** from the antivirus can be standardized to a single field name, such **`src_ip`**, by applying CIM to both logs. This standardization enables analysts to easily link events and details when reviewing these logs, without being hampered by varying terminologies.

Having normalized the data using the CIM, it is now easier to compare and analyze the information from both sources. You may discover that certain IP addresses not only attempt unauthorized network connections but are also linked to known malware. This understanding would allow you to take the necessary steps to further secure your computer and network.

Continuing with our example, after normalizing the data with CIM, you may wish to generate visualizations and reports to better comprehend the security events and trends. Since the data from the firewall and antivirus records now share the same field names and structure, creating these visualizations and reports becomes much simpler.

For instance, you can construct a dashboard that displays the top source IP addresses that generate the greatest number of security events across the firewall and antivirus logs. This would help you identify IP addresses that are repeatedly triggering security alerts and may be malicious. Additionally, you could construct a timeline chart displaying the number of security events per day, allowing you to identify unusual spikes in activity that may indicate a security breach or an ongoing attack.

Benefits of CIM

- **Consistency in Data Analysis**: By adopting CIM, data from various sources are standardized, reducing terminological differences and facilitating and enhancing combined data analysis.
- **Improved Visualization and Reporting**: With the data universally organized, making dashboards, reports, and visualizations is simple. For instance, a security analyst can quickly build a dashboard that displays security events from both firewall and antivirus logs.
- **Improved Threat Detection**: By using CIM to standardize data from many sources, it is simpler to spot trends, correlations, and abnormalities across datasets. This simplified picture can help people spot potential dangers and questionable activity more quickly.
- **Facilitated Collaboration**: Because CIM makes sure that data is presented consistently, cybersecurity experts may communicate their results with CIM-versed colleagues more successfully. Teams that have a common knowledge of data structure will communicate more quickly and work together to mitigate threats.
- **Efficiency in Incident Response**: Incident response teams can immediately comprehend the nature and scale of a security incident with a clear and unified view of security events. They can then contain and lessen the threat more quickly and decisively.
- **Scalability**: CIM makes sure that the addition of new data sources doesn't interfere with current analytical procedures as a firm expands and incorporates more tools into its cybersecurity architecture. The same model can be used to easily include the new data.
- **Promotion of Best Practices**: Organizations naturally embrace a set of best practices for data organization and analysis when they follow a standardized model like CIM. This may result in an overall improvement in the effectiveness and quality of data-related operations.
- **Enhanced Security Posture**: As CIM is consistently used, it can result in better cybersecurity decision-making over time, giving the business a more strong and resilient security posture.

Example Scenario

Suppose AcmeCorp, a sizable business, has several security measures in place, including a Cisco ASA firewall, a web proxy, an endpoint detection program, and others. Splunk is used by AcmeCorp to organize its logs and carry out security analytics.

One day, a probable effort at data exfiltration raises a Splunk alarm. The warning recognizes when a large amount of data is sent outside of the firm quickly using a correlation rule as its foundation.

How CIM helps in this scenario using the Splunk Add-on for Cisco ASA

- **Raw Data Collection**: A device within AcmeCorp's network established a connection to an external IP and sent a sizable amount of data, according to a syslog message sent by the Cisco ASA to Splunk.
- **CIM Normalization by the Add-on**: This raw data is normalized by the Splunk Add-on for Cisco ASA in accordance with the CIM's Network Traffic data model. To match the anticipated CIM data, key fields are removed and renamed.
  - `src_ip` (source IP) becomes `src`
  - `dest_ip` (destination IP) becomes `dest`
  - `bytes_sent` becomes `bytes_out`
- **Correlation with Other Sources**: Since the web proxy logs adhere to the Network Traffic data type, Splunk can now simply correlate this data with them. By comparing the normalized user field between the two data sources, the security team may identify which user was in charge of the traffic.
- **Incident Investigation**: The team investigates the incident and determines that a gadget in the HR division was to blame. After correlating this with data from their endpoint detection solution (also normalized to CIM), they discover that the device had recently been infected with malware.
- **Reaction**: The team rapidly isolates the affected device, eliminates the virus, and blocks the external IP that data was being transferred to using the knowledge learned from the normalized data.

In this situation, the Splunk Add-on for Cisco ASA's (https://splunkbase.splunk.com/app/1620) implementation of CIM was vital. The security team at AcmeCorp could easily correlate ASA data with logs from other tools by making sure that the ASA logs corresponded to the desired data model (in this case, Network Traffic), which allowed for quicker discovery, investigation, and repair of the event.

In conclusion, the CIM provides a standardized method for organizing and analyzing data from various security tools, thereby making it simpler for cybersecurity analysts to detect, analyze, and respond to potential threats and security incidents. By applying the CIM to your security data, you can obtain deeper insights, enhance collaboration, and ultimately strengthen the cybersecurity defenses of your organization.

Best practices for Data Ingestion and Normalization

- **Plan your data strategy:** Before ingesting data into Splunk, it is essential to have a clear strategy for the data you wish to collect and analyze. This involves identifying the data sources, the frequency of data intake, and the anticipated volume and velocity of data.
- **Standardize data formats**: To ensure consistent data ingestion and analysis, it is essential to standardize the data formats across all sources. This includes the application of standard field names, data types, and formats.
- **Use CIM**: CIM is a standardized data model for Splunk security-related data. Using CIM can help ensure that data from all sources is normalized and structured consistently.
- **Real-time monitoring:** To ensure effective data processing, continuously track data utilization, intake rates, system performance, and expenses.
- **Field mapping and standardization:** When converting data during ingestion, clearly define the mappings between the source and destination fields.
- **Document and evolve data models:** Data models should be thoroughly documented and updated on a regular basis in accordance with modifications to data sources and business needs.
- **Adapt to source changes:** Keep an eye out for structural or content changes in data sources and make quick adjustments to the ingestion and normalization procedures.
- **Maintain current documentation:** To keep records accurate and up-to-date, any changes to processes should be promptly documented.
- **Use field extractions**: Use Field Extraction To identify and extract specific fields from the data, use field extraction. This helps make the data simpler to search and analyze.
- **Utilize lookups and mapping tables**: Use lookups and mapping tables to contribute additional context or information to data. This can provide valuable insights and aid in identifying data patterns or anomalies.
- **Use regular expressions (Regex)**: Regular Expressions (Regex) are useful for matching and extracting data patterns from unstructured data. This can help identify particular data fields or events.
- **Utilize event type categorization**: Event type categorization can be used to classify events according to particular attributes or characteristics.

This can aid in identifying data patterns or anomalies and facilitate analysis.

- **Use time-based processing**: Splunk is optimized for time-based processing, so it is essential to use timestamp-based processing to ensure that data is correctly indexed and analyzed.
- **Utilize data preview**: Using Data Preview prior to ingesting data can help identify any issues, such as missing fields or formatting errors. This can help ensure that data is correctly ingested and analyzed.
- **Consistently apply metadata and monitor data quality:** It is crucial to continuously examine the quality of the data for accuracy, completeness, and consistency, as well as to look for data gaps, duplicates, and formatting issues. Additionally, make sure that the metadata applied to resources and hierarchies is uniform and complies with established standards.

By adhering to these data ingestion and normalization best practices, users can ensure that their data is consistent, accurate, and searchable in Splunk. This can help generate valuable insights and guide data-driven decision-making.

Conclusion

This chapter has provided a thorough comprehension of the critical data ingestion process in Splunk, including data parsing, processing, normalization techniques, data models, and the CIM. In addition, we have covered the best practices for data ingestion and normalization, which will ensure that your data is clean, consistent, and well-structured, leading to more accurate and insightful analysis.

As we transition to the upcoming chapter, "*Understanding* SIEM," it is essential to recognize the close relationship between data ingestion, normalization, and Security Information and Event Management (SIEM) systems. The effectiveness of a SIEM solution is significantly dependent on the quality and organization of the ingested data. Using the knowledge acquired in this chapter, you will be able to optimize your SIEM system, ensuring accurate detection, analysis, and response to security incidents and events.

In the upcoming chapter, we will delve deeper into the realm of SIEM by examining its fundamental components, functionalities, and advantages. We will discuss the integration of SIEM systems with various data sources, including ingested and normalized Splunk data. In addition, we will discuss real-world use cases, deployment considerations, and implementation and management best practices for an SIEM solution. The combination of a solid foundation in data ingestion and normalization with an in-depth understanding of SIEM systems will enable you to better safeguard the digital assets of your organization and strengthen its cybersecurity posture.

Points to Remember

- Data ingestion is the process of accumulating and indexing data into Splunk, whereas data normalization is the process of standardizing and structuring the data in preparation for analysis.
- Identifying the sources of data and determining the optimal method for ingesting the data into Splunk is the first stage in data ingestion.
- In addition to guaranteeing data compatibility and fixing any interoperability issues, one should always take into account and evaluate potential security and privacy concerns.
- Multiple data sources, including files, network ports, APIs, and message queues, are supported by Splunk.
- For consistent analysis, it is essential to standardize the data formats across all sources. CIM can be employed to standardize data pertaining to security.
- Field extractions can be used to identify and extract particular data fields, whereas lookups and mapping tables can be used to enrich the data with additional context or information.
- Regular expressions (Regex) are capable of matching and extracting data patterns from unstructured data.
- Event type categorization can be used to categorize events based on specific attributes or characteristics, facilitating the identification of patterns or anomalies in the data.
- Since Splunk is optimized for time-based processing, timestamp-based processing is essential for accurate indexing and analysis.
- Data previewing can help identify any problems with the data before they are ingested, and monitoring data quality over time is essential for ensuring accurate and consistent analysis.
- Planning your data strategy, using standardized data formats, CIM, field extractions, lookups and mapping tables, Regex, event type categorization, time-based processing, previewing data, and monitoring data quality are best practices for data ingestion and normalization.

CHAPTER 5
Understanding SIEM

Introduction

This chapter provides an introduction to Security Information and Event Management (SIEM) and its relationship to Splunk. It begins with a definition of SIEM and its primary functions, which include log management, event correlation, and threat detection.

The following section describes how Splunk can be used as a SIEM platform, including the deployment of the Splunk Enterprise Security (ES) app, which provides additional SIEM functionality, such as security event correlation, threat intelligence integration, and incident response management.

Moreover, the chapter discusses the creation and management of correlation queries, which are used to identify specific activity patterns in log data that may indicate a security threat. In addition, it explores the role of dashboards and visualizations in SIEM, along with the use of real-time alerts and data exploration tools.

This chapter provides an overview of SIEM and how Splunk can be used as a SIEM platform to help organizations detect and respond to security threats more effectively.

Structure

In this chapter, we will cover the following topics:

- Introducing SIEM
- SIEM features and functions
- Common use cases and benefits of SIEM
- Integrating Splunk with SIEM

Introducing SIEM

SIEM is a security solution that enables organizations to centrally monitor and analyze security-related events and alerts from multiple sources. By aggregating and correlating security events from multiple sources into a single console, a SIEM solution aims to provide real-time threat detection, response, and compliance management.

Typical SIEM solutions include the following components:

- **Data collection:** SIEM solutions capture logs and other security-related data from a variety of sources, such as network devices, servers, and security systems like firewalls and intrusion detection systems. The collected data is then normalized, correlated, and stored in a centralized repository for subsequent analysis and reporting.
- **Real-time analysis and alerting:** The SIEM solution performs continuous real-time analysis of aggregated data to detect potential security threats, anomalies, and patterns. It generates an alert for further investigation and response in the event that a potential threat is identified.
- **Reporting and compliance management:** SIEM solutions include dashboards, visualizations, and reports that enable security teams to gain insight into security incidents, trends, and threats.

SIEM solutions enable security teams to detect, investigate, and respond more efficiently to potential security threats by providing a centralized view of security events and alerts. SIEM has become an essential component of an effective cybersecurity strategy for organizations of all sizes due to the rise of advanced persistent threats (APTs), zero-day vulnerabilities, and insider threats.

SIEM solutions can also assist organizations with compliance management in addition to providing a centralized view of security events and alerts. Compliance regulations such as PCI-DSS, HIPAA, and SOX mandate that organizations monitor and analyze security-related events and generate audit reports. SIEM solutions can aid in automating these duties and ensuring that organizations meet compliance standards.

SIEM solutions can also be integrated with endpoint detection and response (EDR) systems, security information management (SIM) solutions, and threat intelligence platforms. This integration can offer a more complete view of security events and enable security teams to respond more effectively to potential threats.

It is crucial to consider the following best practices when implementing a SIEM solution:

- **Define use cases and objectives with precision:** Clearly define the use cases and objectives for your SIEM solution to ensure alignment with the security objectives of your organization.
- **Plan the collection and normalization of data:** Plan the data sources you will collect and how they will be normalized and enriched to facilitate effective analysis.
- **Consider performance and scalability:** Ensure that your SIEM solution can scale to meet your organization's requirements and can operate in real-time to provide effective threat detection and response.
- **Implement a robust security architecture:** Implement security best practices, such as secure communication protocols, access controls, and encryption, to ensure the security and resilience of your SIEM solution.

SIEM solutions are an essential element of an effective cybersecurity strategy, and Splunk offers a robust platform for implementing a SIEM solution that enables organizations to detect and respond to potential security threats in real-time.

SIEM Features and Functions

SIEM solutions are intended to assist organizations in collecting, analyzing, and managing security-related network data from multiple sources in real-time (see *Figure* 5.1).

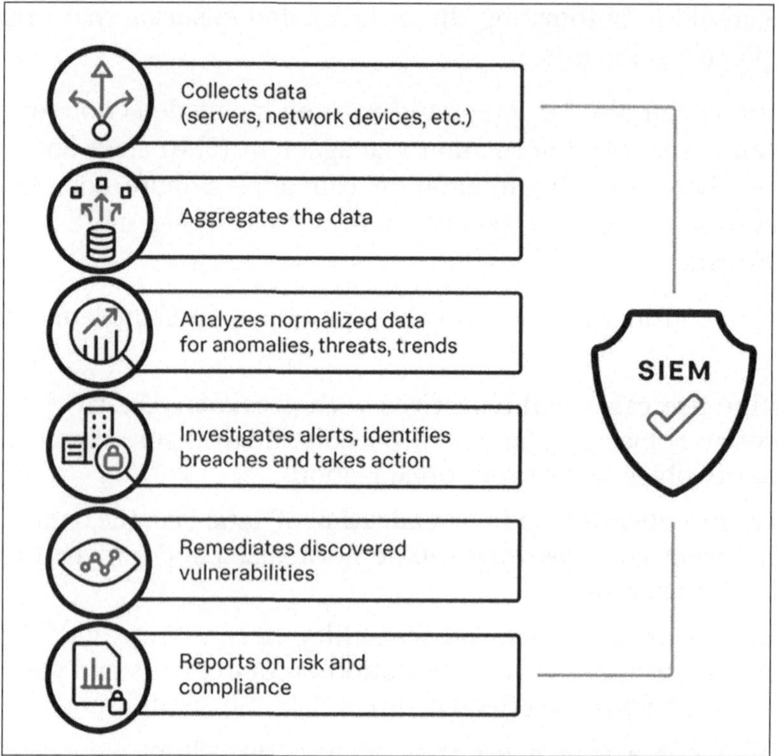

***Figure 5.1**: A SIEM solution (source: What's Cloud SIEM? Security Incident & Event Monitoring in the Cloud. Splunk-Blogs. (Watts, S.). https://www.splunk.com/en_us/blog/learn/cloud-siem.html)*

Among the most important features and functions of SIEM solutions are as follows:

- **Data aggregation:** SIEM solutions can aggregate data from a variety of sources, including firewalls, intrusion detection systems, and antivirus software. For instance, a SIEM can aggregate log data from various network devices and servers to provide a centralized view of all security-related events across the enterprise.
- **Event correlation:** SIEM solutions can correlate events from multiple data sources in order to detect and respond to potential security threats. For example, if a firewall event indicates an attempted intrusion and endpoint logs indicate anomalous user activity, the SIEM can correlate these events to identify a potential security threat.
- **Alerting:** SIEM solutions can generate alerts based on rules and thresholds that have been predefined. For instance, a SIEM can generate an alert when an unauthorized user attempts to access sensitive data or when network traffic suddenly spikes.

- **Incident response:** SIEM solutions offer workflows and tools to assist security teams in responding to and resolving security incidents. For instance, a SIEM can automate the incident response procedure by generating tickets, sending notifications, and initiating predefined workflows to mitigate the security incident.
- **Forensic analysis:** SIEM solutions enable forensic analysis of security incidents, enabling security teams to investigate incidents in detail and determine the source of the problem. For instance, a SIEM can provide forensic data such as packet captures and log files to assist in identifying the origin of a security intrusion.
- **Compliance reporting:** SIEM solutions can generate compliance reports that demonstrate a company's adherence to regulatory standards such as PCI DSS, HIPAA, and SOX. For instance, a SIEM can generate a compliance report that demonstrates how the organization complies with regulatory data security and privacy requirements.
- **Threat intelligence:** SIEM solutions can integrate with threat intelligence feeds to provide additional context and data regarding potential security threats. For instance, a SIEM can integrate with a threat intelligence feed to provide real-time data on the most recent malware or ransomware attacks.
- **User behavior analysis:** SIEM solutions can analyze user behavior across multiple data sources to identify anomalies and potential internal threats. For instance, a SIEM can detect anomalous user behavior, such as when a user accesses sensitive data at odd hours, which could indicate an insider threat.
- **Log management:** SIEM solutions can offer log management capabilities to assist organizations in collecting, storing, and managing log data from various sources. For instance, a SIEM can help organizations meet regulatory compliance requirements by preserving logs for a specified period and providing auditing and reporting capabilities.
- **Real-time monitoring:** SIEM solutions enable real-time monitoring of security events, enabling security teams to respond rapidly to potential security threats. For instance, a SIEM can provide real-time alerts when a security incident is detected, allowing security teams to investigate and respond quickly.
- **Correlation with business context:** SIEM solutions can correlate security events with business context, allowing for a more complete understanding of an organization's security posture. For instance, a SIEM can correlate security events with business applications, thereby revealing the potential impact of a security incident on essential business functions.

- **Anomaly detection:** SIEM solutions can identify potential security hazards by detecting anomalies in security-related data. For instance, a SIEM can detect network traffic anomalies that may indicate a distributed denial of service (DDoS) attack.
- **Threat hunting:** SIEM solutions with sophisticated search and analytics capabilities can facilitate threat-hunting activities. For instance, a SIEM can enable security teams to search for particular events or behavioral patterns that may indicate a potential security threat.
- **Integration with other security tools:** SIEM solutions can integrate with other security tools, such as endpoint protection, identity and access management, and vulnerability management solutions, to provide a more comprehensive security posture. For instance, a SIEM can integrate with an endpoint protection solution to provide a more comprehensive view of network-wide security-related events.
- **Dashboards and reporting:** SIEM solutions can offer customizable dashboards and reporting capabilities to enable security teams to visualize and report on data related to security. For instance, a SIEM can provide a dashboard that displays security-related events and metrics in real-time, such as the number of events, the top event sources, and the top event categories.
- **Machine learning and artificial intelligence:** Some SIEM solutions analyze security-related data and identify potential hazards using machine learning and artificial intelligence (AI) algorithms. For instance, a SIEM with machine learning capabilities can learn to recognize behavioral patterns that may indicate a security threat.
- **Cloud Security:** SIEM solutions can be deployed in the cloud to monitor and provide visibility into cloud-based environments. For instance, a SIEM deployed in the cloud can offer visibility into security events across multiple cloud providers and services.
- **Orchestration of incident response:** SIEM solutions can assist organizations in automating and coordinating incident response activities. For instance, a SIEM can automatically quarantine a system or disable an IP address in response to a security incident.

SIEM solutions provide businesses with a comprehensive collection of tools for managing their cybersecurity posture. By collecting and analyzing security-related data from across the network in real-time, SIEM solutions allow organizations to detect and respond to potential security threats swiftly and effectively, thereby reducing the likelihood of a data breach or other cybersecurity incident.

Common Use Cases and Benefits of SIEM

SIEM solutions offer numerous benefits to organizations seeking to enhance their cybersecurity posture. Among the most important benefits of SIEM solutions are as follows:

- **Enhanced detection and response to threats:** SIEM solutions can help organizations detect and respond to security threats more promptly and effectively. SIEM solutions can assist security teams in identifying and responding to threats before they cause significant damage by providing visibility into enterprise-wide security events in real-time.
- **Enhanced compliance:** Numerous SIEM solutions feature compliance reporting capabilities that aid organizations in meeting regulatory compliance requirements. By providing centralized logging and reporting capabilities, SIEM solutions enable businesses to demonstrate compliance with regulations such as HIPAA, PCI-DSS, and GDPR.
- **Increased efficiency:** SIEM solutions can automate a variety of security-related tasks, enabling security teams to concentrate on more strategic endeavors. For instance, SIEM solutions can automatically correlate security events and generate alerts, eradicating the need for manual intervention.
- **Better resource utilization:** By providing a centralized view of security events across the organization, SIEM solutions enable organizations to utilize their security resources more effectively. By reducing the need for multiple security tools and platforms, SIEM solutions can save organizations time and money.
- **Improved incident response:** SIEM solutions can assist organizations in enhancing their incident response capabilities by providing real-time information about security events. SIEM solutions can assist organizations in mitigating the consequences of security breaches by enabling security teams to swiftly identify and respond to security incidents.
- **Enhanced visibility:** SIEM solutions can provide a comprehensive view of security events across an enterprise, enabling security teams to identify patterns and trends in security-related data. This can assist organizations in gaining a deeper understanding of their security posture and making more informed cybersecurity strategy decisions.
- **Vulnerability management:** SIEM solutions can assist organizations in identifying and prioritizing IT environment vulnerabilities, enabling them to take preventative measures to rectify these vulnerabilities before they can be exploited by attackers.

- **Centralized logging:** SIEM solutions provide centralized logging capabilities, allowing organizations to store and analyze large volumes of security-related data in a central location. This can help organizations streamline their security operations and facilitate the administration of security-related data.
- **Correlation of events:** SIEM solutions can correlate security events from multiple sources to identify patterns and tendencies that may signal a security threat. By aggregating data from multiple sources, SIEM solutions can provide a more comprehensive view of security events across the organization.
- **Integration of threat intelligence:** Many SIEM solutions integrate with threat intelligence feeds, enabling organizations to identify and respond to emerging threats more quickly. By incorporating threat intelligence into their security operations, organizations can stay ahead of the most recent threats and reduce the probability of a security compromise.
- **Customization:** SIEM solutions can be adapted to meet the specific needs of an organization, allowing security teams to modify the solution to their environment. This may include customizable interfaces, alerts, and reports, as well as the ability to integrate with other security tools and platforms.

SIEM solutions provide numerous benefits to organizations seeking to improve their cybersecurity posture, such as enhanced threat detection and response, compliance reporting, increased efficiency, better resource utilization, enhanced incident response, enhanced visibility, centralized logging, event correlation, threat intelligence integration, and customizability.

Integrating Splunk with SIEM

Integrating Splunk and SIEM can provide a robust security monitoring solution, as Splunk's data aggregation and analytics capabilities can augment SIEM's detection and response capabilities. Several methods exist for integrating Splunk with SIEM, including:

- **Data forwarding:** Splunk can forward data to the SIEM in real-time using a variety of protocols, including Syslog, SNMP, and SNMP trap.
- **Ingestion of SIEM data:** The SIEM can be configured to consume Splunk data. This method is beneficial if you have already deployed Splunk and wish to avoid duplicating data ingestion configuration efforts.
- **Event forwarding:** Splunk's event collectors can forward events to a SIEM for event relaying. This method is beneficial when there are only a few events to forward.

- **Correlation searches:** Correlation searches can be used to identify and send to the SIEM events that match specific criteria. This method is beneficial when reducing the volume of data sent to the SIEM.

When integrating Splunk with SIEM, the following recommended practices must be considered:

- **Define a clear data management strategy:** Identify which data sources should be sent to the SIEM and which should remain within Splunk.
- **Configure data normalization:** Normalize the data so that it is consistent and straightforward to analyze.
- **Define correlation rules:** Define correlation rules within Splunk to determine which events should be sent to the SIEM.
- **Monitor the integration:** Ensure that the integration is functioning as expected and that data is being transmitted accurately by monitoring it.
- **Conduct regular audits:** Conduct regular audits to ensure the security of the integration and that data is being handled by regulatory requirements.
- **Map SIEM alerts to Splunk dashboards:** SIEM alerts are mapped to Splunk dashboards: Mapping SIEM alerts to Splunk dashboards enables analysts to view all security events through a single pane of glass.
- **Develop custom dashboards and reports:** Splunk can be used to generate customized dashboards and reports that integrate SIEM data with other data sources to provide a more comprehensive view of security events.
- **Use machine learning algorithms:** Use machine learning algorithms to identify and predict potential security hazards in advance.
- **Automate incident response:** Use Splunk's automation capabilities to automate incident response and reduce response times.
- **Conduct regular performance tuning:** Conduct routine performance tuning to optimize the integration and ensure that it continues to meet the security monitoring requirements of the organization.

Overall, integrating Splunk with SIEM can improve a company's security monitoring capabilities by providing a more comprehensive view of security events, facilitating faster response times, and enhancing the organization's security posture. However, the integration must be meticulously planned and executed to ensure its effectiveness and security.

Conclusion

This chapter concludes with a comprehensive overview of Security Information and Event Management (SIEM) systems, including their essential characteristics and functions. In addition, we have examined the common use cases and benefits of SIEM to demonstrate the importance of these systems in maintaining a robust cybersecurity posture. In addition, we have discussed the integration of Splunk with SIEM solutions, which enables organizations to enhance their security operations by leveraging Splunk's data ingestion and analysis capabilities.

In the upcoming chapter, we will delve into Splunk Enterprise Security (ES), a top-tier SIEM solution building on the concepts outlined here. We'll explore its architecture, features, and optimal practices for deployment and utilization, all aimed at providing profound security intelligence and actionable insights.

By combining the knowledge acquired in *Understanding* SIEM with an in-depth examination of Splunk Enterprise Security, you will be well-equipped to implement and manage a cutting-edge SIEM solution that protects your organization from evolving cybersecurity threats.

Points to Remember

- Security Information and Event Management (SIEM) is a technology that analyzes security alerts generated by network infrastructure and applications in real-time.
- SIEM systems are designed to help organizations detect and respond to security threats promptly by centralizing and correlating data from multiple security-related sources.
- SIEM systems include log management, security event correlation, real-time alerting, incident response, and compliance reporting as essential features and functions.
- Threat detection and response, compliance monitoring, and insider threat detection are frequent use cases for SIEM systems.
- Integrating Splunk with a SIEM system enables organizations to enhance their security monitoring capabilities by leveraging the data analytics and machine learning capabilities of Splunk.
- Configuring the SIEM system to forward data to Splunk, configuring Splunk to receive and extract the data, creating custom dashboards and reports in Splunk, and automating incident response using Splunk's automation capabilities comprise the integration process.
- Setting clear security goals and objectives, selecting the appropriate technology and vendors, defining data sources and data retention policies, and regularly reviewing and updating security policies and procedures are all best practices for implementing and using SIEM systems.

CHAPTER 6

Splunk Enterprise Security

Introduction

This chapter examines Splunk Enterprise Security (ES) and its role in bolstering cybersecurity. It begins by introducing Splunk ES and delineating its advantages in the context of cybersecurity. The chapter then examines the fundamental components of Splunk ES, such as data inputs, forwarders, the Security Information Model (SIM), glass tables, and the Adaptive Response Framework.

In addition, the chapter explores the Security Posture Dashboard, its purpose, customization options, and the interpretation of metrics used to enhance security. It focuses on integrating external data sources and enhancing access controls to highlight the significance of asset and identity management. It explains how threat intelligence inputs can be integrated into Splunk ES to enable proactive threat hunting and response.

Also covered is the significance of anomaly detection and correlation searches in identifying patterns and indicators of compromise. The chapter accentuates the Splunk ES incident review process, workflow customization and automation, and collaborative incident response. It describes typical cybersecurity use cases for Splunk ES, including network security monitoring, advanced persistent threat detection, insider threat mitigation, and compliance monitoring.

The chapter concludes by emphasizing the significance of integrating Splunk and Splunk ES, providing best practices for seamless integration, and leveraging both platforms to improve cybersecurity. It ends with a discussion of the evolving role of Splunk ES in the cybersecurity landscape and the influence of emergent trends and technologies on its capabilities.

Structure

In this chapter, we will cover the following topics:

- Introduction to Splunk Enterprise Security
  - Splunk ES and its Role in Cybersecurity
  - How ES Works
  - Core Components of Splunk ES
  - Key Benefits of Using Splunk ES in Cybersecurity
- Introduction to Correlation Searches and Notable Events
  - Creating and Customizing Correlation Searches
  - Scheduling and Configuring Alert Actions
  - Creating Notable Events for Insider Threat Detection in Splunk ES
- Security Monitoring and Incident Investigation
  - Executive Summary Dashboard
  - Introduction to Security Posture Dashboard and Incident Review Dashboard
  - Navigating and Customizing the Security Posture Dashboard
  - Investigating Notable Events with the Incident Review Dashboard
  - Incident Ownership and Workflow Management
  - Investigating Notable Events
  - Adaptive Response Actions with Splunk ES
  - Integrating MITRE ATT&CK and Kill Chain Methodology
  - Managing Advanced Persistent Threats (APTs)
  - Practical Use Cases of Splunk ES
  - Suppressing Notable Events
- Anomaly Detection and Correlation Searches
  - Introduction to Anomaly Detection and Correlation Searches
  - Importance of Anomaly Detection in Cybersecurity
  - Integrating Anomaly Detection with Other Security Measures
- Investigations in Splunk ES
  - Purpose of Investigations
  - Benefits of Investigations
  - Starting an Investigation in Splunk ES

Introduction to Splunk Enterprise Security

Splunk Enterprise Security (ES) is an advanced security solution designed to improve threat detection, incident response, and operational intelligence. It helps organizations harness machine data by providing an analytics-driven approach to cybersecurity, effectively reducing risk.

Splunk ES and its Role in Cybersecurity

Splunk ES serves as a key component in cybersecurity, utilizing its advanced analytics capabilities to identify and mitigate security threats in real-time. By integrating with various data sources, it enhances visibility into a network, enabling a swift response to security incidents and fortifying an organization's defense against cyber threats.

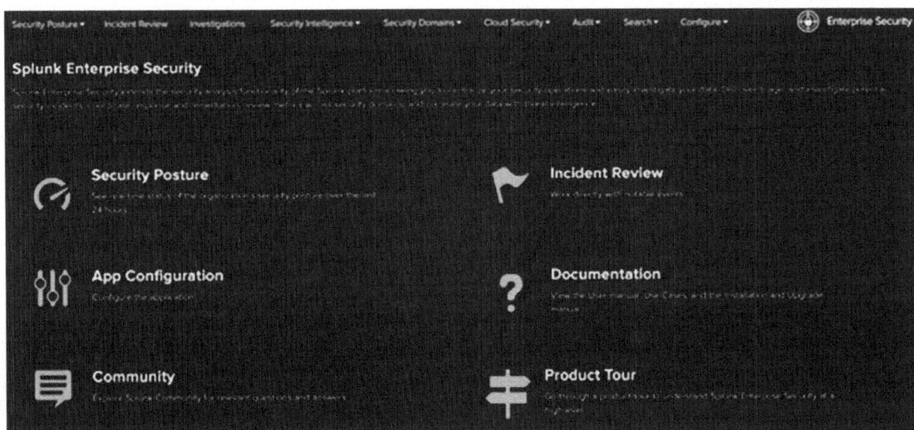

Figure 6.1: *Splunk ES Interface*

How ES Works

Here is a summary of how ES operates:

Through add-ons and data inputs, security-related data is collected from various sources within your enterprise, such as servers, routers, firewalls, and other devices. These add-ons facilitate the collection and parsing of data from various sources, ensuring that the information is compatible with Splunk ES and appropriately formatted.

The collected data is transmitted to Splunk indexers, where it is stored as events. Data is processed, categorized, and stored by Splunk indexers, making it searchable and accessible for analysis.

Splunk ES performs real-time searches on the indexed data to identify indicators of threats, vulnerabilities, or attacks. These searches may be predefined correlation searches or custom searches developed by the security team to identify particular patterns or anomalies. Some of these searches include:

- **Alerting and visualization**: If a search uncovers something that requires attention, such as a potential security hazard or incident, ES displays the information on one or more of its dashboards. These displays provide a visual representation of the data, facilitating the identification and prioritization of issues by security teams.
- **Investigation and analysis**: Security teams can use the investigative capabilities of Splunk ES to delve deeper into the identified issue, monitoring it, analyzing it, and determining the best course of action. This may necessitate the utilization of additional features such as the Incident Review dashboard, Investigations, and various intelligence modules.
- **Incident response and remediation**: Based on the analysis, security teams can take the necessary steps to resolve the issue, such as deploying patches, revising security policies, or initiating incident response procedures.

Splunk Enterprise Security provides organizations with an efficient and effective means to manage, analyze, and respond to security threats and incidents by leveraging its potent search capabilities, data correlation, and visualization features.

Core Components of Splunk ES

The following are some core components:

- **Correlation Searches**

Correlation searches are a vital component of Splunk ES that run continuously in the background, scanning data for evidence of attacks, known threats, or vulnerabilities. These searches can be conducted in real-time or on a predetermined schedule and can be modified or expanded as necessary. When a correlation search identifies a potential problem, an alert is generated, creating a notable event and potentially initiating additional actions such as sending emails, executing routines, or updating risk scores.

- Notable Events

Notable events are generated when correlation searches identify possible security incidents. These events are recorded in the notable index and provide crucial incident investigation data, including pertinent fields, event types, and tags. Analysts can search the index for notable events to obtain insight into potential vulnerabilities or threats.

Real-Life Examples:

Scenario 1: Protecting Against Data Breach Attempts

Scenario Description

To stop data breaches, Jit Inc. must recognize and react to anomalous data access patterns and possible data exfiltration.

Implementation of Correlation Search and Notable Events

- **Correlation Search for Data Access Patterns**: Jit Inc. sets up a search to track unusual data access, like an employee accessing records more frequently than necessary.
- **Notable Events for Data Exfiltration**: When suspicious data transfers occur, the system creates notable events to notify the security team of possible exfiltration attempts. These noteworthy occurrences provide situations priority for examination and handling.

Scenario 2: Combating Advanced Persistent Threats (APTs)

Scenario Description

In order to detect and address APTs, Jit Inc. must keep an eye out for any persistent, subtle hostile activity.

Implementation of Correlation Search and Notable Events

- **Long-term Pattern Correlation Search**: In order to find signs of APTs, the organization configures searches to examine prolonged patterns in user and network behavior.
- **Creating Remarkable Events for APT Indicators**: The search produces remarkable events in response to indications it finds, such as recurring connections to dubious IP addresses or configuration modifications. These incidents facilitate the investigation process by allowing analysts to concentrate on the most important and maybe dangerous tasks.

Scenario 3: Preventing Payment Fraud

Scenario Description

Jit Inc. is vulnerable to payment fraud in its e-commerce operations.

Implementation of Correlation Search and Notable Events

- **Transaction Pattern Monitoring Search**: The business uses searches to find patterns that deviate from the norm, including lengthy or quick successions of transactions.
- **Remarkable Events for Fraudulent Transactions**: A remarkable event is generated each time an anomaly is found. By reviewing and addressing questionable transactions promptly, the security team might potentially halt fraud in its tracks, thanks to these events.

In each of these cases, Jit Inc. uses Splunk ES Correlation Searches to identify potential security threats and to produce noteworthy events for each one. The security team uses these noteworthy occurrences as a focal point, which helps them to effectively prioritize and address the most urgent situations. By integrating noteworthy occurrences into its cybersecurity process, Jit Inc. improves its capacity to handle a variety of cyber threats and guarantees a strong security framework for its online store.

- **The Adaptive Response Framework (ARF)**

It is an ES feature that enables organizations to automate and optimize their security response processes. The framework is intended to assist security teams in responding rapidly to threats, mitigating the impact of incidents, and decreasing the time spent on manual tasks.

Scenario: Implementing Adaptive Response Framework (ARF) for Automated Threat Mitigation

Scenario Overview

Let's look at an example at Jit Inc. where the company wants to integrate the ARF into Splunk ES to improve its cybersecurity response plan. Jit Inc. is especially worried about responding quickly to malware attacks, discovered network intrusions, and any data breaches.

Situation and Challenge

Threats including virus attacks and illegal network access are frequent occurrences for Jit Inc. Delays in the manual analysis of alarms and reaction implementation might raise the possibility of data loss or system compromise.

ARF Implementation

1. **Automated Response to Network Intrusions**
   - **Detection**: Splunk ES's Correlation Searches identify anomalous network traffic patterns that can point to an intrusion.
   - **ARF Activation**: The ARF automatically starts predetermined actions, such as isolating the impacted network segment and blocking the IP address at the firewall, upon detection.
2. **Immediate Action on Malware Detection**
   - **Detection**: By integrating threat intelligence and doing correlation searches, Splunk ES detects a possible malware infection on a company workstation.
   - **ARF Activation**: In response, the ARF automatically quarantines the impacted workstation, starts a malware scan, and notifies the IT security team to do additional research.
3. **Data Breach Containment**
   - **Detection**: Unusual data access patterns and unauthorized data transfers alert a correlation search, which in turn finds a possible data breach.
   - **ARF Activation**: In response, the ARF suspends the concerned user accounts for a short while, blocks erroneous outgoing traffic, and starts backup procedures to guard against data loss.

Benefits for Jit Inc.

- **Quick Reaction**: Jit Inc. can react to threats quickly, thanks to ARF, which reduces the time attackers need to cause damage.
- **Lessened Manual Involvement**: The security team can concentrate on in-depth analysis and strategic responses as automated responses reduce the need for rapid manual involvement.
- **Adaptable and Scalable**: Jit Inc. can adjust ARF activities in accordance with particular threat categories, guaranteeing a customized reaction plan that changes with the business's demands.

The real-time cybersecurity threat management capabilities of Jit Inc. are greatly improved by the Adaptive Response Framework in Splunk ES. The ARF reduces the impact of security incidents and enables the security team to deploy resources more effectively by automating the response process. This allows the team to concentrate on strategic security initiatives rather than on routine threat responses. Jit Inc. is able to maintain a strong and durable defense against a variety of cyber-attacks because of its proactive approach to cybersecurity.

- **Assets and identities**

Assets (devices within the enterprise) and identities (people within the organization) are essential components of ES that assist in determining the significance of noteworthy events. Managed via lookup databases, assets, and identities provide context for security incidents, enabling analysts to prioritize their responses based on the significance of affected devices or users.

- **Investigation timelines**

Splunk ES provides investigation journals to assist security teams in tracking, coordinating, and managing ongoing investigations. These journals allow analysts to visualize and document the progress of incident analyses, collaborate with others, and archive notable events, search results, notes, and other investigation-related content.

- **Beyond notable events**

Splunk ES provides advanced tools for in-depth security analysis, such as risk and threat analysis, web and user intelligence, protocol (stream) intelligence, and adaptive response, in addition to the fundamental components described previously. These tools can be indispensable during forensic investigations, proactive threat hunting, and historical analysis of previous intrusions to better comprehend and prevent incidents.

Splunk Enterprise Security enables organizations to effectively detect, investigate, and respond to security threats and incidents, thereby improving their overall security posture.

Key Benefits of Using Splunk ES in Cybersecurity

Splunk ES offers many benefits in the field of cybersecurity, including:

- **Comprehensive Visibility:** Splunk ES provides a comprehensive view of an organization's security posture by consolidating data from multiple security sources, enabling security teams to identify patterns, trends, and anomalies that may indicate potential threats.
- **Rapid Threat Detection:** Through advanced analytics, correlation searches, and customizable dashboards, Splunk ES enables security teams to detect threats and vulnerabilities rapidly and effectively, thereby reducing the time required to respond to incidents and minimizing the resulting damage.
- **Improved Incident Response:** Splunk ES's Adaptive Response Framework enables automated and semi-automated responses to threats, streamlining the incident response procedure and allowing security teams to concentrate on high-priority duties.
- **Enhanced Collaboration:** Splunk ES facilitates collaboration among security teams with features such as incident review and workflow management, allowing for more effective and coordinated response efforts.
- **Scalability:** Splunk ES is readily scalable to accommodate large amounts of security data from expanding organizations, ensuring that its performance remains consistent and dependable as the volume and complexity of security data increases.
- **Compliance and Reporting:** Splunk ES assists organizations in meeting regulatory compliance requirements by providing built-in reports and customizable dashboards that make it simpler to monitor, analyze, and demonstrate compliance with a variety of security standards.
- **Ease of Integration with Other Security Tools:** Splunk ES integrates seamlessly with a variety of security tools and technologies, including firewalls, intrusion detection systems, endpoint protection platforms, and threat intelligence feeds. This enables organizations to centralize the administration and monitoring of their security infrastructure, thereby reducing complexity and enabling security teams to operate more efficiently.

- **Customizability and Extensibility:** Splunk ES is highly customizable and extensible, allowing organizations to customize the solution to their specific needs and requirements. To better analyze and visualize their security data, security teams can construct personalized dashboards, reports, alerts, and correlation queries. In addition, Splunk ES supports the development of custom applications and add-ons, allowing organizations to extend the platform's functionality and resolve particular security challenges.
- **Machine Learning and Artificial Intelligence Capabilities:** Splunk ES makes use of machine learning algorithms and artificial intelligence to improve its threat detection and response capabilities. These technologies enable Splunk ES to recognize patterns, trends, and anomalies in security data that may indicate potential threats, thereby reducing false positives and enhancing the accuracy of threat detection. Adaptive response capabilities are also powered by machine learning, enabling more intelligent and efficient automated responses to security incidents.
- **Cloud Readiness and Support for Hybrid Environments:** Splunk ES supports both on-premises and cloud-based deployments, making it suitable for businesses of all sizes with diverse IT infrastructures. In addition, it provides seamless integration with popular cloud services, enabling security teams to monitor and analyze security data from their cloud environments alongside on-premises infrastructure. This assures comprehensive security monitoring and visibility across hybrid environments.

Splunk ES is, in conclusion, a robust and adaptable SIEM solution that addresses the diverse cybersecurity requirements of modern organizations. Splunk ES enables security teams to better defend their organizations from cyber threats and maintain a strong security posture by providing comprehensive visibility, rapid threat detection, enhanced incident response, and seamless integration with other security tools. Customizability, extensibility, and advanced capabilities, such as machine learning and support for hybrid environments, make the platform an indispensable asset in an ever-changing cybersecurity environment.

Introduction to Correlation Searches and Notable Events

In this section, we will discuss the process of creating and customizing correlation searches in the context of anomaly detection and cybersecurity. Correlation searches are essential for identifying patterns and indicators of compromise that may signify potential threats.

Creating a new Correlation Search

In Splunk Enterprise Security (ES), correlation searches are essential for spotting anomalies and locating possible security risks. The study of intricate data patterns and compromise signs is made possible by these searches. In the following sections, we delve into great depth on how to create these searches, with resources and examples to help.

Creating a New Correlation Search

- **Getting to Content Management:** In Splunk ES, go to the **`Configure`** menu and choose **`Content Management`**. This section serves as the central location for handling different kinds of content, including correlation searches.
- **Launching a New Correlation Search:** To begin, click **`Create New`** and choose **`Correlation Search`**. The process of defining a new search is started at this phase.
- **Defining Search Parameters:** Enter the search name and description in the creation interface, among other pertinent information. Ensure that the search name is descriptive and reflects the goal of the search.
- **Formulating the Search Query:** The correlation search revolves around the search query. To specify the parameters, use Splunk's Search Processing Language (SPL). Here, resources like the SPL documentation from Splunk might be quite helpful. For query formulation, use knowledge-based datasets pertinent to your security requirements as well.

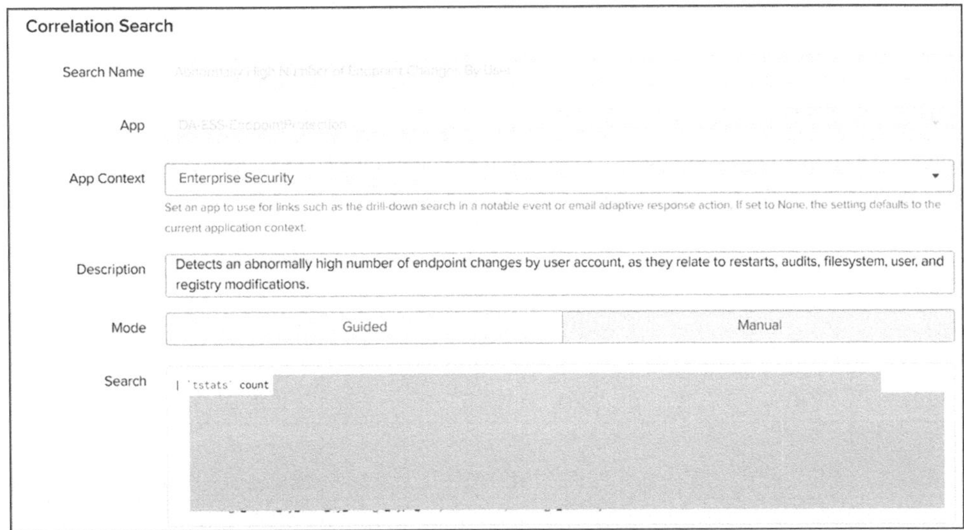

Figure 6.2: *Splunk Correlation Search*

- **Creating the Search Schedule and Alert Actions:** Establish the search schedule (for example, real-time, periodic), decide on the level of detail required in the results, and set up alert actions (for example, email alerts, script executions). It's critical to match these configurations to the unique security goals of the correlation search.
- **Testing and Validation:** Test the correlation search to ensure that it is effective before storing it. As part of this testing, the search may be compared to past data to see how well it detects possible dangers.
- **Preserving and Observing:** Save the correlation search once extensive testing and validation are complete. Keep an eye on its functioning and make any required adjustments in light of the changing cybersecurity environment.

Deep-Dive Resources

- **Splunk Documentation**: Comprehensive instructions for configuring correlation and SPL searches.
- **Splunk Community Forums**: An area for users to converse and exchange ideas.
- **Splunk Education**: Provides training programs and credentials for increased user knowledge and proficiency.

Example: Detecting Data Exfiltration

Scenario

Jit Inc. wishes to keep an eye out for any possible data exfiltration, which entails sending a lot of data to other locations.

Sample Dataset

Consider a simplified dataset from Jit Inc.'s network logs, containing fields like `user`, `file_size`, `destination_ip`, and `timestamp`.

user	file_size (MB)	destination_ip	timestamp
Alice	20	192.168.1.105	2023-11-01 10:30:00
Bob	1500	203.0.113.5	2023-11-01 10:45:00
Alice	25	192.168.1.110	2023-11-01 11:00:00
Bob	1600	203.0.113.5	2023-11-01 11:15:00

A sizable file transfer from Bob to the external IP address 203.0.113.5 is noted in this dataset; this could be a sign of data exfiltration.

SPL Query

In order to find such actions, Jit Inc. could use the following to generate a correlation search:

```
index=network_logs sourcetype=network_traffic | stats sum(file_size) as to-
tal_transferred_MB by user, destination_ip | where total_transferred_MB
> 1000 | search NOT [| inputlookup internal_ip_addresses | fields + des-
tination_ip] | table user, destination_ip, total_transferred_MB
```

Query Breakdown

- **`index=network_logs sourcetype=network_traffic`**: Specifies the log index and sourcetype for network traffic.
- **`stats sum(file_size) as total_transferred_MB by user, destination_ip`**: Aggregates the total data transferred by each user to each IP address.
- **`where total_transferred_MB > 1000`**: Filters for transfers where over 1000 MB of data is moved, indicating potentially large file transfers.
- **`search NOT [| inputlookup internal_ip_addresses | fields + destination_ip]`**: Excludes internal IP addresses, focusing the search on external data transfers.
- **`table user, destination_ip, total_transferred_MB`**: Formats the output in a table for easier analysis.

Unusually significant data transfers to external destinations, which may indicate data exfiltration, are detected by Jit Inc. with the use of this SPL query. The security team can take the necessary action to look into and lessen possible security incidents by evaluating the findings.

Customizing existing correlation searches

To modify an existing correlation search, follow these steps:

1. Navigate to the **Configure** menu and select **Content Management.**
2. Locate the correlation search you wish to modify and click on its name.
3. Update the search fields, settings, or query as needed.
4. Save the modified correlation search.

Scheduling and Configuring Alert Actions

Alert actions are an essential component of efficient correlation searches, as they serve to notify security teams of potential threats and initiate the corresponding response actions. In this section, we will discuss how to schedule and configure alert actions for Splunk ES correlation searches.

Scheduling Correlation Searches

To ensure the timely detection of security events and anomalies, it is essential to schedule correlation searches to run at regular intervals. The process of scheduling entails determining the frequency, time range, and precedence of searches. When planning a correlation search, take into account the following factors:

- The urgency and potential impact of the security event
- The performance and resource consumption implications of running the search
- The intended balance of detection speed and search efficiency

To schedule a correlation search in Splunk ES, navigate to the configuration page for the correlation search and configure the desired cron schedule, time range, and other parameters.

Configuring Alert Actions

After scheduling the correlation search, the next step is to configure the alert actions that will be activated when the search generates notable events. Alert actions can include sending email notifications, creating notable events in the dashboard for Incident Review, executing custom programs, and more. When configuring alert actions, consider the following best practices:

- Select alert actions that correspond to your organization's incident response plan and escalation procedures.
- Customize the alert action's parameters, including email recipients, priority, and subject, to ensure that pertinent information is effectively communicated.
- Use throttling to prevent security teams from being overwhelmed by duplicate or excessive alerts.
- Verify that alert actions function as anticipated and do not generate false positives or negatives by testing them.

To configure alert actions for a correlation search in Splunk Enterprise Security, visit the configuration page for the correlation search and select the `Add New Response Action` button. Select the desired action from the list of available response actions and modify its settings as required.

By scheduling and configuring alert actions for correlation searches, security teams can improve their ability to detect and respond to potential threats, ensuring a proactive and efficient cybersecurity strategy.

Using Splunk ES to Create Notable Events for Insider Threat Detection

To identify possible insider threats, this section will guide you through a methodical procedure for creating noteworthy events in Splunk Enterprise Security (ES). In this scenario, we monitor anomalous user behavior, such as accessing sensitive data at odd hours, which could indicate a security issue.

Situation: Tracking Abnormal After-Hours Access to Private Information

Jit Inc. is worried about insider threats to its sensitive data. They seek to identify any anomalous access to sensitive material by staff after hours to rectify this.

Sample Log File

Consider a simplified dataset from Jit Inc.'s secure data access logs:

User	file_access	edtimestamp
Alice	fileA	2023-11-01 23:00:00
Bob	fileB	2023-11-01 23:15:00
Alice	fileC	2023-11-01 23:30:00
Bob	fileD	2023-11-01 04:00:00

This dataset records instances of users accessing various files, with timestamps indicating after-hours activity.

Step 1: Define the Search Criteria

- **Goal**: The goal is to develop a search that finds sensitive data access outside of regular business hours.
- **Criteria**: Search for logs that show who accessed sensitive data repositories (for example, between 10 PM and 6 AM) after hours.

Step 2: Create the SPL Query

```
index=secure_data_logs sourcetype=user_access | where hour(_time) > 22
OR hour(_time) < 6 | stats count by user, file_accessed | where count > 5
```

Explanation: This query checks for user activities in the secure data logs (`secure_data_logs`) sourcetype, specifically accessing files outside of regular hours and where such access occurrences are more than five times in a night.

Step 3: Set Up Correlation Search in Splunk ES

- **Navigation**: In Splunk ES, choose **`Content Management`** from the **`Configure`** menu.
- **Configuration**: Click **`Create New Content`** and then **`Correlation Search`**. In the designated field, type the SPL query.
- **Specifics**: Provide a descriptive name (for example, **`After-Hours Access to Sensitive Data`**), along with a description and a level of severity.

Step 4: Define Trigger Conditions for Notable Events

- **Criteria**: Define the circumstances, such as any favorable outcome from the SPL query, that lead to a noteworthy event.
- **Thresholds**: Establish thresholds, including multiple after-hours accesses, suggestive of possible insider threats.

Step 5: Configure Notable Event Creation

- **Action Setup**: In the correlation search settings, choose the action to **`Create Notable Event`** when the search criteria are met.
- **Customization**: Make the noteworthy event's title and description more appropriate for the situation by changing it to something like **`Potential Insider Threat Detected: After-Hours Data Access`**.

Step 6: Test and Validate

- **Manual Testing**: Manually carry out the correlation search's initial testing to ensure that it accurately identifies the specified activity.
- **Refinement**: As necessary, based on the results, modify the search query and the remarkable event criteria.

Step 7: Implement Monitoring and Response Protocols

- **Ongoing Monitoring**: Make sure to frequently monitor the Incident Review Dashboard for noteworthy events that have been generated.
- **Reaction Plan**: Formulate a well-defined protocol for addressing these noteworthy incidents, including prompt inquiries and subsequent measures.

Through the use of this Splunk ES configuration, Jit Inc. will be able to detect and address possible insider threats with efficiency. The security team can take immediate action to safeguard sensitive data by being swiftly notified of unexpected and potentially dangerous behaviors when notable events are created based on specified user activity patterns.

Security Monitoring and Incident Investigation

Splunk ES enables continuous security monitoring, allowing for the real-time detection of potential threats and anomalies. Its comprehensive incident investigation features facilitate detailed analyses of security events, providing context and insights that drive effective responses to incidents.

Executive Summary Dashboard

One essential element in Splunk Enterprise Security (ES) is the Executive Summary Dashboard, which gives executive teams and senior management a high-level picture of their company's cybersecurity posture. It simplifies intricate security data into concise, useful insights, empowering leaders to decide on their cybersecurity plans with knowledge.

Key Features of the Dashboard

- **High-Level Security Metrics**: The dashboard shows important security metrics, such as total threat levels, attack type trends, and compliance status, in an understandable manner.
- **Visual Representations of Data**: The dashboard visually shows data using graphs, charts, and heat maps, which helps executives immediately understand the security status and trends.
- **Customizable Views**: This feature enables customization to concentrate on particular topics of interest or concern, including certain company divisions, geographical areas, or categories of security occurrences.

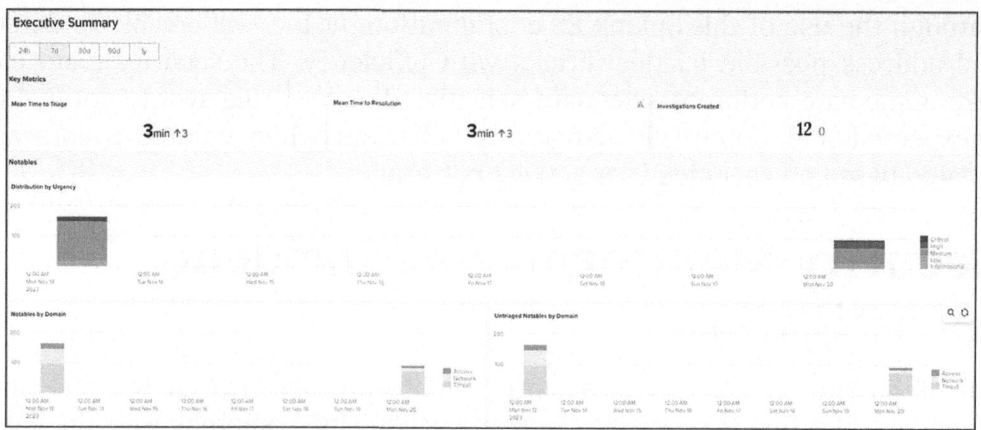

***Figure 6.3**: Splunk ES Executive Summary Dashboard*

Utilization at Jit Inc.

- **Strategic Decision-Making**: The executive team at Jit Inc. uses the dashboard to evaluate the overall success of their cybersecurity initiatives and to make strategic choices, such as directing resources toward regions where threats are more prevalent.
- **Monitoring Compliance and Risk Management**: Jit Inc. is able to manage risk and stay in compliance with regulations thanks to the dashboard's insights on compliance with different standards.
- **Identifying Trends and Patterns**: Jit Inc. executives are able to foresee possible future threats and modify their cybersecurity strategy by examining long-term trends and patterns in security data.

Scenario: Addressing Emerging Threats

Situation: An increase in phishing attempts aimed at the firm is indicated by the dashboard.

- **Management Action**: Jit Inc.'s management team launches a cybersecurity awareness campaign for the entire organization and provides extra funding for cutting-edge phishing detection tools.

Scenario: Regulatory Compliance Monitoring

Situation: Possible non-compliance with data handling procedures is shown by the dashboard.

- **Executive Action**: To guarantee adherence to the most recent legislation, the executives provide the IT and legal departments instructions to examine and update data handling protocols.

Benefits for Jit Inc.

- **Improved Understanding**: Jit Inc.'s leadership can now see the cybersecurity landscape clearly and succinctly without getting bogged down in technical minutiae, thanks to the Executive Summary Dashboard.
- **Proactive Security Posture**: The dashboard enables executives to proactively address security risks prior to their escalation by furnishing them with actionable intelligence.
- **Cybersecurity and Corporate Goal Alignment**: This ensures that security measures promote rather than impede corporate expansion by bringing cybersecurity strategies into line with overarching business goals.

The Executive Summary Dashboard in Splunk ES is a crucial component of Jit Inc.'s strategic cybersecurity management, serving as more than just a reporting tool. It gives the executive team the ability to stay informed, make decisions based on facts, and steer the company in the direction of a compliant and safe digital future.

Introduction to Security Posture Dashboard and Incident Review Dashboard

The Security Posture Dashboard and Incident Review Dashboard are integral components of Splunk Enterprise Security that are designed to enhance a company's security monitoring and incident investigation capabilities. Both dashboards provide security analysts with valuable insights for efficiently managing security incidents, prioritizing responses, and enhancing the security posture as a whole.

- **Security Posture Dashboard:** The Security Posture Dashboard is intended to provide an all-encompassing, high-level view of an organization's security status across multiple security domains. It presents key performance indicators (KPIs) and security metrics that assist security teams in understanding the current state of their organization's security, identifying trends, and prioritizing areas requiring improvement. The Security Posture Dashboard enables security teams to obtain a comprehensive understanding of their organization's risk landscape, monitor the efficacy of security controls, and make data-driven decisions to improve security posture.
- **Incident Review Dashboard:** On the other hand, the Incident Review Dashboard focuses on the investigation and administration of noteworthy events. It provides security analysts with a centralized location to triage, investigate, and manage security incidents. This dashboard provides

essential tools for filtering, sorting, and analyzing notable events, allowing security teams to respond to incidents and mitigate potential threats in an efficient manner. Through the Incident Review Dashboard, security analysts can designate ownership, manage workflows, implement adaptive response actions, and suppress false positive notable events. This streamlines the investigation process and ensures a prompt response to security incidents, thereby minimizing the potential impact of security violations.

In conclusion, the Security Posture Dashboard and Incident Review Dashboard are indispensable Splunk Enterprise Security tools that enable security teams to effectively monitor and manage security incidents, prioritize responses based on risk, and perpetually enhance their organization's security posture. By utilizing these dashboards, security analysts can make informed decisions and proactively address potential threats, thereby protecting their organization's valuable assets and data.

Navigating and Customizing the Security Posture Dashboard

Customization of the Security Posture Dashboard is a key feature that enhances its usability. You can modify the dashboard to display specific panels based on your organization's needs or preferences. This might include focusing on certain threat categories, incorporating data from unique sources, or adjusting the visual presentation of data. This level of customization enables security teams to focus on the most relevant information, leading to more efficient and effective threat detection and response

Accessing the Security Posture Dashboard

To access the Security Posture Dashboard, log in to Splunk Enterprise Security and click the `Security Posture` option in the main menu. This will take you to the dashboard, where you can view the overall security status of your organization across different security domains.

Figure 6.4*: Splunk ES: Security Posture Dashboard*

Understanding dashboard components

The Security Posture Dashboard consists of a number of essential elements, including:

- **Key Indicators**: This section displays the number of noteworthy events per security domain over the previous 24 hours. It provides a summary of recent activity in each security domain, enabling security teams to rapidly evaluate the overall health of the security environment.

  These indicators are organized by security domain and display the total number of noteworthy events and their trajectory for each domain. Here is a summary of each of the main indicators:

  - **Access Notables**: This metric displays the total number and trend of notable events related to access control, such as an excessive number of failed logon attempts, which may indicate potential unauthorized access attempts.
  - **Endpoint Notables**: This indicator displays the total tally and trend of notable events related to endpoint security, such as a host with a recurring malware infection, highlighting potential endpoint protection and malware detection issues.
  - **Network Notables**: This metric displays the total count and trend of network security-related notable events, such as detected network changes, which can help identify unauthorized network modifications or prospective intrusions.

  - **Identity Notables**: This indicator displays the total number and trend of identity-related notable events, such as activity from expired user identities, highlighting potential account management and access control issues.
  - **Audit Notables**: This metric displays the total count and trend of notable events related to auditing and compliance, such as the detection of personally identifiable information (PII), which can assist organizations in identifying and mitigating potential compliance risks.
  - **Threat Notables**: This indicator displays the total number and trend of notable events related to threat intelligence, such as the ATT&CK tactic threshold being exceeded for an object over the previous seven days, which can assist security teams in identifying and prioritizing potential threats.
  - **UBA Notables**: This metric displays the cumulative count and trend of notable User Behaviour Analytics (UBA) events, if Splunk UBA is sending threat data to Splunk Enterprise Security (ES). This can assist businesses in identifying and investigating potential internal threats or compromised accounts.
- **Notable Events By Urgency**: This section displays the notable events in the last 24 hours based on their urgency. The urgency is calculated based on the asset's designated priority and the severity of the correlation search. The drilldown launches the Incident Review dashboard, which displays all noteworthy events with the selected urgency from the previous twenty-four hours.
- **Chronology Of Notable Events**: This visualization displays a chronology of noteworthy events by security domain. It assists security teams in identifying patterns and trends in security event occurrences over time. The drilldown launches the Incident Review dashboard, which displays all noteworthy events for the selected security domain and time period.
- **Top Notable Events**: This section displays the most notable events, organized according to their respective criteria, along with a total count and a sparkline to illustrate activity spikes over time. The drilldown opens the Incident Review dashboard for the notable event rule that was selected.
- **Top Ten Notable Event Sources**: This section displays the top ten noteworthy events by source (src), along with a total count, a count per correlation and domain, and a sparkline to depict activity spikes over time. The drilldown initiates the Incident Review dashboard, concentrating on the selected notable event source for a more targeted analysis.

Hands-On Scenario 1: Addressing Access Control Challenges

Scenario Overview

Concerns regarding possible unauthorized access attempts are raised by Jit Inc.'s unusually high number of unsuccessful logon attempts. For more thorough monitoring and reaction, the organization chooses to use the `Access Notables` indicator on the Security Posture Dashboard in Splunk ES.

Implementation Steps

- **Monitoring Access Notables**: Jit Inc.'s security team keeps a careful eye on the dashboard's `Access Notables` measure, which indicates an upward trend in unsuccessful login attempts.
- **Identifying and Responding to Unauthorized Access Attempts**: The thorough investigation identifies recurrent attempts from particular IP addresses. To reduce the possibility of unwanted access, Jit Inc. reacts by blocking these IPs and starting password resets for the impacted accounts.

Hands-On Scenario 2: Investigating Network Security Anomalies

Scenario Overview

Jit Inc. receives alerts about unforeseen network changes, which could be indicative of illegal changes or invasions. The organization utilizes the Security Posture Dashboard's `Network Notables` metric to conduct comprehensive investigations.

Implementation Steps

- **Monitoring Network Notables**: The IT department monitors the `Network Notables` statistic and has observed a rise in warnings concerning network modifications lately.
- **Diving Deeper into Particular Network Events**: When there is a noticeable increase in notables pertaining to the network, the team uses the Incident Review Dashboard to get a detailed picture of these events, including the devices that were impacted, the kinds of changes that were made, and when they occurred.

- **Recognizing and Reducing Unlawful Network Modifications**: The inquiry identifies unlawful configuration modifications made to vital network equipment. To stop such mishaps, the team quickly undoes these modifications and tightens network access rules.

In both cases, Jit Inc. efficiently monitors, looks into, and addresses security issues pertaining to network security and access control by utilizing the particular metrics available on the Security Posture Dashboard in Splunk ES. The security team will be able to proactively manage potential security threats and uphold the integrity of their cybersecurity posture thanks to these practical applications that showcase the dashboard's capacity to deliver actionable insights.

Customizing the Security Posture Dashboard

You can tailor the Security Posture Dashboard to your organization's requirements by modifying the default panels, adding new panels, and rearranging the layout. To personalize the display, follow these steps:

1. Click **`Edit`** in the upper right-hand corner of the dashboard.
2. To modify the dashboard configuration, select from options such as **`Add Panel`**, **`Edit Panel`**, and **`Remove Panel`**.
3. When adding a new panel, you can select from a variety of visualization types, including charts, tables, and maps, and configure the panel's data source and parameters.
4. The panels can be rearranged by selecting and dragging them to the desired location.
5. Save your modifications by selecting **`Save`**

By configuring the Security Posture Dashboard, you can display the most pertinent data for your organization, enabling more effective security monitoring and decision-making.

Investigating Notable Events with the Incident Review Dashboard

The dashboard for Incident Review is a central location for investigating and managing noteworthy events generated by correlation searches. This dashboard allows analysts to observe event details, drill down into underlying data, and perform actions including assigning ownership, modifying event status, and adding comments. Additionally, the dashboard provides tools for filtering and sorting events based on various criteria, such as urgency, status, and owner, making it simpler to manage and prioritize incidents.

Navigating to the Incident Review Dashboard

To navigate from the Security Posture dashboard to the Incident Review dashboard, follow these steps:

A. **First way**

   To access the Incident Review Dashboard in Splunk Enterprise Security, navigate to the main menu, and click "Incident Review." This dashboard provides a centralized view of all notable events, allowing you to investigate incidents and take appropriate actions.

B. **Second Way**

   1. **Access the Security Posture dashboard:** In Splunk ES, access the Security Posture dashboard to view key metrics such as open incidents, recent noteworthy events, and a breakdown of events by urgency and domain.

   2. **Identify a notable event**: Review the displayed metrics and event categories on the Security Posture dashboard to locate an event of interest.

   3. **Click the notable event**: In the Security Posture dashboard, click the item corresponding to the noteworthy event. This action will automatically access the relevant notable events in the dashboard for Incident Review.

   4. **Investigate the notable occurrence**: After opening the Incident Review dashboard, scrutinize the specifics of each notable event, including event information, related assets and identities, and underlying data.

***Figure 6.5**: Security posture dashboard*

Understanding Dashboard Components

The Incident Review Dashboard is comprised of various elements, including filters, a timeline, and a table of noteworthy events. Filters permit you to refine the displayed events using criteria such as time range, status, urgency, and proprietor. The timeline provides a visual representation of notable events over time, while the table provides information about each event, including its title, description, status, proprietor, and urgency.

Hands-On Scenario: Managing a Ransomware Attack with the Incident Review Dashboard in Splunk ES

Scenario Overview

A significant rise in encryption activity on multiple network endpoints suggests that Jit Inc. is under attack by ransomware. The business manages and looks into the event using Splunk ES's event Review Dashboard.

Incident Detection

- **First Alert**: If Splunk ES detects unusual encryption activity on several endpoints, it may be a sign of an impending ransomware assault.

- **Noteworthy Event Creation**: As a result of the alert, notable events are created and promptly marked on the Incident Review Dashboard.

Utilizing the Incident Review Dashboard

1. **Prioritizing Events Based on Urgency**

   The Jit Inc. security team looks over the `Notable Events By Urgency` section, which indicates that the suspected ransomware assault is of high priority. This prioritizing aids the team in concentrating their short-term efforts.

2. **Analyzing the Chronology of Events**

   The group looks at the `Chronology Of Notable Events` graphic to comprehend how the attack progressed, starting from the first compromise.

3. **Investigating Top Notable Events**

   Based on the attack pattern matching a known ransomware signature, the team determines the exact ransomware strain shown in the `Top Notable Events` section.

4. **Identifying the Source of Attack**

   The group pinpoints the attack's origin using the `Top Ten Notable Event Sources` section, demonstrating that a phishing email was the initial source.

Response and Mitigation

1. **Isolating Affected Systems**

   Jit Inc. swiftly isolates the compromised computers to stop the ransomware from spreading based on the information acquired.

2. **Alerting Relevant Stakeholders**

   The team can communicate succinct information to stakeholders, such as the IT department, management, and possibly impacted users, thanks to the comprehensive analysis provided by the Incident Review Dashboard.

3. **Initiating Recovery Procedures**

   The group starts the recovery process by restoring data from backups and thoroughly cleaning the compromised endpoints of malware.

Post-Incident Analysis

- **Examining incident chronology and reaction**: Using the Incident Review Dashboard, the team examines the full incident chronology and the effectiveness of the reaction following the attack to pinpoint areas where detection and response tactics need to be improved.
- **Updating defensive mechanisms**: Jit Inc. modifies its cybersecurity defensive mechanisms in light of the acquired knowledge to more effectively identify and thwart similar assaults in the future.

This practical example shows how Jit Inc. uses the problem Review Dashboard in Splunk ES to manage a sophisticated cybersecurity problem, such as a ransomware assault. The dashboard offers the tools and insights required for efficient incident management, from initial detection to post-event analysis, allowing the business to react quickly and efficiently to lessen the impact of the assault.

Customizing the Incident Review Dashboard

The Incident Review Dashboard can be tailored to your organization's requirements and preferences. Enhance the dashboard's usability by adding or removing columns, modifying the fields displayed, and modifying the sorting order. Customizing the dashboard enables you to prioritize pertinent data and expedite the incident investigation procedure.

Filtering and sorting notable events

Filtering and categorizing notable events enables you to rapidly identify and prioritize incidents requiring attention. Utilize filters to display events that meet particular criteria, such as high urgency, unassigned ownership, or particular keywords. Sort events according to columns such as urgency, status, or time to prioritize your investigation efforts and ensure a prompt response to critical incidents.

By navigating and customizing the Incident Review Dashboard, you can efficiently manage and investigate noteworthy events, thereby enhancing the security incident response capabilities of your organization.

Incident Ownership and Workflow Management

The dashboard is utilized by analysts to assess event severity, assign events for review, and investigate event specifics. Administrators have the ability to administer and modify the dashboard and its settings. Visualizations and charts, such as pie charts and timeline visualizations, offer insight into notables based on criteria such as urgency, status, proprietor, and domain.

Splunk Enterprise Security identifies noteworthy events via correlation queries that detect suspicious patterns, thereby generating new noteworthy events for further investigation. The dashboard for Incident Review displays these events and classifies them according to severity for efficient triage and monitoring.

Examples of incident assessment workflow components include:

- Administrative analysts monitor the interface, classifying and prioritizing new notable events.
- Assigning events for investigation to reviewing analysts.
- Reviewing analysts who update event status, conduct research, and acquire data.
- Documenting research specifics and executing adaptive response actions as required.
- Resolving incidents and elevating remediation duties.
- Assigning resolved events for verification and closure to a final analyst.

Using filters, categories, and dispositions, the evaluation of notables can be accelerated.

Users can employ techniques such as sorting, filtering, labeling, and adding dispositions to expedite the triage of notables:

- **Sorting notables**: Utilizing filters such as Urgency, Status, Security Domain, Owner, and Type facilitates the categorization, tracking, and assignment of events.
- **Creating and applying filters**: Users are able to create filters to zero in on specific information regarding noteworthy events and rapidly identify potential threats. Filters can be created based on fields including Urgency, Status, Owner, Security Domain, Type, Search type, Time, and Associations.
- **Grouping notables**: Saving filters based on specific fields enables investigators to reuse filter groups. Additionally, they can set a filter as the default and manage filters by modifying, deleting, or selecting them as necessary.
- **Adding dispositions**: Users can add dispositions to notables to precisely identify the threat level, classify notables, and distinguish false positives. Additionally, unique dispositions can be created and applied to notables.

Individually or in bulk, notables can be allocated to specific proprietors. Typically, owners hold the administrator, `ess_admin`, or `ess_analyst` role. As the event progresses through the incident review workflow, the status of a noteworthy can be updated to reflect the actions taken to address the occurrence. Users are able to tailor workflow statuses and progression to their organization's process.

Investigating Notable Events

Follow these steps to investigate a noteworthy event on the Incident Review page of Splunk ES:

1. **Open event details**: This allows you to evaluate the urgency, contributing events, and risk scores associated with the notable event.
2. **Review history**: Examine recent investigation activity, including analyst comments, status changes, and other events-related actions.
3. **Check related investigations**: Determine if the notable event is already the subject of an investigation, and if not, open one if necessary.
4. **Examine the correlation search**: Examine the correlation search by determining why the notable event was created and modifying or reviewing the search as necessary.
5. **View contributing events**: Examine the events that triggered the creation of the notable event.
6. **Review risk scores**: Examine the risk scores for the assets and identities involved. Clicking on a risk score reveals a filtered view of the Risk Analysis dashboard.
7. **Examine the original event**: If a singular event precipitated the notable event, examine its specifics.
8. **Review adaptive responses**: Examine the adaptive response actions taken, their efficacy, and drill down for additional information. View audit events in their unprocessed form for response actions associated with the correlation search.
9. **Verify next actions**: Determine if there are defined next actions for notable event triage.
10. **Create and share a short ID**: Generate a short ID to share with other analysts the notable event. It can also be shared via a link.

By following these steps, you can investigate a notable event exhaustively and collaborate with your team to effectively address security concerns.

Adaptive Response Actions with Splunk ES

Splunk ES incorporates some adaptive response actions that facilitate event investigation. These measures include:

- **Analyzing risk from assets and identities**: Employ adaptive response actions to add risk messages, adjust risk scores, and identify potential threats.
- **Modifying risk scores with risk modifiers**: Use the Risk Analysis adaptive response action to modify risk scores based on correlation searches or significant event specifics.
- **Execute scripts**: Run scripts located in `$SPLUNK_HOME/bin/scripts`.
- **Starting a Splunk Stream stream capture**: Capture transmissions based on specified protocols and IP addresses for a given period of time.
- **Pinging a host**: Use ping to determine whether a host is active on the network.
- **Executing nbtstat**: By executing `nbtstat`, you can learn more about a host and its services.
- **Executing nslookup**: Use `nslookup` to search up domain names or IP addresses.
- **Adding threat intelligence**: Develop threat artifacts for a threat collection in order to improve security analysis.

Note that adaptive response actions such as `ping`, `nbtstat`, and `nslookup` can no longer send results to custom indexes; instead, the results are written to the default index. In addition, certain actions necessitate integration with additional tools, such as Splunk Stream, or implementation of particular utilities on the search head.

Integrating MITRE ATT&CK and Kill Chain Methodology

Security Posture Dashboard

A thorough picture of the organization's security against the range of known attacker tactics and techniques is given by the integration of the MITRE ATT&CK architecture with the Security Posture Dashboard in Splunk ES. This dashboard shows areas of strength and possible vulnerabilities in the way that the framework and the security mechanisms in place are aligned. It provides a strategic perspective on the organization's readiness to counter different attack techniques and synchronizes security posture with industry best practices.

Incident Review Dashboard

In the Incident Review Dashboard, the Kill Chain technique is also essential. The approach is used in this dashboard to rank and classify incidents according to where they are in the attack lifecycle. Through the identification of the incident's location along the kill chain, security teams can enhance their ability to plan and execute countermeasures against potential future threats.

Managing Advanced Persistent Threats (APTs)

Security Posture Dashboard

The Security Posture Dashboard is essential to the ongoing observation required to find APTs. It offers long-term trends and pattern insights that are essential for spotting the subtle signs of APT activity. This ongoing monitoring makes it possible to identify possible APTs early on, improving the organization's capacity to proactively counter these complex threats.

Incident Review Dashboard

The Incident Review Dashboard serves as a primary tool for the thorough examination and handling of these dangers when it comes to APTs. It provides tools for connecting seemingly unrelated occurrences and comprehending the larger context of a possible APT attack, enabling the in-depth investigation of instances that might be a part of an APT campaign.

Practical Use Cases of Splunk ES

1. **Identifying Insider risks:** The identification of insider risks is a critical function of both dashboards. While the Incident Review Dashboard facilitates the thorough investigation of questionable actions, allowing for prompt response and mitigation, the Security Posture Dashboard assists in proactively monitoring for risk indicators.

2. **Data Exfiltration Monitoring:** The Security Posture Dashboard provides information on general trends and potential weaknesses in data security techniques, while the Incident Review Dashboard plays a key role in identifying and looking into data exfiltration attempts.

3. Recognizing and Countering Ransomware Attacks: The Incident Review Dashboard facilitates quick detection and reaction to ransomware threats, while the Security Posture Dashboard helps evaluate the organization's preparedness and susceptibilities to such assaults.

The Security Posture Dashboard and Incident Review Dashboard in Splunk ES can be enhanced to help a company better understand, monitor, and respond to a wide range of cyber threats. This can be achieved through the integration of sophisticated cybersecurity frameworks and processes. Security teams may guarantee a thorough approach to cybersecurity by combining these dashboards, matching their tactics to industry best practices, and quickly addressing new threats.

Suppressing Notable Events

To suppress notable events that are considered false positives, follow these steps in Splunk Enterprise Security's Incident Review:

1. Expand the **`Actions`** menu of the notable event you want to suppress.
2. Select **`Suppress Notable Events`** from the list of options.
3. Enter a description to provide context for why you are suppressing this notable event.
4. Set the start and end dates for the suppression period, during which the notable event will not generate alerts.
5. Click **`Save`** to apply the suppression settings.

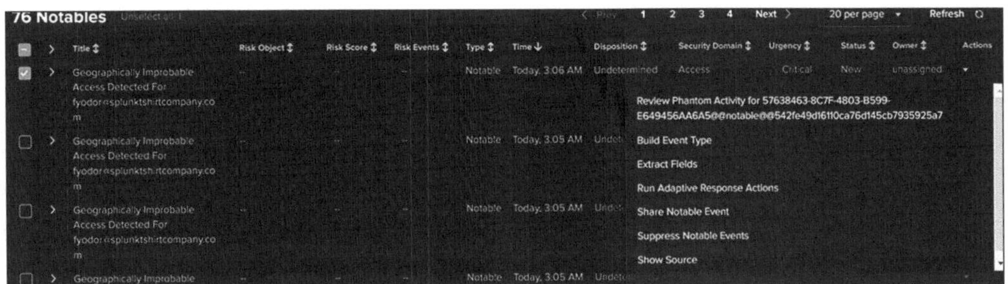

***Figure 6.6**: Notable events*

By following these steps, you can prevent false positives from cluttering your incident review and focus on more relevant security events.

Anomaly Detection and Correlation Searches in Splunk ES

Anomaly Detection and Correlation Searches in Splunk ES provide a robust mechanism to identify unusual patterns and associate related events in real-time, significantly enhancing the platform's ability to detect potential threats and expedite security incident responses.

Introduction to anomaly detection and correlation searches

A comprehensive cybersecurity strategy must include anomaly detection and correlation searches as vital components. Organizations can detect potential hazards and respond to them more effectively by identifying unusual behaviors and patterns. Splunk Enterprise Security offers robust tools for creating and managing correlation queries, enabling security analysts to detect and investigate anomalies in their environment.

The role of anomaly detection in cybersecurity

Anomaly detection involves identifying anomalous system or network behaviors, trends, or events that may indicate a security threat. These anomalies can encompass a wide variety of activities, such as anomalous login attempts, unusual data transfers, and unanticipated configuration changes. By identifying these anomalies, security teams can identify potential threats and implement the necessary countermeasures.

Overview of correlation searches in Splunk ES

Correlation searches in Splunk ES are pre-built queries intended to identify patterns and relationships between events, enabling security analysts to detect anomalies and potential threats. These inquiries can be tailored to specific use cases and environments and used to generate alerts or events worthy of further investigation.

In the following sections, we will delve deeper into the significance of anomaly detection in cybersecurity, explore techniques for identifying patterns and indicators of compromise, and discuss how to construct and customize correlation searches.

Importance of Anomaly Detection in Cybersecurity

In this section, we will discuss the importance of anomaly detection in cybersecurity and how it plays a vital role in identifying potential threats and protecting organizations from various types of cyberattacks.

The role of anomaly detection in cybersecurity

Anomaly detection is an essential component of cybersecurity that identifies anomalous patterns or behaviors in network traffic, system activities, and user actions. By identifying deviations from normal behavior, security teams can rapidly identify potential threats, investigate incidents, and respond to attacks before they cause substantial damage. Anomaly detection is an essential component of a proactive security strategy, complementing firewalls, intrusion detection systems, and antivirus software.

Benefits of anomaly detection

Using anomaly detection in cybersecurity has a number of advantages:

- **Early detection of threats**: Anomaly detection can assist security teams in identifying potential threats and attacks in their earliest stages, enabling quicker response and mitigation.
- **Reduced false positives**: By focusing on deviations from normal behavior, anomaly detection can aid in reducing the number of false positives generated by conventional security tools, resulting in a more efficient and effective incident response.
- **Improved situational awareness**: Anomaly detection gives security teams greater visibility into their organization's network, systems, and users, allowing them to identify patterns and trends that may indicate potential threats.
- **Adaptability to evolving threats**: Anomaly detection can help organizations remain ahead of evolving threats by identifying new attack patterns and techniques that traditional security tools may not recognize.

Challenges of anomaly detection in cybersecurity

Despite its significance, detecting anomalies in cybersecurity can be difficult due to several factors:

- **High volume of data:** Massive quantities of data are generated by organizations, making it difficult to identify unusual patterns or behaviors.
- **Dynamic environments:** IT environments are dynamic because new systems, users, and applications are continually being added and removed. This dynamic nature can make establishing a baseline for typical behavior difficult.
- **Evolving threats:** Cyber threats are perpetually evolving, necessitating that organizations adapt their anomaly detection techniques and remain current with the most recent threat intelligence.
- **False positives and negatives:** Anomaly detection can produce false positives (alerting on normal behavior) and false negatives (failing to alert on malicious behavior), which can compromise the security team's ability to respond effectively.

To overcome these obstacles, organizations must employ effective anomaly detection techniques, leverage advanced analytics and machine learning technologies, and equip their security teams with the skills and resources necessary to analyze and respond to potential threats.

Integrating Anomaly Detection with Other Security Measures

In this section, we will explore how to integrate anomaly detection techniques and correlation searches with other security measures to strengthen your organization's overall cybersecurity posture.

Combining correlation searches with adaptive response actions

Integrating correlation searches with adaptive response actions enables the automation of threat response and remediation processes, thereby reducing the amount of time required to mitigate potential incidents. To accomplish this, keep the following in mind:

- Design correlation searches to identify patterns and indicators of compromise necessitating prompt action.
- Configure adaptive response actions to implement specific tasks or workflows automatically when a correlation search generates a significant event.

- Continuously evaluate and revise your correlation searches and adaptive response actions to ensure their continued efficacy in the face of evolving threats and shifting environments.

Utilizing machine learning and artificial intelligence techniques

- The incorporation of machine learning (ML) and artificial intelligence (AI) techniques can improve the efficacy of anomaly detection and correlation searches by enabling more precise, scalable, and proactive detection of security events. To implement ML and AI in your security strategy, you must:
- Deploy ML algorithms and models to detect anomalies and outliers in your security data, allowing you to identify potential threats that would otherwise go undetected.
- Use AI-driven automation to expedite and optimize your security processes, including incident triage and prioritization.
- Train and update your ML models continuously based on feedback from your security team and lessons learned from past incidents.

Collaborating and sharing information across teams and tools

Improving the security posture of your organization requires effective collaboration and information sharing across teams and tools. To encourage cooperation and information exchange:

- Foster a culture of open communication and collaboration between security analysts, incident responders, and threat intelligence teams, ensuring that insights and findings are disseminated throughout the organization.
- Integrate your organization's security tools and platforms, such as Splunk Enterprise Security, with other solutions in its technology infrastructure to facilitate data sharing and analysis.
- Participate in industry forums, threat-sharing groups, and partnerships to keep abreast of emerging threats, trends, and best practices.

Continuously monitoring and improving detection capabilities

Monitoring and enhancing your anomaly detection and correlation search capabilities on a regular basis is essential for maintaining a strong security posture. To ensure continuous improvement:

- Track key performance indicators, such as false-positive rates, detection accuracy, and response time, to determine the efficacy of your correlation searches and adaptive response actions.
- Conduct routine reviews of your security processes and tools in order to identify opportunities for enhancement and optimization.
- Keep abreast of the most recent research and developments in anomaly detection, machine learning, and artificial intelligence, and incorporate these innovations as appropriate into your security strategy.

By addressing these issues, you can create a more comprehensive and proactive cybersecurity strategy by integrating anomaly detection and correlation searches with other security measures.

Investigations in Splunk ES

Investigations in Splunk ES are a crucial component of the platform's incident response capabilities. They provide a centralized workspace where teams can collaborate, record, and track every step taken in response to a security incident.

The platform allows users to link related notable events, add comments, and attach files to an investigation, creating a comprehensive record of the incident and subsequent response. This consolidated view helps analysts understand the scope and severity of threats, ensuring that all relevant information is easily accessible for informed decision-making.

Furthermore, Splunk ES investigations also serve as a learning tool. By storing a history of past incidents, they provide valuable lessons for future threat detection and prevention, enhancing the overall effectiveness of an organization's cybersecurity strategy.

Purpose of Investigations

Investigations in Splunk Enterprise Security (ES) offer a methodical approach to security incident management and response. By conducting investigations, security analysts can identify, analyze, and resolve security incidents or hazards within the infrastructure of an organization.

Benefits of Investigations

- **Structured Approach**: Splunk ES Investigations enable analysts to follow a structured and documented process for investigating security incidents, ensuring consistency and team-wide effectiveness.

- **Collaboration**: Splunk ES investigations permit analysts to collaborate, share information, and designate tasks, thereby fostering teamwork and the exchange of knowledge.
- **Efficient Incident Management**: By utilizing investigations, analysts can manage incidents more efficiently, decreasing the time required to resolve incidents and minimizing potential damage.
- **Comprehensive Documentation**: Splunk ES investigations provide exhaustive documentation of each incident, making it simpler to evaluate, audit, and learn from past incidents.
- **Customizable**: Splunk ES investigations can be tailored to an organization's particular requirements, policies, and protocols, ensuring seamless integration with existing processes.

In the sections that follow, we will examine how to initiate an investigation, use the investigation workbench, add details to an investigation, manage and collaborate on investigations, track progress, utilize dashboards and visualizations, integrate adaptive response actions, close and archive investigations, and report and share findings. By the end of this chapter, you will have a thorough comprehension of Splunk ES investigations and how they can be used to effectively manage and respond to security incidents.

Starting an Investigation in Splunk ES

Starting an investigation in Splunk ES involves initiating a new workspace where you can gather, analyze, and document information related to a specific security incident. This is typically triggered by a notable event or a series of related events, and the investigation process helps in detailing the incident timeline, associating relevant data, and coordinating a multi-faceted response.

Initiating an investigation

To begin an investigation, navigate to the Investigations page in Splunk ES and perform the following steps:

- Click the `Create Investigation` button, and fill in the necessary details, such as the title, description, and priority of the investigation.
- Assign the investigation to a specific analyst or a group of analysts to collaborate on the case.
- If the investigation is initiated as a result of a notable event or an alert, you can link the investigation to the relevant event or alert for easy reference.

Investigation Workbench

Splunk Enterprise Security's Investigation Workbench provides a centralized workspace for analysts to conduct investigations. The workbench contains numerous panels and instruments to assist analysts:

- Examine the investigation's specifics and context, including its title, description, priority, status, and assigned analysts.
- Access pertinent artifacts, such as logs, events, alerts, and notable events, in order to assemble evidence and information.
- Conduct queries and data analyses within Splunk ES to identify patterns, trends, and anomalies.
- Employ diverse dashboards and visualizations to gain insight into the security incident and monitor the investigation's progress, including details in Splunk ES Investigations.

Adding Artifacts

As the investigation progresses, analysts may discover additional artifacts, such as IP addresses, domain names, file hashes, or user accounts, that are relevant to the case. To add these artifacts to the investigation:

- Use the `Add Artifact` button on the Investigation Workbench to manually enter the details of the artifact.
- If the artifact is discovered as a result of a search or an action within Splunk ES, use the relevant event action to automatically add the artifact to the investigation.

Adding Notes, Files, and Links

Analysts can add notes, files, and links to the investigation to document their findings, observations, and steps taken during the investigation.

This information can be useful for:

- Collaborating with other analysts and sharing insights.
- Providing a comprehensive record of the investigation process for auditing and compliance purposes.
- Facilitating knowledge transfer and learning from past investigations.
- To add notes, files, or links to the investigation, use the appropriate options on the Investigation Workbench.

Collaborating on an Investigation in Splunk ES

Collaborating on an investigation in Splunk ES enables security teams to work together effectively by sharing insights, findings, and actions in real-time within the investigation workspace. This feature allows for efficient team coordination, ensuring that every member has access to the latest information, which aids in a comprehensive and timely response to security incidents.

Assigning and sharing investigations

Splunk ES enables analysts to collaborate on investigations by assigning cases to specific individuals or groups and sharing information and findings. To assign or share an investigation:

- Use the **`Assign to`** field on the Investigation Workbench to select the analysts or groups responsible for the case.
- Share artifacts, notes, files, and links with other analysts through the Investigation Workbench, ensuring that all team members have access to the latest information.

Communicating and tracking progress

Effective communication and progress tracking are crucial for successful collaboration in investigations. Splunk ES provides several tools and features to facilitate communication and monitor progress:

- Use the Investigation Workbench to post updates, ask questions, or share insights with other analysts.
- Track the status and progress of the investigation using the various dashboards and visualizations available in Splunk ES.
- Set deadlines and priorities for tasks within the investigation to ensure timely resolution and resource allocation.

In the next sections, we will discuss how to close and archive investigations, integrate adaptive response actions, and report and share findings from completed investigations in Splunk Enterprise Security.

Closing and Archiving Investigations in Splunk ES

Closing an investigation in Splunk ES marks the completion of incident analysis and response, signifying that all necessary actions have been taken and documented. Once an investigation is closed, it can be archived for future reference, serving as a valuable resource for understanding past incidents, informing future responses, and improving overall cybersecurity strategies.

Closing an investigation

Once the investigation is completed and the security incident is resolved, it's important to close the investigation to ensure proper documentation and maintain an accurate record of the organization's security posture. To close an investigation:

- Navigate to the Investigation Workbench.
- Update the investigation status to `Closed` and provide any necessary details or comments regarding the resolution of the incident.
- If applicable, close any associated notable events or alerts linked to the investigation.

Archiving investigations

Archiving completed investigations allows analysts to maintain a historical record of past incidents and leverage this information for future investigations, reporting, and compliance. To archive an investigation:

- Ensure that the investigation is closed, and all relevant information is documented.
- Archive the investigation using the available options in Splunk Enterprise Security, such as exporting the investigation data or moving it to a designated archive location.

Reporting and Sharing Findings from Completed Investigations

Reporting and sharing findings from completed investigations in Splunk ES is essential for communicating insights, lessons learned, and actions taken during a security incident. These comprehensive reports not only keep all stakeholders informed but also serve as educational resources for enhancing the organization's cybersecurity measures and strategies in the future.

Reviewing the investigation summary

Splunk Enterprise Security's Investigation Summary provides a comprehensive overview of the investigation, including the investigation's title, description, priority, status, designated analysts, artifacts, notes, files, and links. Verify that all pertinent information has been documented and that the investigation has been conducted exhaustively and effectively by reviewing the executive summary.

Sharing the investigation summary

Sharing the investigation summary with stakeholders, such as management or other security teams, is crucial for promoting transparency, fostering collaboration, and demonstrating the value of the security program. To share the investigation summary:

- Export the summary in a suitable format, such as a PDF or CSV file.
- Distribute the summary to relevant stakeholders via email, file-sharing platforms, or internal communication tools.

Printing the investigation summary

In some cases, it may be necessary to print the investigation summary for physical record-keeping or presentation purposes. To print the summary:

- Navigate to the Investigation Workbench and access the Investigation Summary.
- Use the `Print` option available in Splunk Enterprise Security to generate a printer-friendly version of the summary.
- Print the summary using your organization's preferred printing method.

By following these steps and topics, you can effectively conduct, manage, and document investigations in Splunk Enterprise Security, ensuring a comprehensive and efficient approach to security incident response and management.

Best Practices for Investigations in Splunk ES

Best practices for investigations in Splunk ES include maintaining clear documentation, ensuring real-time collaboration among security teams, utilizing the platform's data integration capabilities for comprehensive analysis, and leveraging past investigations to inform future responses and enhance cybersecurity strategies.

Consistent investigation naming and tagging

Establish a naming convention and labeling system for investigations to make searching, filtering, and managing them easier. Analysts can identify and prioritize investigations based on their context and urgency with the aid of descriptive titles and annotations.

Regularly update the investigation status

Ensure that investigation statuses are routinely updated to reflect each case's progress. This contributes to the maintenance of an accurate view of the organization's security posture and enables more efficient resource allocation and prioritization.

Collaborate and communicate with team members

Involve team members in investigations as collaborators and keep them apprised of progress to foster a collaborative environment. Encourage open communication through notes, comments, and shared artifacts to ensure that everyone has access to all pertinent information.

Leverage historical investigation data

Utilize historical investigation data to inform ongoing and future investigations. This can assist in identifying trends, patterns, or recurring problems that may require additional attention or a shift in security strategy.

Continuously improve investigation processes

Regularly review and evaluate investigation processes to identify improvement opportunities. Implement modifications, such as updating correlation searches, refining notable event criteria, and optimizing adaptive response actions, to improve the efficacy and efficiency of security incident response.

Training and education

Ensure that analysts are well-trained in the investigational use of Splunk Enterprise Security. Offer regular training sessions, workshops, or webinars to keep team members abreast of the most recent features, best practices, and investigation methods.

By adhering to these best practices and enumerated topics, you can ensure effective and efficient investigations within Splunk Enterprise Security, thereby improving the security posture and incident response capabilities of your organization.

Evaluating SOC Metrics in the Context of Splunk Enterprise Security

Using Splunk Enterprise Security (ES) in Security Operations Centers (SOCs) greatly improves their capacity to track and assess critical performance indicators. Here's how to apply and evaluate common SOC metrics in the Splunk ES environment:

1. Mean Time to Detect (MTTD)

- **Splunk ES Application**: The MTTD can be computed using real-time analytics and monitoring made possible by Splunk ES. Because of the platform's extensive logging and alerting features, SOCs can detect security events promptly.
- **Improvement Strategy**: Refine alert criteria and cut noise with Splunk's data analytics to possibly lower MTTD.

2. Mean Time to Respond (MTTR)

- **Splunk ES Application**: Use Splunk ES to monitor incident response schedules. Every action done from the time an alert is produced until it is resolved can be recorded via the incident management tools of the platform.
- **Improvement Strategy**: To expedite the response process, make use of Splunk's automated response features and dashboards.

3. Incident Volume and Trends

- **Splunk ES Application**: Track and analyze the volume and types of incidents over time by using Splunk's dashboard and reporting features. This will give you important insights into trends and patterns.
- **Improvement Strategy**: Concentrate on regions with greater incident rates and modify security measures in response to trend studies.

4. False Positive Rate

- **Splunk ES Application**: By separating real threats from false positives, Splunk ES's analytics can assist in figuring out the false positive rate.
- **Enhancement Plan**: Optimize Splunk's alerting and correlation search functions to minimize false positives.

5. Alert Handling Efficiency

- **Splunk ES Application**: Track and log alert responses in real-time with Splunk's logging and tracking capabilities.

- **Strategy for Improvement**: To increase efficiency, optimize Splunk's alert prioritizing and handling procedures.

6. Compliance Adherence

- **Splunk ES Application**: With customized searches and reports for particular compliance needs, Splunk ES can be used to monitor compliance with a range of regulatory standards.
- **Strategy for Improvement**: Update Splunk's compliance tracking functions frequently to keep up with evolving legal requirements.

7. Threat Hunting Success Rate

- **Splunk ES Application**: This program is capable of monitoring and reporting on the results of proactive threat-hunting efforts.
- **Enhancement Strategy**: To improve threat-hunting capabilities, leverage Splunk's data analytics and threat intelligence integration.

8. Customer Satisfaction

- **Splunk ES Application**: Customer evaluations of the SOC's performance can be linked, albeit indirectly, to the effectiveness and efficiency metrics monitored in Splunk ES.
- **Improvement Strategy**: Make modifications to Splunk ES setups and SOC procedures based on input.

9. Employee Training and Development

- **Splunk ES Application**: Monitor training programs and how they affect Splunk ES's SOC performance.
- **Enhancement Approach**: Apply knowledge gleaned from Splunk data to pinpoint areas in which more training is required.

SOCs may more efficiently monitor and optimize these critical KPIs by utilizing Splunk ES's sophisticated features, which will enhance cybersecurity threat detection, response, and management in general. In addition to providing the means to track these data, Splunk ES also has the analytical power to decipher them and help you decide how best to improve SOC operations.

Future Trends

Future trends suggest a continued focus on leveraging artificial intelligence and machine learning in cybersecurity tools like Splunk ES, enhancing their predictive analytics capabilities, automating threat response, and adapting to evolving cyber threats in an increasingly interconnected digital landscape.

Evolving role of Splunk ES in the cybersecurity landscape

Splunk ES has evolved into an indispensable instrument for organizations seeking to enhance their cybersecurity posture. As threats and attacks become more sophisticated, the function of Splunk ES evolves to meet these new challenges. Notable developments in the function of Splunk ES comprise the following:

- Enhanced integration with other security tools and platforms, providing a more complete and unified view of the security landscape for an organization.
- Increased adoption of machine learning and artificial intelligence techniques to allow for more precise and proactive threat detection and response.
- Greater emphasis on collaboration and exchange of information, both within organizations and throughout the broader cybersecurity community.

Emerging trends and technologies in cybersecurity and their impact on Splunk ES

Several trends and technologies are anticipated to have a significant impact on Splunk ES and the broader field of security analytics as the cybersecurity landscape continues to evolve. These include:

- **Increasing reliance on artificial intelligence and machine learning**: The expanding use of AI and ML in cybersecurity will facilitate more sophisticated threat detection and automated response capabilities. Splunk ES is likely to implement additional techniques from this list to improve its anomaly detection and correlation search capabilities.
- **Expanding use of cloud services**: As organizations migrate their infrastructure and data to the cloud at an increasing rate, the need for robust cloud security solutions becomes paramount. Splunk ES will need to offer enhanced support for monitoring and safeguarding cloud-based resources and environments to accommodate this trend.
- **Greater focus on privacy and data protection**: As the importance of data privacy and protection regulations continues to rise, organizations must ensure that their security tools are compliant with these requirements. Splunk ES will require the incorporation of privacy-by-design principles and incorporation of features to assist organizations in managing their compliance obligations.

- **Internet of Things (IoT) and peripheral computing**: The expanding use of IoT devices and periphery computing presents new security challenges and attack vectors. Splunk ES will be required to create solutions for monitoring and securing these environments, including real-time analysis of large volumes of data generated at the network's periphery.
- **Increased emphasis on threat intelligence sharing**: As the importance of collaboration and information sharing in the cybersecurity community grows, Splunk ES will need to support a more robust integration with threat intelligence platforms and facilitate the sharing of insights and findings across organizations.

By remaining ahead of these emerging trends and technologies, Splunk ES can continue to play a crucial role in assisting organizations to improve their cybersecurity posture and respond effectively to the evolving threat landscape.

Conclusion

This chapter has provided a comprehensive analysis of Splunk ES, a prominent SIEM solution that plays a crucial role in cybersecurity. We have reviewed Splunk ES's fundamental components, benefits, and capabilities, including security monitoring, incident investigation, dashboards, and anomaly detection. In addition, we have delved into the complexities of platform-based investigations, adaptive response actions, and correlation queries.

As we transition to the next chapter, *Security Intelligence*, it is crucial to understand the connection between Splunk ES and the broader concept of security intelligence. Splunk ES serves as an effective instrument for gathering, analyzing, and acting on security intelligence. In the following chapter, we will investigate the underlying principles and methodologies of security intelligence and their application in various facets of cybersecurity, such as threat detection, risk management, and incident response.

In the upcoming *Security Intelligence* chapter, we will discuss the acquisition, analysis, and dissemination of security-related data, as well as the incorporation of intelligence-driven approaches into cybersecurity operations. We will investigate how security intelligence can be applied to Splunk ES and other SIEM solutions to enhance their capabilities. In addition, we will discuss emergent cybersecurity trends and technologies that may influence the future of security intelligence and SIEM solutions like Splunk ES.

By connecting the insights from the *Splunk Enterprise Security* chapter to the broader context of security intelligence, you will be better able to utilize advanced techniques and methodologies to defend your organization against evolving cybersecurity threats. This will allow you to make informed decisions, enhance your security posture, and proactively address risks in a digital landscape that is constantly evolving.

Points to Remember

- Splunk Enterprise Security (ES) is a premium security information and event management (SIEM) solution that provides real-time visibility, analytics, and insights into the security posture of an organization.
- ES is designed on the Splunk platform and leverages its powerful search, correlation, and visualization capabilities to process massive amounts of security data.
- Notable Splunk ES features include:
    - **Security Posture Dashboard**: Provides a real-time, comprehensive view of an organization's security events, threats, and hazards.
    - **Incident Review Dashboard**: Allows security analysts to efficiently prioritize, investigate, and monitor security incidents.
    - **Glass Tables**: Customizable visualizations that assist organizations in comprehending their security data and trends.
    - Please visit https://www.splunk.com/en_us/resources/videos/splunk-enterprise-security-glass-tables.html for additional information.
    - **Correlation Searches**: Allows users to construct custom searches for identifying anomalies and patterns indicative of security incidents.
    - **Adaptive Response Framework**: Integrates with third-party security tools to facilitate coordinated and automated incident response actions.
- Splunk ES facilitates integration with a variety of data sources, such as logs, metrics, and threat intelligence feeds, in order to provide comprehensive security monitoring and analysis.
- Splunk ES implementation requires deploying the ES app on a Splunk Enterprise instance, configuring data inputs, configuring correlation searches and alerts, and customizing dashboards and visualizations.

CHAPTER 7

Security Intelligence

Introduction

This chapter explores the idea of security intelligence and its different components, with a particular emphasis on how Splunk Enterprise Security (ES) may be used to acquire insightful information and enhance an organization's overall security posture. The chapter discusses important topics like risk analysis, web intelligence, user intelligence, threat intelligence, and protocol intelligence and exemplifies how Splunk ES may be used to manage and analyze each of these domains. The chapter will instruct readers on how to evaluate and rank risks, identify web-based threats, examine user behavior, incorporate and evaluate threat intelligence feeds, and keep an eye on network protocols. In addition, the chapter discusses how important security intelligence is for improving cybersecurity and looks ahead to possible trends and advancements in this quickly developing area.

Structure

In this chapter, we will cover the following topics:

- Introduction to Security Intelligence
    - Definition and importance of security intelligence
    - Role of security intelligence in Splunk ES
- Risk Analysis
    - Key Components of Risk Analysis in Splunk ES
    - The Risk Analysis dashboard in ES
    - Effective use of Risk Analysis Dashboard

- Web Intelligence
  - HTTP Category Analysis
  - HTTP User Agent Analysis
  - New Domain Analysis
  - URL Length Analysis
- User Intelligence
  - Asset and Identity Investigator
  - User Activity Monitoring
  - User behavior analytics
- Threat Intelligence
  - Introduction to Threat intelligence
  - Threat Activity dashboard
  - Threat Artifacts dashboard
- Protocol Intelligence
  - Protocol Centre
  - Traffic Size Analysis
  - DNS Activity and Search
  - SSL Activity and Search
  - Email Activity and Search
- Case Studies

Introduction to Security Intelligence

Security intelligence is the collective methods and tools used for collecting, analyzing, and responding to security data to prevent, detect, and mitigate potential threats.

Definition and Importance of Security Intelligence

In order to gain knowledge about potential threats, weaknesses, and hazards to an organization's information security architecture, security intelligence is the process of gathering, analyzing, and correlating data from numerous sources. It entails the ongoing observation and assessment of data produced by network devices, applications, and security systems to spot patterns, trends, and abnormalities that could point to malicious activity, security lapses, or potential vulnerabilities.

Security intelligence is crucial because it helps firms to proactively identify and address cyberthreats before they seriously harm their operations. In order to properly manage resources and concentrate on the most serious threats, it also assists businesses in prioritizing their security investments. Utilizing security intelligence, organizations may enhance their overall security, make more informed decisions, and streamline their security posture.

Role of Security Intelligence in Splunk ES

A potent security analytics platform called Splunk Enterprise Security (ES) ensures that businesses efficiently utilize the potential of security intelligence. Splunk ES gives businesses the ability to gather and analyze data from a range of sources to better understand their security architecture, spot potential threats, and take the necessary precautions to reduce risks.

Risk Analysis in Security Intelligence for Splunk ES

The identification, assessment, and prioritizing of risks related to an organization's information security infrastructure are all important parts of risk analysis, which is a subset of security intelligence. It seeks to assess the possibility of security incidents, threats, and vulnerabilities occurring, as well as their possible effects on the company. Organizations can make better judgments about resource allocation, risk mitigation techniques, and security policies by undertaking risk analysis.

Key Components of Risk Analysis in Splunk ES

The capacity to give numerical risk values to things, such as systems or users, is provided by correlation searches. The occurrence of particular circumstances might cause the risk attached to an object to rise. Unlike priority, severity, or urgency, the assignment of risk values can be adjusted for each item and event. This functionality enables users to fine-tune the interpretation of threats or vulnerabilities within the company and evaluate the cumulative risk coming from several events over time. Risk values must be configured by administrators for correlation searches and objects.

Effective risk analysis is supported by various features and capabilities provided by Splunk ES, such as:

- **Risk scoring**: Quantifying the possible impact of assets, identities, and events on the security posture of an organization by assigning numerical values to each.
- **Risk-based prioritization**: Prioritizing security alerts, incidents, and other events according to their risk levels to concentrate on the most pressing problems.
- **Asset and identity correlation**: Linking security incidents to particular assets and persons to give assessments of risk context.
- **Configuring and customizing risk analysis dashboards**: Configuring and tailoring dashboards to display pertinent risk data and insights for certain security domains or business units.

In conclusion, risk analysis is an essential part of Splunk ES's security intelligence that enables businesses to recognize, evaluate, and rank the risks posed by their information security architecture. Organizations may strengthen their security posture, optimize resource allocation, and improve their overall security strategy by utilizing the platform's robust risk analysis capabilities.

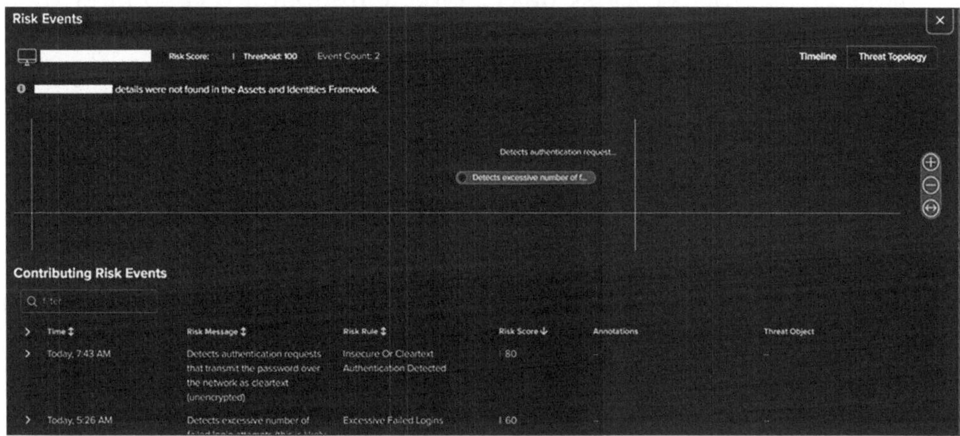

Figure 7.1: Splunk Enterprise Risk events

The Risk Analysis Dashboard in ES

Security analysts can evaluate and track changes in risk scores using the Risk Analysis dashboard in Splunk ES, identify the causes of risk increases, and take any necessary action using this useful tool. You may analyze risk rating changes and their reasons using the various filters and panels on this dashboard.

Gain access to the Risk Analysis Dashboard: Locate the **`Risk Analysis`** Dashboard in the **`Security Intelligence`** section of the Splunk ES app.

Figure 7.2: Splunk Enterprise Risk analysis dashboard

Dashboard filters:

- **Source**: Filter by the correlation search with risk modifiers.
- **Risk Object**: Select a risk object type and input a text to filter by risk object. Risk object type default value is All.

Dashboard panels:

- **Key Indicators**: Displays relevant metrics to the dashboard sources over the past 48 hours.
- **Risk Modifiers Over Time:** Shows changes made to risk modifiers with respect to time. Use filters to narrow down the view.
- **Risk Modifiers by Annotations:** Presents the changes made to risk modifiers with respect to annotations.
- **Risk Score by Annotations**: Shows the risk score with respect to annotations.
- **Risk Modifiers by Threat Object**: Displays the risk modifiers by threat objects.
- **Behavioral Analytics Detections by Type**: Represents the enabled detections in the test index, the risk index, and the disabled detections.
- **Risk Score by Object**: Shows the objects with the highest risk score. The drilldown launches a search that is scoped to the given time and uses the selected risk item.

- **Most Active Sources**: Shows the correlation searches that contribute the highest amount of risk to any object. The drilldown initiates a search using the chosen source.
- **Recent Risk Modifiers**: Lists the most recent modifications to a risk score, their cause, and their target in a table.

Using the filters and panels available in the Risk Analysis dashboard, security analysts can gain valuable insights into the risk landscape of their organization, helping them prioritize security efforts and make well-informed decisions.

Understanding Risk Scoring in Enterprise Security: A Case Study with JIT Inc.

We examine how technology company JIT Inc. uses Splunk Enterprise Security in this case to monitor and manage risk related to its remote employee access system.

Scenario Overview

- JIT Inc. has put in place jit-remote-access.com, a remote access service, to enable its workers to work from home with ease.
- In Splunk Enterprise Security, a correlation search can be set up to monitor anomalous access patterns, like several unsuccessful login attempts, simultaneous access from different locations, or logins during odd hours.

Risk Scoring Process

The system detects an anomaly: many attempts to log in from different countries in a brief period of time. Every questionable login is noted as a notable event, and each one is given a risk modifier. Every odd login attempt is assigned a fairly high-risk score because of the possible security consequences, given the vital nature of the service.

Jit-remote-access.com gains a risk score of 680.0 in a week, indicating a significant possible risk.

Risk Analysis Dashboard

The Risk Analysis dashboard for JIT Inc. shows the following data for jit-remote-access.com:

Risk Object	Risk Object Type	Risk Score	Source Count	Count
jit-remote-access.com	Service	680.0	4	15

Source	Risk Score	Risk Objects	Count
Irregular Access Pattern Detection - Rule	680.0	1	15

Response and Action:

- JIT Inc.'s security team launches a comprehensive investigation in response to the high-risk score.
- They find that most of the attempts to log in were made by personnel traveling abroad on business.
- On the other hand, a specific login attempt is marked as possibly unlawful.

Refinement of Risk Scoring:

- The security team at JIT Inc. adjusts the correlation search criteria to improve the risk scoring system's accuracy.
- They institute a policy whereby logins that are quickly verified through a safe multi-factor authentication procedure are given a lower risk score.
- In order to reduce false alarms, they also create a whitelist that includes the travel plans of the staff.

Constant Evaluation and Modification

- JIT Inc. keeps a close eye on jit-remote-access.com in order to spot and handle any new security threats.
- The correlation searches and risk rating have been adjusted to better distinguish between legitimate and potentially hazardous access attempts.

This case study demonstrates how JIT Inc. uses the dynamic risk assessment capabilities of Splunk Enterprise Security to efficiently monitor their remote access systems and modify their cybersecurity tactics to guarantee a strong defense against changing threats.

Effective use of Risk Analysis Dashboard

Use the Risk Analysis Dashboard in Splunk (ES) by performing the following actions:

- **Understand dashboard components**: Become familiar with the Risk Analysis Dashboard's numerous panels and visualization features. This could include the top risk contributors, a breakdown of risk by object type, and more.
- Use the filters on the dashboard to narrow your view by time, object type (such as user or system), or other pertinent criteria. Use the search bar to locate particular activities or items using keywords or search criteria.

- **Examine risk trends**: Track the recurring patterns and trends in risk scores to spot potential security concerns or weak spots in your organization.
- **Customize risk scoring**: Adapt risk score configurations for particular items or occurrences by working with the security administrators of your company. This enables you to customize the risk analysis process to the unique requirements and threat environment of your firm.
- **Monitor and review**: Keep track of your organization's risk status by frequently checking the Risk Analysis Dashboard. Check the dashboard frequently to make sure the risk score options are still applicable and efficient.

You may increase your entire security posture, better understand your organization's risk profile, and prioritize security initiatives by using these methods and the Risk Analysis Dashboard in Splunk ES.

Web Intelligence

The goal of web intelligence is to identify potential dangers and comprehend network usage patterns by analyzing web traffic and user behavior. To learn more about your network, you can concentrate on the following topics in the context of web intelligence:

- **Explore the types of websites being accessed over your network:**

  You can determine the types of websites that are often viewed on your network by analyzing online traffic categories. You can utilize this information to better understand user browsing patterns and spot any suspicious or inappropriate website visits that could endanger your network.

- **Check the web user agents being applied to your network:**

  Browsers and other apps use web user agents as identifiers when speaking with web servers. You can determine the browsers and programs being used in your network by looking at the user agents. This can assist you in finding any insecure or out-of-date software, as well as possibly unapproved or non-compliant programs.

- **Check the external domains that are being accessed:**

  Examining the external domains that users on your network have accessed might help you spot potential security problems. You may take the necessary steps to secure your network by keeping an eye on domain access to spot any connections to phishing sites, C&C servers, or dangerous domains.

- **Check request URLs for unusual content (Length):**
  You can spot any anomalies that can point to a threat by examining the length and content of request URLs. For instance, unusually long URLs could have encoded SQL commands, XSS attempts, or command and control (C&C) directives. You can identify potential dangers and take the appropriate precautions to minimize them by looking at these URLs.

In conclusion, web intelligence entails keeping an eye on and analyzing many facets of network user activity and web traffic. You may efficiently identify potential risks, assure compliance, and manage the security of your network by investigating the different sorts of websites that are being viewed, looking at web user agents, keeping an eye on connections to external domains, and analyzing request URL contents.

Accessing and Navigating the Web Intelligence Dashboards in ES

To access the Web Intelligence Dashboards, direct your attention to the app navigation bar, where you will find the `Security Intelligence` section. Click this section, and from the dropdown menu, select `Web Intelligence.`

Web Intelligence Dashboards

This section will guide you through the understanding and usage of dashboards like HTTP Category Analysis, HTTP User Agent Analysis, New Domain Analysis, and URL Length Analysis. These dashboards help analyze web data intricately, covering aspects like HTTP traffic, user-agent details, new domain interactions, and URL length patterns for enhanced threat detection.

HTTP Category Analysis Dashboard

To monitor and spot potential risks in your environment, Splunk Enterprise Security's HTTP Category Analysis dashboard offers a thorough view of traffic data categories. This dashboard allows you to:

- Analyze statistical information to spot traffic anomalies that depart from the norm.
- Keep an eye out for category counts that deviate from the usual, since these could indicate potential concerns.
- Locate low traffic volume activities and dig deeper into the compiled data to look at particular events.
- Classify suspicious patterns of behavior using sparklines.

Use the **`Show only unknown categories`** filter to concentrate on unidentified traffic categories. To define which categories are considered unknown, follow these steps:

1. Select **`Settings`** -> **Tags**.
2. Click **`List by tag name`**.
3. Choose a network add-on that is related to **`DA-ESS-NetworkProtection`** or another app context, such as **`TA-websense`**.
4. Click **`New`**.
5. Enter a Tag name of unknown.
6. Enter a Field-value pair as unknown traffic, for example, **`category=undetected`**.
7. Click **Save**.

Figure 7.3: *Http Category Analysis dashboard*

Dashboard filters help in refining the HTTP category list:

- **Time Range:** Select a time range for the data displayed.
- **Advanced Filter**: Click to access a list of category events to be filtered for this dashboard.

Dashboard panels provide insights into various aspects of the data:

- **Key Indicators**: Display relevant metrics from the past 48 hours.
- **Category Distribution**: Category counts are represented as a scatter plot with count and **`src_count`** on the axes, respectively.
- Category Details: Describe HTTP categories, including sparklines that depict activity during the last 24 hours.

HTTP User Agent Analysis dashboard

The HTTP User Agent Analysis dashboard in Splunk Enterprise Security makes it simple to examine user agent strings in your proxy data to look for potential vulnerabilities. Malicious user agent strings can include misspelled browser names, out-of-date version numbers, and unusually long strings, to mention a few. You can examine these strings to look for any dangers by evaluating user agents for command and control (C&C) activities or abnormal HTTP communication activity.

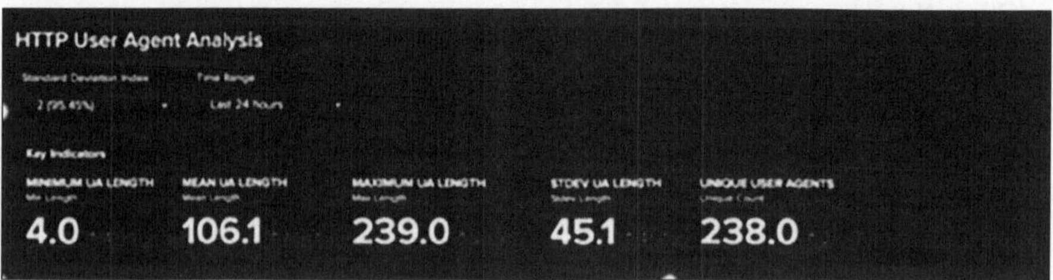

Figure 7.4: *Http user agent Analysis dashboard*

Dashboard filters:

The dashboard offers various filters to refine the user agent list, such as Standard Deviation Index, Time Range, and Advanced Filter. These filters allow you to adjust the level of detail displayed and focus on specific events, timeframes, or categories.

Dashboard panels:

The dashboard consists of several panels that display key information and provide insights into user agent data. These panels include:

- **Key Indicators**: This panel displays relevant metrics from the past 48 hours, providing summary information at the top of the dashboard.
- **User Agent Distribution**: User agent strings are shown in this scatter plot depending on length (x-axis) and count (y-axis). You can get information about the raw data by hovering over an item. When filters or time ranges are modified, the chart changes.
- **User Agent Details**: The string value and a sparkline depicting activity for that user agent string over the previous 24 hours are included in this panel's extensive information about user agents in your environment.

By utilizing these panels and filters, security analysts can effectively monitor and analyze user agent strings to identify potential threats, anomalies, and malicious clients within their network environment.

New Domain Analysis Dashboard

You may track and examine new domains in your environment with the aid of the New Domain Analysis dashboard in Splunk ES. These domains might have just been registered, or the system may have just started to notice them. The dashboard displays data on newly registered domains, newly registered domains by age, newly registered domains by top-level domain (TLD), and newly registered domains by registration information.

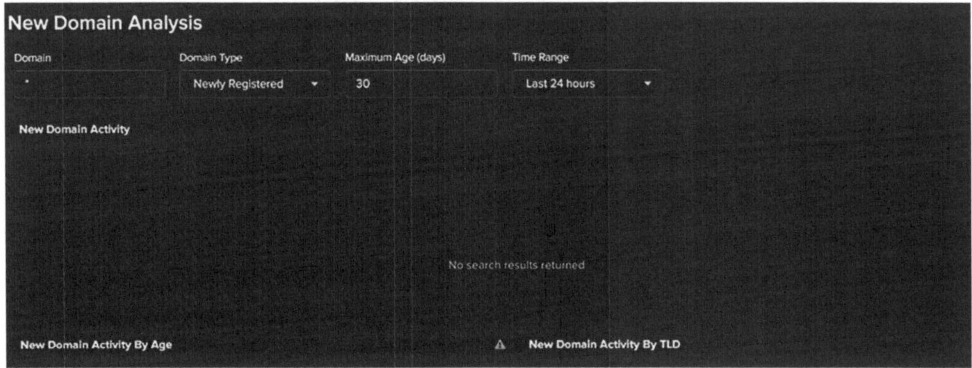

Figure 7.5: *New Domain Analysis dashboard*

With this dashboard, you can:

- Check out hosts that are in contact with recently registered domains.
- In the New Domain Activity by Age panel, look for anomalous activity aimed at recently registered domains.
- Use the New Domain Activity by TLD tab to find unusual top-level domain activity.
- Examine a lot of new domains to see if a Trojan, botnet, or other malicious entity is running on your network.

Dashboard filters help refine the domain list:

- **Domain:** Type the domain (Network, Access, Endpoint).
- **New Domain Type:** Choose from Newly Seen or Newly Registered.
- Set the maximum age (in days) for recently discovered or registered domains. 30 days are the standard.
- **Time Range**: Decide which time period you want to depict.
- **Advanced Filter:** Click to view the category events for this dashboard that can be filtered.

Dashboard panels offer insights into various aspects of the data:

- **New Domain Activity**: Information about new domain activity displayed in a table manner.
- **Age-Related New Domain Activity**: Scatter plot with Age on the x-axis and Count on the y-axis.
- Bar graph with Count on the x-axis and TLD on the y-axis showing new domain activity by TLD.
- Registration Information: A table representation of the data related to a new domain registration.

To view data in the New Domain Analysis dashboard, configure a link to an external domain lookup data source. Domaintools.com, a paid API for WHOIS data, is used in the example displayed. Create a domaintools.com account, gather the API host name and access details, and then configure a modular input in Splunk Enterprise Security. You can also set up the connection by following the specified instructions and using a different domain source.

Remember that requesting information from nonexistent or domains with invalid TLDs is expected to typically result in 404 and 400 errors in logs. If you don't see any new events in the WHOIS index, check that the API URL is using the correct protocol (HTTP or HTTPS).

URL Length Analysis Dashboard

The Splunk ES dashboard for URL Length Analysis looks at proxy or HTTP data that contains URL string or path information. This dashboard is made to support you in:

To find outliers, statistically compare URLs.

- Look into lengthy URLs that have no referrers.
- Look for URLs that are unusually long and may contain malicious material such as SQL injections, cross-site scripting (XSS), embedded command and control (C&C) instructions, or other threats.
- To find out how many assets are interacting with the URL, use the information table.

You can use dashboard filters to narrow down the shown URL length events:

- **Standard Deviation Index (SDI):** The percentage (%) displays the amount of data that was omitted based on the chosen number of SDs. If there are fewer user agent strings, select a greater number of deviations; if there are more, select a lower number.

- **Time Range**: Decide which time period you want to depict.
- **Advanced Filter**: Click to view the category events for this dashboard that can be filtered.

Figure 7.6: *Url length Analysis dashboard*

The dashboard is made up of various panels that offer various insights, including:

- **Key Indicators**: Shows metrics over the previous 48 hours that are pertinent to the dashboard sources. At the dashboard's top, key indicators serve as summaries of information.
- **URL Length Anomalies Over Time**: This graph shows the number of different URL lengths over time. In a line graph with time as the x-axis and count as the y-axis, it displays URL lengths that are longer than the number of standard deviations (2 by default) set in the filter.
- **URL Length Details:** This table shows the URL strings as well as other information, like the complete URI string. The count column displays the number of events observed if a source IP address generates multiple occurrences. The URL length's standard deviations are shown by the letter Z.

You can find possible risks that are larger than the typical sizes (small or large) by analyzing URL lengths. Long URL paths that are not normal from unknown sources or to unknown locations are frequently signs of malicious access and should be investigated.

Hands-On Web Intelligence with Splunk ES at JIT Inc.

Overview

JIT Inc., a growing technology firm, utilizes Splunk Enterprise Security (ES) to bolster its cybersecurity. The company faces a variety of web-based threats and leverages Splunk ES's Web Intelligence capabilities to navigate these challenges. Splunk's Web Intelligence consists of four primary dashboards: HTTP Category Analysis, HTTP User Agent Analysis, New Domain Analysis, and URL Length Analysis. Each of these dashboards plays a crucial role in identifying and analyzing web threats.

Scenario Setup

1. HTTP Category Analysis Dashboard:

- **Scenario**: JIT Inc. is concerned about possible data leakage and non-compliance with corporate standards after noticing an odd rise in web traffic under the `Social Media` and `File Sharing` categories.
- **How It Helps**: JIT Inc. may examine online traffic by category thanks to this dashboard. Through an examination of several categories' trends and patterns, the security team can spot anomalous activity or policy infractions and take appropriate action.

2. HTTP User Agent Analysis Dashboard:

- **Scenario**: The IT department notices odd web requests that appear to come from unusual or out-of-date web browsers, suggesting the possibility of bot activity or a security breach.
- **How It Assists:** With the use of user agent strings, the dashboard facilitates the analysis of online requests. By recognizing possibly harmful traffic from odd user agents, JIT Inc. can locate and look into these anomalies.

3. New Domain Analysis Dashboard:

- **Scenario:** Staff members report receiving suspicious emails that lead them to unidentified websites, leading JIT Inc. to believe that phishing attacks are being carried out using recently registered domains.
- **How It Helps:** Access attempts to recently registered domains can be detected with the help of this dashboard. It can assist JIT Inc. in identifying possible phishing sites early on, enabling the quick blocking of such domains, and training staff members about them.

4. URL Length Analysis Dashboard:

- **Scenario:** The cybersecurity team at JIT Inc. is alert to sophisticated malware and phishing assaults, which frequently mask harmful websites with lengthy, intricate URLs.
- **How It Assists:** JIT Inc. can examine how different URL lengths are distributed throughout online traffic with this dashboard. Unusual lengthy URLs can be promptly recognized and looked into, as they are frequently connected to harmful websites.

Implementation and Analysis

- The JIT Inc. security team can proactively discover and mitigate a wide range of web-based threats by regularly monitoring these dashboards, which each offer particular insights geared to distinct areas of web intelligence.
- The knowledge gathered from these dashboards also helps to improve the business's general cybersecurity plans and procedures.

For JIT Inc., Splunk ES's Web Intelligence dashboards serve as an invaluable tool in their cybersecurity arsenal. By leveraging these dashboards effectively, JIT Inc. can maintain a robust security posture against diverse and evolving web-based threats, ensuring the safety and integrity of their digital assets and operations.

User Intelligence

In a security setting, user intelligence entails keeping an eye on and analyzing user behavior, access patterns, and network activities to spot potential threats, abnormalities, and suspicious activity. The ability to recognize and apply investigators, asset and identity concepts, access abnormalities, and user activity analysis can aid in the detection and mitigation of potential risks coming from within the company.

- **Recognize and employ user activity analysis:**

  This process involves keeping track of user actions such as login attempts, file access, and network resource utilization. You can spot odd behavior patterns that can point to a compromised account, an insider threat, or unauthorized access by keeping an eye on user activity.

- **Use access anomalies to identify suspicious access patterns:**

  Abnormalities in user access patterns, or access anomalies, may be a sign of suspicious activity. You can identify potential dangers, such as unauthorized access to sensitive information or efforts to elevate privileges, by spotting and looking into access anomalies.

- **Recognize the notions of assets and identities**:

  Assets are the many hardware, software, and resource components that make up a network within an organization, whereas identities are the names of specific individuals. Monitoring and restricting user access to critical resources requires an understanding of the connections between assets and identities.

- **Use investigators to analyze activities and events connected to a specific asset or identity:**
  Investigators are tools that security analysts can use to look into activities and occurrences connected to particular assets or identities. You may learn more about user behavior and spot potential security risks by employing investigators.

Some hazards come from within your company, including:

- Social engineering attacks, in which perpetrators trick employees into disclosing private data or allowing illegal access.
- Disloyal workers or subcontractors who commit crimes like data theft, sabotage, or unlawful access to private data.

It is essential to keep an eye on user behavior and respond to the following queries in order to address these threats:

- What user accounts are active, and what are they doing?
- What equipment (servers, and so on) are users accessing?
- Where are users logging on?
- How much risk has been accumulated by each user or device?

By analyzing user behavior, access patterns, and activities, security teams can detect and mitigate potential insider threats, protect sensitive data, and maintain a secure environment within the organization.

Accessing and Navigating the User Intelligence Dashboards in ES

To access the User Intelligence Dashboards, navigate to the Web Intelligence section in Splunk ES Menu Bar and select the relevant dashboard.

User Intelligence Dashboards

This section will provide a comprehensive overview of key dashboards such as the Asset and Identity Investigator dashboards, User Activity Monitoring, and Access Anomalies dashboard, equipping users with tools to analyze and respond to security events effectively. These dashboards facilitate deep-dive investigations, monitor user activity, and identify unusual access patterns to bolster security measures.

Asset and Identity Investigator dashboards

Using swim lanes that are determined by category, the Asset and Identity Investigator dashboards show security-related events over time. They aid security analysts in evaluating and tracking user identities and asset interactions inside the environment, enabling a thorough picture of their operations.

Asset Investigator:

This dashboard shows data on assets for already established event types, such as malware and significant incidents. The Asset Investigator interface allows analysts to track actions across event categories, prioritize interactions with an asset, and do ad hoc searches. Confirming the asset, reducing the time frame, altering swim lanes, examining events, and sharing or further studying events are all steps in the asset investigation procedure.

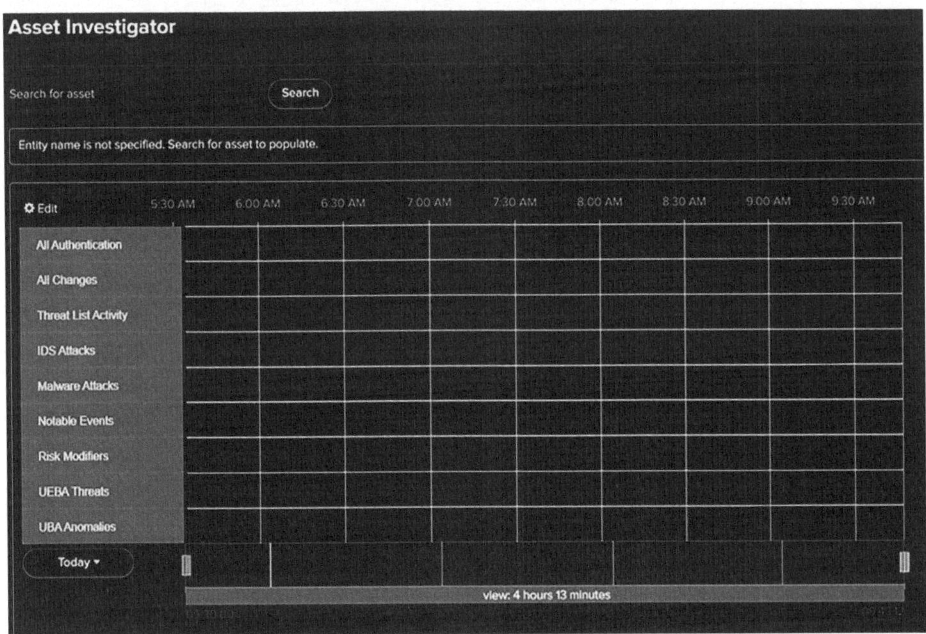

***Figure 7.7**: Asset Investigator dashboard*

Identity Investigator:

This dashboard emphasizes user identities and displays data from predefined event categories, including malware and change analysis. The Identity Investigator dashboard allows analysts to look at a user's activities, follow actions across different event categories, and run ad hoc searches. The workflow for conducting an identity investigation entails verifying the identification, reducing the time frame, altering swim lanes, examining events, and sharing or further researching occurrences.

***Figure 7.8**: Identity Investigator dashboard*

The Edit Lanes menu, which lets you add, remove, or rearrange swim lanes, is supported by both dashboards when it comes to swim lane customization. Custom swim lanes made with ES Content Management or packaged with add-ons can also be included.

Overall, the dashboards for the Asset and Identity Investigator give security analysts a strong tool for investigating and keeping track of user identities and asset activity in their environment. They aid in ensuring a secure workplace by assisting in the detection of potential security threats, unauthorized access, and suspicious activity.

User Activity Monitoring

By displaying panels that depict typical risk-generating actions, the User Activity dashboard in Splunk Enterprise Security is intended to assist analysts in identifying potential insider threats and dangerous user behavior. You can narrow down the results shown on the panels using the dashboard filters, which include user, business unit, watchlisted user, and time period filters.

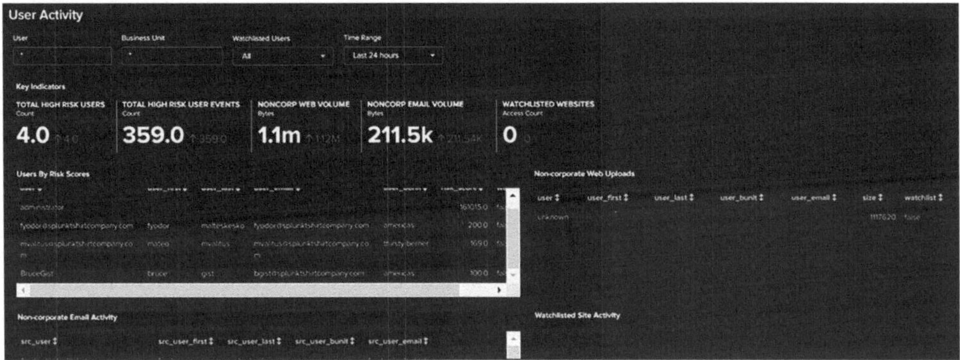

***Figure* 7.9:** *User activity dashboard*

Dashboard Panels for User Activity:

- **Key Indicators**: Provides summary information and displays relevant metrics over the past 48 hours.
- **Users By Risk Scores:** Shows the top 100 highest risk users, helping analysts focus on the riskiest individuals in the organization. Drilldown launches Identity Investigator dashboard and runs a user search on the chosen user.
- **Non-corporate Web Uploads**: Shows user activity in high volume uploads and downloads, which may be a sign of data exfiltration. Launching the Identity Investigator dashboard, Drilldown searches for the selected person.
- **Non-corporate Email Activity:** Displays the top 100 users who send emails in large volumes to non-corporate domains, which could be a sign of data exfiltration. Launching the Identity Investigator dashboard, Drilldown searches for the selected person.
- **Watchlisted Site Activity**: This feature shows users' web access, and activity on particular categories of websites may be a sign of insider threat activities. Launching the Identity Investigator dashboard, Drilldown searches for the selected person.
- **Remote Access:** Displays user-authenticated remote access, including questionable web or email behavior potentially pointing to data espionage or compromised credentials. Launching Identity Investigator dashboard, Drilldown searches users for the selected user.
- **Ticket Activity:** Shows user ticketing activity, with dangerous online or email activity together with ticket submission, perhaps indicating data exfiltration or credential abuse. Launching Identity Investigator dashboard, Drilldown searches users for the selected user.

Access Anomalies dashboard

The Access Anomalies dashboard is intended to reveal questionable authentication patterns, such as simultaneous authentication attempts from various IP addresses and unlikely travel anomalies. Action, app, user, business unit, and time range are all dashboard filters.

Panels on the dashboard for access anomalies are:

- Geographically unusual Accesses: Shows users who have made several attempts for authentication, spaced apart by unusual intervals of time and distance, possibly revealing compromised credentials. The drilldown launches the Access Search dashboard and performs a user search.
- Concurrent Application Accesses: This feature shows users who have made numerous authentication attempts in a short period from various IP addresses, which may be an indication of shared or stolen credentials. Drilldown searches for the selected user on the Access Search panel.

User behavior analytics

This process is used to learn about the daily network events that users create. Information can be used to identify the use of compromised credentials, lateral movement, and other malicious behavior once it has been gathered and evaluated.

The UBA Anomalies dashboard in Splunk Enterprise Security helps you analyze and understand anomalous activity in your environment by displaying various metrics related to user behavior anomalies. To access the dashboard, navigate to **`Security Intelligence`** > **`User Intelligence`** > **`UBA Anomalies`**.

Key features of the UBA Anomalies dashboard include:

- **Key Indicators**: Monitor changes in your environment's count of several metrics over the last 24 hours, including UBA notables, UBA anomaly actors, UBA anomaly signatures, UBA anomalies per threat, and the overall count of UBA anomalies.
- **The Anomalies Over Time panel**: This allows you to look into anomalous activity peaks and contrast the number of actors over time with the number of anomalies in order to spot patterns or trends.
- **Most Active Signatures panel**: This feature helps you focus on high-impact areas by identifying the most prevalent sorts of abnormal activity in your environment.

- **Most Active Actors panel:** Determine which people, devices, apps, and other actors are causing the most abnormal behavior using the Most Active Actors panel to help you focus your investigation efforts.
- **Recent UBA Anomalies panel**: See the latest anomalous activity in your environment, so you can quickly respond to emerging threats or issues.

To view an anomaly in Splunk UBA, click a value on the dashboard to drill down to the search. You can use the event actions on a specific anomaly event to "View Contributing Anomalies" and open Splunk UBA to view the Anomaly Details view.

Hands-On User Intelligence with Splunk ES at JIT Inc.

Overview

The fast-growing startup JIT Inc. uses Splunk Enterprise Security (ES) to enhance its user intelligence capabilities. The increasing threat of insider attacks and the need for extensive user behavior monitoring have led JIT Inc. to utilize Splunk ES's User Intelligence features, which include the Asset Investigator, Identity Investigator, User Activity, Access Anomalies, and User Behavior Analytics dashboards. Each dashboard provides a unique viewpoint on user behavior and potential security threats.

Scenario Setup

1. Asset Investigator Dashboard:

- **Scenario**: JIT Inc. notices odd behavior on a valuable server that holds private customer information. They must look into the nature and sources of this behavior.
- **How It Helps**: JIT Inc. can monitor and visualize all activities related to the particular server, such as alterations in file activity and user access patterns, by using the Asset Investigator Dashboard. This aids in locating any instances of misuse or illegal access.

2. Identity Investigator Dashboard:

- **Scenario**: A few finance department employees may have had their accounts compromised, according to reports.
- **How It Assists**: JIT Inc. is able to investigate the actions and access patterns of particular user identities thanks to the Identity Investigator Dashboard. This helps identify any unusual or out-of-the-ordinary conduct that could point to account compromise or misuse.

3. User Activity Dashboard:

- **Scenario**: JIT Inc. wishes to keep an eye on user activity in general to make sure that internal policies are being followed and to spot any odd behavior.
- **How It Helps**: A thorough overview of user activity throughout the network is provided by this dashboard. Through dashboard monitoring, JIT Inc. can spot any unusual patterns of behavior, such as downloading huge files frequently or accessing sensitive data outside of regular business hours.

4. Access Anomalies Dashboard:

- **Scenario**: JIT Inc. is worried about the security concerns connected with remote access because its employees work from home.
- **How It Assists:** Unusual access patterns, such as many concurrent sessions or logins from geographically unlikely areas, can be highlighted by the Access Anomalies Dashboard and may be a sign of compromised credentials or insider threats.

5. User Behavior Analytics Dashboard:

- **Scenario**: By examining user behavior patterns, JIT Inc. aims to proactively detect possible insider threats or compromised accounts.
- **How It Assists**: By identifying variations from typical user behavior, this dashboard's advanced analytics can identify possible insider threats or compromised accounts. It can spot tiny behavioral irregularities like altered data access patterns or contact with strange external IP addresses.

Implementation and Analysis

- JIT Inc. receives focused information into different facets of user behavior and security from each dashboard.
- By keeping an eye on these dashboards continuously, the security team at JIT Inc. is able to promptly recognize and address possible security incidents.
- The information and patterns found on these dashboards also help JIT Inc. improve its general security guidelines and user access procedures.

The User Intelligence dashboards offered by Splunk ES are crucial resources for JIT Inc. in order to keep its IT infrastructure safe and compliant. Through efficient utilization of these dashboards, JIT Inc. may maintain the security and integrity of their network and data by staying ahead of possible security issues resulting from user activity.

Threat Intelligence

By obtaining and analyzing data on current and potential threats, threat intelligence enables firms to proactively address new cyberthreats.

Splunk Enterprise Security (ES) is a tool that can assist businesses in managing and utilizing threat intelligence data.

- **Understanding threat intelligence feeds:**

  Threat intelligence feeds are constantly updated sources of data on potential threats, weaknesses, and malicious behaviors. These feeds may contain information on IP addresses, domain names, URLs, file hashes, and additional indicators of compromise (IoCs) linked to recognized threats. Feeds can originate from a variety of places, including commercial suppliers, open-source software platforms, governmental organizations, and trade associations.

- **Splunk ES's integration of threat intelligence feeds:**

  Observe these procedures to incorporate threat intelligence feeds into Splunk ES:

  - Configure the necessary apps or add-ons to get threat intelligence data from the feeds of your choice.
  - Set up data inputs to feed Splunk ES with threat intelligence data.
  - Process and standardize the ingested data using Splunk ES's Threat Intelligence architecture.

- **Analyzing and correlating threat intelligence data:**

  After threat intelligence data has been processed and ingested, Splunk ES may be used to analyze and correlate it with internal security data from your company. By doing this, you can see patterns, trends, and IoCs that could point to a danger. To visualize this data and give your security teams useful information, establish alerts, dashboards, and reports.

- **Proactive threat hunting and response:**

  Threat hunting is the proactive process of aggressively seeking out and detecting risks before they cause harm. Utilize threat intelligence data with Splunk ES to proactively search for dangers in your environment. some proactive threat-hunting methods are:

  - Constructing correlation searches to find odd patterns, behaviors, or IoCs.

  - Creating unique dashboards to prioritize investigations and visualize potential hazards.
  - Creating alerts to inform security analysts when certain circumstances or IoCs are found.
  - Combining Splunk ES with other security programs to automate response procedures like blocking malicious IP addresses or isolating affected computers.

Threat Intelligence Dashboards

This section will encompass vital tools such as the Threat Activity and Threat Artifacts dashboards. These dashboards aim to provide a comprehensive view of threat landscapes and deep-dive analysis of threat artifacts, contributing to effective threat detection and response.

Threat Activity dashboard

Through the correlation of threat intelligence source information with events occurring in your environment, the Threat Activity dashboard in Splunk Enterprise Security sheds light on threat activity. Using this dashboard, you may spot potential dangers and take appropriate action.

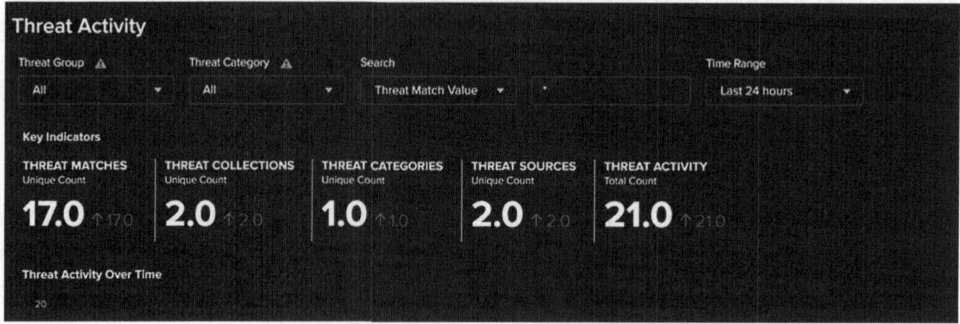

Figure 7.10: *Threat activity dashboard*

Dashboard filters:

The results shown on the dashboard panels can be further filtered using a variety of filters. Key security indicators are not subject to these controls. The filters consist of:

- **Threat Group:** Choose a named group or entity that represents a recognized threat to narrow your search.
- **Threat Category**: Use this filter to narrow your results by threat kind, such as backdoor, financial threat, or advanced persistent threat.

- **Search**: This filter allows you to look for information in areas like Destination, Sourcetype, Source, Threat Collection, Threat Collection Key, Threat Key, Threat Match Field, and Threat Match Value.
- **Time Range**: Choose the time for which the data on the dashboard will be shown.

Dashboard panels:

The dashboard features several panels that provide valuable information about threat activity, including:

- **Key Indicators**: This panel provides a summary of threat activity over the previous 48 hours by displaying metrics pertinent to the dashboard sources.
- **Threat Activity during Time:** The number of incidents for each threat collection during the given time period is displayed in this panel. To see a search that is specific to the selected threat collection and time frame, dive down.
- **Most Active Threat Collections**: This panel shows the most active threat collections based on event matches throughout the given time, with a sparkline denoting the peak of event matches. To view a search using the chosen threat collection, drill down.
- **Most Active Threat Sources:** The top threat sources for the given period are displayed in this panel based on event count matching. To view a search with the chosen threat source, drill down.
- **Threat Activity Details**: The most recent threat matches are broken out in-depth in this panel. To whitelist by threat_match_value or to emphasize certain threat_match_value matches, utilize the event selection box and the Advanced Filter option.

Security analysts can get insights into potential threats, prioritize investigations, and react proactively to limit risks by using the Threat Activity dashboard in Splunk Enterprise Security.

Threat Artifacts dashboard

You may proactively identify and respond to potential threats by using the threat intelligence dashboards in Splunk ES. This lowers the chance of security breaches and lessens the effects of cyberattacks on your company.

The Threat Artifacts dashboard for Splunk Enterprise Security provides a consolidated location to browse and assess threat content downloaded from all listed threat download sources. It helps security analysts acquire additional context by displaying all threat artifacts associated with a user-specified threat source or artifact.

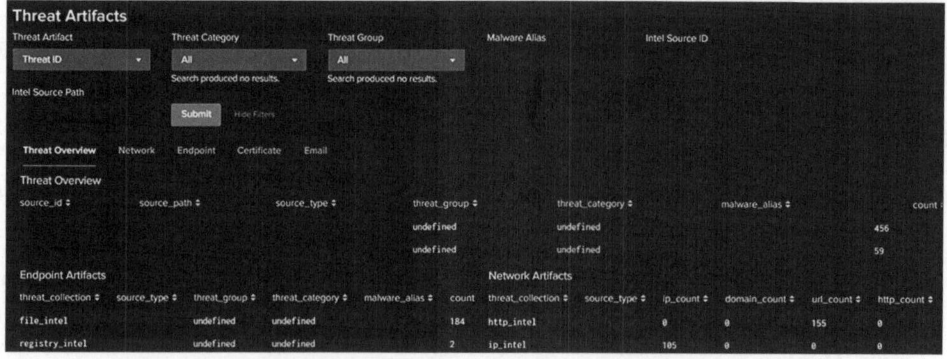

Figure 7.11: *Threat Artifacts dashboard*

The dashboard contains a number of selection filters and sections to let you study the threat content more thoroughly:

1. To choose from the available threat artifact kinds, start by modifying the Threat Artifact filter.
    - Use the Description filter
    - **Threat Artifact**: Objects grouped by threat collection, such as network, file, and service, are referred to as threat artifacts.
2. Depending on your choice, other filters that are accessible may change.
    - **Selection of a threat artifact Text Filter**: (*) Wildcard by Default By Drop-Down Filter
    - **Threat ID**: This includes Threat Category, Threat Group, Malware Alias, Intel Source ID, and Intel Source Path
    - **Network:** This includes IP, HTTP domain. Choose from: User agent, cookie, header, data, URL, or referrer with a string added.
    - **Registry**: This includes Hive, Path, Key Name, Value Name, Value Type, and Value Text.
    - **File**: This includes File Name, File Extension, File Path, and File Hash.
    - **Service:** This includes Name, Descriptive Name, Description, and Type.
    - **User**: User information includes User, Full Name, Group Name, Description
    - **Process**: This includes Process, Process Arguments, Handle Names, and Handle Type.

- **Certificate:** Certificate information includes Serial Number, Subject, Issuer, Validity Not Before, Validity Not After, and Validity Not After.
- **Email:** Email information includes Address, Subject, and Body.

3. Review the threat source context using the tabs:

   Panel Tabs

   - **Overview of the threat:** Endpoint, Network, Email, and Certificate Artifacts
   - Email: Email Intelligence
   - **Certificate**: Certificate Intelligence
   - **Network**: HTTP Intelligence, IP Intelligence, Domain Intelligence
   - **Endpoint**: File Intelligence, Registry Intelligence, Process Intelligence, Service Intelligence, User Intelligence

Security analysts can rapidly analyze and assess threat information using the Threat Artifacts dashboard in Splunk Enterprise Security. This enables them to better understand potential threats and act pro-actively to mitigate risks.

Hands-On Threat Intelligence with Splunk ES at JIT Inc.

Overview

The forward-thinking business JIT Inc. uses Splunk Enterprise Security (ES) to fortify its threat intelligence system. JIT Inc. uses Splunk ES's Threat Intelligence features to counteract the growing threat of cyberattacks, paying particular attention to the Threat Activity and Threat Artifacts dashboards. These dashboards are essential for spotting, evaluating, and dealing with possible online dangers.

Scenario Setup

1. Threat Activity Dashboard:

- **Situation:** JIT Inc. has observed an increase in network traffic aimed at its servers that are visible to the outside world, which prompts concerns about possible cyberattackers using this traffic for reconnaissance.
- **How It Assists:** JIT Inc. receives real-time insights about potential threats discovered throughout their network using the Threat Activity Dashboard. It gathers and presents feeds of threat intelligence, emphasizing dubious IP addresses, domain names, and other signs of compromise (IoCs). JIT Inc. can promptly detect trends suggestive of reconnaissance or other

malevolent activity by keeping an eye on this dashboard, which allows them to take preventative measures.

2. **Threat Artifacts Dashboard:**

- **Scenario:** In order to determine the extent and possible consequences of a suspected phishing attack, JIT Inc. must examine the related artifacts.
- **How It Assists:** The Hazardous Relics Dashboard enables JIT Inc. to investigate particular danger indicators found within the network in further detail. Analyzing URLs, file hashes, and IP addresses connected to the phishing campaign are all part of this process. Through the analysis of these artifacts, JIT Inc. may determine the source, mode, and possible targets of the attack within the company, resulting in more potent mitigation techniques.

Implementation and Analysis

- **Proactive Monitoring:** To stay informed of new dangers, JIT Inc. keeps a close eye on both dashboards. This proactive strategy aids in the early identification and handling of possible security events.
- **Incident Investigation and Response:** These dashboards provide JIT Inc. with extensive insights that facilitate in-depth investigations and the development of effective response plans in the case of an identified danger.
- **Improved Security Posture:** JIT Inc. is able to improve its overall cybersecurity posture by streamlining firewall rules, optimizing security measures, and conducting regular analysis of threat activity and artifacts.

The Threat Activity and Threat Artifacts dashboards from Splunk ES are essential parts of JIT Inc.'s cybersecurity arsenal. These dashboards offer thorough insights into the threat landscape, making it easier to identify and neutralize cyberthreats in a timely manner. Through the utilization of these technologies, JIT Inc. improves its capacity to protect its digital assets and uphold operational integrity in the face of a constantly changing variety of cyber threats.

Protocol Intelligence

In order to identify potential threats, abnormalities, and to improve network security, protocol intelligence entails tracking, analyzing, and comprehending network protocols. Security teams can examine protocol-related occurrences and put preventative measures in place to strengthen their organization's security posture by utilizing protocol intelligence.

- **Monitoring and analyzing network protocols**: Splunk ES is used to gather, process, and store network traffic data for monitoring network protocols. This information offers perceptions into the performance, communication patterns, and general wellness of the network. Security analysts can find possible hazards, spot anomalies, and identify problem areas by evaluating this data.

- **Detecting protocol-based threats and anomalies:** By comparing network traffic data with threat intelligence feeds, user activity, and other security-related data sources, Splunk ES can identify protocol-based threats and anomalies. This procedure aids in the detection of potential assaults like Distributed Denial of Service (DDoS), the spread of malware, or attempts at data espionage. Security teams can promptly respond to crises and minimize potential damage by identifying these dangers early.
- **Using Splunk ES to further examine protocol-related incidents**: When a protocol-related issue is identified, Splunk ES provides a number of tools to do so. In order to comprehend the incident's underlying causes, affected systems, and prospective attack vectors, security analysts can go deeper into the data using search queries, visualizations, and other analytics tools. Analysts can use these technologies to obtain the data they need to fix the problem and stop it from happening again.
- **Using protocol intelligence to boost network security**: Organizations can improve their network security by using protocol intelligence to gain insights into network behavior, identify potential weak points, and swiftly identify assaults. Security teams can utilize this information to establish additional security controls, harden devices, and change network configurations as preventative measures. Additionally, protocol intelligence supports companies in upholding legal and regulatory compliance while protecting the privacy and security of their data.

Protocol Intelligence dashboards

This section will highlight the Protocol Centre and Traffic Size Analysis, along with specific dashboards for DNS, SSL, and Email activity and search. These dashboards offer granular visibility into different protocols and traffic patterns, aiding in the identification and analysis of potential security threats.

Protocol Center

The Protocol Center Dashboard gives a summary of network protocol data that is important for security, enabling analysts to keep an eye on and research network behavior across different protocols. The searches on the dashboard display the results based on the time selected using the dashboard time picker.

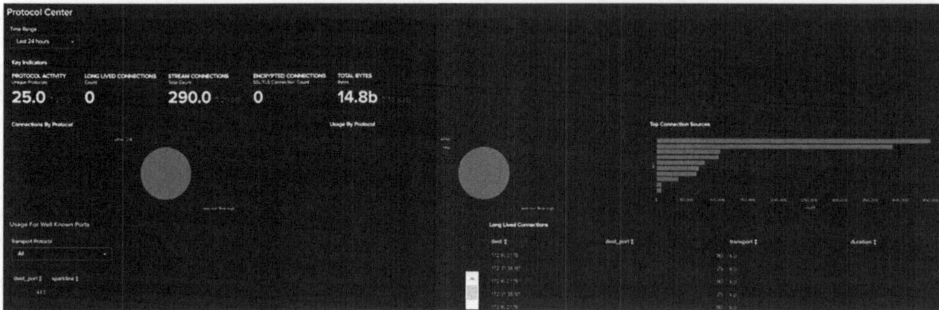

Figure 7.12: *Protocol Center dashboard*

Dashboard Panels

- Important indices for the previous 48 hours, metrics that are pertinent to the dashboard sources are shown. At the dashboard's top, key indicators serve as summaries of information. Protocol Activity, Long Lived Connections, Stream Connections, Encrypted Connections, and Total Bytes are some of the important metrics shown.
- Connections By Protocol Shows the total number of protocol connections over time, organized by protocol. The connection distribution by protocol displays the most often used protocols in a given context, including HTTP/SSL and email protocols. An exploited protocol could display an unusually high number of connections for the service it offers.
- Protocol Usage shows the total amount of protocol traffic, sorted by protocol over time and displayed in bytes. The bandwidth used by each protocol will be consistent when compared to the total network traffic. A protocol that has been exploited might show an out-of-proportion rise in traffic.
    - **Top Sources for Connection** The top 10 hosts in terms of the volume of protocol traffic sent and received over time are shown. A host that shows a lot of connection activity could be overloaded, having problems, or showing suspicious activities. Drilldown searches on the chosen source IP and reroutes the page to the Traffic Search panel.
    - **Application For Well-Known Ports** shows the total amount of protocol traffic over time, organized by ports smaller than 1024. Each port will continue to use the same amount of bandwidth relative to the volume of network traffic as a whole. An improper rise in bandwidth may be visible on a port that has been mishandled. The drilldown sends the user to the Traffic Search dashboard where they may conduct a port-specific search.

- **Long-Lasting Relationships** reveal TCP connections active for more than three minutes. A connection that lasts for a long time between hosts could indicate strange or suspicious behavior. Drilldown launches Traffic Search dashboard and does event search.

Traffic Size Analysis

Analysts can find outliers and anomalies in their network environment by comparing traffic statistics with statistical data using the Traffic Size Analysis dashboard. The traffic data from multiple sources, such as firewalls, routers, switches, and network flows, can be examined using this dashboard.

Investigating traffic data byte lengths, using the graph to identify suspicious data transmission patterns, and digging deeper into the summarized data to search for abnormal source/destination traffic are some of the dashboard's key features.

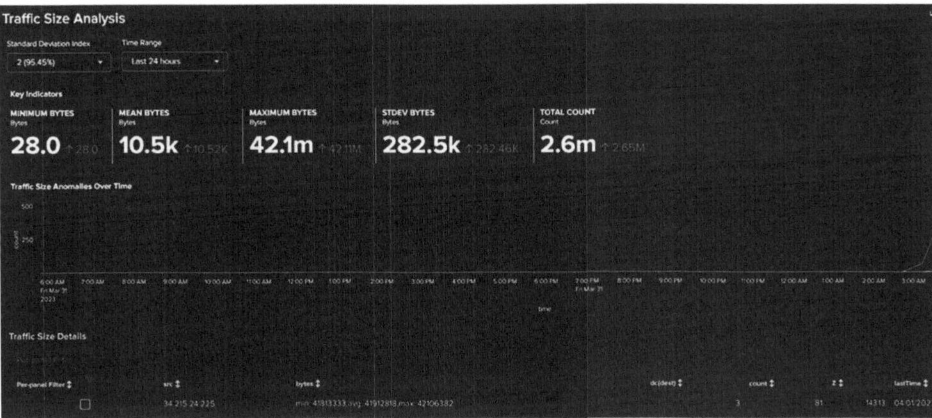

Figure 7.13: *Traffic Size Analysis dashboard*

Dashboard Filters

Filter using Description:

- **Index of Standard Deviation:** The amount of data that will be filtered out if that particular number of standard deviations is chosen is indicated by the percentage (%). Selecting more deviations will result in fewer traffic size anomalies and details, while selecting fewer deviations will result in more anomalies and information.
- **Time Period:** Pick the time frame that will be portrayed. Superior Filter To view the category events that can be filtered for this dashboard, go here.

Dashboard Panels

- Important indices show the metrics from the last 48 hours that are pertinent to the sources of the dashboard. At the dashboard's top, key indicators serve as summaries of information.
- **Changing Traffic Size anomalies: The** graph shows a count of the size of anomalous traffic over time in your environment. With time on the x-axis and count on the y-axis, it displays traffic volume that is more than the number of standard deviations (2 by default) set in the filter.
- **Specifics on Traffic Size:** Each traffic event is listed in a table along with any relevant information, such as its size in bytes. The count column displays the number of events seen for each source IP address if there are multiple events. The minimum, maximum, and average bytes for the traffic event are displayed in the bytes column. The traffic event's standard deviations are shown by the letter Z.

DNS Activity

A summary of the data pertaining to the DNS infrastructure under observation is provided by the DNS Activity dashboard. The time chosen using the dashboard time picker determines the results that are shown.

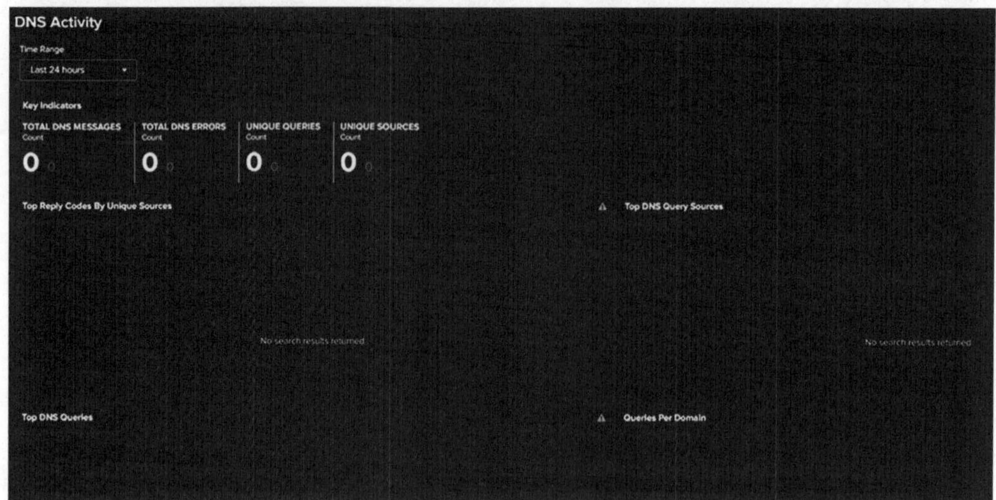

***Figure 7.14**: DNS Activity dashboard*

Dashboard Panels

- Important indicators for the previous 48 hours, metrics that are pertinent to the dashboard sources are shown. At the dashboard's top, key indicators serve as summaries of information.

- Top Reply Codes from Original Sources show the most common DNS reply codes experienced by hosts. A host that launches a lot of DNS queries to unrecognized or inaccessible domains can be trying to exfiltrate data or engaging in other questionable behavior. Drilldown launches DNS Search dashboard and performs a search on the chosen Reply Code.
- Leading DNS query resources show the network's top DNS query sources. A host issuing a lot of DNS queries could be misconfigured, have technical problems, or be engaging in questionable conduct. The drilldown launches the DNS Search dashboard and performs a search using the source IP address that was chosen.
- Leading DNS queries the top 10 DNS QUERY requests over time are shown. The drilldown launches the DNS Search dashboard and conducts a host address search.
- Queries Per Domain shows a list of the most popular searches organized by domain. An attempt at exfiltration or suspicious behavior may be indicated by an unknown domain receiving a lot of inquiries from hosts on the network. The drilldown launches the DNS Search dashboard and does a domain address search.

Current DNS requests reveal additional information for the 50 most recent DNS Response queries. The drilldown launches the DNS Search dashboard and conducts a search at the chosen questioned address.

DNS Search

The DNS Search interface makes it easier to search through filtered DNS protocol data. It serves as the main endpoint for drilldown searches in DNS dashboard panels and is mostly used for ad hoc DNS data searching. No results will be displayed if the DNS Search page is not accessed in response to a drilldown action or after choosing a filter and/or time range and hitting Submit.

SSL Activity

The SSL Activity dashboard, which provides a summary of SSL-encrypted connections and traffic, allows analysts to monitor and examine SSL-encrypted traffic by usage without having to decrypt the payload. The searches on the dashboard return results based on the time period selected using the time picker.

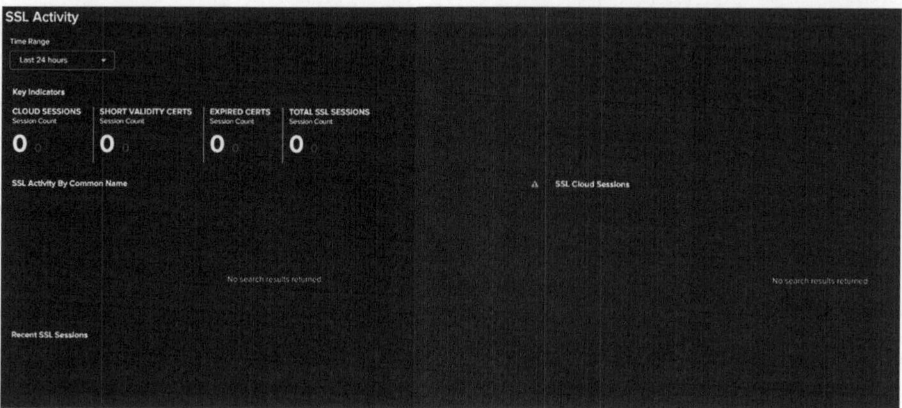

Figure 7.15*: SSL Activity dashboard*

Dashboard Panels

- Important indices for the previous 48 hours, metrics that are pertinent to the dashboard sources are shown. At the dashboard's top, key indicators serve as summaries of information.
- Common Name SSL Activity displays outgoing SSL connections according to the SSL certificate's common name (CN). It can be a sign that something strange or suspect is going on if an unfamiliar domain receives a lot of SSL connections from hosts on the network. The drilldown takes the user to the SSL Search dashboard, where they may conduct a search on the chosen common name.
- Cloud SSL Sessions shows the number of active sessions by CN for each recognized cloud service. The Cloud Domains lookup file contains a list of pre-configured cloud service domains against which the CN is compared. The drilldown accesses the SSL Search dashboard and performs a search using the source IP and common name that were chosen.
- Most current SSL sessions provide extra SSL key information in a table that shows the 50 most recent SSL sessions. Color-coded text is used in the fields **`ssl_end_time`**, **`ssl_validity_window`**, and **`ssl_is_valid`** to identify expired, short-lived, or invalid certificates quickly. The drilldown takes the user to the SSL Search dashboard where the full details of the selected event are displayed.

SSL Search

Search engine-filtered SSL protocol data can be searched using the SSL Search dashboard. It is used for ad hoc scanning of SSL protocol data and is the primary destination for drilldown searches in the SSL Activity dashboard panels. No results will be displayed if the SSL Search page is not accessed in response to a drilldown action or after choosing a filter and/or time range and pressing Submit.

Email Activity

The Email Activity dashboard gives a summary of the information about the tracked email infrastructure. Using the dashboard time picker, the results are presented according to the chosen time frame.

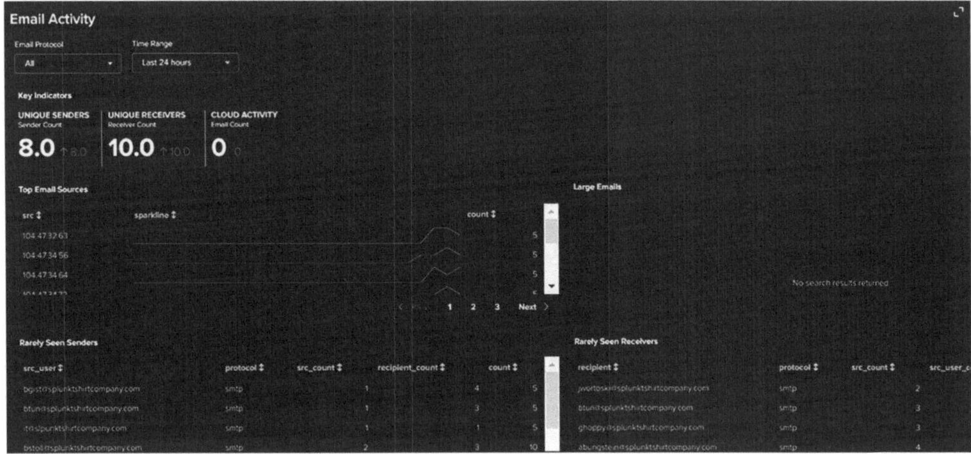

Figure 7.16: *Email Activity dashboard*

Dashboard Panels:

- **Key Indicators**: Shows metrics over the previous 24 hours that are pertinent to the dashboard sources. At the dashboard's top, key indicators serve as summaries of information.
- **Top Email Sources:** The hosts producing the most email protocol traffic are shown in the Top Email Sources section. A host that sends a lot of emails via the network can be engaging in strange or suspicious behavior. Periodicity displayed on the sparklines for different hosts may indicate a planned action. The drilldown launches the Email Search dashboard and does a source IP search.
- **Large Emails**: Shows the senders of emails over 2MB. A host that frequently sends big emails might be engaged in questionable activities or data espionage. The drilldown launches the Email Search dashboard and does a source IP search.
- **Rarely Seen Senders**: Shows email addresses of senders who don't send emails very often. An email address that looks to be a service account or that is being sent by a non-user may be a sign of a phishing attempt

or other questionable activities. The Email Search dashboard, which performs a search on the selected Sender, is accessed by drilling down.

- **Rarely Seen Receivers**: Shows email addresses of recipients who don't usually get emails. A phishing attempt or suspicious activity may be indicated by an email address that corresponds to a service account or a recipient who is not a user. The drilldown launches the Email Search dashboard and does a recipient search.

Email Search

Email Search Dashboard:

- It Aids in using search filters to look up email protocol information.
- It is used as the principal location for drilldown searches from the Email Activity dashboard panels and ad-hoc searches of email protocol data.
- It Does not show any results until a drilldown action is taken, a filter is selected, and/or a time range is entered.

Hands-On Protocol Intelligence with Splunk ES at JIT Inc.

Overview

One of the leading innovators in technology, JIT Inc., uses Splunk Enterprise Security (ES) to improve its network protocol intelligence. JIT Inc. uses the Protocol Intelligence capabilities of Splunk ES, concentrating on dashboards such as Protocol Center, Traffic Size Analysis, DNS Activity, DNS Search, SSL Activity, SSL Search, Email Activity, and Email Search, in an era where network traffic analysis is essential for cybersecurity. Every dashboard offers distinct perspectives on network activity and traffic, assisting in the identification and examination of cyber threats.

Scenario Setup

1. Protocol Center:

- **Scenario:** JIT Inc. wants to get a broad picture of how network protocols are being used in order to spot any unusual usage patterns or behaviors.
- **How It Helps:** A thorough overview of network protocol traffic is provided by the Protocol Center dashboard. This can be used by JIT Inc. to keep an eye out for odd increases in specific protocols, which could be signs of malicious activity or network problems.

2. Traffic Size Analysis:

- **Scenario:** JIT Inc. is experiencing an unanticipated rise in network bandwidth utilization, which raises questions about possible data exfiltration or other nefarious activity.
- **How It Helps:** By analyzing network traffic based on size, this dashboard enables JIT Inc. to identify significant data transfers that might indicate security problems like data breaches.

3. DNS Activity:

- **Situation:** In order to stop users from accessing harmful websites and to identify any attempts at DNS tunneling, JIT Inc. must keep an eye on DNS requests.
- **How It Helps:** All DNS requests made within the network are detailed in the DNS Activity dashboard. This can be used by JIT Inc. to detect possibly harmful DNS patterns and suspicious domain queries.

4. DNS Search:

- **Scenario:** JIT Inc. has to look into certain DNS queries in depth after receiving a warning regarding possible communication with a malicious domain.
- **How It Helps:** JIT Inc. may search for and analyze certain DNS requests thanks to DNS Search, which enables a more thorough investigation into DNS inquiries. This is important for incident response and threat hunting.

5. SSL Activity:

- **Scenario:** As encrypted traffic grows in popularity, JIT Inc. must be sure that SSL/TLS protocols aren't being abused to conceal harmful activity.
- **How It Assists:** The SSL Activity dashboard is useful for tracking SSL/TLS traffic and seeing irregularities that can point to security problems, like improperly recognized certificates or strange encryption techniques.

6. SSL Search:

- **Situation:** JIT Inc. believes that a man-in-the-middle attack could exploit an SSL certificate that has been hacked.
- **How It Helps:** JIT Inc. can look at particular SSL certificates or encrypted traffic patterns thanks to SSL Search's comprehensive search capabilities for SSL/TLS activities.

7. Email Activity:

- **Scenario:** JIT Inc. is concerned about email-based dangers, particularly the spread of malware and phishing emails.
- **How It Helps:** By giving JIT Inc. an overview of email traffic, this dashboard makes it possible to spot odd email patterns like increases in emails from strange domains or ones with attachments.

8. Email Search:

- **Scenario:** JIT Inc. must carry out a thorough investigation in response to a report of a suspicious email.
- **How It Assists:** Email Search makes it possible for JIT Inc. to perform thorough log searches of emails, making it easier to look into particular emails or email addresses.

Implementation and Analysis

- **Continuous Monitoring:** To quickly detect and address possible dangers, JIT Inc. continuously monitors these dashboards.
- **Incident Investigation and Response:** JIT Inc. may investigate data more thoroughly when irregularities are found, enabling an efficient and timely incident response.
- **Enhancement of Network Security:** By enhancing their protocols and security procedures, JIT Inc. is able to lower the danger of cyber threats thanks to the insights gathered from these dashboards.

The Protocol Intelligence dashboards from Splunk ES are crucial to JIT Inc.'s ability to keep a reliable and safe network environment. Through the use of these tools, JIT Inc. is able to keep a close eye on network activity, spot possible threats, and take proactive measures to protect the security and integrity of its network infrastructure.

To sum up, Splunk Enterprise Security's protocol intelligence is crucial for tracking and analyzing network protocols, identifying risks and abnormalities based on protocols, investigating incidents, and increasing overall network security. By using protocol intelligence, organizations may proactively fix potential vulnerabilities and maintain a secure network environment.

Case Studies

Here are four case studies illustrating the successful use of Splunk in various intelligence domains: Web Intelligence, User Intelligence, Threat Intelligence, and Protocol Intelligence. These examples showcase how Splunk can help organizations enhance their security capabilities in different areas.

Case Study: Web Intelligence - E-commerce Company

- **Problem**: An e-commerce company needs to monitor and analyze its web traffic to help detect and respond to potential cyber threats, such as DDoS attacks, web application attacks, and fraudulent transactions.
- **Solution**: The company implemented Splunk in order to gain real-time visibility for its web traffic and application logs. By correlating and analyzing this data, Splunk enabled the company to detect unusual patterns and potential threats targeting its web applications and infrastructure.
- **Results:** The e-commerce company successfully utilized Splunk's web intelligence capabilities to improve its ability to detect and respond to cyber threats targeting its web applications. This led to a reduction in the number of successful attacks and improved the company's overall security posture.

Case Study: User Intelligence - Financial Institution

- **Problem**: A financial institution needed a solution to detect and respond to potential insider threats and unauthorized access attempts to its sensitive data and systems.
- **Solution**: The financial institution used Splunk to monitor and analyze user behavior, including logins, file access, and system activities. Splunk's user intelligence capabilities allowed the institution to identify suspicious activities and anomalies that could indicate potential insider threats or unauthorized access.
- **Results:** By leveraging Splunk's user intelligence capabilities, the financial institution significantly improved its ability to detect and respond to insider threats and unauthorized access attempts. This led to a more secure environment and reduced the risk of data breaches and other security incidents.

Case Study: Threat Intelligence - Healthcare Organization

- **Problem:** A healthcare organization faced challenges in staying informed about the latest cyber threats targeting its industry and needed a solution to incorporate threat intelligence into its security operations.
- **Solution:** The healthcare organization integrated Splunk with various threat intelligence feeds, such as those from commercial vendors and open-source platforms. Splunk correlated this threat intelligence data with the organization's security logs, enabling the identification of potential threats and vulnerabilities in its environment.

- **Results:** The healthcare organization successfully utilized Splunk's threat intelligence capabilities to stay informed about the latest cyber threats and vulnerabilities. This enabled the organization to proactively address potential risks, ultimately improving its overall security posture.

Case Study: Protocol Intelligence - Manufacturing Company

- **Problem:** A manufacturing company needs to monitor and analyze network traffic and protocols while detecting and responding to potential cyber threats targeting its industrial control systems (ICS) and operational technology (OT) environments.
- **Solution:** The manufacturing company implemented Splunk in order to gain real-time visibility in its network traffic and protocol data. By analyzing this data, Splunk allowed the company to identify potential threats and anomalies targeting its ICS and OT environments.
- **Results**: By leveraging Splunk's protocol intelligence capabilities, the manufacturing company significantly improved its ability to detect and respond to cyber threats targeting its ICS and OT environments. This led to a more secure environment and reduced the risk of disruption to its operations.

Conclusion

A comprehensive and successful cybersecurity plan requires a wide range of components, all of which fall under the category of security intelligence. We can measure and rank potential dangers using risk analysis, and we can learn a lot about user behavior and online-based activity via web and user intelligence. By spotting possible threats before they cause harm, threat intelligence makes proactive defense easier, while protocol intelligence helps keep the confidentiality of our electronic conversations intact. Each of these elements contributes significantly to strengthening an organization's security posture.

This foundation will be built upon as we move into the following chapter, "Forensic Investigation in Security Domains," and we'll look at how these intelligence insights may be used to look into and respond to security issues while also boosting the resilience of our cybersecurity systems.

Points to Remember

- Security intelligence focuses on gathering, analyzing, and disseminating data about potential threats, weaknesses, and incidents in the environment of an organization. It entails identifying, evaluating, and prioritizing risks, as well as putting in place the necessary safeguards to reduce or prevent them.
- Real-time monitoring, detection, and response to security threats are made possible by security intelligence technologies and procedures.
- Security dashboards and analytics solutions, like Splunk Enterprise Security, may help prioritize resources and offer insightful information about an organization's security posture.
- Key indicators are summaries of data that are displayed at the top of security dashboards, giving users a quick glimpse at the most crucial parameters.
- Network traffic, DNS activity, SSL activity, and email activity may all be watched to spot any possible security problems like malware infestations, data exfiltration, or unauthorized access.
- More specific information can be obtained by drilling down into particular events or metrics to help with incident response and investigation.
- Effective security intelligence depends on properly configuring, maintaining, and updating security tools with the most recent threat intelligence.
- Improving an organization's overall security posture and increasing the efficacy of security intelligence initiatives can be achieved by establishing a strong security culture and regular personnel training.
- A successful security intelligence approach must emphasize ongoing development and learning from mistakes. Organizations may stay ahead of new dangers by routinely assessing and upgrading their rules, procedures, and tools.

You will build a solid foundation in Security Essential if you keep these crucial ideas in mind as you study through this chapter.

CHAPTER 8

Forensic Investigation in Security Domains

Introduction

This chapter provides a thorough guide to forensic investigation, covering the key security domains of Access, Endpoint, Network, and Identity. The chapter opens with an explanation of the four security domains and the significance of forensic investigation in cybersecurity. The strategies, best practices, and tools necessary for conducting successful research within each domain are then covered in detail.

The integration of forensic inquiry across security domains is next covered in the chapter, emphasizing the significance of correlating events and data for an all-encompassing investigation. It talks about how to leverage security orchestration, automation, and response (SOAR) platforms and how internal and external stakeholders should work together when conducting investigations. The chapter also covers the creation of an extensive incident response strategy.

Readers will obtain a thorough grasp of forensic investigation across the Access, Endpoint, Network, and Identity domains as a result of the coverage of these subjects. They will also be better prepared to conduct successful investigations, thereby improving their organization's cybersecurity posture.

Structure

In this chapter, the following topics will be covered:

- Forensic Investigation
    - Key Aspects of forensic investigation in cybersecurity
    - Key security domains

- Access Domain
    - Key components of ES in the access domain
    - Access Center
    - Access Tracker
    - Access Search
    - Account Management
    - Default Account Activity
- Endpoint Domain
    - Malware Detection
    - System Center
    - Time Center
    - The Endpoint Changes
    - Update Center and Search
- Network Domain
    - Network Traffic Tracking
    - Network Intrusion Tracking
    - Vulnerability Tracking
    - Web Traffic Tracking
    - Network Changes Tracking
    - The Port and Protocol Tracking
- Identity Domain
    - Asset Data
    - Identity Data
    - User Session
- Case Studies

Forensic Investigation in Security Domains

To investigate security incidents and cybercrimes, forensic investigation in the security domains refers to the methodical process of gathering, evaluating, and archiving electronic evidence. Finding the incident's underlying cause, tracing its history, and gathering enough proof to support any potential legal action are the objectives. Several security areas are covered by the inquiry, including network, system, application, and cloud security.

Key aspects of Forensic Investigation in Security Domains include:

- **Evidence collection**: Gathering digital proof from a variety of sources, such as user activity logs, system logs, network logs, and application logs. The integrity of the evidence is guaranteed by maintaining the correct chain of custody and documentation.
- **Evidence Analysis**: Examining gathered evidence to spot trends, outliers, and signs of fraud. This could entail using cutting-edge analytical methods, reconstructing timeframes, and correlating data from various sources.
- **Incident Response**: Putting the right measures in place to lessen the effects of the security incident, such as minimizing the threat, eliminating the root cause, and retrieving affected systems or data.
- **Remediation**: Finding and fixing the fundamental flaws or vulnerabilities that allowed the security incident to happen and taking steps to stop similar incidents in the future.
- **Reporting and Documentation**: Writing thorough summaries of the investigation's findings, presenting the evidence, and keeping accurate records for organizational learning or legal purposes.
- **Legal Considerations**: Understanding legal requirements and ramifications for forensic investigations, such as privacy concerns, jurisdictional challenges, and the admissibility of electronic evidence in court, is considered to be the sixth consideration.
- **Collaboration**: Actively exchanging knowledge, skills, and best practices about forensic investigations with other cybersecurity specialists, law enforcement organizations, and business partners.
- **Continuous Learning**: Keeping abreast of the most recent developments in forensic tools, techniques, and methodologies, as well as new dangers and fashions in the field of cybersecurity.

Key Security Domains

Key security domains are the various areas of focus within the cybersecurity landscape. These domains represent different aspects of information security, and each has its own specific challenges, threats, and best practices. An effective cybersecurity program must address each of these domains to ensure comprehensive protection.

- Access
- Endpoint

- Network
- Identity

Access Domain

This domain focuses on attempts at authentication and events connected to access control, such as login, logout, access granted, and access denied. Security must be maintained by making sure that only authorized users can access sensitive resources. Organizations should use robust authentication techniques, including multi-factor authentication (MFA), and keep an eye on access-related events for indications of unwanted access attempts or potential insider threats to enhance this domain. Effective management of user permissions can also be achieved with the use of access control technologies like role-based access control (RBAC) and attribute-based access control (ABAC).

Key Components of ES in the Access Domain

- **Access control policies**: Strong access control policies that specify user access levels, permissions, and restrictions based on their roles and responsibilities should be put in place. By doing this, users are guaranteed to have access to only the resources they require to carry out their duties.
- **Monitoring and alerting**: Continually keeping an eye on events connected to authentication and access enables the quick detection of odd or suspicious activity. Security teams can respond more rapidly to possible security incidents by setting up notifications for specific events, like access to restricted privileges or repeated failed login attempts.
- **User authentication**: Strong user authentication techniques, such as multi-factor authentication (MFA), can be implemented to dramatically lower the risk of unwanted access. Requesting additional data or elements from users to verify their identity gives an extra degree of protection.
- **Privileged access management**: Managing privileged user access and keeping an eye on it is essential for preventing unwanted access to sensitive information and systems. Elevated access should only be allowed when necessary, by implementing a privileged access management solution to manage and monitor privileged user actions.
- **Identity and access management (IAM):** Integrating IAM solutions with Enterprise Security can assist with controlling user access, provisioning, and de-provisioning, as well as enforcing access control policies throughout the company.
- **Reporting and auditing**: Insights into user behavior, access patterns, and potential security threats can be gained by routinely auditing

access-related events and producing reports. This data can be utilized to pinpoint vulnerabilities, enhance access control procedures, and establish regulatory compliance.

- **Incident response**: Setting up a clear incident response plan for access-related security problems can assist firms in finding, containing, and fixing security flaws as soon as possible.

By focusing on these key components, ES in the access domain can help organizations enhance their overall security posture and reduce the risk of unauthorized access to critical systems and data.

Access Domain Areas

This section will cover dashboards including the Access Center, Access Tracker, Access Search, Account Management, and Default Account Activity. These dashboards offer a holistic view of system access, tracking and searching activities, account operations, and default account activities to strengthen security controls and mitigate unauthorized access risks.

Access Center

Monitoring authentication events and spotting potential security incidents depend on the Access Center dashboard. Organizations can identify occurrences like brute-force attacks, the use of clear-text passwords, or unwanted access outside of regular business hours since it gives a summary of all authentication events. The dashboard has a number of panels and filters that may be used to modify the data and make it simpler to comprehend and take action on.

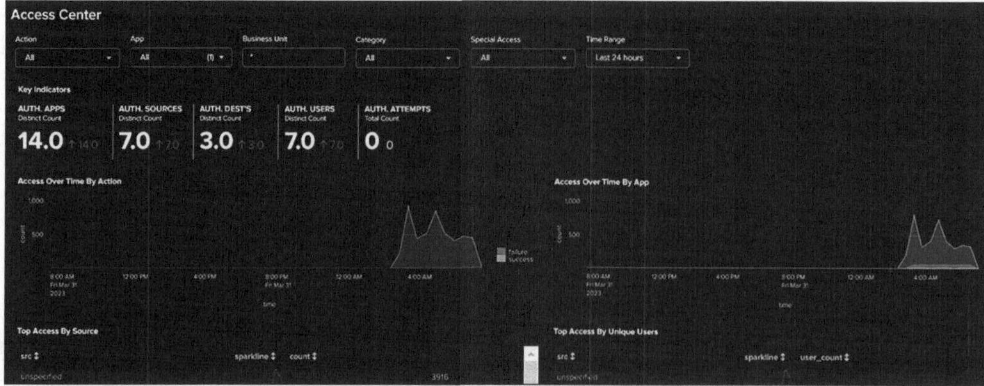

Figure 8.1: Access Center Dashboard

Some key points to remember about the Access Center dashboard are:

- **Dashboard filters**: Filters such as action, app, business unit, category, special access, and time range allow you to narrow down the results displayed on the dashboard panels. Note that filters don't apply to key security indicators.
- **Access Over Time By Action panel**: This panel displays the count of authentication events over time by action, helping you visualize trends and identify anomalies.
- **Access Over Time By App panel**: This panel shows the count of authentication events over time by app, providing insights into which applications are experiencing the most authentication activity.
- **Top Access By Source panel**: This table displays the highest access counts by source, which can help detect brute-force attacks by showing an unusually high number of authentication requests from a single source.
- **Top Access By Unique Users panel**: This table shows the sources generating the highest number of unique user authentication events, giving insight into user access patterns.

A strong cybersecurity strategy should include the Access Center dashboard, which enables enterprises to monitor authentication events, identify potential security incidents, and make sure access to critical data and systems is properly restricted. An organization's security posture can be greatly enhanced by routinely examining the Access Center dashboard and acting on the insights it offers.

Access Tracker

This dashboard gives an overview of account statuses. This dashboard helps identify newly active or inactive accounts, as well as those that have been inactive but recently became active. It also helps detect accounts that haven't been properly de-provisioned or inactivated when a user leaves the organization.

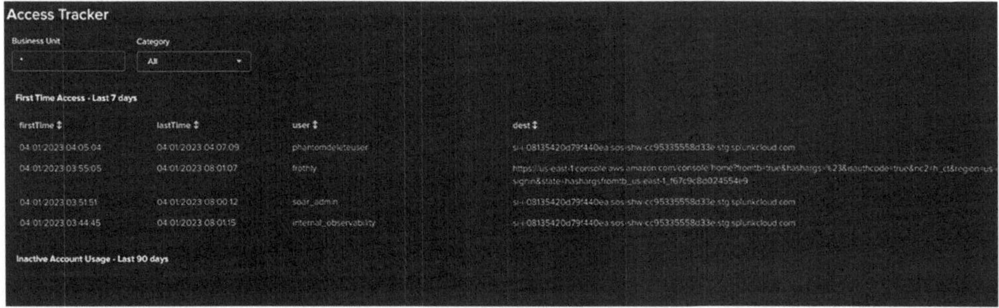

Figure 8.2: *Access Tracker Dashboard*

Key points to remember about the Access Tracker dashboard:

- **Dashboard filters**: Filters such as business unit, category, and time range enable you to refine the results displayed on the dashboard panels. Note that filters don't apply to key security indicators.
- **`First Time Access - Last 7 days` panel**: This panel displays new account access by user and destination, helping you identify recently created accounts.
- **`Inactive Account Usage - Last 90 days` panel:** This panel shows accounts that were inactive for a while but have shown recent activity, which can help detect unauthorized access to inactive accounts.
- **`Completely Inactive Accounts - Last 90 days` panel**: This panel displays accounts with no activity, assisting you in identifying accounts that should be suspended or removed.
- **`Account Usage For Expired Identities - Last 7 days` panel**: This panel shows activity for accounts that are suspended within the specified timeframe, helping you ensure that inactive accounts aren't in use.

Regularly monitoring the Access Tracker dashboard is crucial for maintaining the security of your organization. Identifying and managing inactive accounts or accounts with suspicious activity can prevent unauthorized access and reduce the risk of security breaches.

Access Search

The Access Search dashboard is helpful for ad-hoc searching of authentication data and for locating specific login occurrences. The drilldown searches done in the Access Anomalies dashboard panels usually end up there as well.

Key details to keep in mind regarding the Access Search dashboard:

- **Dashboard filters**: The results shown on the dashboard panels can be further filtered by using filters like action, app, source, destination, user, and time range. Note that critical security indicators are not covered by filters.
- Only when the Access Search page is accessed in response to a drilldown action or after you specify a filter and/or time range and click Submit will results be shown.

Account Management

This dashboard displays alterations to user accounts, including password resets, account creations, account lockouts, and account disabling. This dashboard assists in ensuring that privileges for managing accounts are properly controlled and that accounts are being managed effectively.

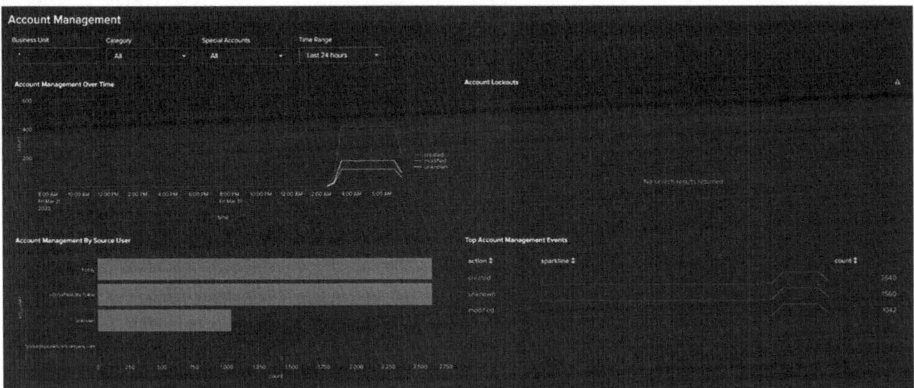

Figure 8.3: *Account Management Dashboard*

Key points to remember about the Account Management dashboard:

- **Dashboard filters**: Filters such as business unit, category, special accounts, and time range allow you to refine the results displayed on the dashboard panels. Note that filters don't apply to key security indicators.
- **`Account Management Over Time` panel**: Displays all account management events over time, helping you identify trends and potential security concerns.
- **`Account Lockouts` panel:** Shows all account lockouts, including the number of authentication attempts per account, which can help detect brute force attacks or other suspicious activity.
- **`Account Management by Source User` panel**: Tracks the total account management activity by source user, showing the source users with the most account management events. This panel helps identify accounts that shouldn't be managing other accounts and shows spikes in account management events.
- Top Account Management Events panel: Shows the most frequent management events in the specified time, assisting you in identifying any unusual account activities.

Default Account Activity

This dashboard displays activity on "default accounts" or accounts that are enabled by default on a variety of platforms, including databases, applications, and network infrastructure devices. Default accounts frequently aren't properly disabled when a system is launched and have well-known passwords.

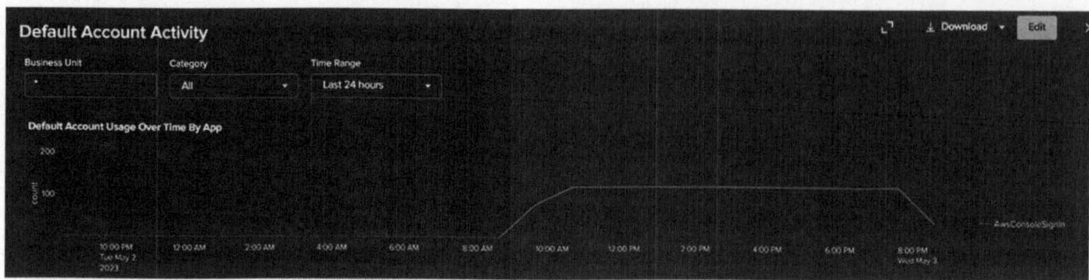

Figure 8.4: *Default Account Activity Dashboard*

Key points to remember about the Default Account Activity dashboard:

- **Dashboard filters**: Filters such as business unit, category, and time range enable you to refine the results displayed on the dashboard panels. Note that filters don't apply to key security indicators.
- **`Default Account Usage Over Time by App` panel:** Shows default account activity on all systems and applications during the selected time frame, split by application.
- **`Default Accounts in Use` panel:** Shows all default user accounts with a high number of login attempts on different hosts, including the last attempt made.
- **`Default Local Accounts` panel**: Lists all default accounts that are active on enterprise systems, including accounts "at rest".

Monitoring these dashboards regularly can help ensure that your organization's Access domain security policies are being properly followed, reducing the risk of unauthorized access or security breaches.

Hands-On Access Domain Investigation with Splunk ES at JIT Inc.

Overview

The forward-thinking company JIT Inc. uses Splunk Enterprise Security (ES) to conduct thorough access domain investigations. Access-related risks, like illegal access and account compromises, are major worries in the complicated world of cybersecurity. JIT Inc. uses the suite of dashboards in Splunk ES's **`Access domain`**, which includes **`Access Center`**, **`Access Tracker`**, **`Access Search`**, **`Account Management`**, and **`Default Account Activity`**. Each of these dashboards has unique features for handling and looking into security events involving access.

Scenario Setup

1. Access Center:

- **Scenario**: With more workers working remotely, JIT Inc. requires a centralized perspective to keep an eye on all access-related actions.
- **How It Helps**: An organization-wide perspective of access-related events and notifications is provided via the Access Center dashboard. This makes it possible for JIT Inc. to respond to possible threats promptly by enabling the company to swiftly detect patterns of illegal access attempts or odd access patterns.

2. Access Tracker:

- **Scenario**: Unusual access patterns in private sections of JIT Inc.'s network are a source of concern.
- **How It Helps**: Access Tracker makes it possible to keep thorough records of all access attempts, both approved and denied. JIT Inc. can improve their capacity to respond to and manage these risks by identifying any security breaches or policy violations by examining these patterns.

3. Access Search:

- **Situation**: An employee has reported a specific access event and JIT Inc. has to look into it because they believe there was unauthorized access to their account.
- **How It Helps**: To investigate certain access occurrences, the Access Search dashboard offers sophisticated search options. This makes it possible for JIT Inc. to thoroughly investigate the reported occurrence by delving into the details of the access attempt, including its timing, origin, and nature.

4. Account Management:

- **Situation**: In order to stop the exploitation of dormant or rogue accounts, JIT Inc. is putting into place a new policy for routine account review and management.
- **How It Helps**: By monitoring account creation, modification, and deletion, this dashboard helps with user account management. Through the use of this dashboard, JIT Inc. can monitor adherence to their regulations regarding account management and promptly detect any unauthorized or questionable account modifications.

5. Default Account Activity:

- **Scenario**: JIT Inc. is concentrating on monitoring activity related to default and service accounts, which are frequently targets for attackers, in order to strengthen security.

- **How It Assists**: The activity of default system and service accounts is the focus of the Default Account Activity dashboard. By monitoring this dashboard, JIT Inc. is able to identify any odd activity or patterns of access related to these accounts, which are frequently signs of a breach or misuse.

Implementation and Analysis

- **Proactive Identification and Response**: JIT Inc. is able to proactively identify and respond to security incidents connected to access through the ongoing monitoring of these dashboards.
- **Incident Analysis and Investigation**: JIT Inc. can use these dashboards for comprehensive analysis and investigation in the event that an access-related security event is detected, which will result in efficient incident resolution.
- **Policy Enforcement and Compliance**: These dashboards' insights assist JIT Inc. in upholding regulatory requirements and enforcing access control regulations.

The Access domain dashboards in Splunk ES are essential to JIT Inc.'s upkeep of a secure access environment. JIT Inc. may safeguard the integrity of their systems and data against unauthorized access and potential security breaches by using these dashboards to give them the tools they need to monitor, evaluate, and respond to threats linked to access.

Endpoint Domain

Securing gadgets like desktops, laptops, cellphones, and tablets falls within the endpoint security area. Organizations can identify and address possible security issues by tracking and analyzing malware infections, system configuration, system state (CPU utilization, open ports, uptime), patch status and history, and time synchronization data. Organizations should implement antivirus and anti-malware programs, make sure that software and operating systems are patched on time, and keep an eye out for endpoints that have been compromised in order to protect them.

Key components of ES in the access domain include:

- **Endpoint protection:** Ensuring that the most recent security updates and up-to-date antivirus and anti-malware software are installed on all endpoints.
- **Vulnerability management**: Performing routine endpoint vulnerability scans and deploying the required patches or updates to reduce the risk of attacker exploitation.

- **System configuration and hardening**: Adopting best practices for system configurations, such as turning off superfluous services, getting rid of unused software, and giving user accounts the least amount of privilege possible.
- **Monitoring and alerting**: Continually keeping an eye on endpoint actions, events, and security logs to spot and warn about potentially dangerous activities.
- **Incident response**: Establishing an effective and efficient incident response procedure to deal with security incidents impacting endpoints.
- **Access control**: Putting robust access control mechanisms in place to stop illegal access to endpoints, like multi-factor authentication and proper user account management.
- **Encryption**: Encrypting sensitive data held on endpoints and ensuring secure endpoint-to-server connectivity.
- **Asset management**: To help identify and fix vulnerable systems, keep an up-to-date inventory of all endpoints, their configurations, software, and patch levels.
- Implementing endpoint detection and response (EDR) solutions will give you sophisticated threat detection, investigation, and response capabilities.
- **Security education and training**: Informing users on recommended practices for endpoint security, such as secure password management, phishing awareness, and how to report potential security issues.

Endpoint Domain Areas

This section will discuss dashboards such as the `Malware Detection System Center`, `Time Center`, `Endpoint Changes`, `Update Center`, and `Search`. These dashboards help monitor malware activity, system changes, and updates, and provide a temporal analysis of endpoints, aiding in strengthening endpoint security and ensuring system integrity.

Malware Center

A crucial tool for spotting potential malware outbreaks in your environment is the Malware Center dashboard. Based on information gathered by Splunk, it shows the current status of malware incidents and how that status varies over time. Using the Malware Search feature on the dashboard, you can directly look for malware events and dig down to the raw events for additional details. Through the Settings menu, you can also configure new data inputs.

The dashboard provides several filters, including **Action, Business Unit**, **Category**, and **Time Range**, to help you narrow down the events displayed. You can concentrate on particular malware events in your environment using these filters.

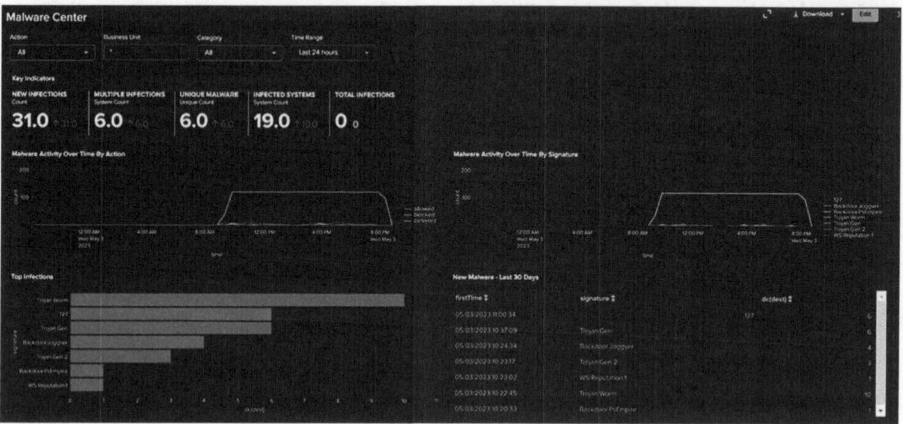

Figure 8.5: *Malware Center Dashboard*

The Malware Center dashboard contains several panels, including:

- **Key Indicators**: This panel displays the metrics relevant to the dashboard sources over the past 48 hours, providing a summary of essential information.
- **Malware Activity Over Time By Action**: This chart shows all detected malware over the specified time, split by action (allowed, blocked, deferred), helping you identify whether too many malware infections are allowed.
- **Malware Activity Over Time By Signature**: This chart displays all detected malware over the specified time, split by signature (for example, **Mal/Packer**, **LeakTest**, **EICAR-AV-Test**, **TROJ_JAVA.BY**), allowing you to identify dominant infections in your environment.
- **Top Infections**: This panel presents a bar chart of the top infections in your environment, split by signature, to help you identify outbreaks related to specific types of malware.
- **New Malware - Last 30 Days**: This panel shows new malware detected on the network over the last 30 days, including the date and time each malware signature was first detected and the total number of infections. This information is crucial, as first-time infections are most likely to cause outbreaks.

By utilizing the Malware Center dashboard, you can effectively monitor and manage malware threats in your environment, ensuring the security of your organization.

Malware Search and Operations Dashboard

The Malware Search dashboard and the Malware Operations dashboard are two essential tools for managing malware threats in your environment.

Malware Search Dashboard

This dashboard assists in searching malware-related events based on search filters like **`Action, Signature, File, Destination, User`**, and **`Time Range`**. It is primarily used for ad-hoc searching of malware data and drilldown searches from the Malware Center dashboard panels. The dashboard doesn't display results unless it's opened in response to a drilldown action or you update a filter, select a time range, and click **`Submit`**.

Malware Operations Dashboard

This dashboard tracks the status of endpoint protection products deployed in your environment. It helps you monitor the overall health of systems and identify systems that need updates or modifications to their endpoint protection software. It also allows you to see how the endpoint protection infrastructure is being administered.

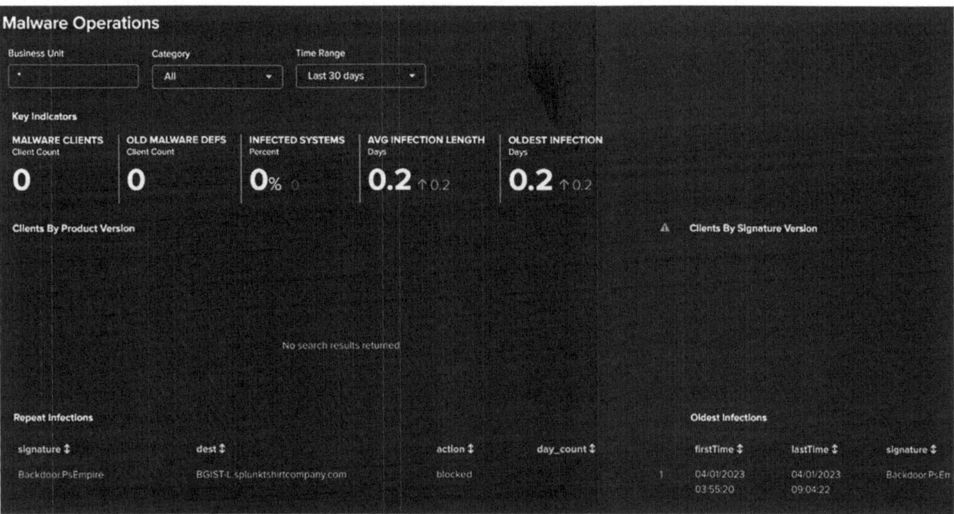

Figure 8.6: *Malware Operations Dashboard*

Filters for the Malware Operations dashboard include **`Business Unit, Category`**, and **`Time Range`**. The dashboard contains several panels, such as:

- **`Key Indicators`**: Displays the metrics relevant to the dashboard sources over the past 48 hours, providing summary information.
- **`Clients by Product Version`**: Shows a bar chart of the number of clients with a certain version of the endpoint protection product installed.
- **`Clients by Signature Version`**: Shows a bar chart of the number of clients with a certain signature version.
- **`Repeat Infections`**: Displays repeated malware infections, sortable by signature, destination, action, or number of days.
- **`Oldest Infections`**: Shows the oldest malware infections in your environment, sortable by the date of detection, signature, destination host, or days the infection has been active.

By utilizing the Malware Search and Malware Operations dashboards, you can effectively search for malware events, monitor endpoint protection, and manage the overall security of your organization.

System Center

Beyond what is given by deployed antivirus or host-based IDS solutions, the System Center dashboard in Splunk offers an overview of endpoint data and statistics. The system setup and performance data for hosts, such as memory, CPU, and disk utilization, are the main topics of this dashboard.

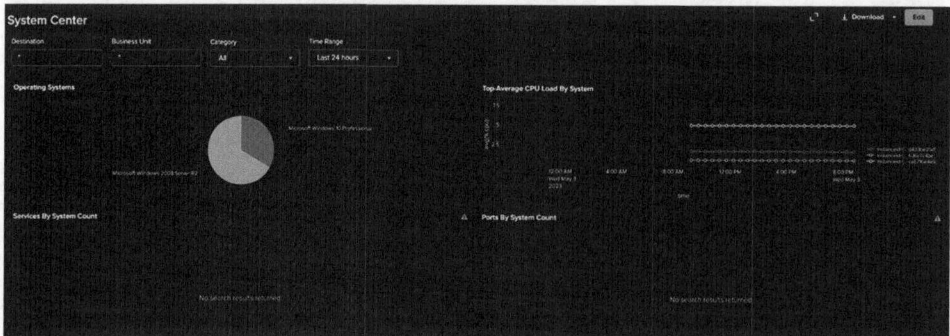

Figure 8.7: *System Center Dashboard*

You can use filters to refine the events displayed on the dashboard, including Destination, Business Unit, Category, and Time Range.

The panels in the System Center dashboard are as follows:

- **`Operating Systems:`** This panel shows the various operating systems deployed on the network. It helps you detect operating systems that should not be present in your environment.
- **`Top-Average CPU Load by System:`** This panel displays the systems on the network with the highest average CPU load. It can be useful for identifying systems that may require further investigation or optimization.
- **`Services by System Count`**: This panel shows the services ordered by the number of systems on which they are present. It provides insights into the distribution of services across your environment.
- **Ports By System Count:** This panel displays the transport method (for example, TCP) and destination ports, ordered by the number of systems. It helps you understand the network communication patterns within your environment.

Remember that if incorrect or missing data appears in the System Center dashboard, you should ensure that the technology add-ons supplying the data for this dashboard are installed on the full forwarders in your deployment. Technology add-ons containing knowledge needed for parsing data must be installed on the full forwarders.

Time Center

Splunk's Time Center dashboard is made to help discover hosts that are not correctly synchronized with their clocks to help assure data integrity. When a system with a timing difference is found, it can create warnings that let you dive down to the raw data and conduct more research.

You can use filters to refine the events displayed on the dashboard, such as **`Show only systems that should timesync`**, **`Business Unit`**, **`Category`**, and **`Time Range`**.

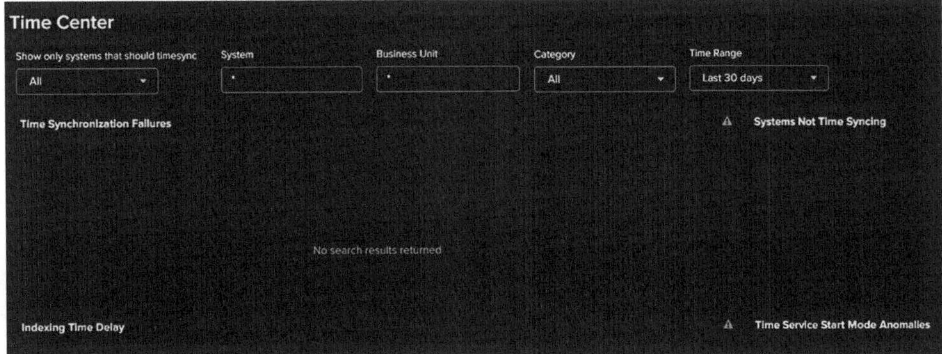

***Figure 8.8**: Time Center Dashboard*

The panels in the Time Center dashboard include:

- **Time Synchronization Failures:** This panel displays a list of systems where time synchronization has failed. It helps you identify the hosts with potential time-related issues.
- **Systems Not Time Synching:** This panel shows a list of systems that have not synchronized their clocks within the specified time frame. It allows you to monitor and address potential time-related discrepancies in your environment.
- **Indexing Time Delay**: This panel displays hosts with significant discrepancies between the timestamp the host places on the event and the time the event appears in the Splunk platform. For example, if the timestamp on an event is later than the time that Splunk indexes the event, the host is timestamping events as future events. A large difference (on the order of hours) indicates improper time zone recognition.
- **Time Service Start Mode Anomalies:** This panel displays hosts that have a time service start mode, such as Manual, that others do not. It helps you identify inconsistencies in the time service start mode configurations across your environment.

By monitoring and addressing time synchronization issues in your environment, you can ensure data integrity and improve the overall reliability of your systems.

The Endpoint Changes

You may see trends and uncover potential security incidents by using Splunk's Endpoint Changes dashboard, which focuses on tracking file-system and registry changes in the endpoints in your environment. For instance, a sharp increase in modifications can be a sign of malware activity or a security breach.

Figure 8.9: *Endpoint Changes Dashboard*

To refine the events displayed on the dashboard, you can use filters such as **`Business Unit, Category`**, and **`Time Range.`**

The panels in the Endpoint Changes dashboard include:

- **`Endpoint Changes by Action:`** This panel summarizes changes over time. A significant increase in changes could suggest the presence of a security incident, such as a virus or worm, causing alterations on the endpoints.
- **`Endpoint Changes by Type`**: This panel summarizes the types of changes observed on the endpoints, including file and registry changes. It helps you understand the nature of the changes and identify any unusual activity.
- **`Changes by System`**: This panel displays changes summarized by the system. It allows you to identify specific systems with an abnormal number of changes, which could indicate a security issue or unauthorized access.
- **`Recent Endpoint Changes`**: This panel shows the most recent endpoint changes observed in your environment. It helps you keep track of the latest alterations and quickly spot any suspicious activity.

By monitoring endpoint changes and staying alert to unexpected trends, you can enhance the security of your environment and quickly respond to potential incidents.

Update Center and Search

The **`Update Center`** dashboard in Splunk provides valuable insights into the update status of systems in your environment. Regularly reviewing this dashboard helps ensure that systems are updated properly and security risks are minimized.

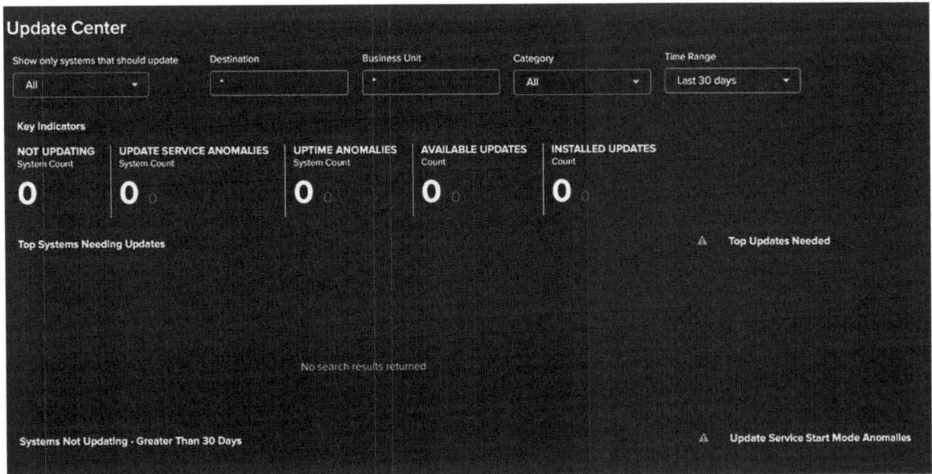

Figure 8.10: *Update Center Dashboard*

Filters like Show only systems that should update, Destination, Business Unit, Category, and Time Range help refine the events displayed on the dashboard.

The panels in the Update Center dashboard include:

- **`Key Indicators`**: Displays the summary information and relevant metrics for the dashboard sources over the past 48 hours.
- **`Top Systems Needing Updates`**: A bar chart showing the top systems in your environment that require updates to be installed.
- **`Top Updates Needed`**: A bar chart displaying the most critical updates needed across the environment, sorted by signature, such as the KB number.
- **`Systems Not Updating - Greater Than 30 Days`**: A list of systems that haven't been updated for over 30 days, sorted by the number of days since their last update.
- **`Update Service Start Mode Anomalies`**: Shows all systems where the update startup task or service is disabled, which can help identify cases where administrators might have forgotten to re-enable the process after a restart.

Patches and updates are highlighted by package or device on the **`Update Search`** panel. When troubleshooting problems brought on by a certain patch, it is especially helpful to be able to identify devices that have those patches installed.

Display only systems that require update. **`Update Status`**, **`Signature`**, **`Destination`**, and **`Time Range`** are some of the filters for the Update Search dashboard.

You can keep your environment secure and stable by routinely checking **`the Update Center`** and **`Update Search`** dashboards to make sure systems are patched and up to date.

Hands-On Endpoint Domain Investigation with Splunk ES at JIT Inc.

Overview

The technologically astute company JIT Inc. uses Splunk Enterprise Security (ES) to protect its endpoint security domain. Endpoints are frequently the first line of defense and a frequent target for attacks in the constantly changing world of cyber threats. To efficiently manage and look into endpoint-related security issues, JIT Inc. makes use of Splunk ES's endpoint domain dashboards, which include Malware Detection, System Center, Time Center, Endpoint Changes, Update Center, and Search.

Scenario Setup

1. Malware Detection:

- **Scenario:** With the emergence of sophisticated zero-day threats, JIT Inc. is concerned about possible malware infestations in its network.
- **How It Helps**: JIT Inc. can track and examine malware activity on all of its endpoints thanks to the Malware Detection dashboard. This dashboard facilitates the early detection and response to such threats by assisting in the identification of patterns and trends in malware infections.

2. System Center:

- **Situation**: JIT Inc. must guarantee that every network endpoint is running the most recent security updates and system configurations.
- **How It Assists** A comprehensive view of system configurations and security patch levels across all endpoints is provided via the System Center dashboard. This makes it possible for JIT Inc. to locate and fix endpoints that don't adhere to the most recent security standards.

3. Time Center:

- **Scenario**: Time drift or manipulation on vital systems raises questions and may be a sign of an impending security compromise.
- **How It Helps:** All endpoints' system time configurations are tracked by the Time Center dashboard. For JIT Inc. to maintain time synchronization and identify any irregularities that would point to a security breach, this is essential.

4. Endpoint Changes:

- **Situation:** JIT Inc. desires to keep an eye out for any illegal modifications or dubious activity on its endpoints.
- **How It Helps:** This dashboard shows changes performed to the endpoints, such as file alterations, software installations, and configuration adjustments. By keeping an eye on these alterations, JIT Inc. may promptly identify and address any illegal changes that might point to a security breach.

5. Update Center:

- **Scenario**: JIT Inc. prioritizes keeping all endpoints up to date with the most recent software versions and fixes in order to prevent vulnerabilities.
- How It Assists Software update status across endpoints is tracked by JIT Inc. with the help of the Update Center dashboard. It assists in guaranteeing that all systems are current and free from known vulnerabilities brought about by out-of-date software.

6. Search (Endpoint Domain):

- **Scenario**: A specific security incident that was reported on an endpoint requires an investigation by JIT Inc.
- **How It Helps**: JIT Inc. can perform in-depth investigations into particular endpoint-related issues thanks to the comprehensive search capabilities provided by the Search dashboard within the endpoint domain. This is necessary for forensic examination and comprehending the extent of an occurrence.

Implementation and Analysis

- **Continuous Monitoring and Alerting**: To facilitate prompt detection and notification of possible threats, JIT Inc. uses these dashboards for continuous monitoring of endpoint security and health.
- **Forensics and incident investigation**: Using these dashboards, JIT Inc. can conduct in-depth analysis in the case of a security incident, assisting with efficient forensic investigation and incident resolution.
- **Endpoint Security Compliance and Management**: By using these dashboards for routine monitoring and analysis, JIT Inc. can make sure that its endpoints are safe and in compliance with both internal and external regulations.

The endpoint domain dashboards in Splunk ES are extremely helpful to JIT Inc. in ensuring strong endpoint security. Through the use of these technologies, JIT Inc. is able to protect its network from a variety of cyber threats by efficiently managing the health of their endpoints, keeping an eye out for threats, and responding quickly to endpoint-related security problems.

Network Domain

In this field, data regarding network traffic is gathered and analyzed from hardware like firewalls, routers, network-based intrusion detection systems, network vulnerability scanners, proxy servers, and hosts. The use of firewalls, intrusion detection and prevention systems (IDPS), secure network topologies, and encryption protocols are examples of network security methods. Organizations can find anomalies, spot potential risks, and look into security issues by monitoring network traffic.

Protecting an organization's network infrastructure and linked devices from attacks and vulnerabilities is the core goal of network domain security. Network security experts must act fast and adhere to the proper response processes when intrusion detection systems (IDS) discover suspicious activity.

Key components of ES in the access domain include:

- **Suspicious activity spotted by intrusion detection systems**: Intrusion detection systems that pick up on questionable activities: If your IDS notices any suspicious or malicious activity, look into the matter right away. This can entail studying traffic patterns, looking at logs, or linking occurrences. Once you've established the threat's nature, take the necessary precautions to reduce it, such as blocking the originating IP address, modifying firewall settings, or isolating the impacted systems.
- **Vulnerabilities**: Check your network frequently for vulnerabilities and make sure your systems and software are patched with the most recent updates. The process of identifying, evaluating, prioritizing, and remediating vulnerabilities ought to be ongoing. Implement a reliable patch management procedure to guarantee that vulnerabilities are fixed quickly, reducing the risk of exploitation.
- **Unusual ports being opened:** Keep an eye out for unauthorized or unexpected port openings on your network devices since they may indicate a compromised system or an intrusion attempt. Firewalls should be set up to block unused ports and limit incoming and outgoing traffic to the bare minimum required for your company's activities. To maintain security, evaluate and update firewall rules frequently.
- Unusual DNS activity Keep an eye out for any odd behavior in the DNS traffic, such as a high volume of requests, unexpected domain lookups, or connections to known malicious sites. Put DNS security mechanisms in place, such as DNS filtering, DNSSEC, or DNS sinkholes, to stop attackers from abusing DNS. Perform an investigation into any odd DNS activity to see if it points to a more serious security problem, such as data exfiltration or command and control communication, or malware infection.
- **Port scanning**: Attackers employ port scanning to find open ports and possibly risky services on network devices. To identify and stop attempts at port scanning, implement network intrusion detection and prevention systems (IDS/IPS). Utilize network segmentation to further limit the reach of potential assaults and impose access restrictions on delicate systems.

In conclusion, a proactive and comprehensive strategy that incorporates ongoing monitoring, threat detection, vulnerability management, and incident response is needed for network domain security. Organizations may efficiently detect and respond to suspicious activity by having strong security controls and procedures, reducing the likelihood of security incidents and breaches.

Network Domain Areas

This section will outline the use of dashboards like Network Traffic Tracking, Network Intrusion Tracking, Vulnerability Tracking, Web Traffic Tracking, Network Changes Tracking, and the Port and Protocol Tracking. These dashboards facilitate in-depth network monitoring, intrusion detection, vulnerability assessment, and tracking changes in network traffic and protocols to maintain robust network security.

Network Traffic

The Traffic Center dashboard offers information on the general patterns of network traffic, assisting in the detection of trends and potential security problems. It is possible to do more specific, ad hoc studies of network data using the Traffic Search dashboard. Both dashboards provide several options to help you narrow down the information shown and locate certain incidents or problems.

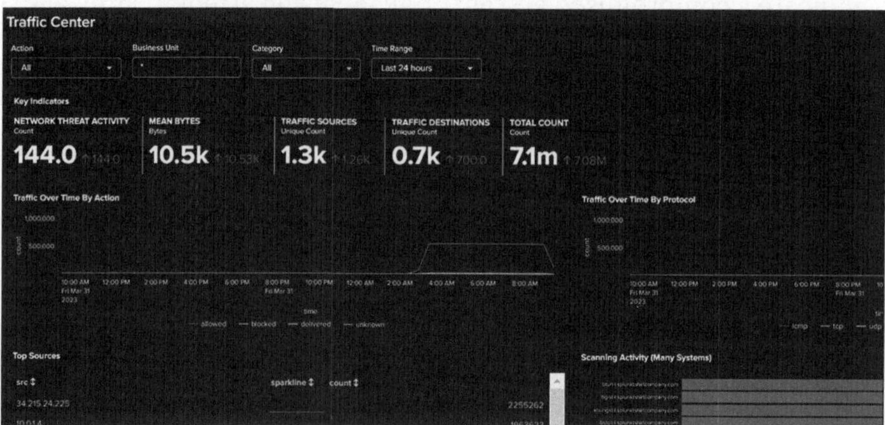

***Figure 8.11**: Traffic Center Dashboard*

Traffic Center Dashboard:

- `Key Indicators`: Provides an overview of relevant metrics for the past 48 hours to quickly assess the network traffic situation.
- `Traffic Over Time by Action`: Shows network traffic based on firewall rule actions, with drilldowns leading to the Traffic Search dashboard for more detailed investigations.
- `Traffic Over Time By Protocol`: Displays the number of events per day for a specified protocol, with drilldowns leading to the Traffic Search dashboard for more detailed investigations.

- `Top Sources`: Highlights the top sources of total traffic volume, with a sparkline representing peak event matches. Drilldowns open the Traffic Search dashboard for further investigation.
- **`Scanning Activity (Many Systems)`:** Displays network activity from port or vulnerability scanners, helping to identify unauthorized instances of these scanners. Drilldowns lead to the Traffic Search dashboard for further investigation.

Traffic Search Dashboard:

Drilldown searches from the Traffic Center dashboard panels typically end up on the Traffic Search dashboard, which is made for ad-hoc network data searching.

Security teams may monitor network traffic patterns and immediately spot potential security vulnerabilities by using these dashboards and their corresponding filters, enabling a more effective response to attacks and incidents.

Network Intrusion

The dashboard for the intrusion center gives a thorough overview of network intrusion events gathered from intrusion detection and prevention systems (IPS) devices. The dashboard helps with IDS activity analysis and reporting, allowing you to see trends in the frequency and intensity of IDS occurrences.

Figure 8.12: *Intrusion Center Dashboard*

To refine the displayed events, you can use the following filters:

- **IDS Type**: Filter events based on a specific type of IDS.
- **IDS Category**: Filter events matching vendor-defined categories.
- **Severity**: Filter events based on their severity.
- **Business Unit**: Filter events based on a group or department classification for the identity.
- **Category**: Filter events based on the categories to which the host belongs.
- **Time Range**: Select a time range for the displayed events.

The dashboard contains the following panels:

- **Key Indicators**: Displays summary information and metrics relevant to the dashboard sources over the past 48 hours.
- **Attacks Over Time By Severity**: Shows the top attacks over time, categorized by severity. Drilling down opens the Intrusion Search dashboard, searching on the selected severity and time range.
- **Top Attacks**: Displays the top attacks by count and signature. Drilling down opens the Intrusion Search dashboard, searching on the selected signature.
- **Scanning Activity (Many Attacks)**: Shows source IPs with a pattern of attacks. Drilling down opens the Intrusion Search dashboard, searching on the selected source IP and time range.
- **New Attacks - Last 30 Days**: Displays attacks identified for the first time. New attack vectors may indicate a change in the network or the presence of a new threat, such as a malware infection. Drilling down opens the Intrusion Search dashboard, searching on the selected signature and time range.

Based on the parameters specified by the search filters, the Intrusion Search dashboard assists in searching IDS-related events, such as assaults or reconnaissance-related activity. The major location for drilldown searches utilized in the Intrusion Center dashboard panels is this dashboard, which is used for ad-hoc network data searching. Unless the dashboard is opened in response to a drilldown action or you alter a filter, choose a time range, and click Submit, no results will be shown.

Vulnerability

The dashboard for the Vulnerability Center offers a thorough overview of vulnerability occurrences gathered from device data. It aids with the analysis and reporting of vulnerability data, enabling the detection and mitigation of potential security issues.

Figure 8.13: *Vulnerability Center Dashboard*

To refine the displayed events, you can use the following filters:

- **Severity:** Filter events based on their severity.
- **Business Unit**: Filter events based on a group or department classification for the identity.
- **Category:** Filter events based on the categories to which the host belongs.
- **Time Range**: Select a time range for the displayed events.

The dashboard contains the following panels:

- **Key Indicators**: Displays summary information and metrics relevant to the dashboard sources over the past 60 days.
- **Top Vulnerabilities**: Shows the most common issues reported by vulnerability scanners, aggregated by host. Drilling down opens the Vulnerability Search dashboard, searching on the selected signature and time range.
- **Most Vulnerable Hosts**: Displays the hosts with the highest number of reported issues. Drilling down opens the Vulnerability Search dashboard, searching on the selected severity, host, and time range.
- **Vulnerabilities by Severity**: Shows issues by severity assigned by the vulnerability scanner. Drilling down opens the Vulnerability Search dashboard, searching on the selected severity and time range.

- **New Vulnerabilities**: Displays the most recent new vulnerabilities detected and the date they were first observed. Drilling down opens the Vulnerability Search dashboard, searching on the selected signature and time range.

The status and activity of vulnerability detection products installed in your environment are tracked by the Vulnerability Operations dashboard. It enables you to keep track of the general health of your scanning systems, spot persistent problems, and locate systems that are no longer subject to vulnerability scanning.

Based on the criteria specified by the search filters, the Vulnerability Search dashboard shows a list of all vulnerability-related occurrences. The drilldown searches used in the Vulnerability Center dashboard panels use it as the primary location for ad hoc searches of vulnerability data. Unless the dashboard is opened in response to a drilldown action or you alter a filter, choose a time range, and click Submit, no results will be shown.

Web Traffic

By reporting on online traffic acquired by Splunk via proxy servers, the online Center dashboard is made to profile web traffic occurrences in your deployment. Debugging potential problems like excessive bandwidth utilization or proxies that are no longer sending content to proxy clients, can be helpful. The Web Center also assists in profiling the kind of content that clients are requesting as well as each client's bandwidth usage.

Figure 8.14: *Web Center Dashboard*

Filters available for the Web Center dashboard include:

- **Business Unit**: Filter events based on a group or department classification for the identity.
- **Category:** Filter events based on the categories to which the host belongs.
- **Time Range**: Select a time range for the displayed events.

Dashboard panels in the Web Center dashboard are as follows:

- **`Key Indicators`**: Displays summary information and metrics relevant to the dashboard sources over the past 48 hours.
- **`Events Over Time by Method`**: Shows the total number of proxy events over time, aggregated by Method (POST, GET, CONNECT, and so on).
- **`Events Over Time by Status`**: Shows the total number of proxy events, aggregated by Status (HTTP status of the response).
- **`Top Sources:`** Identifies sources associated with the highest volume of network traffic, which is useful for detecting sources using excessive network traffic or frequently requested destinations generating significant network traffic.
- **`Top Destinations:`** Identifies destinations associated with the highest volume of network traffic, which is useful for detecting sources using excessive network traffic or frequently requested destinations generating significant network traffic.

Based on the criteria specified by the search filters, the Web Search dashboard aids in the search for web events. In addition to being the main location for drilldown searches used in the online Search dashboard panels, it is utilized for ad-hoc online data searching. Unless the dashboard is opened in response to a drilldown action or you alter a filter, choose a time range, and click Submit, no results are shown.

Network Changes

You can keep track of configuration changes made to firewalls and other network devices in your environment using the Network Changes dashboard. Due to recent configuration changes, firewalls or other devices may go offline, making this dashboard helpful for debugging device issues.

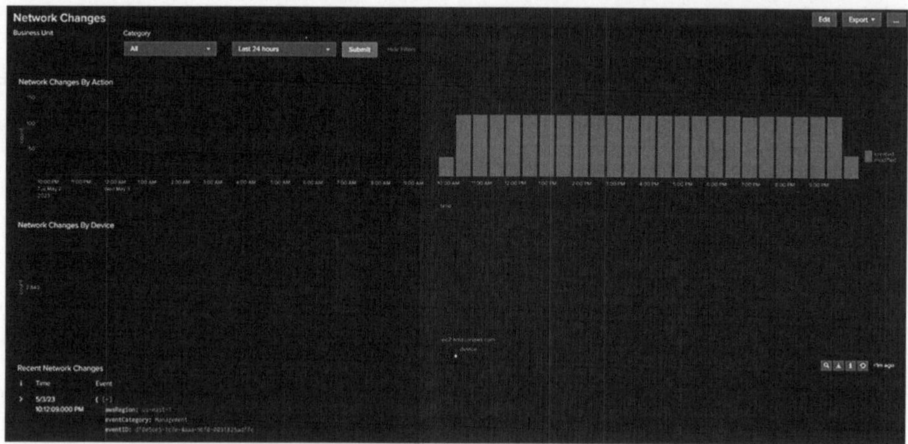

Figure 8.15: *Network Changes Dashboard*

Filters available for the Network Changes dashboard include:

- `Business Unit`: Filter events based on a group or department classification for the identity.
- `Category`: Filter events based on the categories to which the host belongs.
- `Time Range`: Select a time range for the displayed events.

Dashboard panels in the Network Changes dashboard are as follows:

- `Network Changes by Action`: This panel shows all changes to devices by the type of change, or whether a device was added, deleted, modified, or changed. The drilldown opens the "New Search" dashboard and searches on the selected action and time range.
- `Network Changes by Device`: This panel shows all devices that have been changed as well as the number of changes, sorted by the devices with the highest number of changes. The drilldown opens the "New Search" dashboard and searches on the selected device and time range.
- `Recent Network Changes`: This panel shows a table of the most recent changes to network devices in the last day.

Using this dashboard, you can monitor and analyze changes in your network devices to help identify and troubleshoot issues caused by configuration changes.

The Port and Protocol Tracking

Based on the restrictions established in the Enterprise Security, the Port and Protocol Tracker dashboard monitors port and protocol activity. This dashboard is helpful for monitoring, recognizing devices that don't adhere to business regulations, and spotting traffic that shouldn't be there.

***Figure 8.16**: Port and Protocol Tracker Dashboard*

Filters available for the Port and Protocol Tracker dashboard include:

- **`Business Unit:`** Filter events based on a group or department classification for the identity.
- **`Category:`** Filter events based on the categories to which the host belongs.

Dashboard panels in the Port and Protocol Tracker dashboard are as follows:

- **`Port/Protocol Profiler:`** Displays the volume of network transport and port activity over time to evaluate if the port activity is trending upwards or downwards. Sudden increases in unapproved port activity may indicate a change in the networked devices, such as an infection. The drilldown opens the **`New Search`** dashboard and searches on the selected transport destination port and time range.
- **`New Port Activity - Last 7 Days`**: Displays a table of transport and port traffic communication over time. The drilldown opens the Traffic Search dashboard and searches on the selected transport and time range.
- **`Prohibited Or Insecure Traffic Over Time - Last 24 Hours`**: Displays the volume of prohibited network port activity over time and helps determine if the unapproved port activity is trending upwards or downwards. The drilldown opens the **`New Search`** dashboard and searches on the selected transport destination port and time range.

- `Prohibited Traffic Details - Last 24 Hours`: Displays a table of the number of prohibited network traffic events. The drilldown opens the `New Search` dashboard and searches on the selected source IP, destination IP, transport, port, and time range.

Using this dashboard, you can monitor port and protocol activities, identify non-compliant devices, and detect prohibited traffic to maintain a secure network environment.

Hands-On Network Domain Investigation with Splunk ES at JIT Inc.

Overview

Splunk Enterprise Security (ES) is used by JIT Inc., a forward-thinking business that specializes in technological solutions, to handle network security completely. Network invasions and vulnerabilities provide serious hazards in today's digital environment. Network Traffic Tracking, Network Intrusion Tracking, Vulnerability Tracking, Web Traffic Tracking, Network Changes Tracking, and Port and Protocol Tracking are some of the Splunk ES network domain dashboards that JIT Inc. uses to address these issues. Every dashboard provides distinct perspectives on various facets of network security.

Scenario Setup

1. Network Traffic Tracking:

- **Scenario**: In order to identify irregularities that can point to a security breach, JIT Inc. must keep an eye on the quantity and kind of network traffic.
- **How It Helps**: JIT Inc. can see detailed information on network traffic patterns thanks to this dashboard. It assists in spotting anomalous data transfers or traffic surges that might be signs of cyberattacks or attempts at data exfiltration.

2. Network Intrusion Tracking:

- **Scenario**: JIT Inc. is concentrating on identifying and countering network intrusions in light of the growing threat of cyberattacks.
- **How It Assists**: JIT Inc. can keep an eye on and evaluate network intrusion attempts thanks to the Network Intrusion Tracking dashboard. In order to enable quick action to secure the network, this involves monitoring illegal access attempts, scanning activities, and other indicators of possible breaches.

3. Vulnerability Tracking:

- **Scenario**: In order to stop such exploits, JIT Inc. strives to proactively manage network vulnerabilities.
- **How It Helps**: This dashboard aids in locating and monitoring known network vulnerabilities. JIT Inc. can enhance network security by prioritizing patching and cleanup operations by identifying susceptible systems and applications.

4. Web Traffic Tracking:

- **Scenario**: JIT Inc. must track and examine web traffic in order to protect against attacks originating from the internet.
- **How It Assists**: By providing insights into all web traffic, the Web Traffic Tracking dashboard helps JIT Inc. prevent web-based assaults by helping to identify illegal online activity, possible data leaks, and suspicious website accesses.

5. Network Changes Tracking:

- **Scenario**: Unauthorized network configuration modifications have the potential to jeopardize network security, which worries JIT Inc.
- **How It Helps**: To ensure network integrity, monitoring changes is essential. This dashboard assists JIT Inc. in monitoring all network configuration changes and notifies them of any unauthorized or questionable alterations.

6. Port and Protocol Tracking:

- **Situation**: JIT Inc. must make sure that protocols and network ports are not abused or left open to attack from outside sources.
- **How It Helps**: This dashboard offers comprehensive information on how ports and protocols are used throughout the network. This data can be used by JIT Inc. to detect unauthorized or unusual use of network ports and protocols, which is crucial for identifying possible security flaws or active assaults.

Implementation and Analysis

- **Constant Monitoring and Alerting:** JIT Inc. uses these dashboards to continuously monitor network activity, which allows for the early identification of possible problems and the sending of alerts on time.
- **Incident Analysis and Response:** Using these dashboards, JIT Inc. can conduct in-depth analysis in the event of a network-related security incident, resulting in the incident's successful mitigation and resolution.

- **Network Security Enhancement**: By using these dashboards for regular monitoring and analysis, JIT Inc. is able to improve its network security posture over time and guarantee that security policies and standards are being followed.

The network domain dashboards in Splunk ES are essential to JIT Inc.'s ability to keep a safe and reliable network environment. Through efficient use of these technologies, JIT Inc. can keep an eye on network activity, spot possible dangers, and take proactive measures to defend the network from a variety of cyberthreats.

Identity Domain

In order to make sure that persons and devices accessing resources within an organization are correctly verified and allowed, the identity security domain focuses on analyzing identity and asset lookup data. Systems for managing user IDs, authenticating users, and enforcing access control regulations are known as identity and access management (IAM) systems. Implementing robust authentication systems, such as multi-factor authentication (MFA), managing user provisioning and deprovisioning, and employing role-based access control (RBAC) to manage user permissions are all considered best practices in this area. Organizations can identify insider threats, unlawful access, and identity theft by monitoring identity-related data.

In cybersecurity, the identity domain is concerned with controlling and securing user identities, access privileges, and network activity. To ensure secure access to sensitive data and resources, certain threats and risks within this area can be monitored and managed. The Identity domain is frequently related to the following dangers:

- **Brute force attacks:** These are attempts to obtain unauthorized access to a system by repeatedly attempting different users and password combinations. Attackers employ automated technologies to swiftly test a huge number of options. Organizations should develop account lockout procedures, enforce strong password regulations, and employ multi-factor authentication to defend against brute force assaults.
- **Misuse of privileged accounts:** Privileged accounts have enhanced access rights and permissions within a system, such as root or administrator accounts. The infrastructure and data of an organization may suffer serious harm if these accounts are misused. Organizations should follow the concept of least privilege, keep an eye on privileged account activity, and employ privileged access control tools to reduce the risk of privileged account exploitation.

- **Access by uncommon or new accounts**: If uncommon or new accounts are not adequately monitored and managed, they may present a risk. Unusual behavior from these accounts may be a sign of intrusion or malicious intent. To guarantee compliance with security regulations and identify potential dangers, organizations should monitor and assess the activities of new accounts, especially those with enhanced rights.
- **Access by expired or disabled accounts:** Access to any system resources should not be permitted by expired or disabled accounts. However, if these accounts are not handled appropriately, attackers may use them to gain illegal access. Organizations should periodically check dormant accounts, disable them, and keep an eye out for any attempts to log into these accounts.
- **Unusual application access**: Attackers may utilize SSH or VNC, among other programs, to enter networks without authorization or carry out destructive deeds. It can be useful to keep an eye out for atypical program usage to spot insider threats or possible security lapses. To spot any suspect or unauthorized activities, organizations should set application control policies and keep an eye on application usage.

By addressing these threats within the Identity domain, organizations can better protect their network, data, and resources, ensuring a secure environment for their users and operations.

Identity Domain Areas

This section will cover key dashboards such as Asset Data, Identity Data, and User Session. These dashboards focus on monitoring and analyzing asset and identity information along with user session activities, offering essential insights to identify potential security issues and improve overall identity management.

Asset Data

The Enterprise Security Asset Center dashboard is a tool for perusing and looking up things in the asset data. Along with other details on each asset, it offers a thorough view of the hosts, IP addresses, and subnets used by the firm. This dashboard provides information, such as asset location and priority level, to help link asset properties with indexed events.

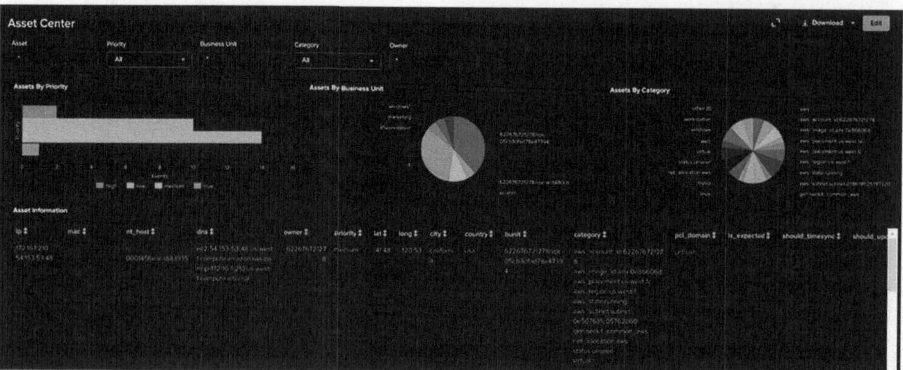

Figure 8.17: *Asset Center Dashboard*

Dashboard filters enable users to refine the results shown on the dashboard panels:

- **Asset**: A known or unknown asset
- **Priority**: Filter by the Priority field in the Asset table
- **Business Unit:** A group or department classification for the asset
- **Category**: Filter by the Category field in the Asset table
- **Owner:** Filter by the Owner field in the Asset table
- **Time Range**: Select the time range to represent

The dashboard panels provide insights into various aspects of the assets, including:

- **Assets by Priority**: Displays the number of assets by priority level, with a drilldown that opens a search with the selected priority level.
- **Assets by Business Unit**: Displays the relative amount of assets by business unit, with a drilldown that opens a search with the selected business unit.
- **Assets by Category**: Displays the relative amount of assets by category, with a drilldown that opens a search with the selected category.
- **Asset Information:** Shows all assets matching the current dashboard filters. The drilldown opens the Asset Investigator dashboard if the `ip`, `nt_host`, `mac`, or `dns` fields are selected; otherwise, it opens a search with the selected field.

Identity Data

Users of Enterprise Security can browse and look for things within the identity data using the Identity Center dashboard. Identity information for each identity comprises account names, legal names, nicknames, alternate names, and other related details. This information is used to link user information to indexed events, adding further context.

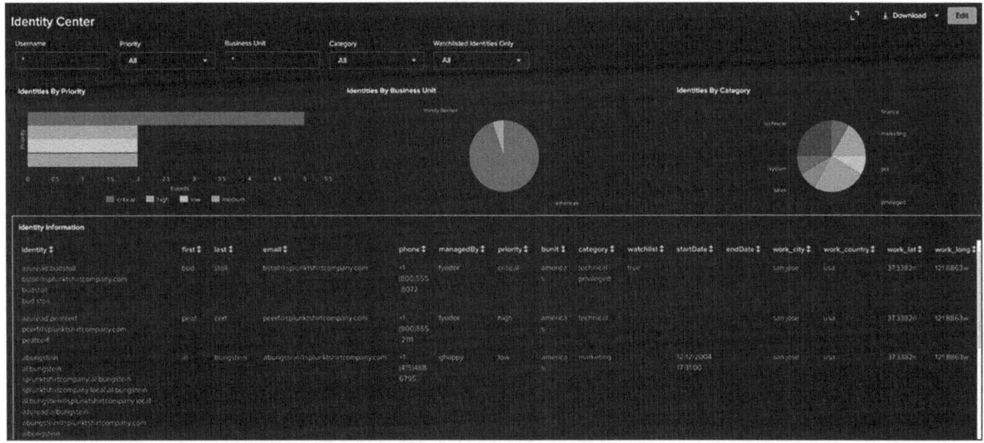

Figure 8.18: *Identity Center Dashboard*

To filter identities in the Identity Center dashboard, a `key=value` pair search field is used. Users can enter `key=value` pairs instead of plain text strings, such as `email=*acmetech.com` or `nick=a_nickname`.

Dashboard filters help refine the results displayed on the dashboard panels, as follows:

- **Username:** A known or unknown user
- **Priority:** Filter by the Priority field in the Identities table
- **Business Unit:** A group or department classification for the identity
- **Category**: Filter by the Category field in the Identities table
- **Watchlisted Identities Only**: Filter by the identities tagged as "watchlist" in the Identities table
- **Time Range**: Select the time range to represent

The dashboard panels offer insights into various aspects of the identities, as follows:

- **Identities by Priority**: Displays the count of identities by priority level, with a drilldown that opens a search with the selected priority level.
- **Identities by Business Unit**: Displays the relative number of identities by business unit, with a drilldown that opens a search with the selected business unit.

- **Identities by Category**: Displays the relative number of identities by category, with a drilldown that opens a search with the selected category.
- **Identity Information**: Shows all assets matching the current dashboard filters. The drilldown opens the Identity Investigator dashboard if the identity field is selected; otherwise, it opens a search with the selected field.

User Session

Enterprise Security's Session Center dashboard offers a summary of network sessions that are used to link user-provided session data from DHCP or VPN servers to network activities. Users can access the dashboard to examine session records and locate the device or person that used an IP address during a session. Users and device association data from Splunk UBA or the Network Sessions data model can be used to review network session information.

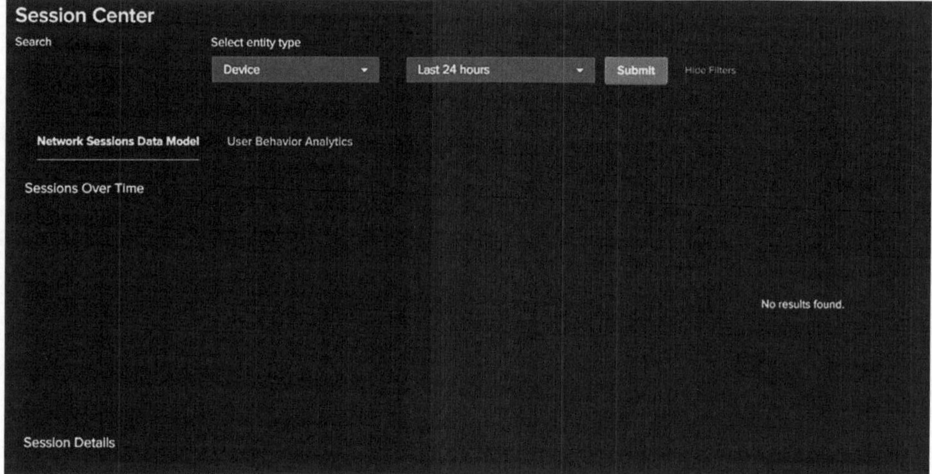

***Figure 8.19**: Session Center Dashboard*

The dashboard panels are divided into two tabs: Network Sessions and User Behavior Analytics.

Network Sessions tab:

- **Sessions Over Time**: Displays the total count of network sessions over time, with a drilldown that opens a search with the selected session and time range.
- **Session Details**: Displays the top 1000 network sessions most recently opened, based on session start time. The drilldown opens a search with the selected session details.

User Behavior Analytics tab:

- **Sessions of Associated Entities**: Based on the search filter, this panel displays sessions of users and devices associated with a device that you search, or devices associated with a user that you search. Hover over a session to learn more about the session activity.
- **Session Details**: Shows the entity ID from Splunk UBA, the name of the entity, the type of entity, the start and end times of the session, and event data from Splunk UBA. Users can expand a row to view more details.

Hands-On Identity Domain Investigation with Splunk ES at JIT Inc.

Overview

JIT Inc., a company specializing in advanced technology solutions, utilizes Splunk Enterprise Security (ES) to ensure robust identity and access management. In the realm of cybersecurity, managing and safeguarding identity data is crucial. To effectively handle these aspects, JIT Inc. employs Splunk ES's identity domain dashboards: Asset Data, Identity Data, and User Session. Each dashboard plays a specific role in monitoring and investigating identity-related security aspects.

Scenario Setup

1. Asset Data:

- **Scenario**: JIT Inc. is worried about making sure that all of the hardware and software that its workers utilize is monitored and protected.
- **How It Assists**: JIT Inc. has comprehensive insight into all registered assets inside the company thanks to the Asset Data dashboard. This contains details regarding the ownership, location, and status of the asset. Through the dashboard's monitoring, JIT Inc. can detect any unregistered or illegal assets within the network, hence assisting in the reduction of potential security threats linked to asset misuse.

2. Identity Data:

- **Scenario**: With more workers working remotely, JIT Inc. must control and protect employee identity.
- **How It Helps**: The Identity Data dashboard provides in-depth information on each employee's identity profile. Information on user roles, access rights, and behavior patterns is included in this. Using this dashboard, JIT Inc. can look for unusual user behavior, possible account breaches, or privilege escalations that might point to security risks.

3. User Session:

- **Scenario:** JIT Inc. needs to keep an eye on user session activity to spot any unusual behavior because insider attacks and account takeovers are becoming a bigger danger.
- **How It Assists**: The network's active user sessions are monitored and examined via the User Session dashboard. This entails keeping an eye on access trends, session lengths, and login times. With the use of this data, JIT Inc. will be able to spot anomalous session activity, such as access to critical resources, sessions at strange times, or sessions lasting unusually long, all of which could point to a compromised account or insider threat.

Implementation and Analysis

- **Continuous checking for Asset and Identity Management:** JIT Inc. can keep accurate records of its assets and user identities by routinely checking the dashboards for asset and identity data. This ensures that any inconsistencies or abnormalities are promptly found and fixed.
- **Proactively Detecting Security events**: JIT Inc. can potentially avert security events related to insider threats or compromised accounts by using the User Session dashboard to proactively detect and respond to odd user behaviors.
- **Security Policies and Compliance:** JIT Inc. may improve its asset and identity management security policies with the use of these dashboards' insights, ensuring that they adhere to legal and industry requirements.

The identity domain dashboards in Splunk ES are essential for JIT Inc. to manage and secure their identities and digital assets. By successfully utilizing these dashboards, JIT Inc. may ensure the integrity and security of their network and sensitive data by monitoring, analyzing, and responding to identity-related security issues.

Case Studies

Here are three case studies illustrating the successful use of Splunk in forensic investigations within the security domain. These examples showcase how Splunk can help organizations identify, analyze, and respond to cyber threats and incidents more effectively.

Case Study: Financial Services Company - Insider Threat Investigation

- **Problem**: A financial services company suspected an insider threat after detecting unusual activity in its network. The company needed to identify the source of the suspicious activity, determine if any sensitive data had been compromised, and implement appropriate remediation measures.

- **Solution**: The company used Splunk to conduct a forensic investigation, collecting and analyzing data from various sources, including system logs, network traffic, and user activity. Splunk's advanced analytics capabilities allowed the company to identify patterns and anomalies, ultimately tracing the suspicious activity back to a rogue employee.
- **Results:** The financial services company used the insights gained from the Splunk investigation to take appropriate action against the rogue employee and implement stronger security measures to prevent future insider threats. The company also improved its monitoring and detection capabilities by leveraging Splunk's real-time analytics.

Case Study: E-commerce Company - Data Breach Investigation

- **Problem**: An e-commerce company experienced a data breach resulting in the exposure of customer payment information. The company needed to identify the root cause of the breach, assess the extent of the damage, and implement appropriate remediation measures.
- **Solution**: The e-commerce company engaged a forensic investigation team that leveraged Splunk to conduct a thorough analysis of its systems, network, and logs. The team used Splunk's powerful search and data visualization capabilities to identify the source of the breach and track the attackers' activities.
- **Results:** The forensic investigation, aided by Splunk, helped the e-commerce company pinpoint the vulnerabilities exploited by the attackers, assess the scope of the breach, and remediate the issue. As a result, the company improved its security posture, implemented more robust monitoring and detection capabilities, and was able to provide a detailed report of the incident to relevant stakeholders.

Case Study: Healthcare Organization - Ransomware Attack Investigation

- **Problem:** A healthcare organization fell victim to a ransomware attack, with critical systems and patient data being encrypted and held for ransom. The organization needed to identify the source of the attack, assess the extent of the damage, and restore its systems as quickly as possible.
- **Solution**: The healthcare organization utilized Splunk to perform a forensic investigation, collecting and analyzing data from affected systems, network traffic, and security logs. Splunk's advanced analytics helped the organization identify the ransomware's infection vector, trace its propagation within the network, and understand its behavior.
- **Results:** With the insights gained from the Splunk-based forensic investigation, the healthcare organization was able to effectively

respond to the ransomware attack, mitigate its impact, and restore affected systems. The organization also used the information gathered to strengthen its security measures, improve monitoring and detection capabilities, and better prepare for future cyber threats.

Conclusion

The chapter on *Forensic Investigation in Security* Domains has come to a close. We have looked at the key elements of a forensic investigation and examined domains including Access, Endpoint, Network, and Identity. Each domain contributed a distinct viewpoint to the investigative process and was essential in identifying, evaluating, and reducing security vulnerabilities. The case studies demonstrated the complexity of cyber forensics and offered useful real-world applications of these principles.

We will expand on these ideas as we move into our next chapter, *Splunk Integration with Other Security Tools*, and examine how Splunk ES, a flexible security platform, can be improved by being integrated with other security tools to create a more complete and robust cybersecurity framework.

Points to Remember

- To ascertain the reason of a security issue or to assist legal procedures, forensic investigations systematically gather, preserve, analyze, and present digital evidence.
- Digital artifacts that can be used to recreate the sequence of events leading up to a security incident include logs, files, emails, network traffic, and other digital artifacts.
- The chain of custody must be followed to protect the validity of digital evidence. It records how evidence is handled and preserved in order to guarantee its admissibility in court.
- Forensic investigation and incident response go hand in hand. While forensic investigation focuses on determining the source and scope of the breach, incident response concentrates on containment and recovery.
- The steps of a forensic inquiry normally go as follows: Establish the policies, methods, and tools needed for the inquiry as part of your preparation. (a) Identification: Identify and notify others of a possible security incident. (b) Gathering: Maintain the integrity of digital evidence while gathering and storing it. (c) Analysis: Look over the information gathered to ascertain the reason for the incident, its scope, and its

effects. (d) Reporting: Summarize findings, offer suggestions, and update pertinent parties. (e) Corrective action: Take steps to stop similar occurrences in the future.

- To assist with the investigative process, a number of forensic tools are available, including disk imaging tools, file recovery tools, network forensics tools, and malware analysis tools.
- Dead forensics deal with gathering data from a system that has been shut down, whereas live forensics gather data from a system that is still in use. Both approaches have advantages and disadvantages, and the choice depends on the particulars of the research.
- To precisely reconstruct the timeline of the occurrence and connect events across many systems, time synchronization is crucial in forensic investigations.
- To make sure that their investigations abide by relevant laws and professional standards, forensic investigators should be knowledgeable on legal, ethical, and privacy rules.
- For a forensic investigation to be effective, cooperation and communication between many teams and stakeholders, including security analysts, IT employees, legal counsel, and law enforcement, are crucial.

CHAPTER 9

Splunk Integration with Other Security Tools

Introduction

The advantages and best practices for integrating Splunk with different security technologies, including SIEM systems, Threat Intelligence Platforms, Vulnerability Management technologies, Endpoint Security systems, and Network Security Tools, are covered in this chapter.

An overview of Splunk and its function in Security Operations Centers (SOCs) opens the chapter. It emphasizes the value of Splunk integration with other security solutions as well as the necessity of integrating security products for efficient threat detection and response.

The parts that follow concentrate on best practices for integrating Splunk with security products, such as data standardization and enrichment, using Splunk Add-ons and Apps, configuring alerts and notifications, and creating efficient correlation rules and use cases.

Following that, the chapter delves into particular instances of how Splunk may be integrated with security software, including IBM QRadar, LogRhythm, McAfee Enterprise Security Manager, AlienVault USM, Anomali ThreatStream, ThreatConnect, Qualys, Cisco Firepower, and CrowdStrike Falcon. Each example is followed by a brief description of the security solution, the advantages of integrating it with Splunk, and the actions necessary to set up the integration in the chapter.

The chapter ends by summarizing the important ideas to keep in mind when integrating Splunk with other security tools, including the value of automation and customization in enhancing security analytics, threat detection, and response capabilities, the significance of data normalization and enrichment, and the advantages of creating efficient correlation rules and use cases.

Structure

In this chapter, we will cover the following topics:

- Introduction to Splunk and Security Tool Integrations
    - The role of Splunk in Security Operations Centers (SOCs)
    - The importance of integrating security tools for effective threat detection and response
- Best Practices for Integrating Splunk with Security Tools
    - Data normalization and enrichment
    - Use of Splunk Add-ons and Apps
    - Establishing effective correlation rules and use cases
- Splunk Integration with SIEM Solutions
    - Integration Benefits with SIEM Solutions
    - Integration with IBM QRadar
    - Integration with McAfee Enterprise Security Manager
    - Integration with other SIEM Solutions
- Splunk Integration with Threat Intelligence Platforms
    - Integration Benefits with SIEM Solutions
    - Integration with Anomali ThreatStream
    - Integration with other Threat Intelligence Platforms
- Splunk Integration with Vulnerability Management Tools
    - Integration Benefits with Vulnerability Management Tools
    - Integration with Qualys
    - Integration with other Vulnerability Management Tools
- Splunk Integration with Endpoint Security Solutions
    - Integration Benefits with Endpoint Security Solutions
    - Integration with CrowdStrike Falcon
    - Integration with other Endpoint Security Solutions

- Splunk Integration with Network Security Tools
    - Integration Benefits with Network Security Tools
    - Integration with Cisco Firepower
    - Integration with other Network Security Tools
- Case Studies

Introduction to Splunk and Security Tool Integrations

By combining several data sources for better visibility and analysis, Splunk and Security Tool Integrations provide a potent combination to streamline security operations. This integration makes security data more actionable and efficient by enabling thorough threat detection, enhanced incident response, and proactive risk reduction.

The role of Splunk in Security Operations Centers (SOCs)

With the help of the potent data analytics platform Splunk, businesses can gather, examine, and display data from numerous sources. Splunk is the main processing and analysis tool used in Security Operations Centers (SOCs) to handle and analyze security-related data. The platform lets security analysts find, look into, and address potential vulnerabilities by giving real-time visibility into an organization's security posture.

The Importance of Integrating Security Tools for Effective Threat Detection and Response

Splunk integration with different security technologies enables businesses to get a complete picture of their security environment. Security teams are better able to recognize, prioritize, and react to risks when they combine data from many sources. Integrating security technologies with Splunk has several advantages, such as:

- **Increased visibility:** By combining data from several security technologies, a more complete picture of an organization's security posture is provided, making it simpler to spot risks that might otherwise go unnoticed.

- **Improved productivity:** By centralizing data on a single platform, integrating security tools enables analysts to carry out duties like incident investigation, threat hunting, and remediation more quickly.
- **Improved collaboration**: By offering a common platform for exchanging and analyzing security data, integration makes it possible for various teams within the business to collaborate more successfully.
- **Reduced false positives:** Correlating data from multiple sources helps minimize false positives by providing more context around security events.

Best Practices for Integrating Splunk with Security Tools

Following are some best practices to adhere to while integrating Splunk with other integration tools.

Data Normalization and Enrichment

Integrating Splunk with security technologies requires several essential processes, including data normalization and enrichment. These procedures guarantee the consistency of data from many sources and give pertinent context for analysis.

- **Standardize field names and data formats:** To ensure consistency between diverse sources, it is crucial to standardize field names and data formats when integrating data from different security solutions. Analysts may more efficiently search for and correlate data thanks to this.
- **Contextualize data collection**: Contextualizing the data obtained enables analysts to better comprehend and rank security occurrences. Information like asset criticality, user roles, and geolocation data may be included in this.
- **Make use of Splunk's Common Information Model (CIM):** This offers a standard framework for normalizing and classifying data from various sources. The efficiency of searches and correlations is increased by adopting CIM, which provides smooth data integration.

Use of Splunk Add-ons and Apps

- Splunk Add-ons and Apps, which offer pre-built interfaces and configurations for particular security products, can simplify and accelerate the integration process.

- **Use authorized Splunk Add-ons**: Since these add-ons are created and maintained by Splunk or its partners, compatibility and support are guaranteed. For particular security products, these add-ons frequently offer data gathering, standardization, and visualization capabilities.
- **Use applications created by the community**: The Splunk user community frequently creates and shares apps that can be useful for integrating particular security products. Even though they might not have official backing, community-developed apps can nonetheless offer useful functionality and insights.

  These apps can be accessed at the address listed here:

  https://splunkbase.splunk.com/apps?page=1&filters=categories%3Asecurity_compliance
- **Customize apps and add-ons:** Depending on the needs of your business, you might need to modify already-existing applications or add-ons or even create your own to better suit your unique security tools and use cases.

Establishing effective correlation rules and use cases

Security teams can discover complex threats and trends that might not be obvious from individual security events with the help of effective correlation rules and use cases.

- Determine the most important security use cases for your firm, such as phishing attempts detection, insider threats, or data exfiltration. Concentrate on creating correlation rules that cover these particular use situations.
- Use the correlation engine in Splunk to develop sophisticated searches and rules that mix data from several sources. Inferring correlations between events that might not be obvious when analyzing different data sources can be done with this.
- **Continuously improve rules**: Review and update correlation rules on a regular basis to make sure they are still applicable and effective in light of the changing threat environment facing your organization.

For maximizing the value of your security data and guaranteeing prompt and efficient threat detection and response, it is essential to implement best practices for integrating Splunk with security products. Organizations can develop a more thorough and effective security posture by concentrating on data normalization, utilizing Splunk Add-ons and Apps, and implementing good correlation rules.

Splunk Integration with SIEM Solutions

Numerous advantages of integrating Splunk with SIEM technologies include increased operational efficiency, improved threat detection, and response capabilities, and improved security posture.

Integration Benefits with SIEM Solutions

Some of the key benefits include:

- **Complete visibility**: Integrating SIEM technologies with Splunk enables security teams to centralize and correlate data from many sources. This gives a complete picture of the security environment of the company, which makes it simpler to spot patterns, trends, and potential threats.
- **Improved threat detection:** Organizations may use advanced analytics and correlation capabilities to detect threats more efficiently by combining the benefits of Splunk and SIEM technologies. Finding strange patterns, signs of compromise, and potentially hostile activity are all included in this.
- **Better incident response:** Security teams can prioritize occurrences based on risk by integrating Splunk with SIEM technologies, which can speed up the incident response procedure. To speed up investigations and get a more complete picture of security occurrences, analysts can examine and evaluate data from both platforms.
- **Data enrichment:** By integrating with SIEM systems, security teams may add extra context to their Splunk data, such as threat intelligence, asset data, and vulnerability data. During the threat detection and response phase, this aids in better decision-making.
- **Flexibility and customization:** By integrating Splunk with different SIEM technologies, businesses may adjust their security analytics and threat detection capabilities to suit their particular requirements. This entails developing customized correlation rules, use cases, and dashboards that are tailored to the needs and environment of the firm.
- **Scalability**: Organizations can grow their security operations more successfully by utilizing the combined capability of Splunk and SIEM technologies, handling higher amounts of data and events without sacrificing performance.

- **Better collaboration**: Integration with SIEM solutions can help security teams work together more effectively by enabling them to share information, data, and results. This aids in creating a SOC that is more cohesive and effective.

Organizations may use the combined capability of Splunk and SIEM products to strengthen their security posture, increase environment visibility, and improve threat detection and response capabilities.

Integration with IBM QRadar

A Security Information and Event Management (SIEM) tool called IBM QRadar aids enterprises in real-time monitoring and analysis of security incidents. Organizations can utilize the benefits of both systems by integrating Splunk and QRadar, resulting in a more complete security analytics solution.

- **Data forwarding:** Set up Syslog or a Universal Forwarder in Splunk to send pertinent security events and logs to QRadar. As a result, Splunk data can be processed and correlated with information from other security data sources by QRadar.

Steps to Integrate:

1. **Plan the integration**: Choose the Splunk data sources and event types you wish to deliver to QRadar. To forward to QRadar, you must choose the right Splunk index, source type, and source.
2. **Set up Splunk's data forwarding:**
    a. If a Universal Forwarder isn't already present on the Splunk instance, install it and set it up. From Splunk to QRadar, data must be forwarded through the Universal Forwarder.
    b. Set up `outputs.conf` on the Universal Forwarder to send information to the QRadar SIEM. To send the data, you must specify the IP address and port number of the QRadar instance.
3. **Configure QRadar's data inputs**:
    a. Open the `Log Sources` section of the `Admin` page in the QRadar console.
    b. To add a new log source, click `Add`. Select the `Syslog` protocol, then pick the right type of log source for the information coming from Splunk.
    c. Enter the appropriate data, such as the `Log Source Identifier` (often the hostname or IP address of the Splunk instance), and modify the event parameters in accordance with your needs.
    d. Save the settings.

4. **Examine the fusion**:
    a. Employ the Universal Forwarder to send a sample of Splunk data to QRadar. Either create test events in Splunk or wait for fresh events to be indexed to accomplish this.
    b. Verify in QRadar that the forwarded events are being received and correctly interpreted by looking at the `Log Activity` page.
    c. Confirm that the correlation and analysis of the events in QRadar are as anticipated.
5. **Bi-directional integration:** To enable bi-directional communication across the platforms, use the IBM QRadar App for Splunk. As a result, QRadar users may access Splunk data and dashboards while Splunk users can examine offense statistics and event details within Splunk.

Installing and setting up the Splunk IBM QRadar App:

1. Access Splunkbase and download the IBM QRadar App for Splunk (https://splunkbase.splunk.com/app/3541).
2. Using the `Manage Apps` section of the Splunk Web UI, install the app on your Splunk instance.
3. Configure the app by entering the required data, such as the IP address and QRadar API credentials.
4. Save the setup and confirm that Splunk allows you to examine QRadar offensive data and event specifics.

Integration with McAfee Enterprise Security Manager

A Security Information and Event Management (SIEM) solution called McAfee Enterprise Security Manager (ESM) offers real-time monitoring, analytics, and threat detection capabilities. By combining security data and analytics from Splunk and McAfee ESM, enterprises can get a more complete picture of their security posture.

Adding Splunk to McAfee Enterprise Security Manager involves the following steps:

1. **Arrange for the integration**:
    a. Choose the Splunk data sources and event types that you want to send to McAfee ESM. To forward to McAfee ESM, you must choose the right Splunk index, source type, and source.

2. **Set up Splunk's data forwarding**:
   a. If a Universal Forwarder isn't already present on the Splunk instance, install it and set it up. Data transmission from Splunk to McAfee ESM is handled via the Universal Forwarder.
   b. Set outputs.conf on the Universal Forwarder to use the Syslog protocol to send data to McAfee ESM. To transfer the data, you must include the IP address and port number of the McAfee ESM Receiver instance.
3. **McAfee ESM data input configuration**:
   a. After logging in, go to the `Data Sources` area of the McAfee ESM console.
   b. Select the proper data source type that corresponds to the Splunk data being delivered by clicking **`Add Data Source`**.
   c. Provide the appropriate details, including the name of the data source, the Splunk instance's IP address or hostname, and the data format.
   d. After configuring the data processing settings to your specifications, save the configuration.
4. **Test the integration**:
   a. Employ the Universal Forwarder to send test data from Splunk to McAfee ESM. Either create test events in Splunk or wait for fresh events to be indexed to accomplish this.
   b. Check that the transmitted events are received, correctly processed, and connected as anticipated in McAfee ESM.

Splunk integration with other SIEM Solutions

Splunk may be linked with numerous other SIEM systems to improve security analytics, threat detection, and response capabilities, in addition to IBM QRadar and McAfee Enterprise Security Manager. Organizations can successfully integrate IBM QRadar with other SIEM platforms by using the same procedures that were previously described for IBM QRadar. These SIEM tools include, among others:

- **LogRhythm**: A SIEM platform with capabilities for log management, security analytics, and incident response, LogRhythm.
- **AlienVault USM**: AlienVault Unified Security Management (USM) is an all-in-one security platform with features for SIEM, behavioral monitoring, asset discovery, vulnerability assessment, and intrusion detection.

- **Exabeam**: Exabeam is a SIEM platform that uses user behavior analytics and machine learning to identify sophisticated threats.
- **Rapid7 InsightIDR:** This cloud-based SIEM system from Rapid7 provides capabilities for threat detection, incident response, and compliance management.
- **Fortinet FortiSIEM:** Combining log management, security analytics, and incident response, Fortinet FortiSIEM provides a comprehensive security platform.
- **SolarWinds Security Event Manager (SEM)** is a SIEM tool that delivers capabilities for automated incident response, real-time log analysis, and event correlation.

These are just a few illustrations of SIEM solutions that can be combined with Splunk to improve the security posture of a business. Organizations can get a more complete understanding of their security environment and enhance threat detection and response capabilities by combining Splunk with different SIEM solutions.

Splunk Integration with Threat Intelligence Platforms

Threat Intelligence Platforms (TIPs) give businesses useful knowledge about new and ongoing cyberthreats. Security teams can use this information by integrating Splunk with threat intelligence platforms to improve threat detection, response, and overall security posture.

Integration Benefits with Threat Intelligence Platforms

Some of the key benefits include:

- **Improved security data**: Integrating TIPs with Splunk enables security teams to add useful threat intelligence to their data. By providing more context, analysts are better able to comprehend security incidents and respond to threats on time.
- **Better threat detection**: Organizations can enhance their threat detection capabilities by utilizing threat intelligence from TIPs within Splunk. This entails more accurately spotting indicators of compromise (IOCs), patterns of malicious behavior, and emerging threats.

- **Proactive threat hunting**: Integrating with TIPs enables security teams to use the most recent threat intelligence to actively look for risks in their environment. This assists organizations in identifying and reducing hazards before they have a chance to do serious harm.
- **Simplified incident response**: Security teams may prioritize issues based on risk and the most recent threat information by combining Splunk data with threat intelligence from TIPs. This lessens the potential impact of security issues by enabling more effective reaction and cleanup operations.
- **Personalization and automation:** By integrating Splunk with TIPs, businesses can adapt their security analytics, threat detection, and incident response procedures to suit their particular requirements. The development of unique correlation rules, warnings, and automated actions based on the most recent threat intelligence is part of this process.
- **Improved collaboration**: TIP integration can help security teams and other stakeholders work together more effectively by enabling them to share knowledge, threat information, and findings. This aids in creating a SOC that is more cohesive and effective.
- **Lessened false positives**: Security teams may lessen false positives by integrating threat intelligence from TIPs into Splunk, allowing them to concentrate their efforts and resources on real threats while reducing the amount of noise in their environment.

Organizations may take advantage of the strength of both platforms by integrating Splunk with Threat Intelligence Platforms to improve their threat detection and response capabilities, gain better visibility into their environment, and make more educated decisions based on the most recent threat intelligence.

Integration with Anomali ThreatStream

The comprehensive Threat Intelligence Platform known as Anomali ThreatStream gathers, evaluates, and organizes threat data from many sources.

Steps for integration are as follows:

1. Download and install the Splunkbase Anomali ThreatStream App (https://splunkbase.splunk.com/app/2951) from Splunk.
2. Configure the app by entering the required data, such as the ThreatStream API login details and server configuration.

3. Set up alerts, customize dashboards, and add threat intelligence to your Splunk data using the app.

Integration with other Threat Intelligence Platforms

Splunk may be linked with a number of different Threat Intelligence Platforms in addition to Anomali ThreatStream to improve security analytics, threat detection, and response capabilities. Businesses can successfully integrate with different threat intelligence platforms by using the same procedures described earlier for Anomali ThreatStream. These threat intelligence platforms include, among others:

- **ThreatConnect**: ThreatConnect is a well-known threat intelligence platform with administration, analysis, and threat data aggregation capabilities.
- **Recorded Future**: A leading provider of real-time threat intelligence, Recorded Future is a worldwide cybersecurity organization.
- **MISP (Malware Information Sharing Platform)**: An open-source platform for threat intelligence, MISP enables businesses to share, store, and work together on threat data.
- **IBM X-Force Exchange**: An online platform for threat intelligence, IBM X-Force Exchange enables companies to share and access threat information.
- **CrowdStrike Falcon X** is a threat intelligence platform that automates threat analysis and provides tailored intelligence based on the particular environment of the enterprise.

These are just a few instances of Threat Intelligence Platforms that can be combined with Splunk to enhance the security environment of a company. Organizations can acquire a more complete understanding of their environment and be better able to recognize and react to threats by combining Splunk with a variety of Threat Intelligence Platforms.

Splunk Integration with Vulnerability Management Tools

Numerous advantages of integrating Splunk with Vulnerability Management Tools include improved threat detection and response capabilities, improved security posture, and effective management of vulnerabilities in the environment.

Integration Benefits with Vulnerability Management Tools

Some of the main advantages are:

- **Centralized visibility**: Security teams can centralize and correlate vulnerability data with other security information by integrating Vulnerability Management Tools with Splunk. This gives a more complete picture of the organization's security environment, which makes it simpler to pinpoint problems and order repair actions.
- **Improved risk assessment**: Organizations can better understand the risks they face by merging vulnerability data with other security information in Splunk. This makes it possible for security teams to prioritize vulnerabilities for remediation depending on the potential impact and threat level.
- **Simplified vulnerability management**: Organizations can automate and simplify their vulnerability management operations by integrating Splunk with Vulnerability Management Tools. Automating data collection and analysis, ranking vulnerabilities according to risk, and monitoring remedial efforts are all part of this.
- **Improved threat detection and response**: Organizations can improve their threat detection capabilities by identifying potential attack vectors and compromised assets by utilizing vulnerability data within Splunk. Since security teams can immediately evaluate the impact of a security event and take necessary action based on vulnerability information, this information can also be used to enhance incident response procedures.
- **Customization and automation**: By integrating Splunk with Vulnerability Management Tools, businesses may adapt their security analytics, vulnerability management, and incident response procedures to suit their particular requirements. On the basis of vulnerability data, this entails developing unique correlation rules, alerts, and automated actions.
- **Improved collaboration**: Integration with vulnerability management tools can help security teams and other stakeholders work together more effectively by enabling them to share knowledge, vulnerability information, and findings. This aids in creating a SOC that is more cohesive and effective.
- **Compliance and reporting:** By giving consolidated visibility into vulnerability data and remediation efforts, integrating Splunk with Vulnerability Management Tools can assist enterprises in demonstrating compliance with various industry standards and regulations. This can help in producing thorough reports for both internal and external audits.

Organizations may effectively manage vulnerabilities while enhancing threat detection and response capabilities by combining Splunk with Vulnerability Management Tools. This combines the strengths of both platforms and improves security posture.

Integration with Qualys

Leading suppliers of cloud-based security and compliance solutions, such as Qualys, include scanning online applications, managing vulnerabilities, and policy compliance. Organizations may improve their threat detection and response capabilities, gain more insight into their security environment, and streamline vulnerability management procedures by integrating Splunk with Qualys.

Steps for integration are as follows:

1. Splunkbase (https://splunkbase.splunk.com/app/3418/) offers the Qualys Technology Add-on (TA) for Splunk. Data gathering from the Qualys API and ingestion into Splunk are made possible by this add-on.
2. Configure the Qualys TA by giving it the required data, such as the Qualys API login credentials, the server configuration, and the proxy settings (if any).
3. Set up data inputs to gather Qualys data on assets, vulnerabilities, and policy compliance. The TA accepts a variety of input formats, including policy compliance scans, knowledge base searches, asset tagging, and vulnerability scans.
4. (Optional) Utilize Splunkbase to get the Qualys App for Splunk (https://splunkbase.splunk.com/app/3415/). For Qualys data in Splunk, this app offers pre-built dashboards, reports, and visualizations that make it easier for security teams to examine vulnerability data.
5. Create custom correlation rules, alerts, and dashboards for your organization's needs using the Qualys data in Splunk.

Integration with other Vulnerability Management Tools

To improve security analytics, threat detection, and response capabilities, Splunk may be linked with a number of different Vulnerability Management

Tools in addition to Qualys. These Vulnerability Management Tools include, among others:

- **Tenable SecurityCenter (Nessus)** is a complete vulnerability management system that comes with the well-known Nessus scanner.
- **Rapid7 InsightVM** (formerly Nexpose) is a potent vulnerability management tool that helps businesses to find, evaluate, and fix vulnerabilities.
- **OpenVAS (Greenbone Vulnerability Management)**: OpenVAS is a free and open-source vulnerability management program that provides extensive scanning and evaluation features.
- **Tripwire IP360:** Tripwire IP360 is a vulnerability and risk management tool that aids businesses in locating and repairing vulnerabilities throughout their environment.
- **Ivanti Patch for SCCM:** This vulnerability management tool works with Microsoft System Center Configuration Manager (SCCM) to help businesses find and fix vulnerabilities.

These are just a few instances of Vulnerability Management Tools that can be combined with Splunk to enhance the security environment of a business. Organizations may acquire a more complete understanding of their environment and improve their capacity to detect and respond to attacks while also managing vulnerabilities by combining Splunk with a variety of Vulnerability Management Tools.

Splunk Integration with Endpoint Security Solutions

Numerous advantages of integrating Splunk with endpoint security solutions include improved threat detection and response capabilities, improved security posture, and effective management of endpoint security.

Integration Benefits with Endpoint Security Solutions

Some of the key benefits include:

- **Increased visibility from a single location**: Integrating Endpoint Security Solutions with Splunk enables security teams to aggregate and link endpoint security data to other security data. This gives a complete picture of the security environment within the firm, making it simpler to spot hazards, identify threats, and organize remedial operations.

- **Improved threat detection**: Organizations can increase the effectiveness of their threat detection processes by merging endpoint security data with other security data in Splunk. Finding indicators of compromise (IOCs), odd behavioral patterns, and potentially malicious endpoint activity are all included in this.
- Splunk and Endpoint Security Solutions integration can aid security teams in prioritizing issues based on risk and streamlining the incident response procedure. To speed up investigations and get a more complete picture of security occurrences, analysts can examine and evaluate data from both platforms.
- **Data enrichment**: By integrating with endpoint security solutions, security teams may add more context to their Splunk data, such as endpoint status, user behavior, and process details. During the threat detection and response phase, this aids in better decision-making.
- **Personalization and automation**: By integrating Splunk with Endpoint Security Solutions, businesses may adapt their security analytics, threat detection, and incident response capabilities to suit their particular requirements. This entails developing customized correlation rules, use cases, and dashboards that are tailored to the needs and environment of the firm.
- **Improved collaboration**: Integrating with endpoint security solutions can help security teams and other stakeholders work together more effectively by enabling them to exchange information, data, and results. This aids in creating a security operations center (SOC) that is more cohesive and effective.
- **Proactive threat hunting**: By integrating with endpoint security solutions, security professionals may use the most recent endpoint security data to actively look for dangers in their environment. This assists organizations in identifying and reducing hazards before they have a chance to do serious harm.

Organizations may use the combined strength of Splunk and Endpoint Security Solutions to strengthen endpoint threat detection and response capabilities, increase environment visibility, and strengthen security posture.

Integration with CrowdStrike Falcon

Endpoint detection and response (EDR), threat hunting, and next-generation antivirus are all features of CrowdStrike Falcon, a cloud-native endpoint security system. Organizations may improve threat detection and response, streamline endpoint security management, and gain better visibility into their security landscape by integrating Splunk with CrowdStrike Falcon.

Steps for integration are as follows:

1. Download the CrowdStrike Falcon Splunk Add-on from Splunkbase at https://splunkbase.splunk.com/app/4379/. With the help of this add-on, Splunk may import data from the CrowdStrike Falcon API.
2. Set up the CrowdStrike Falcon Add-on by entering the required data, such as the CrowdStrike API credentials and server configuration.
3. Configure data inputs to get CrowdStrike Falcon detection, prevention, and reaction data. The add-on is compatible with a variety of input formats, including detection events, incidents, and device data.
4. (Optional) Splunkbase (https://splunkbase.splunk.com/app/4380) offers the CrowdStrike Falcon App for Splunk. This software makes it easier for security teams to examine endpoint security data in Splunk by offering pre-built dashboards, reports, and visualizations for CrowdStrike Falcon data.
5. Create custom correlation rules, alerts, and dashboards for your organization using the CrowdStrike Falcon data in Splunk.

Organizations may acquire a more complete understanding of their security environment, enhance threat detection and response capabilities, and effectively manage endpoint security in their environment by integrating Splunk with CrowdStrike Falcon.

Integration with other Endpoint Security Solutions

Splunk may be linked with a number of different endpoint security solutions in addition to CrowdStrike Falcon to improve security analytics, threat detection, and response capabilities. These Endpoint Security Solutions include, among others:

- **Carbon Black (VMware Carbon Black Cloud):** Carbon Black is a full-featured endpoint security program that includes advanced antivirus, EDR, and threat-hunting features.

- **Microsoft Defender for Endpoint (formerly Windows Defender ATP):** This enterprise-grade endpoint security tool offers sophisticated threat prevention, automated investigation and remediation, and threat intelligence.
- **Symantec Endpoint Security (Broadcom):** Symantec Endpoint Security is an all-encompassing endpoint security program that provides cutting-edge threat prevention, detection, and response capabilities.
- **Cisco AMP for Endpoints**: An endpoint security solution that offers enhanced malware prevention, EDR, and threat hunting capabilities is Cisco AMP for Endpoints.
- **Palo Alto Networks Cortex XDR:** Cortex XDR is a next-generation endpoint security solution with EDR, threat hunting, and next-generation antivirus features.

These are just a few instances of Endpoint Security Solutions that may be combined with Splunk to enhance the security environment of a company. Organizations may acquire a more complete understanding of their environment and improve their ability to detect and respond to threats while effectively managing endpoint protection by integrating Splunk with a variety of endpoint security solutions.

Splunk Integration with Network Security Tools

Numerous advantages of integrating Splunk with network security tools include improved threat detection and response capabilities, improved security posture, and effective network protection management.

Integration Benefits with Network Security Tools

Some of the key benefits include:

- **Centralized visibility**: Integrating Splunk with Network Security Tools enables security teams to centralize and compare network security data with other security-related data. This gives a more complete picture of the security environment within the firm, making it simpler to spot hazards, identify threats, and organize remedial operations.
- **Improved threat detection**: Organizations can enhance their threat detection capabilities by merging network security data with additional

security information in Splunk. Finding IOCs, odd behavioral patterns, and potentially malicious network activity are all included in this.

- **Improved incident response**: Security teams can prioritize issues based on risk by integrating Splunk with Network Security Tools, which will also speed up the incident response procedure. To speed up investigations and get a more complete picture of security occurrences, analysts can examine and evaluate data from both platforms.
- **Data enrichment:** Through the integration of Network Security Tools, security teams may add extra context to Splunk data by integrating it with logs from firewalls, intrusion detection systems (IDS), and network traffic. During the threat detection and response phase, this aids in better decision-making.
- **Personalization and automation**: By integrating Splunk with Network Security Tools, businesses may adapt their security analytics, threat detection, and incident response capabilities to suit their particular requirements. This entails developing customized correlation rules, use cases, and dashboards that are tailored to the needs and environment of the firm.
- **Improved collaboration:** Integration with Network Security Tools can help security teams and other stakeholders work together more effectively by enabling them to share information, data, and findings. This aids in creating a security operations center (SOC) that is more cohesive and effective.

Organizations may use the combined capability of Splunk and Network Security Tools to strengthen their security posture, get a better understanding of their environment, and increase threat detection and response capabilities at the network level.

Integration with Cisco Firepower

With its next-generation firewall (NGFW), intrusion prevention system (IPS), and sophisticated threat protection features, Cisco Firepower is a complete network security solution. Organizations may improve threat detection and response, centralize network security data, and have better visibility into their security environment by integrating Splunk with Cisco Firepower.

Steps for integration are as follows:

1. Download and install the Splunk Cisco Firepower eStreamer eNcore Add-on from Splunkbase (https://splunkbase.splunk.com/app/3662). With the help of this add-on, Splunk may import data from the Cisco Firepower eStreamer API.

2. Configure the Cisco Firepower eStreamer eNcore Add-on by entering the required data, such as SSL certificates and Cisco Firepower eStreamer server settings.

3. Configure data inputs to gather connection information, intrusion events, and security events from Cisco Firepower. Numerous input formats, such as intrusion events, connection events, and security intelligence events are supported by the add-on.

4. (Optional) Utilize Splunkbase to get the Cisco Firepower App for Splunk (https://splunkbase.splunk.com/app/3663). This software makes it easier for security teams to examine network security data in Splunk by offering pre-built dashboards, reports, and visualizations for Cisco Firepower data.

5. Create custom correlation rules, alerts, and dashboards using the Cisco Firepower data in Splunk that are suited to the needs of your company.

6. Organizations may acquire a more complete understanding of their security environment, enhance threat detection and response capabilities, and effectively manage network security in their environment by integrating Splunk with Cisco Firepower.

Integration with other Network Security Tools

Splunk may be linked with a variety of different network security tools in addition to Cisco Firepower to improve security analytics, threat detection, and response capabilities. These network security tools include, among others:

- **Palo Alto Networks**: Palo Alto Networks provides a range of network security products, such as advanced threat protection solutions, intrusion prevention systems, and next-generation firewalls (NGFWs).
- FortiGate firewalls, FortiSandbox advanced threat prevention, and FortiWeb web application firewalls are just a few of the network security products offered by Fortinet.
- **Check Point**: Check Point provides a range of network security solutions, such as NGFWs, IPS, and technologies for threat prevention.
- **Juniper Networks**: Juniper Networks offers a variety of network security products, including SRX firewalls, Sky Advanced Threat Prevention (ATP), and intrusion detection and prevention (IDP) systems.

- **F5 Networks**: F5 Networks provides a range of network security options, such as web application firewalls (WAF), DDoS protection, and application security.

These are just a few illustrations of Network Security Tools that can be combined with Splunk to enhance the security environment of a company. Organizations may acquire a more complete understanding of their environment and improve their ability to detect and respond to attacks while effectively managing network protection by combining Splunk with a variety of network security tools.

Case Studies

Here are three case studies illustrating successful integrations of Splunk with other security tools, showcasing its ability to enhance security operations, improve incident response capabilities, and streamline threat detection and mitigation.

- **Case Study: Technology Company**
  - **Problem**: A technology company faced challenges in correlating and analyzing data from multiple security tools, such as firewalls, intrusion detection systems (IDS), and endpoint protection platforms. This lack of a centralized view made it difficult for the security team to quickly detect and respond to threats.
  - **Solution**: The technology company integrated Splunk with its existing security tools, allowing it to collect and analyze data from multiple sources on a single platform. Splunk's integration with tools such as Palo Alto Networks, Cisco, and CrowdStrike provided the company with a unified view of its security landscape, enabling advanced threat detection, analytics, and incident response.
  - **Results:** The successful integration of Splunk with other security tools allowed the technology company to improve its threat detection and response capabilities significantly. The company experienced a reduction in false positives and increased efficiency in its security operations center (SOC), ultimately enhancing its overall security posture.
- **Case Study: E-commerce Company**
  - **Problem**: An e-commerce company experienced a growing number of cyberattacks targeting its web applications and customer data. The company needed a solution to help detect and respond to these threats more effectively.

  - **Solution**: The e-commerce company integrated Splunk with its existing security tools, such as web application firewalls (WAFs) and distributed denial-of-service (DDoS) protection services. This integration allowed the company to collect and analyze data from various sources in real-time, enabling rapid detection and response to potential threats.
  - **Results:** The successful integration of Splunk with other security tools significantly improved the e-commerce company's ability to detect and respond to cyberattacks targeting its web applications and customer data. The company experienced a reduction in the number of successful attacks and an improvement in its overall security posture.
- **Case Study: Manufacturing Company**
  - **Problem:** A manufacturing company faced challenges in securing its industrial control systems (ICS) and operational technology (OT) environments from cyber threats. The company needed a solution that could help detect and respond to potential threats quickly and efficiently.
  - **Solution**: The manufacturing company integrated Splunk with its existing security tools, such as Nozomi Networks for ICS/OT security monitoring and Fortinet for network security. This integration allowed the company to collect and analyze data from various sources in real-time, enabling rapid detection and response to potential threats targeting its ICS and OT environments.
  - **Results:** The successful integration of Splunk with other security tools significantly improved the manufacturing company's ability to detect and respond to cyber threats targeting its ICS and OT environments. The company experienced a reduction in the number of successful attacks and an improvement in its overall security posture.

Conclusion

The integration of Splunk with several security platforms, such as SIEMs, threat intelligence platforms, vulnerability management tools, endpoint security solutions, and network security tools, is covered in this chapter to show how it improves threat detection, incident response, and overall security operations. This chapter has illustrated the priceless advantages of using Splunk Add-ons and Apps, efficient correlation rules, and data normalization while also offering useful case study-based insights.

As we go on to *Chapter 10,Splunk for Compliance and Regulatory Requirements*, showing the broad possibilities of this powerful platform, we will concentrate more on how Splunk may be used to ensure that your business remains compliant with applicable laws and regulations.

Points to Remember

- By centralizing data and presenting a more thorough picture of the organization's security landscape, integrating Splunk with other security solutions improves security analytics, threat detection, and response capabilities.
- The advantages of integration vary depending on the individual category of security technology, such as SIEM systems, Threat Intelligence Platforms, Vulnerability Management Tools, Endpoint Security systems, and Network Security Tools. Benefits may include increased incident response, improved threat detection, simpler management, and data enrichment.
- Installation and configuration of the relevant Splunk applications or add-ons for the particular security tool constitute integration. These add-ons allow data to be ingested into Splunk from the appropriate security tool's APIs or data sources.
- After integration, security teams can design alerts, dashboards, and custom correlation rules that are specific to the needs of their organization. These tools make it easier to identify and address security issues.
- In order for the ingested data to be consistent, comprehensible, and easily connected with other security data in Splunk, data normalization and enrichment play a critical part in the integration process. In order to effectively identify and respond to security events, setting up alerts and notifications is a crucial component of integrating security technologies with Splunk.
- To fully utilize Splunk integration with other security solutions, it is essential to establish efficient correlation rules and use cases. It makes it simpler to spot dangers by recognizing patterns, correlations, and trends across a variety of data sources

CHAPTER 10

Splunk for Compliance and Regulatory Requirements

Introduction

The use of Splunk to assist enterprises in meeting compliance and regulatory standards in the sphere of cybersecurity is covered in this chapter. The necessity of compliance and regulatory standards, as well as how non-compliance can have negative legal and financial repercussions, are covered at the beginning of the chapter.

The following section of the chapter discusses the many compliance and regulatory regulations that firms may have to follow, such as GDPR, HIPAA, and PCI DSS. In the chapter, examples of how Splunk can assist enterprises in meeting these demands are also given, including log management and reporting.

The chapter also discusses the technical elements of regulatory and compliance requirements, such as audit trails and data retention regulations. The significance of access control and policy enforcement in compliance is also covered in this chapter.

This chapter explains the significance of meeting compliance and regulatory standards in the world of cybersecurity and how Splunk may assist enterprises in doing so.

Structure

In this chapter, we will cover the following topics:

- Introduction to Compliance and Regulatory Requirements
  - Importance of compliance and regulatory requirements in organizations
  - Common regulations and standards affecting businesses (for example, GDPR, HIPAA, PCI-DSS, SOX, and so on)
- Overview of Splunk for Compliance
  - Data Retention
  - Data Encryption
  - Monitoring and Reporting
  - Role-Based Access Control and Auditing
  - Incident Response and Remediation
- Continuous Improvement and Automation
  - Exploring popular Splunk apps for specific regulatory requirements
  - Splunk App for PCI Compliance
  - Splunk App for GDPR Compliance
  - Integrating third-party tools for additional compliance capabilities
- Leveraging machine learning and artificial intelligence to enhance compliance efforts
- Case Studies

Introducing Compliance and Regulatory Requirements

This section unveils how Splunk, a powerful technology, serves as a critical tool for organizations striving to align their data management, monitoring, and analysis processes with prevailing industry norms and legislative stipulations.

Importance of Compliance and Regulatory Requirements in Organizations

To retain their brand, safeguard sensitive data, and stay out of legal and financial trouble, firms across all industries must comply with regulatory regulations.

Following these guidelines enables businesses to protect the interests of their stakeholders–including clients, employees, and customers–while conducting business morally and responsibly. The following are some major justifications for the significance of compliance and regulatory requirements:

- **Legal repercussions:** Depending on how serious the infraction was, failure to comply with regulations can lead to hefty fines, penalties, and even criminal charges.
- **Business reputation**: Compliance shows a company's dedication to moral behavior and has a big impact on how well-liked it is by clients, partners, and investors.
- **Data protection**: Organizations can protect sensitive information by adhering to data protection regulations, which lowers the likelihood of data breaches and illegal access.
- **Improved operational effectiveness**: Compliance initiatives may result in the adoption of more effective and standardized procedures, which will enhance overall corporate operations.
- **Competitive advantage**: Companies that follow regulations are more likely to be trusted by clients and investors, giving them an advantage over rivals.

Common Regulations and Standards Affecting Businesses

Distinct sectors and areas are governed by distinct laws and norms. The following are some of the most typical regulations and standards affecting businesses:

- **The General Data Protection Regulation** (**GDPR**) is a law that was passed by the European Union to safeguard the privacy and personal information of its residents. No matter where a business is located, if it processes the personal data of EU citizens, it must comply.
- **Health Insurance Portability and Accountability Act** (**HIPAA**): The US law requires the security of patients' private health information. It covers healthcare providers, insurance companies, clearinghouses, and their commercial partners.
- **PCI-DSS**, or **Payment Card Industry Data Security Standard**, is a global standard for businesses that process credit card payments. It provides instructions on how to safeguard cardholder data and maintain a secure network infrastructure.
- **Sarbanes-Oxley Act** (**SOX**): This US law seeks to safeguard investors by enhancing the veracity and accuracy of business financial statements. It is applicable to all American publicly traded businesses.

- **The Personal Data Protection Act (PDPA)** in India is a framework created to safeguard people's private information. It sets rules for how businesses and government agencies must manage personal data, much like the GDPR. The PDPA establishes guidelines for handling sensitive personal data, processing, storing, and obtaining consent. Furthermore, it delineates the entitlements of persons about their personal data and enforces stringent guidelines for notifying data breaches.

Depending on their industry, location, and type of operations, firms must adhere to a wide range of regulations. These are just a few examples. Organizations can successfully and efficiently comply with these regulatory obligations by implementing the proper tools and procedures, such as Splunk.

Overview of Splunk for Compliance

A vital part of data-driven corporate operations is comprehending Splunk's position in upholding compliance. The numerous features of how Splunk complies with legal obligations and institutionalizes adherence to industry standards will be covered in this section. First, we'll look at *Data Retention*, with a particular emphasis on how Splunk helps with data storage and retrieval under relevant laws and regulations. We will then examine Splunk's features for protecting sensitive data to thwart illegal access under the heading *Data Encryption*. The *Monitoring and Reporting* subsection describes how Splunk enables real-time data surveillance, producing in-depth reports to support proactive compliance. We'll talk about how Splunk makes sure that only people with the right permissions may access certain data in the paragraph titled *Role-Based Access Control and Auditing*. At the same time, Splunk keeps a thorough audit trail. Last but not least, the section on *Incident Response and Remediation* will give you information about Splunk's effective procedures for handling potential security issues and resolving them, which is essential for preserving regulatory compliance.

Data Retention

Organizations must appropriately index, retain, and encrypt their data in order to stay in compliance with numerous rules. Splunk offers powerful data management tools that can be tailored to meet certain compliance needs:

- **Data retention**: With the help of Splunk, businesses may set up data retention guidelines depending on time, data quantity, and data type. This makes it possible for them to follow laws that impose time limits on how long data must be stored.

Indexer buckets are a notion used by Splunk to control data retention. Splunk organizes the data it receives into time-based indexer buckets that go through the hot, warm, cold, and frozen stages of their lifetime. Different performance traits and storage considerations apply to each stage.

Organizations can select two main settings for each index to configure data retention in Splunk:

- **Retention period**: The `frozenTimePeriodInSecs` parameter in the `indexes.conf` configuration file specifies the retention duration. The duration of data retention before it is deemed `frozen` and deleted from the index is determined by this parameter. The default setting for the value, which is set in seconds, is 188697600 seconds, or around six years.
- **Maximum size**: The `maxTotalDataSizeMB` parameter, which can also be found in the `indexes.conf` configuration file, specifies the largest possible size for an index. The maximum size of the index can be determined using this parameter. In order to make room for fresh data, Splunk begins rolling the oldest data to the frozen stage once this limit is reached.

These characteristics for each index can be altered by organizations to satisfy their unique data retention needs. For instance, they might have to keep log data for a shorter time in order to comply with legal obligations or conserve storage space. Organizations may efficiently manage their data storage, follow regulatory guidelines, and save storage expenses by defining data retention policies in Splunk.

Data Encryption

Splunk offers data encryption for both data at rest and data in transit in order to safeguard sensitive information. By doing this, data is protected both during storage and transmission within the system and between components.

Data Encryption at-Rest

Data at rest encryption, or the security of data saved on disk, is supported by Splunk. The methods listed below can be used by businesses to encrypt data in Splunk while it is at rest:

- **Filesystem-level encryption**: Organizations can encrypt every aspect of their Splunk deployment, including indexes, configuration files, and knowledge objects, by employing an encrypted filesystem, such as dmcrypt on Linux or BitLocker on Windows. By using this technique, the data saved on the underlying disk is guaranteed to be encrypted, guarding it against unauthorized access.

- **Index-level encryption**: In addition, Splunk offers a function called SmartStore that enables businesses to store indexed data remotely in cloud storage services like Amazon S3. Data can be encrypted when using SmartStore thanks to server-side encryption offered by the cloud storage provider. By doing this, it is made sure that indexed data is encrypted before it leaves the Splunk environment and that it is still encrypted while being kept in the remote storage.

Data Encryption in Transit

Data encryption in transit refers to the security of data as it travels over a network or between various system components. Splunk supports the following techniques for encryption in transit:

- **Secure Socket Layer (SSL) / Transport Layer Security (TLS)**: Splunk may encrypt data while it is being transmitted using SSL/TLS, a popular security protocol that ensures safe connection between various Splunk components, that is, forwarders, indexers, and search heads. To ensure that data is protected while it travels between different Splunk components or across networks, organizations can set up SSL/TLS for these components.
- **HTTPS for web-based communication**: HTTPS (HTTP over SSL/TLS) can be used to encrypt communication between users' web browsers and the Splunk server in Splunk Web, the web-based interface for Splunk. Sensitive data, including login credentials and search queries, are safeguarded during transmission as a result.

Organizations can effectively safeguard sensitive information from unauthorized access and meet compliance standards for data protection by deploying data encryption at rest and in transit.

Monitoring and Reporting

Organizations can use Splunk to monitor compliance-related events and produce reports to show that they are following regulations:

- **Data Aggregation and Real-Time Monitoring**: Splunk excels at collecting and indexing data from various sources, such as logs, server data, network devices, and more. This capability allows businesses to have a centralized view of their entire IT infrastructure. By providing real-time monitoring, Splunk helps in identifying potential compliance issues as they arise, enabling prompt responses.

- **Customizable Dashboards for Compliance Data**: Splunk offers customizable dashboards that can be tailored to display key compliance metrics and indicators. These dashboards can be configured to track specific compliance requirements relevant to regulations like GDPR, HIPAA, PCI-DSS, SOX, and PDPA. This visual representation aids in understanding the compliance posture at a glance and facilitates quick decision-making.
- **Alerts for Compliance Breaches**: One of the critical features of Splunk is setting up alerts for specific events that might indicate a compliance violation. These alerts can be configured to notify the relevant personnel immediately, ensuring that any potential breach is addressed swiftly to mitigate risks and possible penalties.
- Reporting and Auditing: Splunk's robust reporting features allow organizations to generate detailed reports on compliance-related activities and incidents. These reports can be used for internal auditing purposes or to demonstrate compliance with regulatory bodies. The ability to customize and automate reports saves time and resources while ensuring accuracy and consistency in compliance reporting.
- **Advanced Analytics and Forensics**: Splunk provides advanced analytics tools that can be used to delve deeper into compliance issues. It enables the investigation of incidents by tracing the root cause and understanding the impact. This forensic capability is crucial for resolving compliance breaches and preventing future occurrences.
- **Adaptable to Various Regulations**: Since Splunk is highly adaptable and can be configured to monitor various aspects of IT operations, it's well-suited to help businesses comply with different regulations. The flexibility to tailor its functionalities to specific regulatory requirements makes Splunk a versatile tool in the compliance arsenal of any business.

In summary, Splunk's ability to aggregate data, provide real-time monitoring, customizable dashboards, alerting mechanisms, detailed reporting, advanced analytics, and adaptability make it an invaluable asset for businesses looking to maintain compliance in an increasingly regulated world.

Case Study: JIT Inc. - Enhancing Compliance with Splunk

Background:

A fictitious international company called JIT Inc. works in the healthcare and banking industries. JIT Inc. has to deal with the problem of adhering to several standards, including GDPR, HIPAA, PCI-DSS, SOX, and India's PDPA, because of its varied range of operations that cover multiple nations, including the United States and India. Due to the intricacy and extent of these requirements, an effective method for tracking and reporting compliance-related events is needed.

Challenge:

Disjointed data monitoring systems caused JIT Inc. to suffer, which resulted in inefficiencies and possible compliance issues. The business required a way to effectively handle the reporting needs for various regulations, centralize its monitoring procedures, and provide real-time visibility into compliance status.

Splunk implementation:

JIT Inc. made the decision to put Splunk into use for its reporting and compliance monitoring requirements. The subsequent actions were performed:

- **Data Integration:** To gather and index compliance-related data, Splunk was combined with a number of data sources from around the company, including databases, network devices, and server logs.
- **Custom Dashboard Creation:** To give real-time insights into compliance status, custom dashboards were made for each regulatory requirement. For example, one dashboard tracked requests from data subjects and reports of breaches under GDPR, while another tracked access to protected health information (PHI) in order to monitor HIPAA compliance.
- **Alert Setup:** JIT Inc. set up Splunk to send out warnings in response to particular occurrences that would point to possible violations of compliance, like illegal access to private information or departures from accepted data processing practices.
- **Compliance Reporting:** To track audits, issues, and compliance-related actions, automated reports were put up. These reports were customized to meet the demands of various regulatory organizations.

Outcome:

- **Improved Real-Time Monitoring**: By identifying and addressing compliance concerns quickly, JIT Inc. was able to lower the risk of fines and reputational harm due to Splunk's real-time monitoring capabilities.
- **Better Compliance Posture**: JIT Inc. was able to manage compliance risks pro-actively thanks to the customized dashboards, which gave them a clear picture of their compliance posture across several legislations.
- **Effective Incident Response:** By enabling prompt reaction to possible violations of compliance, the warning system reduced risks and made sure that problems were resolved on time.

- **Streamlined Reporting**: JIT Inc. was able to effectively satisfy the reporting needs of multiple regulatory authorities, guaranteeing accountability and openness, thanks to automated, customized reporting.

JIT Inc. greatly enhanced its capacity to track, log, and handle compliance-related events across several regulatory frameworks by putting Splunk into practice. This case study highlights how well Splunk works to provide a centralized, effective, and flexible compliance management solution in a complicated, multi-regulatory setting.

Role-based Access Control and Auditing

For many compliance needs, it's essential to implement appropriate access restrictions and keep thorough audit logs. Splunk provides tools that enable businesses to efficiently manage system access and audits, including:

- **Role-based access control**: Role-based access control (RBAC) is a technology that Splunk enables enterprises to use to restrict access to sensitive data and guarantee that only authorized workers can view or edit particular information.
- **Auditing**: Splunk gives enterprises the ability to audit user activity, system configurations, and modifications, which can help them monitor and document their compliance efforts.

By giving particular permissions to various user roles, RBAC in Splunk enables enterprises to restrict access to critical data and system capabilities. Contrarily, auditing enables businesses to monitor user actions and system modifications, assisting them in maintaining a secure environment and satisfying compliance standards. The actions to establish RBAC and audits in Splunk are as follows:

Creating and Defining User Roles

- Determine the various user roles necessary, such as administrators, power users, and general users, by assessing the needs of your organization.
- In the Splunk Web interface, select **`Settings`** > **`Access Controls`**.
- To create a unique role, select **`Roles`** and click **`New Role`**.
- If necessary, adjust the role settings, such as the role name, description, and inheritance from existing roles.
- Give each role the necessary permissions, such as the ability to search, modify, remove, or manage settings.

Assigning Users to Roles

- Select **Settings** > **Access Controls** from the Splunk Web interface.
- Click **New User** under **Users** to add a new user or change an existing one.
- Set up the user preferences, such as the username, password, and email.
- Based on the user's duties inside the organization, assign the appropriate position or roles to them.

Configuring Access to Data and Objects

- Limit access to data by giving each role access to only certain indexes.
- Set permissions for each knowledge item, giving read and/or write access for particular roles, to manage access to knowledge objects (such as saved searches, dashboards, and alerts).

Enabling Auditing

- User activities, system changes, and configuration modifications are all captured in the internal logs that Splunk automatically creates.
- Establish and set up a specific index for internal audit data in order to keep track of these records.
- Create a data input to feed the specialized audit index using Splunk's internal logs (_internal index).

Monitoring and Reviewing Audit Data

- Build personalized dashboards, alerts, and searches to track and view audit data in real time.
- Regularly examine audit data to spot any shady behavior or security lapses.

These methods will help firms install Splunk's RBAC and audits efficiently, ensuring that users have access to only the information and system features they require. By doing so, a secure environment is maintained, and compliance standards for data access and user activity tracking are met.

Incident Response and Remediation

Splunk can facilitate faster identification, investigation, and remediation of security incidents and compliance violations:

- **Detecting and responding to security incidents**: With its powerful search and analytics capabilities, Splunk enables organizations to quickly identify potential security incidents or compliance breaches.

- **Managing incident investigations and remediation efforts**: Splunk can assist in managing investigations by providing insights into the root cause of incidents and streamlining the remediation process.

Continuous Improvement and Automation

Organizations can use Splunk's automation tools, machine learning, and artificial intelligence capabilities to further their compliance efforts.

- **Machine learning and AI**: Organizations may use Splunk's machine learning- and AI-driven capabilities to find patterns, outliers, and trends in their data, which can help them develop and refine their compliance management strategies.
- **Automation**: Splunk can automate repetitive compliance-related tasks and procedures, saving businesses time and money while lowering the risk of human error.

In conclusion, Splunk is a useful tool for businesses trying to manage and uphold compliance with a range of legal standards. Organizations can efficiently satisfy their compliance needs and lower the risk of non-compliance because of its comprehensive data management, monitoring, reporting, and automation capabilities.

Exploring popular Splunk apps specific regulatory requirements

Splunk provides a wide range of apps and add-ons to assist businesses in adhering to various regulatory standards. These add-ons and apps frequently include pre-built dashboards, reports, and alarms that are customized to a specific rule or standard. Several well-liked Splunk add-ons and applications for particular regulatory requirements include:

- Splunk App for PCI Compliance
- Splunk App for GDPR
- Splunk Add-on for NIST Compliance

These are just a few examples of the many Splunk apps and add-ons available for specific regulatory requirements. By leveraging these tools, organizations can streamline their compliance management efforts, easily monitor their environment for potential violations, and generate compliance reports for auditing and documentation purposes.

These are just a few of the numerous Splunk add-ons and apps that are available for particular regulatory requirements. Utilizing these solutions enables firms to automate compliance management processes, quickly keep an eye on any infractions in their environment, and provide compliance reports for auditing and documentation needs.

Splunk App for PCI Compliance

To monitor and uphold compliance with the Payment Card Industry Data Security Standard (PCI DSS), enterprises can use the full Splunk App for PCI Compliance. All firms that store, handle, or transport cardholder data must adhere to the PCI DSS security standards in order to do so.

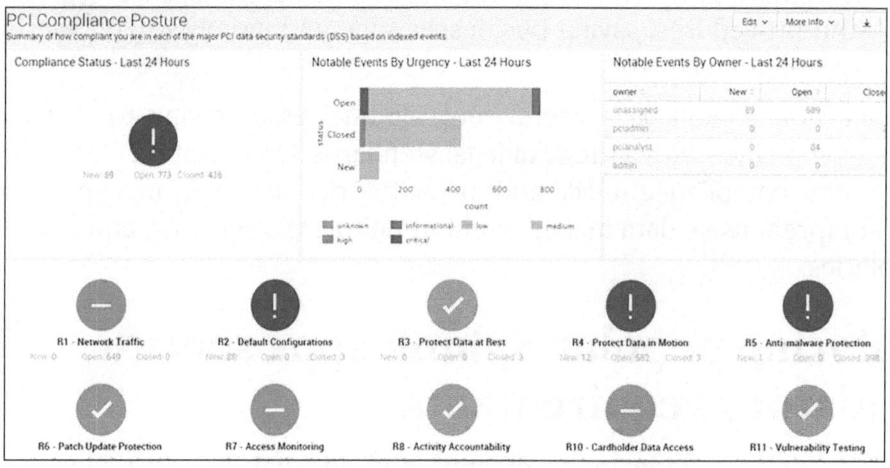

Figure 10.1: *Splunk app for PCI compliance (source: Splunk App for PCI Compliance - Splunk Enterprise Security | Splunkbase. (n.d.). Splunk App for PCI Compliance - Splunk Enterprise Security | Splunkbase. https://classic.splunkbase.splunk.com/app/2897/*

Key Features of the Splunk App for PCI Compliance are:

- **Pre-built Dashboards and Panels**: The app includes a number of pre-built dashboards and panels that offer real-time visibility into an organization's cardholder data environment's (CDE) security posture. The user access, network traffic, vulnerabilities, and security events are just a few of the PCI DSS topics that are covered by these dashboards.
- **Continuous Monitoring and Reporting**: The Splunk App for PCI Compliance provides automated reporting and continuous monitoring features that let businesses monitor and report on their PCI compliance

levels. The program provides PCI DSS-compliant reports, streamlining the documentation process and making it simpler for enterprises to prove compliance to auditors.

- **Predefined Searches and notifications**: The app comes with predefined searches and notifications to assist enterprises in identifying potential security incidents, policy violations, or other events that may have an influence on their PCI compliance status. These alerts can be tailored to a company's unique requirements and set up to deliver notifications via email or other channels of communication.
- **Splunk Enterprise Security integration**: This Security Information and Event Management (SIEM) tool's Splunk App for PCI Compliance is fully integrated with Splunk Enterprise Security (ES). Through this integration, businesses may use Splunk ES's threat intelligence, risk assessment, and incident response features to strengthen their PCI compliance initiatives.
- **Customization and Extensibility**: The Splunk App for PCI Compliance is built on the Splunk platform, which enables customization and extensibility. Organizations have the option of customizing the app to meet their particular needs, building their own dashboards and reports, or even building their own apps and add-ons to handle particular PCI DSS controls.

Organizations may discover potential risks and vulnerabilities, get a complete picture of their PCI DSS compliance status, and automate the creation of compliance reports by using the Splunk App for PCI Compliance. In the end, this aids businesses in minimizing the time and effort needed to maintain PCI DSS compliance, lowering the risk of data breaches, and avoiding exorbitant fines and penalties for non-compliance.

Splunk App for GDPR Compliance

The Splunk App for GDPR is intended to assist enterprises in adhering to the General Data Protection Regulation (GDPR) of the European Union. Aiming to safeguard the personal information of EU citizens and residents as well as provide them with more choice over how their data is used, GDPR is a comprehensive data privacy policy. The Splunk App for GDPR offers crucial resources and tools to track, document, and uphold compliance with the law.

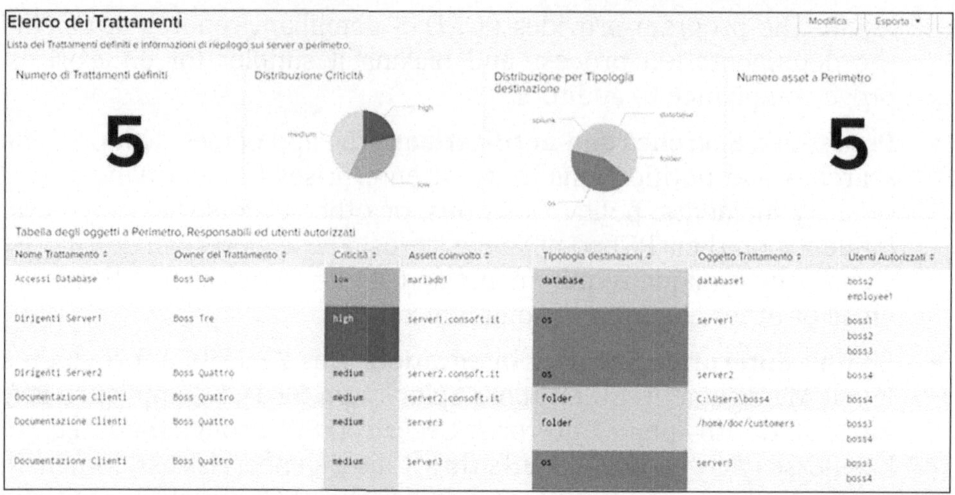

Figure 10.2: *Splunk app for GDPR compliance (source: Compliance GDPR | Splunkbase. (n.d.). Compliance GDPR | Splunkbase. https://apps.splunk.com/app/4281/)*

This app is made to specifically meet the requirements of businesses that must abide by the GDPR. The following list of features and functions are included in the app:

- **Comprehensive Monitoring of Perimeter System Access**: The software enables businesses to keep track of every user who accesses their perimeter systems, which can include servers, databases, files, and documents. With the aid of this thorough monitoring, it is possible to spot illegal access, potential data breaches, and other security issues that can jeopardize GDPR compliance.
- **Integrity and intransigence Verification of Collected Data**: The app verifies that collected data is accurate and unaltered, making it appropriate for use as evidence in the event of a GDPR audit or investigation. Organizations can have peace of mind knowing that their data is correct and unchangeable, thanks to this functionality.
- **Integration with Records of Processing Activities**: The app interfaces with an organization's records of processing activities to give users a comprehensive overview of all data processing activities and the degree to which they are GDPR compliant. Organizations now find it simpler to monitor and control their data processing activities in accordance with GDPR rules, thanks to this integration.
- **Correlation of Access Information with Processing Activity Records**: Using the software, businesses may compare access data to their processing activity records. This capability aids in the quick resolution of compliance issues by assisting in the identification of potentially non-compliant data processing processes or unlawful access to personal data.

- **Extensive Log Management**: The app's extensive log management features let businesses gather, examine, and archive all the data pertaining to a GDPR infringement. With the use of this tool, companies can better understand security incidents, identify their underlying causes, and take the necessary precautions to avoid similar incidents in the future.
- **Flexible and Customizable Reporting for Compliance**: The app offers a variety of flexible and customizable reporting options that are designed to be GDPR compliant. Reports can be produced by organizations to indicate their GDPR compliance status, evaluate the efficiency of their data protection measures, and demonstrate their dedication to data privacy.

For businesses wishing to handle the difficulties of GDPR compliance, Consoft Sistemi's Splunk App for GDPR Compliance provides an all-encompassing solution. The app assists organizations in maintaining GDPR compliance, reducing the risk of non-compliance fines, and protecting the personal data of their clients and users by combining robust monitoring capabilities, data integrity verification, integration with processing activity records, and customizable reporting.

Integrating third-party tools for additional compliance capabilities

An organization's compliance capabilities can be improved, and a more complete compliance management solution can be delivered, by integrating third-party products with Splunk. Organizations can make use of these connectors to combine Splunk's strong data analytics and visualization capabilities with extra features provided by third-party technologies. Several well-liked integrations for compliance consist of:

- **Tools for Identity and Access Management (IAM)**: IAM systems like Okta, Microsoft Azure Active Directory, or OneLogin can be integrated with Splunk to enable enterprises to track and manage user access to critical data and resources in real time. This is especially helpful for complying with laws like GDPR, HIPAA, and PCI DSS that demand stringent access restrictions and auditing.
- **Data Loss Prevention (DLP) solutions**: Organizations may monitor and stop unwanted access or data leakage by combining Splunk with DLP systems like Symantec DLP, Forcepoint, or Digital Guardian. With the use of these interfaces, enterprises may identify potential compliance violations and take corrective action before any data breaches happen.
- **Tools for managing vulnerabilities**: Organizations may find and fix security flaws in their infrastructure by integrating Splunk with solutions

for managing vulnerabilities like Qualys, Tenable, or Rapid7. This is necessary to stay in compliance with the numerous laws that call for frequent vulnerability assessments and repairs.

- **Endpoint Detection and Response Solutions**: Splunk can be linked with EDR technologies like CrowdStrike, Carbon Black, or SentinelOne to detect and address security threats on endpoints. Endpoint Detection and Response (EDR) solutions. With real-time threat detection and incident response capabilities required by regulations, this can assist firms in staying in compliance.
- **Governance, Risk, and Compliance (GRC) systems**: Organizations can consolidate their compliance efforts and streamline the administration of risks, rules, and controls throughout their environment by connecting Splunk with GRC solutions like ServiceNow GRC, RSA Archer, or MetricStream.
- **Security Orchestration, Automation, and Response (SOAR) tools**: To automate and orchestrate incident response tasks, Splunk can be linked with SOAR systems such as Splunk Phantom, Palo Alto Networks Cortex XSOAR, or IBM Resilient. As a result, firms may respond to issues involving compliance more quickly and with fewer negative effects.
- Organizations can use pre-built add-ons or create bespoke integrations utilizing Splunk's REST API and SDKs to integrate external technologies with the search engine. The advantages of numerous solutions are combined through these interfaces to build a comprehensive compliance management ecosystem that enables businesses to more efficiently monitor, manage, and uphold compliance with a variety of standards.

Leveraging Machine Learning and Artificial Intelligence to Enhance Compliance Efforts

By automating data analysis, seeing trends and abnormalities, and forecasting future hazards, machine learning (ML) can dramatically enhance an organization's compliance efforts. An illustration of how machine learning can be used to help enforce compliance with a particular legislation, such as the General Data Protection legislation (GDPR), is provided below:

Step 1: Define the compliance goal

Identify the specific GDPR compliance obligations that the firm needs to pay attention to, such as tracking user access to personal data, spotting potential data breaches, and making sure data subject access requests (DSARs) are handled promptly.

Step 2: Gather and prepare the data

Pre-process the data by cleaning, converting, and aggregating it to make it acceptable for machine learning analysis by gathering relevant data from multiple sources within the enterprise, such as logs, databases, and apps.

Step 3: Pick the best machine learning algorithms

Select suitable ML techniques that can assist in achieving the specified compliance objectives. The handling of DSARs can be automated with the use of natural language processing (NLP) algorithms, clustering algorithms, anomaly detection algorithms, and other techniques. For instance, clustering methods can be used to spot trends in user access.

Step 4: Train and verify the ML models

Utilize the pre-processed data to train the chosen ML models, and then use a different dataset to confirm their effectiveness. Adjust the models as needed to maximize performance and guarantee precise forecasts.

Step 5: Include ML models in the workflow for compliance

Utilize tools like the Splunk Machine Learning Toolkit (MLTK) to integrate the learned ML models into the organization's compliance workflow. To monitor the real-time outputs of the ML models and set up alerts and warnings for potential compliance issues, bespoke dashboards, and visualizations may be created.

Step 6: Automate corrective measures

To automate the execution of remediation steps in response to compliance-related issues, combine the ML-powered compliance monitoring with automation tools like Security Orchestration, Automation, and Response (SOAR) platforms. This can ensure a prompt response and lessen the effect of potential infringement.

Step 7: Keep track of, assess, and improve the ML models

Keep an eye on the ML models' performance, assess how well they achieve the compliance goals, and make adjustments as necessary. This can entail updating the models to reflect changes in the regulatory environment or retraining the models with fresh data.

By automating data analysis, spotting patterns and abnormalities in user access to personal data, identifying potential data breaches, and automating the response to DSARs, machine learning is used in this case to enforce GDPR compliance. The firm may greatly enhance its GDPR compliance efforts, lower the risk of non-compliance fines, and safeguard the personal information of its users and customers by incorporating ML models into its compliance workflow and automating remediation steps.

Case Studies

- **Financial Services Organization**: A large financial services organization used Splunk to automate the monitoring and reporting of their PCI DSS compliance efforts. By leveraging Splunk's data analytics capabilities and pre-built PCI DSS dashboards, the organization gained real-time visibility into their cardholder data environment and was able to quickly identify and remediate potential issues, ultimately reducing the risk of non-compliance and data breaches.
- **Healthcare Provider**: A healthcare provider implemented Splunk to meet HIPAA compliance requirements by monitoring access to protected health information (PHI) and ensuring the confidentiality, integrity, and availability of PHI. Using Splunk, the organization was able to detect unauthorized access to PHI, identify potential data breaches, and generate compliance reports for auditing purposes.
- **Government Contractor**: A government contractor leveraged Splunk to comply with NIST 800-171 requirements by monitoring the security of controlled unclassified information (CUI) in their non-federal systems. With Splunk's NIST Compliance add-on and custom visualizations, the contractor gained real-time insights into their security posture, identified vulnerabilities, and ensured the proper implementation of required security controls.

These case studies demonstrate how organizations across various industries can leverage Splunk's powerful data analytics capabilities, pre-built apps and add-ons, and integration options to meet their compliance and regulatory requirements more efficiently and effectively.

Conclusion

We have explored many aspects of how Splunk navigates the intricate web of regulatory requirements throughout this chapter. We began with a summary of these complex standards before moving on to a thorough analysis of Splunk's contribution to maintaining compliance, covering details like data retention, encryption, monitoring, role-based access control, and incident response. We also looked at how continuous improvement, automation, and the use of machine learning and artificial intelligence could be used to boost the effectiveness of compliance initiatives. Case studies provided real-world illustrations of Splunk's capabilities in this area, which supplemented our conversation. As this chapter comes to a conclusion, it should be clear that Splunk is more than simply a tool; it also serves as a strategic partner in improving and strengthening an organization's compliance posture.

In the following chapter, *Security Orchestration, Automation, and Response* (SOAR) *with Splunk*, we will examine how these Splunk features work together as a single entity to combat security threats, orchestrating, automating, and responding to security incidents, ensuring a resilient and effective defense against potential vulnerabilities.

Points to Remember

- Recognize the particular rules and requirements that apply to your organization.
- Gather and compile information about compliance from multiple sources.
- Implement encryption and data retention rules in Splunk.
- Configure audits and role-based access control.
- Design unique dashboards and visualizations for monitoring compliance in real time.
- Set up notifications and alerts for compliance-related occurrences.
- Produce current compliance reports with Splunk.
- Integrate Splunk with external products like SOAR platforms, EDR, GRC, vulnerability management, IAM, DLP, and DLP.
- Use Splunk's machine learning and artificial intelligence features to analyze data automatically and forecast risks.
- To adjust to changes in the regulatory environment, you should constantly evaluate and improve your Splunk compliance setup.

CHAPTER 11

Security Orchestration, Automation and Response (SOAR) with Splunk

Introduction

This chapter offers a thorough overview of integrating Splunk, a top platform for security operations, with Security Orchestration, Automation, and Response (SOAR). We will examine Splunk's involvement in SOAR operations and how it supports these activities through a variety of capabilities and integrations. We will also examine the essential elements and features of a SOAR platform.

We go into the fundamentals of Splunk SOAR, covering its introduction, salient characteristics, advantages, and use. In addition to providing examples of orchestrating and automating security processes using Splunk SOAR and its interactions with third-party technologies, this chapter emphasizes the use of playbooks in streamlining security operations.

With interfaces with Microsoft Office 365, Carbon Black Response, Tenable, ThreatConnect, Cuckoo Sandbox, ServiceNow, and Jira, among others, the chapter discusses real-world use cases of security orchestration, automation, and incident management with Splunk SOAR. These examples show how Splunk SOAR may be used to tackle numerous security concerns, from vulnerability monitoring and patching to endpoint detection and response (EDR) and phishing incident response.

The chapter concludes with recommended practices for implementing SOAR with Splunk, highlighting the significance of determining how prepared your organization is for SOAR, creating a cross-functional SOAR team, and spending money on SOAR analyst training and skill development.

The principles, elements, and real-world implementations of SOAR with Splunk will be thoroughly understood by the readers by the end of this chapter, enabling them to make use of the platform for improved security operations in their businesses.

Structure

In this chapter, we will cover the following topics:

- Introduction to Security Orchestration, Automation, and Response (SOAR)
    - Definition and importance of SOAR
    - The role of SOAR in improving security operations
    - Key components and functions of a SOAR platform
- Splunk's role in SOAR operations
    - How Splunk supports SOAR operations with its various features and integrations
- Splunk SOAR: Streamlining security operations
    - Introduction to Splunk SOAR
    - Key features of Splunk SOAR
    - Splunk SOAR Playbooks
    - Benefits of Splunk SOAR
    - Implementing Splunk SOAR
- Security orchestration with Splunk SOAR
    - Phishing incident response with Splunk add-on for Microsoft Office 365
    - EDR with Splunk Add-on for Carbon
    - Vulnerability management and patching with Splunk add-on for Tenable

- Security automation with Splunk SOAR
  - Threat intelligence enrichment with Splunk add-on for ThreatConnect
  - Malware analysis with Splunk Add-on for Cuckoo Sandbox
- Incident management with Splunk SOAR
  - Incident response with Splunk SOAR and ServiceNow add-on
  - Incident management with Splunk SOAR and Jira integration
- Additional important tool integrations with Splunk SOAR
- Case studies
- Best practices for implementing SOAR with Splunk
  - Assessing your organization's readiness for SOAR
  - Building a cross-functional SOAR team
  - Training and skill development for SOAR analysts

Introduction to Security Orchestration, Automation, and Response (SOAR)

This section provides a comprehensive introduction to this state-of-the-art security technology and emphasizes how vital a role it plays in enhancing security operations. As we embark on this journey through the sophisticated landscape of cybersecurity, we'll commence by understanding the 'Definition and Importance of SOAR.' This will set the stage for comprehending why SOAR has become an integral part of modern security strategies. Subsequently, we will delve into *The Role of SOAR in Improving Security Operations*, exploring how this technology has been transforming and fortifying the realm of cybersecurity. The section will conclude with an exploration of the 'Key Components and Functions of a SOAR Platform,' providing a comprehensive overview of the individual elements that constitute a SOAR solution and their functions. As we navigate through each subsection, we aim to build a robust understanding of SOAR and its crucial role in orchestrating, automating, and enhancing security operations.

Definition and Importance of SOAR

By integrating numerous security tools and automating routine processes, the Security Orchestration, Automation, and Response (SOAR) method aids enterprises in streamlining and enhancing their security operations. SOAR platforms orchestrate workflows, automate procedures, and offer a centralized platform for incident response, enabling security teams to manage, respond to, and mitigate security issues effectively.

In its capacity to increase the effectiveness and efficiency of security operations, SOAR is crucial. Security teams are faced with an overwhelming amount of data and warnings as cyber threats continue to increase in quantity and sophistication. SOAR solutions assist enterprises in overcoming this difficulty by:

- Improving collaboration among security team members
- Reducing manual, repetitive activities for security analysts
- Speeding up incident response times
- Giving a comprehensive picture of the security posture of the firm

Figure 11.1: *SOAR in Splunk (source: H. (2023, March 13). Splunk SOAR Managed Services - Hurricane Labs. Hurricane Labs. https://hurricanelabs.com/splunk-soar/)*

Incorporating the SOAR Maturity Model

Knowing SOAR's Maturity Model is essential to putting it into practice. This approach helps businesses move toward more advanced phases of SOAR adoption by giving them a framework to evaluate their present SOAR deployment. Typically, the SOAR Maturity Model comprises phases, such as:

- **First Implementation**: Companies begin by automating basic, repetitive operations and integrating a small number of security products.
- **Developing Proficiency**: At this point, more intricate automation and orchestration procedures are implemented, along with a wider integration of security solutions.
- **Advanced Automation**: In this scenario, companies make use of sophisticated incident response automation and threat intelligence integration, among other advanced SOAR capabilities.

- **Proactive Security Operations**: At the most advanced stage, businesses go beyond reactive security measures by utilizing SOAR for proactive threat hunting and predictive analytics.

Organizations can gradually optimize their security operations and maximize the advantages of SOAR solutions in their particular security settings by comprehending and navigating through these stages of the SOAR Maturity Model.

Role of SOAR in Improving Security Operations

By focusing on the following areas, SOAR plays a key role in boosting security operations:

- **Orchestration**: SOAR platforms assist businesses in integrating a variety of security tools and systems, speeding workflows and enhancing communication amongst security solutions. Security teams can respond to threats more quickly and effectively as a result.
- **Automation**: SOAR solutions can perform specified activities or playbooks in response to particular triggers, like as alerts or issues, using automation. Security analysts will have less work to do as a result, freeing them up to concentrate on important jobs and more strategic projects.
- **Response**: SOAR solutions give security teams the tools they need to respond rapidly to incidents by centralizing incident management and response capabilities. As a result, security issues are resolved more quickly, and the risk of damage is reduced.

Insights from the 2023 Gartner® Market Guide for SOAR Solutions

Important information about how the security, orchestration, automation, and response (SOAR) market is changing can be found in the 2023 Gartner® Market Guide for SOAR Solutions. A few important lessons learned are:

- **Trends in SOAR Adoption:** In an ever-changing threat landscape, enterprises are increasingly turning to SOAR solutions to strengthen their security posture. This is highlighted in the handbook.
- **Emerging Technologies:** AI integration, machine learning, and advanced analytics are just a few of the features and technologies covered in this research that are becoming essential to combating sophisticated cyber threats.

- **Best Practices:** The Gartner report offers best practices for putting SOAR solutions into effect, stressing the significance of coordinating SOAR projects with more general security plans and corporate goals.
- **Vendor Evaluation:** The guide also offers evaluation guidelines for SOAR suppliers, emphasizing the significance of selecting solutions that are most appropriate for the operational environment and unique security requirements of an organization.

Key Components and Functions of a SOAR platform

Typically, a SOAR platform has the following essential elements and capabilities:

- **API support and integration**: SOAR platforms should be able to integrate with a variety of security solutions, including SIEM, endpoint security, threat intelligence platforms, and more. This makes it possible for various security systems to seamlessly share and interact with data.
- **Playbook and workflow management:** SOAR solutions ought to provide a library of programmable playbooks and workflows to automate and coordinate a range of security functions, including alarm triage, forensic data gathering, and the launching of corrective measures.
- **Automation engine**: The automation engine is in charge of carrying out automatic tasks in accordance with preset triggers and regulations. It ought to be adaptable and extendable so that businesses can build special automation to meet their own needs.
- **Incident management:** SOAR solutions ought to offer thorough incident management features, such as incident tracking, prioritizing, and collaboration tools. This aids in the rapid management and response to occurrences by security staff.
- Reporting and analytics: SOAR solutions ought to include strong reporting and analytics capabilities that let businesses assess the success of their security operations, spot trends, and constantly strengthen their security posture.

In conclusion, SOAR is a critical part of contemporary security operations, assisting businesses in streamlining processes, automating time-consuming procedures, and enhancing overall security incident management. Organizations can improve their capacity to recognize, respond to, and mitigate cyber risks more quickly and effectively by using a SOAR platform.

Splunk's Role in SOAR Operations

Splunk supports SOAR operations significantly while being largely renowned for its log management and data analytics capabilities. Splunk's features and integrations can be used to improve security posture and streamline security operations for enterprises.

How Splunk supports SOAR operations with its various features and integrations

Splunk's contribution to SOAR in key areas is as follows:

- **Data collection and analysis**: Splunk gathers and analyzes data from a variety of sources, including security tools, network gadgets, and applications, to present a thorough picture of a company's security landscape. This makes it possible for security professionals to spot patterns, identify dangers, and gather insightful information about prospective security issues.
- **Integrations with third-party security tools**: Splunk provides connectors with a wide range of security platforms and solutions, including SIEM, endpoint security, threat intelligence feeds, and others. Through these integrations, security teams can improve the efficiency of their current security solutions by utilizing Splunk's data analytics capabilities.
- **Adaptive Response Framework**: Security teams can develop automatic responses to particular triggers or situations using Splunk's Adaptive Response Framework (ARF). With the help of this platform, businesses can create unique workflows and automate security procedures, which speed up incident response and minimize manual intervention.
- **Splunk SOAR**: An extension of Splunk's SOAR capabilities, Splunk SOAR is a security automation and orchestration platform. In order to assist enterprises in more efficiently automating and orchestrating their security activities, it offers a wide range of functions, such as playbook creation, automation, and incident management.

Splunk SOAR: Streamlining Security Operations

The Security Orchestration, Automation, and Response solution from Splunk will be covered in this part as a crucial tool for streamlining and bolstering organizational security frameworks. We start with an Introduction to Splunk

SOAR, which describes the platform's features and how they fit into the larger Splunk ecosystem. The *Key Features of Splunk* SOAR, which makes it a potent asset in any cybersecurity strategy, will next be closely examined. Then, we'll delve deeper into *Splunk* SOAR *Playbooks*, investigating how these pre-built routines improve security operations efficiency. Next, we'll explore the 'Benefits of Splunk SOAR,' highlighting its key benefits and the value it provides for businesses. In order to help those wishing to incorporate this potent technology into their own security operations, we'll also give a guide on *Implementing Splunk* SOAR. Each section strives to provide you with a comprehensive overview of the SOAR solution from Splunk and its revolutionary effects on cybersecurity operations.

Introduction to Splunk SOAR

The SOAR platform Splunk SOAR, formerly known as Phantom, enables businesses to orchestrate and automate their security operations. Organizations may boost their overall security posture, accelerate response times to security issues, and increase the effectiveness of their security teams by utilizing Splunk SOAR. The main attributes and advantages of Splunk SOAR will be covered in this chapter, along with information on how to utilize and apply it.

Key Features of Splunk SOAR

Splunk SOAR provides a range of features to improve security operations, including:

- **Orchestration:** With the powerful orchestration features offered by Splunk SOAR, integrating different security products within an IT ecosystem is made easy. This function ensures that all parts function together by assisting in the coordination of actions across various platforms. Splunk SOAR's orchestration feature functions as a conductor, coordinating various security tools–from firewalls to endpoint security–to ensure that they are all operating effectively and simultaneously.
- **Automation:** One of Splunk SOAR's most notable advantages is its ability to automate tasks. Using playbooks enables security teams to automate tedious and repetitive operations. The mean time to detect (MTTD) and respond (MTTR) to incidents can be greatly decreased by using these playbooks, which can quickly carry out a sequence of activities in response to particular triggers. Because of the automation editor's ease of use, analysts may quickly construct and alter playbooks to meet their needs.
- **Event and Alert Management:** When it comes to organizing and arranging incoming notifications, Splunk SOAR is exceptional. It guarantees high

efficiency and accuracy by automating the research process. This feature makes it possible to manage a high amount of warnings effectively, allowing security professionals to concentrate on the most important problems.

- **Integration of Threat Intelligence:** Splunk SOAR interfaces with multiple sources of threat intelligence, giving security professionals the most recent details about new dangers. Scoring options are included in this integration to assist analysts in prioritizing and concentrating on the most pertinent intelligence.
- **Case Management and Cooperation:** The platform enables cross-security team cooperation and provides thorough case management. It makes it possible to combine and escalate several alerts or events into a single case, which expedites the incident response procedure and enhances team communication.
- **Metrics and Reporting:** Splunk SOAR offers comprehensive reporting and metrics functions that are necessary to assess the efficiency of security operations and pinpoint areas in need of development. The ROI of the SOAR implementation can be calculated with the use of these insights.
- **Mobility:** Splunk SOAR provides mobile functionalities in recognition of the necessity for on-the-go access. These functionalities enable analysts to engage with the platform, execute playbooks, and react to incidents straight from their mobile devices.
- **Scalability:** Splunk SOAR expands with an organization's size. It can handle growing workloads and escalating operational needs by supporting both vertical and horizontal scaling.
- **Open and extensible:** Splunk SOAR's open architecture makes it simple to add new security scenarios, products, actions, and playbooks, guaranteeing that it can be adjusted to meet changing security requirements.
- **Community-Powered:** Splunk SOAR promotes an open ecosystem for app development by supporting a community-driven model. This strategy guarantees that the platform can adjust to evolving technologies without interfering with automated procedures and prevents vendor lock-in.

In conclusion, Splunk SOAR is unique due to its metrics, mobility, scalability, openness, threat intelligence, orchestration, automation, event and alert management, and community-driven methodology. Together, these capabilities enable businesses to better manage their security operations, react quickly to crises, and keep a strong security posture.

Splunk SOAR Playbooks

The platform's automation and orchestration skills are built on Splunk SOAR playbooks. They give a visual picture of the incident management process' decision-making processes, workflows, and actions. The creation and execution of Splunk SOAR playbooks will be covered in this chapter, along with a real-world example of how to use them.

Playbook Components and Design

Various elements make up a Splunk SOAR playbook, including:

- **Triggers**: Specify the circumstances or occurrences that start a playbook's execution.
- **Actions**: Depict the specific activities or actions that need to be carried out, such as data extraction, enrichment, or correction procedures.
- **Filters and Decision Points:** Manage the playbook's flow by approving or rejecting the execution of specific actions in accordance with predetermined criteria.
- **Assets**: These points of external tool and service integration, such as threat intelligence platforms, ITSM programs, or security products, are represented.

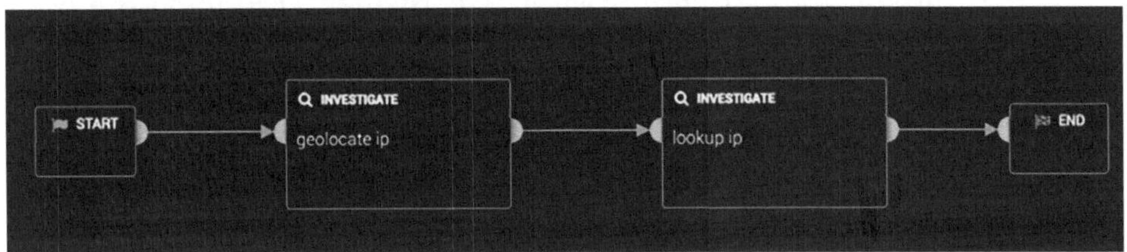

Figure 11.2: *Splunk SOAR playbook (source: Determine your Splunk Phantom playbook flow - Splunk Documentation. (n.d.). Determine Your Splunk Phantom Playbook Flow - Splunk Documentation. https://docs.splunk.com/Documentation/Phantom/4.10.7/Playbook/VPEPlaybookFlow.)*

Playbook Design Best Practices

The following best practices should be taken into account while creating a Splunk SOAR playbook:

- **Define clear objectives**: Specify the playbook's aims and desired results, such as automating triage, enhancing data, or carrying out corrective measures.

- **Modularize and reuse:** To make playbook creation and maintenance easier, break down complex procedures into smaller, reusable components.
- **Test and validate**: Playbooks should be thoroughly tested to make sure they work as intended and produce the desired results.
- **Version control and documentation**: To promote collaboration and speed up updates, have your playbooks well-documented and under version control.

Benefits of Splunk SOAR

There are many advantages that Splunk SOAR (Security Orchestration, Automation, and Response) provides to businesses that want to improve their cybersecurity posture. The following are some of the main benefits:

- **Increased Productivity and Efficiency:** Splunk SOAR drastically lowers the strain on security teams by automating repetitive and routine operations. In addition to accelerating reaction times, automation frees up analysts' time to concentrate on more intricate and strategic work, which boosts output overall.
- **Enhanced Incident Response:** The incident response procedure is streamlined by Splunk SOAR. Its orchestration features make it possible to act quickly and in concert with different security technologies. As a result, threats are met with greater effectiveness, reducing the possible damage to the organization.
- **Improved Use of Threat Intelligence:** Splunk SOAR offers thorough and current information on emerging risks by integrating many threat intelligence sources. This aids security teams in staying ahead of any dangers and providing more accurate and contextual responses to threats.
- **Consolidated Security Operations:** To manage different security responsibilities, Splunk SOAR acts as a consolidated platform. It becomes simpler to identify, look into, and address threats as a result of this convergence, which improves visibility and control over security operations.
- **Flexibility and Scalability:** The platform can expand together with an enterprise. Because of its adaptability, new tools and technologies may be integrated with it, allowing the security infrastructure to change to meet changing business needs and the ever-changing threat landscape.
- **Improved Coordination and Communication**: Splunk SOAR's case management and collaboration tools let security team members work

together more effectively. Through the consolidation of warnings into comprehensive cases, teams may collaborate more successfully to address situations.

- **Data-Driven Decision Making:** Splunk SOAR's extensive reporting and metrics features offer insightful information about how well security plans and operations are working. These data-driven insights support the ongoing improvement of security processes and the ability to make well-informed judgments.
- **Decreased Mean Time to Detect and Respond:** Automation and orchestration greatly reduce the amount of time needed to identify and address security issues, which lowers the organization's total risk.
- **Compliance and Regulatory Adherence:** By automating data collecting, analysis, and reporting procedures, Splunk SOAR ensures that businesses effectively fulfill their compliance requirements. This aids in maintaining compliance with a variety of regulatory standards.
- **Cost-Effectiveness:** Splunk SOAR lowers operating expenses by automating and optimizing security operations. Being more efficient and requiring less manual involvement results in more efficient resource allocation, which makes it an affordable security operations management solution.

To sum up, Splunk SOAR provides efficiency, efficacy, and scalability in security management through a thorough and integrated approach. It is a priceless tool for businesses looking to strengthen their cybersecurity defenses because of its capacity to automate and coordinate difficult security processes as well as its sophisticated intelligence and reporting functions.

Implementing Splunk SOAR

Enhancing cybersecurity capabilities inside a business can be achieved through a strategic process called Splunk SOAR (Security Orchestration, Automation, and Response) implementation. Here's a how-to for using Splunk SOAR effectively:

- **Assessment of Current Security Infrastructure:** Start by analyzing the security procedures and instruments that are currently in place. Recognize the weaknesses and difficulties in the current configuration, as well as the places where automation and orchestration can make a big difference.
- **Outlining the Needs and Goals:** Clearly state the objectives of the company using Splunk SOAR. Establish quantifiable, precise goals for incident response, threat intelligence, compliance, and other areas. This

stage is essential for customizing the implementation to the specific requirements of the company.

- **Planning and Design:** Create a thorough plan outlining how the SOAR will be implemented. This entails selecting the points of integration with already available security technologies, creating automated playbooks and workflows, and describing the general architecture of the SOAR solution inside the IT infrastructure of the company.
- **Stakeholder Engagement:** Involve important parties from a range of departments, such as executive leadership, IT, security, and compliance. Getting their support and learning about their viewpoints guarantees a more seamless implementation process and improved alignment with company objectives.
- **Phased Implementation and Testing:** Begin by automating and orchestrating simple tasks before moving on to more complex ones. Make gradual progress to more intricate processes. Make sure that the system functions as intended, cutting reaction times and simplifying procedures by thoroughly testing each step.
- **Training and Capacity Building:** Give the security team and other pertinent employees thorough instruction on how to use Splunk SOAR. Make sure they know how to use the platform, create and edit playbooks, and use the tool to respond to problems.
- **Integration of Tools and Data Sources:** Combine Splunk SOAR with currently in-use security tools, including intrusion detection systems, firewalls, and antivirus software. To enable efficient orchestration and response, make sure there is a smooth data flow between these tools and Splunk SOAR.
- **Ongoing Monitoring and Optimization:** After Splunk SOAR is put into place, keep an eye on its functionality at all times. After getting user input, modify playbooks, workflows, and integration points as necessary. Update the system often to take advantage of new tools, threats, and operational modifications.
- **Metrics and Reporting:** To monitor the effectiveness of Splunk SOAR, make use of its reporting and metrics features. Analyze results in relation to the predetermined goals to assess implementation success and pinpoint areas in need of improvement.
- **Expandability and Prospectivity:** Consider future scalability as the company expands. Make that Splunk SOAR can grow as needed, integrate with new technologies, and adjust to changing security demands.

Improving an organization's security posture can be achieved in large part by putting Splunk SOAR into practice. Although careful planning, execution, and continuous monitoring are necessary, the advantages in terms of increased productivity, quicker reaction times, and stronger cybersecurity capabilities are significant and well worth the work.

Security Orchestration with Splunk SOAR

In this section, particular Splunk Add-ons will be utilized to demonstrate how Splunk SOAR may be used to improve security workflows in real-world circumstances.

Phishing Incident Response with Splunk add-on for Microsoft Office 365

The Splunk Add-on for Microsoft Office 365 can be used to implement an efficient phishing incident response procedure that will significantly improve an organization's capacity to promptly detect and neutralize phishing assaults. Here's how to use this integration to manage phishing incidents step-by-step:

Step 1: Set up the Microsoft Office 365 Splunk Add-on.

- **First Setup**: Set up the Microsoft Office 365 Splunk Add-on by installing and configuring it. Setting up the required connections and permissions to access Office 365 data, including email logs–which are essential for phishing detection–is part of this process.

Step 2: Monitoring and Ingestion of Data

- **Gathering Data:** Make sure the add-on is correctly consuming Office 365 data, especially email logs, which include metadata about incoming emails and their senders.
- **Constant Monitoring**: Configure Splunk to scan ingested data continuously for indicators of phishing, such as dubious email senders, odd email content, or connections to websites that are known to be dangerous.

Step 3: Configure Alerts

- **Creating Alerts**: Set up alerts in Splunk to inform the security team of any possible phishing attempts. These notifications can be set up to react to particular email characteristics, including having attachments with dubious file formats, coming from unreliable sources, or including specific keywords in the email body.

Step 4: Splunk SOAR Integration

- **Automated Response with SOAR**: If available, connect Splunk to Splunk SOAR to enable automated incident response. For phishing events that begin with a Splunk alert, create playbooks in Splunk SOAR.
- **Automation Playbooks**: Create playbooks to automate early reaction tasks, like identifying and removing links or attachments from suspicious emails, alerting the impacted users, and quarantining the email.

Step 5: Research and Evaluation

- **Incident inquiry**: Perform a thorough inquiry as soon as an alert is set out. Look for any signs of malicious activity in the email's content, sender, attachments, and links.
- **User Verification**: Get in touch with the recipient of the email to find out if and how much they have interacted with it.

Step 6: Mitigation and Remediation

- **Containment**: If it is verified that the email is phishing, take action to lessen its effect. This can entail clearing the email out of every mailbox, blocking access to harmful URLs, and changing passwords in the event that credentials are stolen.
- **User Education**: Educate and warn the impacted user or users about email security best practices and phishing.

Step 7: Documentation and Reporting

- **Document the Incident**: For future reference, include the specifics of the phishing attempt and the steps taken in response in Splunk.
- **Generate Reports**: To build comprehensive reports on the incident, utilize Splunk's reporting features. For compliance, auditing, and enhancing phishing response tactics, this data is helpful.

Step 8: Ongoing Enhancement

- **Feedback Loop**: Examine the efficiency of the response procedure and pinpoint areas in need of development.
- **Update Detection Rules**: Based on the most recent intelligence and phishing patterns, regularly update Splunk and Splunk SOAR's detection rules and response playbooks.

By following these procedures, companies can establish a strong and efficient phishing incident response process by utilizing the Splunk Add-on for Microsoft Office 365, Splunk's rich analytics, and Splunk SOAR's automation capabilities.

This method not only improves the organization's overall cybersecurity resilience but also aids in quickly responding to phishing efforts.

Endpoint Detection and Response (EDR) with Splunk add-on for Carbon Black Response

An organization's Endpoint Detection and Response (EDR) capabilities are improved by integrating Splunk with the Carbon Black Response add-on. A thorough view and management of endpoint security events are made possible by this integration. Here's how to use the Carbon Black Response for the EDR Splunk Add-on step-by-step:

Step 1: Integration and Configuration

- **Set up the Extra**: Installing the Carbon Black Response Splunk Add-on is the first step. Verify that it works with the Splunk version you have.
- **Set Up Data Inputs**: Configure Splunk's data inputs for Carbon Black Response. This will enable Splunk to get alerts, endpoint activity, and system events from Carbon Black and index them.

Step 2: Normalization and Ingestion of Data

- **Ingest Endpoint Data**: After the add-on is set up, Splunk will get endpoint data from Carbon Black. Processes, network connections, registry modifications, and other endpoint actions are all covered by this data.
- **Normalize Data**: By standardizing the data into a uniform format, the add-on facilitates faster analysis and correlation with other Splunk data sources.

Step 3: Analyzing and Monitoring in Real-Time

- **Dashboard Utilization**: For real-time endpoint activity monitoring, make use of the pre-built dashboards that the add-on offers. You can personalize these dashboards to showcase particular metrics or trends that are pertinent to your setting.
- **Threat Hunting:** Proactively look for possible threats on endpoints by utilizing Splunk's robust search and analysis features. Use the query language in Splunk to find odd behavior or trends.

Step 4: Notification and Reaction to Events

- **Configure Alerts:** In Splunk, create alerts for particular endpoint events or indicators of compromise (IoCs) that Carbon Black has identified. Notifications or automated response actions may be initiated by these alerts.

- **Automated Response:** Create automated playbooks for handling typical endpoint threats if your system is integrated with Splunk SOAR. This could entail obtaining more context, separating impacted endpoints, or starting remediation procedures.

Step 5: Investigating and Forensics

- **Detailed Forensics**: Utilize the comprehensive endpoint data gathered by Carbon Black and indexed in Splunk to carry out an exhaustive forensic examination in the case of a security incident.
- **Timeline reconstruction**: To comprehend the extent and consequences of an occurrence, reconstruct the timeline by figuring out how the threat originated, propagated, and carried out its actions.

Step 6: Compliance and Reporting

- **Produce Reports**: Create thorough reports on incident responses, endpoint security status, and policy compliance with Splunk.
- **Compliance Monitoring**: Using the comprehensive endpoint data and logs, keep an eye out for and report on compliance with external regulations as well as internal policies.

Step 7: Ongoing Enhancement and Modification

- **Frequent Updates**: To guarantee compatibility and access to new capabilities, make sure the Carbon Black Response add-on for Splunk is updated frequently.
- **Playbooks and Alerts:** Constantly improve and modify SOAR playbooks and Splunk alerts in response to changing endpoint and threat dynamics.

Organizations may improve their endpoint security management (EDR) capabilities, gain better visibility into endpoint activities, detect and respond to threats more effectively, and maintain a strong posture by utilizing the Splunk Add-on for Carbon Black Response. Within the larger cybersecurity strategy, this connection makes it easier to take a more proactive and data-driven approach to endpoint security.

Vulnerability Management and Patching with Splunk add-on for Tenable

The Tenable Add-on's connection with Splunk improves an organization's vulnerability management and patching procedures. This combination provides a thorough understanding of vulnerabilities and helps with the effective prioritization and remediation of security flaws. Here's how businesses can make use of this integration:

Step 1: Configuring Integration

- **Set up Tenable's Splunk Add-on:** Installing and setting up the add-on in your Splunk environment should come first. Verify that it works with the Splunk version you are currently using.
- **Set Up Data Inputs**: Configure Tenable's data inputs in Splunk. This makes it possible for Splunk to obtain and index vulnerability data from Tenable SecurityCenter or Tenable Nessus scans, including details on assets that are impacted and the severity of vulnerabilities that are found.

Step 2: Normalization and Data Gathering

- **Continuous Data Ingestion**: To keep Splunk up to date, the add-on will ingest vulnerability data from Tenable on a regular basis.
- **Data Normalization**: To ensure consistency, the imported data is normalized. This makes it simpler to examine alongside other security data in Splunk.

Step 3: Prioritization and Vulnerability Analysis

- **Dashboard Utilization**: Make use of the pre-made dashboards that the add-on offers to learn more about your environment's vulnerability status. Tailor these dashboards to highlight important elements, such as systems that are regularly impacted or high-severity vulnerabilities.
- **Give Vulnerabilities Priority**: Prioritize vulnerabilities using Splunk's data according to their seriousness, exploitability, and how important the impacted assets are. This makes it easier to concentrate patching efforts where they are most required.

Step 4: Repair and Cleaning

- **Integrate Patch Management solutions**: For more efficient patch deployment, if possible, integrate your patch management solutions with Splunk.
- **Automatic Patching Workflows**: Create automatic patching processes using Splunk (or Splunk SOAR, if it's available). This can entail determining which systems are impacted, applying patches, and confirming that the patches are applied.

Step 5: Reporting and Compliance

- **Compliance Monitoring**: Keep an eye on adherence to internal and external policies and standards for vulnerability management.

- **Produce Reports**: Provide thorough reports for different stakeholders, such as IT management and security teams, on vulnerability exposure, patching status, and compliance.

Step 6: Handling Incidents for Vulnerabilities That Were Exploited

- **Alert Configuration**: Set up Splunk to notify you when network vulnerabilities are exploited. Procedures for incident response may be triggered by these warnings.
- **Incident Investigation**: If an exploit is discovered, utilize Splunk to look into the incident's details, including the extent of the damage and the efficiency of the patches that have been applied.

Step 7: Ongoing Enhancement

- **Frequent Updates and Scanning**: To find new vulnerabilities, update your Tenable solutions on a regular basis and run frequent scans.
- **Improve Processes**: Continually improve your vulnerability management and patching procedures by drawing on Splunk's insights. Your remediation and priority procedures should be modified to account for new threats and vulnerabilities.

Organizations can greatly improve their vulnerability management and patching capabilities by integrating Splunk with the Tenable Add-on. Through a more thorough, analytical, and proactive approach to vulnerability identification, prioritization, and remediation, this integration strengthens the organization's overall cybersecurity posture.

Security Automation with Splunk SOAR

A crucial part of Splunk SOAR is security automation, which enables businesses to speed up incident response and minimize manual work. Security teams can concentrate on duties that are more important and work more efficiently by automating repetitive operations and streamlining procedures. This chapter will give practical examples of how Splunk SOAR may be utilized to utilize particular Splunk Add-ons to automate various security activities.

Threat Intelligence Enrichment with Splunk add-on for ThreatConnect

Using the Splunk Add-on for ThreatConnect to implement security automation improves an organization's capacity to proactively identify and mitigate cybersecurity threats. Organizations can automate responses to possible threats, improve their security data with external threat intelligence, and streamline their security operations by utilizing this integration. Here's how to put this into practice inside the framework of security automation:

Step 1: Configuring Automation and Integration

- **Install ThreatConnect's Splunk Add-on:** Make that the Splunk environment's add-on is installed and set up to connect to ThreatConnect.
- **Autonomous Data Ingestion**: Configure the add-on to automatically take in threat intelligence feeds (such as IoCs, threat actor details, and other threat data) from ThreatConnect.

Step 2: Enriching Threat Intelligence Automatically

- **Data Normalization and Enrichment**: Automate the procedure of standardizing the imported data so that it may be readily analyzed in a uniform format. Add ThreatConnect's threat intelligence data to Splunk's internal security logs and events.
- **Correlation Rules**: In order to identify possible threats or malicious activity, create automated correlation rules in Splunk by matching internal event data with enriched threat intelligence.

Step 3: Incident Creation and Automated Alerting

- **Automatic Alert Configuration**: Utilizing ThreatConnect intelligence, create automatic alerts in Splunk that are triggered by particular IoCs or threat patterns.
- **Incident production**: To ensure prompt reaction to possible dangers, automate the production of incidents in response to triggered alarms.

Step 4: Using Splunk SOAR for Automated Incident Response

- **SOAR Integration**: To automate response activities, integrate Splunk SOAR with the Splunk-ThreatConnect configuration.
- **Playbook Development**: Using ThreatConnect intelligence, create SOAR playbooks for common threat situations. The reactions that these playbooks can automate include banning IP addresses, isolating impacted systems, and starting additional research.

Step 5: Ongoing Evaluation and Modification

- **Automated Monitoring**: Configure your security systems and Splunk environment to automatically update in response to emerging or new threats that are notified by ThreatConnect.

- **Dynamic Rule Adjustment**: Put in place a system where response plans and correlation rules are dynamically modified in response to changing threat intelligence and input from past incidents.

Step 6: Automation of Reporting and Analysis

- **Automated Reporting**: Utilize Splunk's automated reporting feature to gain insights into attack patterns, threat trends, and the efficiency of automated defenses.
- **Analysis for Strategic Decisions**: Make strategic security decisions, including strengthening defenses or altering policies, with the help of automated reports.

Step 7: Adaptive and Collaborative Security Position

- **Feedback Mechanism**: To continuously enhance threat intelligence and response procedures, set up an automatic feedback loop.
- **Collaborative Threat information**: To gain from and add to collective threat information, automatically share insights with security communities or industry associations.

Organizations may more effectively and quickly handle cybersecurity risks by utilizing the Splunk Add-on for ThreatConnect for security automation. This integration improves the organization's overall security posture and resilience by enabling automatic, quick, and educated responses to new security threats, in addition to enriching security data with thorough threat information.

Malware analysis with Splunk add-on for Cuckoo Sandbox

The Cuckoo Sandbox add-on can be integrated with Splunk to provide a potent automated malware analysis solution. With this combination, businesses may examine dubious files and URLs in a secure setting and use the information gathered to improve their cybersecurity protocols. Here's how to put this integration into practice and reap its benefits:

Step 1: Configuration and Setup

- **Set up the Cuckoo Sandbox Splunk Add-on**: Make that the Cuckoo Sandbox add-on is installed and configured correctly in your Splunk system.
- **Get into the Cuckoo Sandbox**: Set up the add-on to interact with your Cuckoo Sandbox instance so that Splunk may transmit files and URLs for examination and obtain the findings of that examination.

Step 2: Automated Submission of Malware

- **Detection and Submission**: Configure automatic procedures to identify and forward dubious files or URLs from your network to Cuckoo Sandbox. Splunk's data monitoring features can be used to do this by seeing possible malware in downloads, email attachments, and other entry points.
- **Safe Analysis Environment**: To avoid any possible harm to your actual network, Cuckoo Sandbox examines the provided files or URLs in a controlled, isolated environment.

Step 3: Data Ingestion and Analysis

- **Detailed Analysis**: Cuckoo Sandbox analyzes files and URLs both dynamically and statically, offering insights into their behavior, including attempted registry edits, network calls, and file alterations.
- **Ingestion of Data into Splunk**: Following analysis, the findings are re-ingested into Splunk for additional processing and correlation.

Step 4: Incident Response and Alerting:

- **Set Up Alerts**: Create alerts in Splunk according to the Cuckoo Sandbox analysis results. For instance, an alert may be set off if it is found that a file is harmful.
- **Automated Incident Response**: If Splunk SOAR integration is available, use it to automate responses to these warnings. Examples of automated responses include quarantining compromised systems, obstructing malicious IP addresses, or starting cleanup procedures.

Step 5: Threat hunting and data correlation

- **Correlation with Other Data Sources**: To obtain a complete picture of the threat landscape, use Splunk to correlate the Cuckoo Sandbox results with information from other data sources, such as threat intelligence feeds, network traffic logs, and endpoint security logs.
- **Proactive Threat Hunting**: Spot and eliminate any threats before they have a chance to do damage by using the richer data found in Splunk.

Step 6: Trend analysis and reporting

- **Automated Reporting**: Utilizing Splunk, create automated reports that enumerate the malware analysis results, including the kinds of malware found, the systems impacted, and the steps taken.
- **Trend Analysis:** Examine patterns over a period of time to find recurrent malware strains or popular attack vectors. This data can help direct advances in strategic security.

Step 7: Ongoing Enhancement

- **Improve Detection and Analysis**: Based on input from previous analyses and the changing threat landscape, continuously improve the criteria for malware submission and analysis.
- **Update and Adjust**: To take advantage of the newest capabilities and guarantee compatibility, update Cuckoo Sandbox and Splunk on a regular basis.

With the Splunk Add-on for Cuckoo Sandbox, businesses can safely and automatically carry out in-depth malware investigations. Organizations may boost their overall cybersecurity framework by combining this with Splunk's potent data analysis and correlation capabilities, which will improve their capacity to identify, evaluate, and respond to malware threats.

Incident Management with Splunk SOAR

Businesses may automate and simplify their security incident response process by combining Splunk SOAR with IT Service Management (ITSM) technologies.

Incident Response with Splunk SOAR and ServiceNow add-on

A strong incident response architecture can be created by combining the ServiceNow Add-on with Splunk SOAR (Security Orchestration, Automation, and Response). By automating workflows between Splunk SOAR and ServiceNow, a well-known IT service management software, this connection simplifies the incident management procedure. Here are some ways that businesses might use this connectivity to handle incidents more effectively:

Step 1: Configuring Integration

- **Install the Splunk ServiceNow Add-on**: Start by setting up the ServiceNow Add-on in your Splunk setup. ServiceNow integration with Splunk is made possible by this add-on.
- **Configure Splunk SOAR**: Make sure Splunk SOAR is configured to interface with ServiceNow as well as Splunk. This entails setting up the links and guaranteeing that data is transferred between these systems.

Step 2: Logging and Detecting Incidents

- **Automated Incident Detection**: Keep an eye out for security events throughout your network by utilizing Splunk's potent analytics. This involves looking for irregularities, security lapses, and other possible dangers.

- **Recording Incidents in ServiceNow**: Automate the production of an incident record in ServiceNow as soon as an occurrence is discovered. Splunk should have retrieved all pertinent information for this record in order to take appropriate action.

Step 3: Analysis of Incidents and Setting Priorities

- **Data Enrichment**: Add more context from Splunk to incident data in ServiceNow. Logs, user activity, and threat intelligence data may all fall into this category.
- **Prioritization**: Using the Splunk analysis's results for severity, impact, and urgency, automate the process of ranking events in ServiceNow.

Step 4: Using Splunk SOAR for Automated Response and Playbook Activation: Playbooks can be automatically executed by using Splunk SOAR. These playbooks can carry out a number of tasks, including contacting impacted parties, blocking malicious IPs, and isolating compromised systems.

- **Integration with ServiceNow**: Make sure that the ServiceNow incident record reflects the activities performed by Splunk SOAR, giving a synchronized picture of the issue response process.

Step 5: Interaction and Teamwork

- **Automated Communication**: Configure ServiceNow to send incident updates automatically. This includes updating the IT support staff and stakeholders on the status of the issue, any necessary measures, and the resolution's progress.
- **Collaboration capabilities**: Make use of ServiceNow's collaboration capabilities to facilitate productive teamwork across disparate teams during issue resolution.

Step 6: Resolving and Concluding the Incident

- **Monitoring with ServiceNow**: Track the development of the ServiceNow incident resolution process. This entails keeping track of the actions performed, the resources used, and the resolution time.
- **Documentation and Resolution**: After a problem has been fixed, make sure Splunk SOAR updates the ServiceNow incident record with the details of the fix as well as any reports or post-incident analysis.

Step 7: Improvement and Reporting

- **Automated Reporting**: Create in-depth reports on incidents, responses, resolution timeframes, and trends using ServiceNow's reporting features.

- **Continuous Improvement**: Examine these reports to find out where your incident response and security posture could use some tweaking.

An effective and smooth method for handling incident response is offered by the combination of Splunk SOAR with the ServiceNow Add-on. This potent combination preserves transparent communication and documentation while enabling quick detection, in-depth analysis, automatic reaction, and efficient resolution of security events. Organizations can greatly increase their incident response capabilities by utilizing these tools, which will result in speedier resolutions, less impact, and improved security overall.

Incident Management with Splunk SOAR and Jira Integration

A strong incident management system can be achieved by integrating Jira, a popular project and problem-tracking tool, with Splunk SOAR (Security Orchestration, Automation, and Response). The effectiveness of monitoring, controlling, and resolving security events is improved by this combination. Here is a thorough method for making use of this integration:

Step 1: Integration Configuration

- **Install Splunk SOAR's Jira Integration**: Set up the Jira integration in Splunk SOAR first. In order to guarantee smooth communication between Splunk SOAR and your Jira instance, this entails setting up the connection parameters.
- **Adjust Integration Preferences**: Adjust the integration so that it fits your process for handling incidents. This entails aligning Jira's issue fields with Splunk SOAR's incident fields to make sure pertinent data is exchanged between the two platforms.

Step 2: Identifying incidents and creating tickets

- **Automated Incident Detection**: To keep an eye out for security incidents on your network and systems, use Splunk SOAR. To find possible risks, make use of its analytics and detection features.
- **Making tickets on Jira**: Automate the Jira ticket-generating process after an issue is discovered. Fill in the incident ticket with all relevant information, including the threat's type, the systems that were impacted, and the preliminary conclusions.

Step 3: Assigning and Prioritizing Incidents

- **Jira prioritization**: Utilize Jira's features to rank incidents according to their immediacy, effect, and severity. Based on the predetermined standards established in Splunk SOAR, this can be automated.
- **Assigning Tickets**: Using Jira, automatically assign tickets to the right team members or response teams so that events are handled by the right personnel.

Step 4: Automated Response Playbooks and Orchestrated Response with Splunk SOAR Playbooks in Splunk SOAR can be used to automate incident response. These playbooks are capable of carrying out a number of tasks, including performing initial containment steps, obtaining further intelligence, and isolating impacted systems.

- **Coordinating Actions with Jira:** Make sure that every action performed by Splunk SOAR is recorded and updated in the relevant Jira ticket, offering a thorough overview of the response operations.

Step 5: Cooperation and Interaction

- **Team Collaboration**: Make use of Jira's collaboration tools to help the team members working on the problem communicate and coordinate effectively. This covers adding comments, sending files, and exchanging updates.
- **Stakeholder Communication**: Use Jira's automated updates and reports to tell stakeholders about the status of problems.

Step 6: Documentation and Incident Resolution

- **Tracking Progress**: Keep tabs on Jira's incident resolution process. Keep track of the actions done, the materials used, and the resolution time.
- **Settlement and Concluding**: After the issue has been fixed, make sure to update the Jira ticket with comprehensive resolution details, documenting all actions and conclusions for future reference.

Step 7: Analysis and Reporting Following the Incident

- **Jira reporting**: To create thorough reports on incident response metrics, timetables for resolution, and reoccurring issues, use Jira's reporting features.
- **Ongoing Improvement**: Examine these reports to spot patterns, indicate areas that need work, and hone your incident response plan.

Automation of the detection, response, and tracking procedures is achieved by integrating Splunk SOAR with Jira to streamline incident management. This connection makes sure that incidents are handled efficiently, with transparent documentation and communication, which speeds up resolution times and creates a more structured strategy for dealing with security risks. Through the integration of Splunk SOAR and Jira, entities may establish a more agile and effective incident management process.

Additional Important Tool Integrations with Splunk SOAR

From a cybersecurity standpoint, the following are five other significant tool integrations with Splunk SOAR:

- **Palo Alto Networks**: Automated incident response, threat information sharing, and network security policy management are made possible thanks to Splunk SOAR's integration with Palo Alto Networks' next-generation firewalls and PAN-OS. Organizations may detect threats more quickly and effectively thanks to this integration.
- **Cisco Threat Grid**: Using this integration, Splunk SOAR may analyze suspicious files and URLs using Cisco's Threat Grid threat intelligence platform. Security teams can swiftly assess a threat's nature and take appropriate action by automating the process of submitting samples and getting analysis results.
- **CrowdStrike Falcon**: The cloud-native endpoint protection platform CrowdStrike Falcon is integrated with Splunk SOAR. This gives security teams more visibility into endpoint behavior and threats and enables automation of operations like threat hunting, endpoint containment, and remediation.
- **Okta Identity Cloud**: Splunk SOAR can automate identity and access management processes, including user provisioning, de-provisioning, and password resets by connecting with Okta. Ensuring that only authorized individuals have access to sensitive systems and data aids companies in maintaining a secure environment.
- **VirusTotal**: Splunk SOAR may query the platform for file and URL analysis thanks to the integration with VirusTotal, a well-known online malware and URL scanning service. By automating the process of comparing files and URLs to a variety of antivirus engines and other threat intelligence sources, security teams may better comprehend and contextualize potential threats.

Security teams can detect, analyze, and react to threats in their environment more quickly thanks to the automation of key cybersecurity activities made possible by these connectors.

Case Studies

Here are three case studies illustrating the successful implementation of Splunk SOAR (formerly Phantom) in various organizations. These examples demonstrate how Splunk SOAR can help businesses improve their security posture, enhance incident response capabilities, and streamline security operations.

Case Study 1: Large Financial Institution

- **Problem**: A large financial institution faced challenges in managing and responding to the high volume of security alerts generated by its numerous security tools. The organization's manual processes were time-consuming and prone to errors, making it difficult to prioritize and respond to critical threats efficiently.
- **Solution**: The financial institution implemented Splunk SOAR to automate its incident response process, allowing the security team to respond to alerts more efficiently. With Splunk SOAR, the organization was able to create custom playbooks to automate repetitive tasks, such as gathering threat intelligence, identifying malicious IPs, and blocking them at the firewall level.
- **Results:** By leveraging Splunk SOAR, the financial institution reduced its mean time to respond (MTTR) to incidents by over 50%. Additionally, the organization experienced a significant improvement in its ability to prioritize and respond to critical threats, reducing the risk of data breaches and other security incidents.

Case Study 2: Energy Sector Organization

- **Problem:** An organization in the energy sector faced challenges in protecting its industrial control systems (ICS) and other critical infrastructure components from cyber threats. The organization needed a solution that could help detect, analyze, and respond to potential threats quickly and efficiently.
- **Solution**: The energy sector organization deployed Splunk SOAR to automate its ICS security processes. Splunk SOAR was integrated with the organization's existing security tools, such as intrusion detection systems (IDS) and firewalls, to automate threat detection, investigation, and response tasks.
- **Results**: By implementing Splunk SOAR, the energy sector organization was able to improve its ability to detect and respond to potential threats targeting its critical infrastructure. The organization experienced a significant reduction in incident response times, which helped minimize the risk of disruption to its operations and services.

Case Study 3: Higher Education Institution

- **Problem**: A higher education institution struggled to manage and respond to the growing number of cybersecurity threats targeting its network and systems. With limited resources and a small security team, the institution needed a way to improve its incident response capabilities and overall security posture.
- **Solution**: The higher education institution implemented Splunk SOAR to automate its incident response processes. By integrating Splunk SOAR with its existing security tools, the institution was able to create custom playbooks that automated tasks such as gathering threat intelligence, detecting malicious activity, and containing compromised devices.
- **Results:** With the help of Splunk SOAR, the higher education institution experienced a significant improvement in its ability to detect and respond to cyber threats. The institution was able to reduce its mean time to detect (MTTD) and mean time to respond (MTTR) to incidents, ultimately improving its overall security posture and reducing the risk of data breaches and other security incidents.

Best Practices for Implementing SOAR with Splunk

Careful planning, cross-functional cooperation, and skill development are required for Security Orchestration, Automation, and Response (SOAR) implementation in a company. We will go over how to create a cross-functional SOAR team, evaluate your organization's SOAR preparedness, and create the necessary training for SOAR analysts in this chapter.

Assessing Your Organization's Readiness for SOAR

Evaluating your organization's readiness is critical before implementing a SOAR solution. Think about the following elements:

- **Security Maturity**: Evaluate the security operations maturity and existing security posture of your firm. To fully capitalize on the advantages of SOAR, a security environment that is established and has established procedures, rules, and technology is preferred.
- **Incident Volume and Complexity**: Evaluate whether your firm deals with complex threats or a high volume of security issues that necessitate manual investigation and comprehensive action. The automation and

orchestration features of SOAR are more likely to help organizations deal with these issues.

- **Integration Capabilities**: Determine whether the existing security tools and technologies used by your firm are compatible with the chosen SOAR platform. For your SOAR installation to be as efficient and effective as possible, seamless integration is crucial.
- Availability of Resources: Take into account the availability of the funds, staff, and time needed for a successful SOAR implementation.

Building a Cross-Functional SOAR Team

Establishing a cross-functional team with representatives from several departments within the organization is essential to guaranteeing the success of the SOAR deployment. The group should include:

- Security analysts are in charge of creating and updating playbooks, as well as researching and responding to security events.
- **IT Operations:** Work together with security analysts to put corrective measures in place and make sure SOAR is seamlessly integrated with the current IT architecture.
- **Compliance and Risk Management:** Make sure that the SOAR deployment complies with the organization's regulatory and risk management standards.
- **Business Stakeholders:** Offer feedback on the organization's priorities and expectations. They should also support the SOAR effort by advocating for it to get the funding and support it needs.

Training and Skill Development for SOAR analysts

It is crucial to make investments in the training and skill advancement of SOAR analysts in order to optimize the success of a SOAR implementation. Priority regions include:

- **SOAR Platform Training**: Analysts need thorough instruction on the SOAR platform they have chosen, including all of its features, functions, and integrations with other security technologies.
- **Playbook Development**: To enable efficient and effective automation and orchestration of security procedures, analysts should receive training in playbook design, deployment, and administration.

- **Threat Intelligence**: Improve analysts' knowledge of sources, methods, and best practices for threat intelligence to help them recognize, rank, and respond to threats.
- **Incident Response**: To guarantee a consistent and efficient response to security incidents, offer training on incident response techniques, best practices, and frameworks, such as the NIST Cybersecurity Framework.
- **Communication and Collaboration**: Give analysts training in these areas to encourage cross-functional cooperation and enable efficient coordination of incident response activities.

Conclusion

We have thoroughly examined this chapter in order to gain a thorough understanding of the intricate environment of SOAR. We've seen how Splunk plays a key role in orchestrating and automating security operations, starting with an introduction to this broad field. We have discussed Splunk SOAR's function in security orchestration and automation as well as how it streamlines security operations. We've seen how Splunk SOAR functions in a larger security ecosystem by looking at other tool integrations, and our trip through real-world case studies has illuminated useful applications and outcomes. It is abundantly obvious from our discussion of the best practices for integrating SOAR with Splunk that thoughtful use and ongoing improvement of these strategies result in a robust cybersecurity approach.

As we transition into the next chapter, 'Cloud Security with Splunk,' we will extend our exploration into how Splunk's robust security capabilities can be applied in the cloud environment, ensuring a secure and resilient digital presence across multiple platforms.

Points to Remember

- SOAR technologies, such as Splunk, automate repetitive processes and orchestrate complicated workflows to streamline security operations, freeing security staff to concentrate on tasks with high priority and make decisions.
- Through a number of capabilities and integrations, including Splunk Enterprise Security (ES) and Splunk SOAR, Splunk supports SOAR operations.
- A variety of functionalities, such as security orchestration, automation, playbooks, and integrations with third-party tools and services, are offered by Splunk SOAR.

- Playbooks created with Splunk SOAR are essential for automating and coordinating security operations. They provide a visual representation of the incident management process's decision-making processes, workflows, and actions.
- By integrating Splunk SOAR with outside technologies like Microsoft Office 365, Carbon Black Response, and Tenable, you can improve security orchestration for handling phishing incidents, endpoint detection and response (EDR), vulnerability management, and patching, respectively.
- Integrations like ThreatConnect for threat information enrichment and Cuckoo Sandbox for malware analysis can be used to automate security with Splunk SOAR.
- Integrating Splunk SOAR with well-known ITSM tools like ServiceNow and issue-tracking tools like Jira helps expedite incident management.
- Steps for a successful deployment include evaluating your organization's readiness for SOAR, assembling a cross-functional SOAR team, and spending money on SOAR analyst training and skill development.

CHAPTER 12
Cloud Security with Splunk

Introduction

The chapter begins by delving into the unique challenges that organizations face when securing their cloud environments. These challenges include understanding the shared responsibility model, ensuring data protection and privacy, maintaining compliance with various regulations, gaining visibility and control over cloud assets, and managing security across multi-cloud environments. This overview provides a foundational understanding of the complex landscape of cloud security and sets the stage for exploring how Splunk can help address these concerns.

The chapter then transitions to a detailed exploration of Splunk's solutions for cloud security, including monitoring and analyzing cloud security data, integrating Splunk with popular cloud services such as Amazon Web Services (AWS), Microsoft Azure, and Google Cloud, as well as other third-party cloud security tools. Furthermore, the chapter provides real-world use cases to demonstrate how Splunk's capabilities can be applied to enhance cloud security. Finally, the chapter concludes with a comprehensive summary of best practices for cloud security with Splunk and key points to remember, empowering readers with the knowledge needed to secure their cloud infrastructure effectively.

Structure

In this chapter, we will cover the following topics:

- Overview of cloud security challenges
    - Shared responsibility model

    - Data protection and privacy
    - Compliance and regulations
    - Visibility and control
    - Multi-cloud environments
- Splunk solutions for cloud security
- Monitoring and analyzing cloud security data with Splunk
    - Collecting cloud security data
    - Analyzing cloud security data
- Integrating Splunk with cloud security services
    - Integrating Amazon Web Services (AWS)
    - Integrating Microsoft Azure
    - Integrating Google Cloud
    - Integrating with third-party cloud security tools
- Case studies
- Best practices for cloud security with Splunk

Overview of Cloud Security Challenges

The difficulties associated with cloud security are complex and relate to many facets of cloud operation. First, the Shared Responsibility Model frequently results in ambiguity in both the client's and the cloud service provider's security responsibilities, increasing the vulnerability. Second, privacy and data security are major issues. It is a difficult undertaking to guarantee that sensitive data is encrypted, safely stored, and unable to be accessed illegally. Third, it can be quite difficult to comply with different international and regional rules because they can vary greatly depending on where you are in the world. Fourth, organizations must manage several processes and access points while maintaining a secure environment, creating the problem of visibility and control. The adoption of multi-cloud systems, which is growing, further exacerbates these issues because it requires careful management and sophisticated tactics to coordinate security across many platforms and providers. These combined problems make securing the cloud a difficult but necessary undertaking.

Cloud Shared Responsibility Model

A key idea in cloud computing is the cloud shared responsibility model, which describes how security responsibilities are divided between the cloud service provider (CSP) and the cloud service user (customer). Organizations must comprehend this approach in order to manage cloud security and compliance efficiently. Take a close look at this model:

Basic Concept

- **Shared Responsibility:** The CSP and the client share security and compliance duties under the cloud shared responsibility paradigm. Depending on the cloud service paradigm being used, this category varies (IaaS, PaaS, SaaS).

Responsibilities of Cloud Service Providers (CSPs)

- **Security of the Underlying Infrastructure:** CSPs are in charge of safeguarding the infrastructure that underpins cloud services. This covers the hardware, networking, storage, and data center physical security.
- **Platform and Application Maintenance:** CSPs also look after the security of the operating systems, middleware, and runtime environments that make up the platform or application layers in PaaS and SaaS models.
- **Compliance Certifications:** For their infrastructure and services, CSPs frequently possess a variety of compliance certifications, like ISO 27001, SOC 2, or GDPR compliance.

Responsibilities of Customers

- **Data Security:** Users are in charge of protecting their data on cloud servers. This involves making sure sensitive data is handled in accordance with compliance regulations, enforcing access rules, and encrypting data.
- **Application Security:** Users deploying apps in the cloud under IaaS and PaaS models must ensure their apps are safe. This entails keeping secure coding standards and putting in place the appropriate security controls within the program.
- **Identity and Access Management:** Users' access to cloud services must be managed by customers, who are also responsible for user activity monitoring, authorization, and authentication.
- **Network Security:** In Infrastructure as a Service (IaaS) model, clients are in charge of protecting their virtual network, which includes configuring intrusion detection systems, firewalls, and secure network traffic.

Shared Areas

- **Patch Management:** Customers are in charge of making sure their apps and virtual machines are patched and updated, even while CSPs are in charge of updating the underlying infrastructure.

- **Configuration Management:** Users must appropriately set up cloud resources and services. Cloud security incidents are frequently caused by misconfigurations.

The Value of Comprehending the Model

- **Risk Management:** To effectively manage risk in the cloud, one must comprehend the shared responsibility paradigm. In order to put in place the proper security procedures, customers must understand their responsibilities.
- **Compliance:** Knowing which parts are under the control of the CSP and which are the customer's obligation is essential for regulatory compliance.
- **Security Best Practices:** To guarantee a secure cloud environment, CSPs and clients alike must follow security best practices within their respective purviews.

Under the cloud shared responsibility model, consumers and CSPs work together to maintain security. Customers are still responsible for protecting their data, apps, and network configurations even while CSPs safeguard the cloud infrastructure. Upholding a safe and legal cloud environment requires a thorough comprehension of these duties and conscientious handling of them.

Data Protection and Privacy

Given that data is stored and processed remotely in the cloud, protecting data and preserving privacy can be difficult. Data frequently travels via several distinct geographic regions, subjecting it to various privacy standards. To protect sensitive data and guarantee compliance with various data protection and privacy standards, such as GDPR and CCPA, organizations must employ strong encryption and access restrictions.

Compliance and Regulations

When employing cloud services, businesses in regulated sectors like healthcare and finance are subject to stringent compliance regulations. It can be difficult to ensure compliance in the cloud since it calls for businesses to have a thorough awareness of both their obligations and the security measures offered by CSPs. To make sure they continue to comply with current requirements, organizations must constantly monitor and evaluate their cloud infrastructures.

Visibility and Control

Since cloud environments are dynamic and distributed, it can be tricky to constantly monitor and manage assets, making it challenging to gain visibility into and maintain control over them. To improve visibility and control over their cloud environments, organizations need to establish extra tools and processes as well as a thorough understanding of the security measures provided by CSPs. This includes creating access controls, monitoring and analyzing logs, and automating security procedures.

Multi-cloud Environments

Many businesses today use numerous CSPs to satisfy their various needs while operating in multi-cloud settings. Although this strategy has many advantages, it also has drawbacks, because businesses must manage and secure various, frequently dissimilar cloud environments. Organizations must create a unified security strategy that tackles the particular issues faced by each CSP and provides uniform security rules and controls across all environments to properly safeguard multi-cloud environments.

These difficulties with cloud security show how difficult it is for businesses to protect their cloud systems. Organizations must create a thorough cloud security strategy that makes use of cutting-edge security solutions like Splunk to improve visibility, control, and overall security posture to successfully manage these concerns.

Splunk Solutions for Cloud Security

Splunk provides a full range of cloud security solutions that aid businesses in improving visibility, control, and overall security posture in their cloud environments. Important Splunk cloud security solutions include:

- **Splunk Enterprise Security (ES):** It gathers, examines, and correlates data from a variety of sources, including cloud environments, to offer enhanced security analytics and threat detection capabilities.
- **Splunk Infrastructure Monitoring:** Provides in-depth insights into the performance and health of cloud infrastructure through real-time monitoring and analytics, assuring optimum performance and availability.
- **Splunk SOAR (Security Orchestration, Automation, and Response):** By integrating with different cloud security products, automating activities, and coordinating workflows, Splunk SOAR streamlines security operations and enhances incident response.

- **Splunk Mission Control:** This platform for unified security operations unifies different Splunk security products into a single user interface, allowing businesses to manage and coordinate their security operations across diverse cloud environments.

Organizations can create a thorough and unified cloud security strategy by utilizing these Splunk solutions to successfully manage the particular problems presented by cloud environments.

Monitoring and Analyzing Cloud Security Data with Splunk

Splunk plays a crucial role in boosting cybersecurity strategy as a potent tool for monitoring and analyzing cloud security data. The gathering of information on cloud security is the first stage. With the help of Splunk, complete data may be gathered from a variety of sources, such as network traffic, server logs, and other security equipment. Organizations can retain a consolidated view of their cloud infrastructure because of this reliable data collection, which improves visibility and control.

In order to enable enterprises to proactively combat cybersecurity risks, cloud security data analysis is then carried out while turning raw cloud security data into actionable insight.

Collecting Cloud Security Data

There are several methods to amass cloud security data, which include:

- **Cloud-native services logs and metrics**

  Large amounts of logs and metrics are produced by various cloud-native services used by organizations. These logs include useful data about the performance, security, and usage of the services. Through its many add-ons, agents, and interfaces, Splunk enables businesses to gather and ingest logs and data from cloud-native services like Amazon Web Services (AWS), Microsoft Azure, and Google Cloud Platform (GCP). Splunk helps security teams understand their cloud infrastructures and find potential security threats and abnormalities by ingesting this data.

- **Cloud Access Security Broker (CASB) data**

  A CASB is a security tool that aids in the monitoring and management of an organization's cloud-based data and applications. Logs and notifications about user behavior, access restrictions, and possible security problems in the cloud are produced by CASBs. Splunk can ingest CASB data to give users a thorough understanding of the security posture of the cloud and to keep track of user activity across different cloud applications. As a result, security personnel can immediately respond to incidents and identify potential security concerns such as unauthorized access or data exfiltration attempts.

- **Cloud infrastructure logs**

  The underlying infrastructure elements that support cloud services, such as virtual machines, containers, and networking equipment, produce cloud infrastructure logs. These logs can offer insightful data regarding the functionality, safety, and general condition of the cloud infrastructure. Through a variety of integrations, add-ons, and agents, Splunk can gather and ingest cloud infrastructure logs, giving security teams thorough visibility into their cloud environments. Security teams may respond to incidents more successfully and identify prospective threats, such as unauthorized access attempts or incorrect configurations, by evaluating this data.

Analyzing Cloud Security data

Organizations can use Splunk to analyze and correlate cloud security data after it has been gathered to acquire insights into their cloud security posture. Essential analysis tasks include:

- **Identifying threats and anomalies**

  Splunk's advanced analytics capabilities enable security teams to uncover threats and abnormalities by correlating data from different sources and spotting trends that could point to possible security problems. Security teams can keep an eye out for unexpected activity in their cloud environments and react fast to possible risks by developing custom searches, alerts, and dashboards.

- **Investigating security incidents**

  Splunk enables security teams to examine suspected security incidents by digging into the gathered data and reviewing the pertinent logs and metrics. This aids security personnel in comprehending the incident's extent and effects, locating its origin, and choosing the best course of action.

- **Creating custom dashboards and alerts for cloud security monitoring**

  Security teams can design unique dashboards and warnings with Splunk to meet their individual requirements for cloud security. These dashboards can show real-time information on the state of cloud security, including user activity, access control violations, and security incidents. Security teams can be informed of potential risks and incidents as they happen by setting up alerts based on certain conditions or thresholds, enabling a quicker reaction to new security issues.

  Organizations can improve their overall cloud security posture, gain comprehensive visibility into their cloud environments, and discover potential threats and vulnerabilities by efficiently collecting and analyzing cloud security data with Splunk.

Integrating Splunk with Cloud Security Services

Splunk is capable of being integrated with the following cloud providers:

Integrating Amazon Web Services

The Splunk Add-on for AWS may gather several kinds of data from AWS, offering insightful security information. The following is a list of some significant data sources that the add-on can access:

- **AWS CloudTrail Logs:** Gathers API activity logs for your AWS account, recording details such as the source IP address, user, and actions taken during API calls.
- **Amazon GuardDuty Findings:** Retrieves information from the GuardDuty threat detection service, which keeps an eye out for illegal behavior and hostile activity inside your AWS environment.
- **Amazon Inspector Assessment Results:** Results of the Amazon Inspector examination are collected here. Amazon Inspector is a service that identifies potential security flaws in your AWS resources.
- **AWS Config Rules:** This method retrieves configuration compliance information from AWS Config and offers details on resource configuration changes and adherence to predetermined guidelines.
- **VPC Flow Logs:** Gathers IP traffic data from network flow logs for your VPCs to aid in identifying potential security issues and keeping track of network activities.

- **Amazon S3 Server Access Logs:** This feature allows you to retrieve the access logs for your S3 buckets and see the requests made to access your stored data.
- **Amazon RDS Logs:** Gathers information about database activities and events from Amazon Relational Database Service (RDS) logs.
- **AWS WAF Logs:** This feature allows you to retrieve web access logs from the AWS Web Application Firewall (WAF), which gives you information about online traffic and possible security risks aimed at your applications.
- **AWS Security Hub Findings:** Compiles security findings from a variety of AWS services and integrated third-party solutions, giving you a complete picture of your security status.
- **Amazon Macie Findings:** This feature allows you to access sensitive data discoveries and warnings from Amazon Macie, a service that employs machine learning to detect, categorize, and safeguard sensitive material kept in S3 storage.

You can monitor your AWS infrastructure, spot potential security issues, and handle problems more skillfully by ingesting these data sources into Splunk.

Amazon Web Services (AWS) Security Hub and GuardDuty

The security warnings and compliance status for various AWS accounts are comprehensively displayed via the AWS Security Hub. GuardDuty is a threat detection service that constantly scans your AWS environment for harmful activities and unlawful behavior. Organizations can gather, examine, and display security findings and alerts in one place by integrating Splunk with AWS Security Hub and GuardDuty. This can be accomplished by utilizing Splunk add-ons, like the Splunk Add-on for AWS, to ingest data from GuardDuty and the AWS Security Hub, develop personalized dashboards, and send out alerts for better incident response.

The following steps can be used to combine GuardDuty and AWS Security Hub with Splunk:

1. **Enable AWS Security Hub and GuardDuty**:

   Make sure GuardDuty and AWS Security Hub are activated in your AWS account. You can enable them through the AWS Management Console.

2. **Set IAM permissions and roles**:

   Create a Security Hub and GuardDuty data access IAM role on AWS with the required permissions. The security hub should be in the role:Guardduty:Get* and BatchImportFindings permissions.

3. **Install the AWS Splunk Add-on**:

   The Splunk Add-on for AWS can be downloaded and installed from Splunkbase (https://splunkbase.splunk.com/app/1876/). With the help of this add-on, Splunk can import data from a number of AWS services, such as Security Hub and GuardDuty.

4. **Configure AWS account in Splunk**:

   Go to the Splunk Add-on for AWS in the Splunk Web UI, select the Configuration tab, and enter the information for your AWS account. To grant Splunk the necessary access rights to your AWS services, you may either utilize your AWS access key and secret key or take on an IAM role.

5. **Set up data inputs for Security Hub and GuardDuty**:

   After setting up your AWS account in Splunk, create data inputs to gather information from GuardDuty and AWS Security Hub.

   a. For Security Hub:

      - Go to the **`Inputs`** tab in the Splunk Add-on for AWS.
      - Click **`Create New Input`** and choose **`Security Hub`** from the list of available AWS Services.
      - Give the input a distinctive name, select your location and AWS account, and specify the right data collection interval.
      - Save the entry.

   b. For GuardDuty:

      - Go to the **`Inputs`** tab in the Splunk Add-on for AWS.
      - Click **`Create New Input`** and choose **`GuardDuty`** from the list of available AWS Services.
      - Give the input a distinctive name, select your location and AWS account, and specify the right data collection interval.
      - Save the entry.

6. **Verify data ingestion in Splunk**:

   Verify that Splunk is absorbing data from AWS Security Hub and GuardDuty after establishing data inputs. To check if the data is being correctly digested, you can run a search query in Splunk such as `sourcetype=aws:securityhub` or `sourcetype=aws:guardduty`.

7. **Create custom dashboards and alerts**:

   Utilize the data Security Hub and GuardDuty have ingested to build unique dashboards and alerts in Splunk. This makes it possible for you to keep track of security discoveries, spot prospective threats, and handle situations more skillfully.

Using the Splunk Add-on for AWS, you may use a similar process to get other kinds of security information from AWS.

Integrating Microsoft Azure

The Splunk Add-on for Microsoft Cloud Services may gather different kinds of data from Azure and offer insightful security analysis. The following is a list of some significant data sources that the add-on can access:

- **Azure Activity Logs:** Gathers logs pertaining to actions taken on resources in your Azure subscription, such as resource management, access control, and updates.
- **Azure AD Audit Logs:** Retrieves logs for activities such as user sign-ins, group changes, and role assignments that took place in Azure Active Directory.
- **Azure AD Sign-in Logs:** Gathers Azure Active Directory sign-in activity logs, including details on user access and authentication.
- **Alerts from the Azure Security Center:** This feature allows you to retrieve alerts from the Azure Security Center, which offer threat detection and security advice for your Azure resources.
- **Azure Diagnostics Logs:** Gathers diagnostic logs from a variety of Azure resources, including Virtual Machines, App Services, and Storage Accounts, to assist in monitoring and resolving security-related problems.
- **Azure Network Security Group (NSG) Flow Logs:** This feature allows you to retrieve flow logs for your Azure Network Security Groups, recording IP traffic data to help you spot potential security concerns and keep tabs on network activities.

- **Azure Web Application Firewall (WAF) Logs:** This feature gathers web access logs from the Azure Web Application Firewall (WAF), giving you information about online traffic and potential security risks aimed at your apps.
- **Azure Monitor Logs:** This feature allows you to retrieve metrics and logs from Azure Monitor, which you can use to keep an eye on the efficiency and security of your Azure resources.
- **Azure Sentinel Logs:** Gathers logs and alerts from Microsoft's cloud-native SIEM and SOAR service Azure Sentinel, giving information on security incidents and threats.

When you include these data sources in Splunk, you can monitor your Azure environment, spot potential security risks, and handle problems more skillfully.

Microsoft Azure Security Center and Sentinel

The unified infrastructure security management system known as the Azure Security Center improves the security posture of your Azure environment. Providing intelligent security analytics at a cloud-scale, Azure Sentinel is a cloud-native SIEM (Security Information and Event Management) and SOAR (Security Orchestration, Automation, and Response) solution. Organizations can gather and analyze security alerts, suggestions, and logs in a consolidated platform by integrating Splunk with Azure Security Center and Sentinel. You may import data from Azure Security Center and Sentinel into Splunk using the Splunk Add-on for Microsoft Cloud Services or other pertinent add-ons, enabling the construction of personalized dashboards and alerting to improve security monitoring and incident response.

The following steps can be used to integrate Microsoft Azure Security Center and Sentinel with Splunk:

1. **Install and configure the Splunk Add-on for Microsoft Cloud Services**:
    - Visit the following link to download and install the Splunk Add-on for Microsoft Cloud Services from Splunkbase: https://splunkbase.splunk.com/app/3110/
    - After installation, set up the add-on with the relevant Azure login information, subscription information, and other settings.
2. **Enable data collection from Azure Security Center and Sentinel**:
    a. For Azure Security Center:
        - Go to `Security Center` in the Azure interface and select `Security Policy.`

  - Select your subscription and then select **`Data export`**.
  - Click **`Add new export settings`** and select **`Export to an event hub.`**
  - Set the event hub name, event hub policy, and event hub namespace. Save the changes.

b. For Azure Sentinel:

  - Go to **`Azure Sentinel`** in the Azure portal and select **`Data connectors.`**
  - Locate the **`Azure Security Center`** connector and then select **`Open connector page`**.
  - To enable the integration, click **`Configure Azure Security Center`** and adhere to the prompts.

3. **Configure data inputs in Splunk Add-on for Microsoft Cloud Services:**
   - Navigate to the **`Configuration`** section of the Splunk Add-on for Microsoft Cloud Services.
   - Click on **`Create New Input`** and choose the appropriate input type (such as Event Hub for Azure Security Center or Azure Sentinel).
   - Give the input a name, choose the index where the data will be saved, and establish additional parameters like the event hub namespace, name, policy, and any other necessary data.
   - Save the input settings.
4. **Verify data ingestion**:
   - Go to the **`Search & Reporting`** app in Splunk once the data input has been set up.
   - To ensure that the information from Sentinel and Azure Security Center is being absorbed into Splunk, run a search query. You may, for instance, use the query **`index =<your_index> sourcetype=<your_sourcetype>.`**
5. **Create custom dashboards and alerts**:
   - Utilize the Sentinel and Azure Security Center data that has been ingested to build unique Splunk dashboards and alerts. This makes it possible for you to keep track of security discoveries, spot prospective threats, and handle situations more skillfully.

By utilizing the Splunk Add-on for Microsoft Cloud Services, you can carry out comparable actions to gather other kinds of security data from Azure.

Integrating Google Cloud

The Splunk Add-on for the Google Cloud Platform may gather multiple Google Cloud data types, including insightful security information. The following is a list of some significant data sources that the add-on can access:

- **Google Cloud Audit Logs:** Gathers audit logs pertaining to actions taken on resources in your Google Cloud projects, such as administrator activity logs, data access logs, and system event logs.
- **Google Cloud Security Command Center Findings:** The Google Cloud Security Command Center offers a centralized view of security alerts, policy violations, and vulnerabilities.
- **Google Cloud Security Command Center Findings:** Retrieves security findings from the Google Cloud Security Command Center.
- **Google Cloud Identity and Access Management (IAM) Logs:** Gathers logs pertaining to IAM policies, role assignments, and service account usage, giving details on user access and permissions.
- **Google Cloud Pub/Sub:** This service allows users to retrieve messages and logs from the Google Cloud Pub/Sub service, which may be used to ingest logs from a variety of Google Cloud services and third-party tools.
- **VPC Flow Logs:** Gathers IP traffic data from network flow logs for your VPCs to aid in identifying potential security issues and keeping track of network activities.
- **Google Cloud Storage Access Logs:** This feature retrieves the access logs for the Cloud Storage buckets you have created, giving you insight into the requests made to access the data you've stored.
- **Google Cloud Load Balancer Logs:** Gathers information from the Google Cloud Load Balancer service's logs, including details on load-balancing traffic and potential security concerns.
- **Google Cloud Functions Logs:** This feature allows you to retrieve logs from Google Cloud Functions, giving you information about the performance and behavior of your serverless applications.
- **Google Kubernetes Engine (GKE) Logs:** This feature gathers logs from your GKE clusters, which may be used to keep an eye on the security and functionality of your containerized applications.

You can monitor your Google Cloud environment, spot potential security issues, and handle problems more skillfully by ingesting these data sources into Splunk.

Google Cloud Security Command Center and Chronicle

An extensive security management and data risk platform for Google Cloud, the Google Cloud Security Command Center (SCC), aids businesses in preventing, detecting, and countering threats. The Chronicle platform for enterprise security telemetry aids security teams in investigating occurrences and spotting threats at scale. Organizations may gather and examine security findings, logs, and alerts from their Google Cloud environment by integrating Splunk with Google Cloud SCC and Chronicle. The Splunk Add-on for Google Cloud Platform or other pertinent add-ons can be used to accomplish this, allowing the development of unique dashboards and alerts for enhanced security monitoring and incident response.

The following steps can be used to combine Splunk with Chronicle and Google Cloud SCC:

1. **Install and configure the Splunk Add-on for the Google Cloud Platform:**
   a. Access Splunkbase to obtain the Google Cloud Platform add-on: https://splunkbase.splunk.com/app/3088
   b. After installation, set up the add-on with the relevant Google Cloud login information, project information, and other options.
2. **Enable data export from Google Cloud Security Command Center**:
   a. Go to the `Security Command Center` in the Google Cloud Console.
   b. Select `Data Exports` from the left-hand menu's `Settings` option.
   c. Select `Pub/Sub` as the export type by clicking on `Create Data Export`.
   d. Set up the export options, which include the `Pub/Sub` topic, the data types you want to export, and any filters you want to use. Save the changes.
3. **Configure data inputs in the Splunk Add-on for the Google Cloud Platform**:

   For Google Cloud Security Command Center:

   a. Go to the `Configuration` page of the Splunk Add-on for Google Cloud Platform and select the `Data inputs` tab.
   b. Click `Create New Input` and then choose `Google Cloud Pub/Sub`.

   c. Give the input a name, choose the index where the data will be saved, and set up any other necessary parameters, such as the Google Cloud project and `Pub/Sub` subscription.

   d. Save the input settings.

4. **Integrate Splunk with Chronicle**:

   a. Chronicle does not have a specific Splunk add-on, but you can ingest data into Splunk by using the Chronicle API.

   b. Create a custom script or application that makes use of the Chronicle API to gather information from your Chronicle, for instance, such as logs and alerts.

   c. To be compatible with Splunk ingestion, the custom script or application should be built to handle API login, data retrieval, and data formatting.

   d. To import the prepared data from the custom script or application into Splunk, use the HTTP Event Collector (HEC) feature of Splunk or another data input mechanism.

5. **Verify data ingestion**:

   a. Go to the `Search & Reporting` app in Splunk once the data inputs have been set up.

   b. Run search queries to ensure that Splunk is receiving data from the Google Cloud Security Command Center and Chronicle. You may use a query like `index=<your_index> sourcetype=<your_sourcetype>`, for instance.

6. **Create custom dashboards and alerts**:

   a. Utilize the data that has been imported from the Chronicle and the Google Cloud Security Command Center to build unique Splunk dashboards and alerts. This makes it possible for you to keep track of security discoveries, spot prospective threats, and handle situations more skillfully.

Using the Splunk Add-on for AWS, you may use a similar process to get other kinds of security information from AWS.

Integrating with Third-party Cloud Security Tools

Splunk can be linked with numerous third-party cloud security solutions, including Cloud Access Security Brokers (CASBs), cloud-based firewalls, and intrusion detection systems, in addition to native cloud security services. These connectors give businesses the ability to gather and examine security information from various sources, giving them a complete picture of their cloud security posture. Organizations can improve their overall security monitoring and incident response capabilities by ingesting data from third-party cloud security technologies using the right Splunk add-ons or by establishing custom connectors.

Organizations may get a consolidated view of their cloud security posture, more effectively identify possible risks, and react to security incidents by integrating Splunk with a variety of cloud security services and technologies.

Case Studies

Here are three case studies illustrating the successful implementation of cloud security in various organizations using Splunk. These examples demonstrate how Splunk can help businesses improve their cloud security posture.

- Detecting and responding to misconfigurations in the cloud:

Use Case: Unsecured Amazon S3 Buckets

The AWS infrastructure of a large e-commerce company, which contained several Amazon S3 buckets containing client data, was monitored by Splunk. Splunk was set up to collect data from AWS Config and provide alerts for any S3 buckets that have open read and write access. One day, an alert signaling the creation of a new S3 bucket with public read access was triggered. The security team was alerted right away, and they were able to lock down the bucket to stop unwanted access to private customer information.

- Monitoring and securing cloud-based applications:

Use Case: Securing a Serverless Application

With the help of AWS Lambda, a financial services company converted its payment processing application to a serverless architecture. To ingest logs and data from AWS Lambda, Amazon API Gateway, and other services utilized in the application, the company used Splunk. The security team was able to identify an increase in unsuccessful authentication attempts through the analysis of this data, which pointed to a probable application-targeting brute-force assault. They rapidly discovered the source IP addresses using Splunk, and they made unique alerts to immediately stop malicious activity.

- Identifying and mitigating data exfiltration attempts:

Use Case: Preventing Data Exfiltration in a Multi-Cloud Environment

Splunk was utilized by a healthcare firm with several clouds to combine logs and security events from the AWS, Azure, and Google Cloud Platform. They tracked user activity across all three cloud platforms using Splunk's machine learning and user behavior analytics (UBA) features. Splunk discovered anomalous data access behaviors by a worker who had just handed in their two-week notice. The worker was trying to obtain a significant amount of private patient data from various cloud storage platforms. The employees' access permissions were swiftly terminated by the security team after they were notified, preventing a large data breach.

Best Practices for Cloud Security with Splunk

In today's digital environment, cloud security is of the utmost importance. Splunk, a popular platform for data analysis and monitoring, has a lot of tools and capabilities that can assist businesses in ensuring strong security in their cloud environments. Here are some recommendations for using Splunk for cloud security:

- **Implementing least privilege access controls**:

  Users have the bare minimum of permissions required to carry out their job responsibilities, thanks to the least privilege access constraints. To uphold this rule, you can manage user roles and permissions in Splunk. This entails designating users to particular roles and granting each role only the necessary capabilities. By restricting access, the possibility of insider threats is diminished and illegal acts are prevented.

- **Leveraging machine learning and AI for advanced threat detection**:

  Splunk offers a number of machine learning and artificial intelligence features that can improve an organization's ability to identify threats and take appropriate action. These techniques can find patterns and anomalies in enormous volumes of data that might point to possible security concerns. While applications like Splunk Enterprise Security (ES) offer built-in AI-driven analytics for advanced threat detection, Splunk's Machine Learning Toolkit (MLTK) and the Splunk Security Suite can be used to construct bespoke models for detecting attacks.

- **Continuously monitoring cloud environments for security and compliance**:

  By gathering, analyzing, and correlating data from numerous sources, such as logs, metrics, and events, Splunk may assist you in continuously monitoring your cloud environment. Dashboards, alarms, and reports may be made using this data to give you a real-time view of your cloud security position. Additionally, you can monitor your cloud infrastructure with the aid of the Splunk App for AWS, Azure, and Google Cloud to make sure it complies with all applicable laws and requirements.

- **Automating incident response with playbooks and automation**:

  For security breaches to have as little of an impact as possible, a quick and effective incident response is essential. By integrating with applications like Splunk Phantom, which enables you to develop playbooks that specify the precise steps to be taken in response to particular security occurrences, Splunk can aid in automating incident response operations. These playbooks may contain robotic tasks like ticket creation, notification sending, or blocking malicious IP addresses. Automating incident response allows you to minimize possible damage by speeding up the detection, investigation, and remediation of security problems.

  In conclusion, implementing least privilege access controls, utilizing machine learning and AI for advanced threat detection, continuously monitoring cloud environments for security and compliance, and automating incident response with playbooks and automation tools are all part of leveraging Splunk for cloud security. Organizations may greatly enhance their cloud security posture and lower the likelihood of security incidents by adhering to these best practices.

Conclusion

This chapter has described how Splunk provides complete solutions for handling a variety of cloud security issues. The subtleties of the Shared Responsibility Model, data protection and privacy, compliance, visibility, control difficulties, and the challenges of multi-cloud systems have all been covered. We've seen how Splunk's strong data-collecting and analytical capabilities help with the ongoing observation and comprehension of these intricacies. Splunk offers a unified platform for better security management with its flexible connection with multiple third-party security technologies and key cloud service providers like AWS, Azure, and Google Cloud.

As we proceed to the next chapter, *DevOps and Security Operations*, we will build on this knowledge of cloud security to examine how Splunk enables the union of development and operations (DevOps). We will explore how to use Splunk's capabilities for seamless DevOps activities, providing both quick service delivery and strong security, combining the best of both worlds.

Points to Remember

- Implement access restrictions to reduce the risk of unwanted actions and insider threats by giving users only the minimal access rights required to complete their responsibilities.
- Make better use of Splunk's machine learning and artificial intelligence tools, such as Splunk Enterprise Security (ES) and the Machine Learning Toolkit (MLTK), to identify and counteract sophisticated attacks.

  Use Splunk to gather, examine, and correlate data from diverse sources, including logs, metrics, and events, to continually monitor your cloud environment. This makes it possible to see your cloud security posture in real-time.
- Monitor your cloud infrastructure with the help of the Splunk App for AWS, Azure, and Google Cloud to make sure it complies with all applicable laws and requirements.
- Integrate Splunk with applications like Splunk Phantom to build playbooks that automate incident response procedures, cutting down on the amount of time needed to find, analyze, and fix security events.

Chapter 13

DevOps and Security Operations

Introduction

This chapter examines the critical interface between DevOps and Security Operations, highlighting the significance of incorporating security practices within the DevOps lifecycle to improve an organization's general security posture. A secure and successful software delivery process is made possible by the chapter's insights on how Splunk may be used in DevOps and Security Operations.

The first section of the chapter introduces the idea of DevOps, outlining its fundamental ideas and the advantages of using a DevOps strategy. The necessity to integrate security measures into the DevOps process is then covered, leading to the secure development methodology known as DevSecOps. In order to make sure that security is a crucial component of the entire software development lifecycle, this section emphasizes the significance of moving security considerations to the left.

The chapter then explores Splunk's role in assisting Security Operations and DevOps. It addresses a range of use cases, including tracking configuration changes, discovering security vulnerabilities, and monitoring CI/CD pipelines. To build a cohesive and efficient workflow, the chapter also offers instructions on integrating Splunk with various DevOps and security solutions.

For security experts and DevOps practitioners wishing to integrate Splunk into their development and operations processes, the *DevOps and Security Operations* chapter is a great resource. Organizations can create a secure and effective software delivery pipeline by adhering to the guidelines presented in this chapter, ensuring that security is given top attention throughout the development lifecycle.

Structure

In this chapter, we will cover the following topics:

- Introduction to DevOps and security operations
  - Importance of integrating security into the DevOps lifecycle
  - Security Operations (SecOps) and its objectives
  - Key principles of DevSecOps
  - Tools and technologies for DevSecOps
  - Challenges in implementing DevSecOps
  - Measuring the success of DevSecOps
- Integrating Splunk into DevOps and SecOps
  - Overview of Splunk's capabilities for DevOps and SecOps
  - Key components of Splunk for DevOps and SecOps integration
  - Benefits of using Splunk for DevOps and Security Operations
- Continuous Integration and Continuous Deployment (CI/CD) with Splunk
  - Monitoring and managing CI/CD pipelines with Splunk
  - Leveraging Splunk to identify and address security vulnerabilities in CI/CD pipelines
- Use cases

Introducing DevOps and Security Operations

Software development (Dev) and IT operations (Ops) are two fields that can be combined to create DevOps, a set of practices that aims to shorten the development life cycle and offer continuous delivery of high-quality software. DevOps attempts to build a more effective and agile software development process by encouraging strong cooperation between the development and operations teams.

DevOps is essential in the context of cybersecurity because it makes sure that security is a natural component of the development process. Organizations can reduce the risk of data breaches and other security events by implementing

DevOps principles because they can spot and fix security flaws early in the development cycle. The need for integrating security practices and technologies throughout the whole software development life cycle is emphasized by this proactive approach to security, known as DevSecOps.

Importance of Integrating Security into the DevOps Lifecycle

Security has frequently been overlooked in the software development process in the past. This method may result in vulnerabilities being found later in the development process or even after deployment, making remediation expensive and time-consuming. Organizations can incorporate security into the DevOps lifecycle:

- **Shift security left:** Vulnerabilities can be found and handled more quickly by adding security practices and tools early in the development process.
- **Lower risk**: Security breaches and other events are much less likely when vulnerabilities are found and fixed quickly.
- **Promote improved communication and collaboration**: By incorporating security into the DevOps lifecycle, development and security teams are encouraged to work more closely together.
- **Quicker software deployment**: Organizations can reduce security-related delays by taking security into account at every stage of software development.
- Delivering secure and dependable software contributes to consumer trust, which is crucial for any organization's long-term success.

Security Operations (SecOps) and Its Objectives

A cooperative strategy that unites IT security and operations teams is called Security Operations (SecOps). Its goal is to guarantee that all IT systems and operations are smoothly linked with security. The following outlines the main goals of SecOps as well as the "shift right" approach concept:

Core Objectives of SecOps

- **Enhanced Security Posture:** Increasing an organization's overall security is the main goal of SecOps. Proactive monitoring, threat identification, incident response, and ongoing security enhancements are used to accomplish this.

- **Operational Efficiency:** The goal of SecOps is to improve workflows, cut down on redundancies, and boost overall efficiency by incorporating security into operational procedures. This entails making sure that operational agility is not hampered by security measures and automating regular security chores.
- **Compliance Management:** SecOps makes sure that security measures are properly implemented and tracked throughout all IT systems, which helps to maintain compliance with pertinent rules and standards.
- **Risk Mitigation:** The goal of SecOps is to detect and reduce risks before they become security events. This calls for the ongoing evaluation of risks and the application of suitable risk-reduction techniques.
- **Collaboration and Communication:** Improving communication and coordination between security and operations teams is a primary objective of SecOps. This contributes to the development of a more unified and integrated approach to IT and security management.

Shift Right Approach in SecOps

- **Classical "Shift Left" Philosophy:** A traditional strategy that emphasizes integrating security early in the development lifecycle, especially in software development and DevOps processes, has been the center of attention.
- **Emergence of "Shift Right":** By emphasizing the integration of security practices into the later phases of the development lifecycle and post-deployment, the **shift right** method is a complement to the **shift left** strategy. This covers operational security in live situations, incident response, and real-time monitoring.
- **Real-Time Security Monitoring:** Making the shift to the right entails ongoing observation of the systems and applications within their operational environment in order to identify and address threats as they arise.
- **Post-Deployment Testing:** In order to find vulnerabilities that might not have been obvious at an earlier stage, it involves thorough security testing and analysis in production systems.
- **Feedback Loop:** Using the **shift right** method, security measures are improved and informed throughout the IT lifecycle by using insights from monitoring and testing in real-world scenarios.
- **Incident Response and Recovery:** Creating strong incident response and recovery plans is essential to **shift right** in order to promptly handle security breaches and lessen their effects.

SecOps, which focuses on boosting security, increasing operational effectiveness, and guaranteeing compliance, is a crucial component of contemporary IT operations. The SecOps **shift right** method highlights the significance of security in the post-deployment stage, guaranteeing ongoing defense, observation, and enhancement in operational environments. Organizations can establish a more comprehensive and effective security posture by combining reactive and adaptable techniques ("shift right") with proactive security measures ("shift left").

Key Principles of DevSecOps

A concept called DevSecOps incorporates security procedures into the DevOps workflow. The goal is to integrate security throughout the entire process of developing and implementing software. These are the main ideas that characterize the DevSecOps approach:

- **Embedded Security:** DevSecOps incorporates security from the outset of the development cycle, in contrast to traditional models where security is a distinct, final step. To do this, security must be taken into account at every stage, including design, development, testing, deployment, and operations.
- **Automation:** To smoothly incorporate security into the DevOps workflow, DevSecOps mostly relies on automation. Continuous integration and delivery pipelines use automated security tools and procedures to guarantee reliable and effective security checks and tests.
- **Open Communication and Collaboration:** DevSecOps encourages open communication and cooperation between the security, operations, and development teams. Because of this cooperative approach, security is made to be a shared responsibility and is taken into account while making decisions.
- **Continuous Security:** DevSecOps views security as a continuous process. It is imperative to have response systems, threat detection, and ongoing monitoring. This includes automated reactions to possible attacks and real-time security notifications.
- **Shift Left and Right:** DevSecOps acknowledges the significance of **shift right** methods, which concentrate on security after deployment, but also stresses the value of **shift left** practices, which integrate security early in the development process. Throughout the lifecycle, complete security coverage is ensured by this dual approach.
- **Iterative Improvement:** DevSecOps approaches security in an iterative manner, much like DevOps does with software development. Security procedures and methods are always being refined in response to user input and lessons learned from past versions.

- **Code for Compliance:** DevSecOps handles legal and compliance obligations like code. The development process incorporates and codifies compliance requirements to guarantee that they are automatically verified and upheld.
- **Pragmatic Risk Management:** A key component of DevSecOps is the effective, practical assessment and management of hazards. By ranking security jobs according to their possible impact and likelihood of attacks, it makes sure that resources are distributed efficiently.
- **Holistic Security View:** DevSecOps necessitates a comprehensive understanding of the security posture of the company. It considers the broader organization-wide effects of security choices and tactics in addition to specific projects.
- **Education and Training:** An integral part of DevSecOps is ongoing education and training in security best practices. This gives every team member the ability to participate in a secure development process and make knowledgeable security decisions.

DevSecOps guarantees that security is an essential and ongoing component of the development lifecycle by abiding by these principles, which results in better secure products and quicker, safer delivery cycles.

Tools and Technologies for DevSecOps

A collection of tools and technologies created to smoothly incorporate security into the DevOps pipeline is necessary for an efficient DevSecOps implementation. In addition to automating several security check processes, these systems guarantee ongoing compliance and monitoring all the way through the development lifecycle. This is a summary of the main tool and technology categories utilized in DevSecOps:

1. Static Application Security Testing (SAST)

- **Goal**: SAST tools find security flaws by analyzing source code while it's at rest.
- **Examples:** Fortify, Checkmarx, and SonarQube.
- **Integration Point**: During code commits or pull requests early in the development process, integration.

2. Dynamic Application Security Testing (DAST)

- **Goal:** DAST tools check for vulnerabilities in programs that are currently operating, usually from an external viewpoint.
- **Examples**: Veracode, Burp Suite, and OWASP ZAP.

- **Integration Point**: Used in development or staging environments for testing deployed applications.

3. **Interactive Application Security Testing (IAST)**

- **Goal**: Applications are analyzed from within using IAST tools, which incorporate parts of both SAST and DAST, frequently during runtime.
- **Examples**: Veracode Greenlight and Contrast Security.
- **Integration Point**: Usually integrated into the QA and testing stage.

4. **Software Composition Analysis (SCA)**

- **Goal:** SCA tools locate open-source parts in codebases in order to monitor licensing and vulnerabilities.
- **Examples**: Black Duck, Snyk, and WhiteSource.
- **Integration Point**: Integrated to check dependencies throughout the development stage.

5. **Container Security Tools**

- **Goal:** These tools protect containerized apps, as well as the environments used for container orchestration and container images.
- **Examples**: Twistlock, Sysdig, and Aqua Security are a few examples.
- **Integration Point**: Incorporated into the build, deployment, and runtime stages of the CI/CD pipeline.

6. **Configuration Management Tools**

- **Goal**: Assure that systems are kept up to date and configured securely in a reliable state.
- **Examples:** Ansible, Chef, and Puppet.
- **Integration Point**: Utilized during the operational and deployment stages.

7. **Secrets Management Tools**

- **Goal**: Protect, control, and monitor user access to private keys and credentials.
- **Examples:** Azure Key Vault, AWS Secrets Manager, and HashiCorp Vault are a few examples.
- **Integration Point**: incorporated into the CI/CD pipeline to control access securely.

8. Compliance as Code Tools

- **Goal:** Automate compliance audits using pre-established guidelines or standards.
- **Examples:** Terraform, Chef Compliance, and InSpec are a few examples.
- **Point of Integration**: Incorporated into the CI/CD pipeline, especially in the testing stage.

9. Security Information and Event Management (SIEM)

- **Goal**: Offer in-the-moment security warning analysis from network hardware and apps.
- **Examples**: IBM QRadar, Sumo Logic, and Splunk.
- **Integration Point:** Used in production situations during the monitoring phase.

10. Incident Response and Forensics Tools

- **Goal:** Assist in the identification, study, and handling of security incidents.
- **Examples:** PagerDuty, Demisto, TheHive.
- **Integration Point**: Following deployment, integrated at the operational stage.

The careful selection and incorporation of these tools are essential to the successful execution of DevSecOps. By managing vulnerabilities, automating security tests, ensuring compliance, and quickly responding to security incidents, these tools assist in integrating security into every stage of the DevOps pipeline.

Challenges in Implementing DevSecOps

When attempting to apply DevSecOps techniques, organizations may run into a number of difficulties, such as:

- **Change reluctance**: The development, operations, and security teams can be wary of implementing novel procedures, devices, and approaches.
- **Skills gap**: To acquire the knowledge and abilities required for implementing DevSecOps techniques, team members may need training.
- **Integration problems**: It may be difficult to develop a smooth workflow when using existing tools and systems that do not seamlessly interact with DevSecOps technology.
- **Budget restrictions**: A company's capacity to invest in the new tools, technology, and training required for a successful DevSecOps implementation may be hampered by a lack of funds.

Measuring the Success of DevSecOps

It is imperative for enterprises to assess the efficacy of their DevSecOps initiatives in order to ascertain the return on investment and to consistently enhance their security protocols. Evaluating several key performance indicators (KPIs) that show how security is incorporated into the DevOps process is part of measuring success in DevSecOps. These are the key performance indicators and factors for evaluating the success of DevSecOps:

1. Reduction in the Number of Security Incidents

- **Metric**: Determine how frequently security lapses or incidents occur both before and after DevSecOps is implemented.
- **Objective**: DevSecOps implementation success should result in a discernible drop in security incidents.

2. Time to Detect and Respond to Security Threats

- **Metric**: Calculate the average time it takes to detect security threats (MTTD) and to respond to them (MTTR).
- **Objective**: DevSecOps should enhance the company's capacity to promptly detect and address security issues and vulnerabilities.

3. Vulnerability Detection and Management

- **Metric:** Track the quantity, seriousness, and turnaround time for vulnerabilities found.
- **Objective**: Early vulnerability detection and timely mitigation should result from effective DevSecOps procedures.

4. Compliance and Audit Readiness

- **Metric:** Determine how simple and prepared compliance audits are, as well as how many compliance problems are discovered.
- **Objective**: DevSecOps should improve regulatory standard compliance and lower the frequency of compliance problems.

5. Automation in Security Processes

- **Metric**: Determine how much automation has been used for security testing and monitoring.
- **Objective**: One of the main signs of an advanced DevSecOps strategy is increased automation in security processes.

6. Deployment Frequency and Failure Rate

- **Metric:** Monitor the deployment rate and the deployment failure rate as a result of security vulnerabilities.
- **Objective**: DevSecOps seeks to lower the failure rate resulting from security-related issues while raising the frequency of deployments.

7. Feedback Loop Efficiency

- **Metric:** Evaluate how well the security, development, and operations teams communicate with each other.
- **Objective:** An effective and fruitful feedback loop is fostered by a successful DevSecOps effort, enhancing cooperation and communication.

8. Team Knowledge and Skills Improvement

- **Metric:** Evaluate the development and operational teams' security knowledge and proficiency.
- **Objective**: DevSecOps should lead to improved security expertise and abilities among all participating teams.

9. Cost-Effectiveness

- **Metric:** Examine the financial savings brought about by a decline in security incidents and an increase in operational effectiveness.
- **Objective**: DevSecOps practice implementation should ultimately be financially advantageous for the company.

10. Customer Satisfaction

- **Metric**: Evaluate client satisfaction and feedback, especially with regard to program security and dependability.
- **Objective**: One of the most important signs of a successful DevSecOps integration is increased customer satisfaction with the security and dependability of goods and services.

DevSecOps success measurement is a complex process that calls for the analysis of both quantitative and qualitative data. Better security postures, better teamwork, more effective procedures, and eventually higher customer satisfaction and trust are signs of a successful deployment. The success and development of DevSecOps techniques within an organization depend on constant measurement and improvement.

Integrating Splunk into DevOps and SecOps

This section will guide you through the vast array of Splunk's features that are tailored exclusively for DevOps and SecOps. We'll open the door to Splunk's essential elements, which are crucial to their seamless integration with these operations. We will also go into great detail about the inherent advantages of using Splunk for DevOps and Security Operations. This chapter will help you learn how this potent tool can improve organizational performance by streamlining development processes, revolutionizing your understanding of data, and enhancing security measures.

Overview of Splunk's capabilities for DevOps and SecOps

Splunk is a fantastic solution for both DevOps and SecOps initiatives because it offers a robust platform for data collection, processing, and visualization. Splunk offers helpful insights into application performance, infrastructure health, and security incidents thanks to its capacity to ingest and process enormous volumes of data from numerous sources in real time. The following are some of Splunk's crucial DevOps and SecOps capabilities:

- **Real-time monitoring and analysis**: Splunk gives businesses the ability to track and examine data from security, infrastructure, and application events in real-time, giving them useful information for quick decision-making.
- **Advanced search and reporting**: Users can easily spot patterns, abnormalities, and possible problems in their IT environment because of Splunk's strong search and reporting capabilities.
- **Customizable dashboards**: Splunk provides visualizations and dashboards that enable teams to more effectively communicate and comprehend their data, promoting better decision-making and collaboration.
- **Extensibility and integration**: Splunk is extensible and easy to combine with other tools and technologies thanks to a large variety of add-ons, apps, and integrations that it supports.

Key Components of Splunk for DevOps and SecOps Integration

Organizations can utilize a number of essential components and capabilities of Splunk to successfully incorporate it into DevOps and SecOps workflows, including:

- **Splunk Enterprise**: The main platform for real-time data collection, indexing, search, and analysis.
- **Splunk IT Service Intelligence (ITSI):** An analytics-driven solution that aids businesses in keeping tabs on the functionality and health of their IT systems.
- **Splunk App for Infrastructure (SAI):** A comprehensive tool for managing and monitoring the efficiency of servers, containers, and other cloud resources.
- **Splunk Enterprise Security (ES):** A complete security information and event management (SIEM) tool that gives SecOps teams access to real-time visibility, sophisticated analytics, and incident response tools.
- **Splunkbase:** A storefront offering a variety of add-ons, apps, and integrations that may be used to enhance the functionality of Splunk and connect it to other software and hardware.

Benefits of Using Splunk for DevOps and Security Operations

Integrating Splunk into DevOps and SecOps workflows offers several benefits, such as:

- **Increased visibility**: Because Splunk offers a thorough overview of the whole IT environment, teams can discover and handle performance problems, security incidents, and other issues right away.
- Better communication and collaboration between development, operations, and security teams are made possible by Splunk's shared dashboards and visualizations.
- **Faster incident response**: Splunk's real-time monitoring and powerful analytics enable organizations to quickly identify, look into, and address security problems, thereby minimizing their potential impact.
- **Reduced downtime**: Organizations may reduce the risk of downtime and guarantee the continuous delivery of high-quality software by identifying and resolving issues early in the development cycle.

Continuous Integration and Continuous Deployment (CI/CD) with Splunk

DevOps essential practices Continuous Integration (CI) and Continuous Deployment (CD) allow businesses to automate the processes of integrating code changes, developing, testing, and deploying software. By accelerating the delivery of high-quality software, teams can decrease time-to-market and improve customer satisfaction. CI/CD enables businesses to incorporate security audits and vulnerability assessments throughout the development pipeline in the context of SecOps, ensuring that security issues are dealt with promptly and continually.

Monitoring and Managing CI/CD pipelines with Splunk

By giving users visibility of the whole CI/CD pipeline, Splunk plays a critical part in supporting Continuous Integration (CI) and Continuous Deployment (CD) procedures. Splunk can be included in CI/CD workflows in several ways, such as:

- **Monitoring and managing CI/CD pipelines**: Splunk can ingest data from CI/CD technologies to monitor and manage the performance of pipelines, assisting teams in locating and resolving bottlenecks and other problems.

  As an illustration, let's say Jenkins is the CI/CD technology used by your company. Installing the Splunk plugin for Jenkins will allow you to integrate Jenkins with Splunk. This plugin will gather and send Jenkins data to Splunk for analysis and visualization, such as build status, deployment status, and test results.

- **Analyzing build and deployment data**: Splunk is able to gather and analyze data from build and deployment processes, revealing patterns, abnormalities, and potential problems that could have an impact on the caliber of the software being delivered.

  As an illustration, when the Jenkins plugin sends data to Splunk, you may design your own dashboards and visualizations to examine build and deployment data, assisting you in spotting patterns and potential problems that could have an impact on the application's quality.

- **Code quality and vulnerability scanning**: Splunk can assist teams in locating security vulnerabilities and issues with code quality early in the development process by integrating with code analysis and vulnerability scanning tools.

  As an illustration, let's imagine you scan for vulnerabilities and analyze code using SonarQube. You can set SonarQube up to transmit Splunk's analysis results. Splunk can assist you in identifying and resolving security vulnerabilities and issues with code quality early in the development process by indexing and analyzing this data.

- **Monitoring and troubleshooting deployment environments**: Splunk enables teams to quickly discover and address issues that may affect application performance or availability by monitoring the health and performance of various deployment environments, such as staging, testing, and production.

  Let's take the case when your application is first promoted to production after being deployed to a staging environment. You may set up Splunk to gather logs and data from both environments, enabling you to keep an eye on the application's health and performance and immediately spot any potential problems.

- **Performance testing and monitoring:** Performance test data can be collected and analyzed using Splunk in conjunction with performance testing tools, assisting teams in making sure that their applications meet performance requirements prior to launch.

  Consider the example of performance testing with JMeter. By sending test results and performance information to Splunk for analysis, you may combine JMeter with Splunk. The performance of the application may then be tracked to make sure it meets the necessary standards before deployment, using customized dashboards and visualizations.

- **Change management and release tracking**: Splunk can help teams decide when to deploy new releases by gathering and analyzing data from tools for change management and release tracking. This information can be used to understand how changes affect the stability and security of the IT system.

  In this instance, Jira is used by your company to track releases and handle changes. The Splunk Add-on for Atlassian JIRA allows you to combine Splunk and Jira. This add-on gathers information from Jira, including issue updates, project modifications, and release statistics, giving users insights into how changes affect the stability and security of the IT infrastructure.

You can acquire a comprehensive understanding of your application pipeline by integrating these technologies with Splunk. This will enable you to oversee and control every step of the development and deployment process and, eventually, provide your clients with high-quality, secure software.

Leveraging Splunk to Identify and Address Security Vulnerabilities in CI/CD pipelines

Pipelines for continuous integration and deployment (CI/CD) have become an essential component of contemporary software development techniques. They ensure the stability of the product while enabling quicker distribution of software upgrades and problem fixes. If these pipelines are not adequately maintained and monitored, they may also present security flaws. These security flaws in CI/CD pipelines can be found and fixed using Splunk, a top platform for data analysis and visualization. This is how:

- **Data Collection and Ingestion**:

  Splunk can gather and ingest logs, events, and metrics from a variety of CI/CD pipeline components, including build systems, version control systems, and deployment tools. These data sources shed light on the condition, functionality, and security of the pipeline.

- **Real-time Monitoring and Alerting:**

  Real-time monitoring and warnings on potential security flaws are made possible by Splunk. Teams can be informed of any anomalies, failed builds, or suspicious behaviors within the CI/CD pipeline by setting up custom alerts and dashboards.

- **Vulnerability Detection and Analysis**:

  Splunk may examine ingested data to find trends and patterns that might point to security flaws. It is able to identify and correlate things like unauthorized code changes, configuration drifts, and unsuccessful authentication attempts. Splunk's robust search and query features make it simple to identify and look into these problems.

- **Compliance and Auditing**:

  To make sure that the CI/CD pipeline complies with industry standards and laws like GDPR, HIPAA, or PCI DSS, Splunk can be employed. Splunk assists teams in maintaining a thorough audit trail by recording and reviewing changes made along the pipeline, which is essential for proving compliance.

- **Incident Response and Remediation**:

  In the event of a security breach, Splunk can assist teams in locating the issue's primary cause, evaluating its effects, and taking prompt action. Splunk integration with incident response and ITSM technologies helps speed up the remediation process and reduce possible harm.

- **Continuous Improvement**:

  Splunk offers significant insights for teams to identify areas for improvement by continuously monitoring and analyzing data from the CI/CD pipeline. Teams may continuously improve their security posture and lower the attack surface thanks to this iterative process.

In conclusion, utilizing Splunk to find and fix security flaws in CI/CD pipelines entails gathering and ingesting data from various sources, monitoring and alerting on potential problems, detecting and analyzing vulnerabilities, ensuring compliance, handling incidents, and continuously enhancing the overall security posture. Organizations may maintain a secure, compliant, and effective software delivery process by incorporating Splunk into the CI/CD pipeline.

Use Cases

Here are four case studies illustrating the successful implementation of devSecOps in various organizations using Splunk.

- **Secure Continuous Integration and Continuous Deployment (CI/CD) for a Fintech Company**:

The CI/CD pipeline of a financial company has to be safe and consistent with industry standards. Splunk was linked with the company's CI/CD technologies, including Jenkins and GitLab, to monitor and control the security of the pipeline. The company's ability to regularly evaluate the security posture of its codebase was made possible by data collection from code analysis and vulnerability scanning technologies like SonarQube. The development and security teams were able to proactively resolve vulnerabilities and maintain a high degree of security throughout the software development lifecycle thanks to Splunk's customized dashboards and warnings.

- **Incident Response and Threat Hunting for a Government Agency**:

To safeguard its sensitive data and important infrastructure, a government agency wished to strengthen its incident response and threat-hunting skills. Splunk was utilized by the organization to gather and examine data from a variety of security sources, including endpoints, network gadgets, and threat intelligence feeds. The agency's DevOps and security teams were able to find trends and anomalies suggestive of security concerns with the use of Splunk's advanced analytics and machine learning features. This decreased the overall risk to the agency's infrastructure and data by allowing them to promptly analyze and address security incidents.

- **Secure Configuration Management for a Manufacturing Company**:

A manufacturer had to make sure that its IT infrastructure was configured safely and in accordance with industry requirements. The organization utilized Splunk to manage and keep an eye on how its servers, network equipment, and other IT assets were configured. The business was able to regularly evaluate the security posture of its infrastructure by gathering information from configuration management technologies like Ansible and Puppet and integrating with vulnerability scanners like Nessus and Qualys. The DevOps and security teams were able to discover and correct misconfigurations and vulnerabilities proactively thanks to customized alarms and reports, maintaining a high level of security and compliance throughout the enterprise.

- **Microservices Security Monitoring for a Media and Entertainment Company**:

A media and entertainment firm needed to guarantee that its microservices were secure and compliant after adopting a microservices-based architecture for its applications. The business uses Splunk to keep an eye on the security of its microservices and the orchestration and container infrastructure that supports them, including Docker and Kubernetes. The organization was able to learn more about the security of its microservices environment by gathering data from container security products like Aqua Security and Twistlock. The DevOps and security teams were able to proactively detect and fix security risks and vulnerabilities thanks to customized dashboards and alerts, assuring the secure and reliable delivery of the company's apps and services.

Conclusion

The intersection of DevOps and Security Operations (SecOps) has been thoroughly explored in this chapter, emphasizing the significance of integrating these specialties for better software development and security practices. We investigated how the potent platform Splunk, which can be easily incorporated into both DevOps and SecOps workflows, can support a proactive, data-driven approach to security.

We have learned how Splunk assists with automating processes, enabling real-time error detection, and offering insights for these processes' optimization through our investigation of Continuous Integration and Continuous Deployment (CI/CD). We have seen via the use cases how these ideas are put into practice in actual situations, highlighting the useful advantages of including Splunk in the CI/CD process.

After delving into the subtle dynamics of DevOps, SecOps, and its integration with Splunk, let's move on to our final chapter, *Best Practices for Splunk in Cybersecurity*. In the following chapter, we'll go into the finer points of how Splunk may be used to its maximum capacity, particularly in bolstering our cybersecurity posture. Expect a practical handbook filled with effective tactics, tips, and practices for leveraging Splunk's strength in securing digital assets.

Points to Remember

- **Collaboration and communication**: Effective collaboration and communication between the Development and Operations teams are the cornerstones on which DevOps is built. This collaborative approach, emphasizing open communication, shared responsibility, and group decision-making must be upheld when integrating Security Operations.
- **Shift security left**: By including security controls early in the development process (also known as shifting security left), vulnerabilities can be found and countered before they become serious. This method produces better secure software while reducing risk and saving time.
- **Continuous integration and delivery (CI/CD):** Setting up an automated testing and deployment pipeline with a CI/CD pipeline makes it easier to identify security issues and enables speedier remediation. This strategy ensures a more resilient infrastructure and shortens the time it takes to release security patches.
- **Automation:** Wherever possible, automate security procedures, including configuration management, code analysis, and vulnerability scanning. Automation reduces human error, simplifies processes, and aids in maintaining a constant security posture.
- **Monitoring and visibility**: Implement real-time monitoring and logging to get visibility into your apps, infrastructure, and security events. This provides a proactive security approach and enables quicker detection of potential attacks, vulnerabilities, or anomalies.
- **Incident response and recovery**: To address security issues swiftly and successfully, create well-defined incident response and recovery plans. Make sure that all team members are aware of their roles and

responsibilities by periodically reviewing and updating these plans to keep them up-to-date.

- **Culture of constant learning and improvement**: DevOps and Security Operations should adopt this philosophy. Assess your security posture frequently, judge how well your security procedures are working, and make adjustments for new threats and cutting-edge technologies.
- **Shared accountability**: Rather than falling solely on the security staff, security should be the responsibility of the entire team. Develop a culture where security, operations, and development staff collaborate to create and maintain secure systems.
- **Compliance and governance**: Make that your DevOps and Security Operations procedures comply with applicable industry standards, laws, and best practices. To prove compliance to stakeholders and regulators, keep accurate records and audit trails.
- **Tooling and integration**: Choose the best DevOps and Security Operations workflow tools and technologies. To ensure a smooth, effective, and safe software development and delivery process, make sure these tools are well-integrated.

References

- https://www.splunk.com/en_us/blog/learn/devops-roles-responsibilities.html
- https://www.splunk.com/en_us/blog/learn/devops-monitoring.html

Chapter 14

Best Practices for Splunk in Cybersecurity

Introduction

This chapter delves into the critical best practices for properly employing Splunk in cybersecurity. Its goal is to provide a complete guide to optimizing your Splunk implementation and maximizing its ability to address security concerns. The chapter is divided into sections, each focusing on a different facet of Splunk's use in cybersecurity, such as data ingestion, scalability, and real-world case studies.

The chapter opens with an introduction to cybersecurity best practices, emphasizing the necessity of cybersecurity in today's digital landscape, fundamental cybersecurity principles, and the critical role of data analytics in cybersecurity. It then delves into numerous ways to use Splunk efficiently in cybersecurity, with an emphasis on understanding its architecture, connecting with other security tools, and creating security use cases.

Subsequent sections discuss best practices for data intake and standardization, search and analytics, alerting and reporting, as well as Splunk scalability and performance. These sections provide step-by-step instructions for optimizing your Splunk deployment for security use cases, ensuring that your organization is well-prepared to handle and respond to security threats.

In conclusion, the chapter Best Practices for Splunk in Cybersecurity is a thorough guide for security professionals aiming to optimize the value of Splunk in their cybersecurity efforts. You may optimize your Splunk deployment, improve your security posture, and effectively handle security concerns in your organization by following the best practices provided in this chapter.

Structure

In this chapter, we will cover the following topics:

- Overview of best practices in cybersecurity
  - Fundamental cybersecurity principles
  - Role of data analytics in cybersecurity
- Techniques for effective use of Splunk in cybersecurity
  - Understanding Splunk's architecture and components
  - Integrating Splunk with various security tools and data sources
  - Identifying security use cases and requirements
- Best practices for data ingestion and normalization with Splunk
  - Choosing the right data inputs and forwarders
  - Implementing data normalization using the Common Information Model (CIM)
  - Managing data retention and storage policies
- Best practices for search and analytics with Splunk
  - Writing efficient and optimized search queries
  - Creating meaningful and actionable visualizations and dashboards
  - Leveraging machine learning and advanced analytics for proactive threat hunting
- Best practices for alerting and reporting with Splunk
  - Configuring meaningful alerts and notifications
  - Creating comprehensive and actionable security reports
  - Integrating Splunk with incident response and IT Service Management (ITSM) tools
- Best practices for scalability and performance with Splunk
  - Designing a scalable Splunk deployment architecture
  - Optimizing search performance and resource management
  - Monitoring and maintaining the health of your Splunk environment

Overview of Best Practices in Cybersecurity

Our reliance on technology has increased dramatically in the modern world. Digital platforms and services are used by businesses, governments, and individuals for a range of functions. However, as our reliance has grown, so have cyber threats, making cybersecurity more vital than ever. A cyberattack can have serious implications, ranging from financial losses and reputational harm to the compromise of sensitive data and significant legal responsibilities.

Fundamental Cybersecurity Principles

Protecting against a variety of digital risks, cybersecurity is a crucial component of contemporary digital operations. System, network, and data security require a continuous application of some basic concepts. Anyone wishing to safeguard their digital assets must comprehend these fundamental ideas. Here is a summary of the core ideas in cybersecurity:

1. Confidentiality

- Ensuring that only those with permission can access information. Protecting private and corporate information from unauthorized people or systems is the goal of confidentiality.
- Usually implemented using strong authentication procedures, access controls, and encryption.

2. Integrity

- Ensuring the correctness and consistency of data throughout its whole lifecycle. This implies that information cannot be changed in an unlawful or covert way.
- To trace changes and modifications, techniques including audit trails, version controls, hashes, and checksums are used.

3. Availability

- Ensuring that resources and information are accessible to authorized users at the appropriate time. This branch of cybersecurity focuses on guarding against and minimizing disruptions to service, such as hardware malfunctions and Denial of Service (DoS) assaults.
- Among the strategies are reliable disaster recovery plans, frequent software updates, and redundant systems.

4. Authentication

- Checking that a system, entity, or user is who they say they are before allowing them to access resources. Authentication guarantees that people or systems are who they say they are.
- May entail digital certificates, biometrics, two-factor authentication, and passwords.

5. Authorization

- The act of approving or rejecting a certain set of rights to access data and resources. A person, program, or process that has been authorized is guaranteed to be granted authorization to access resources in a proper and suitable manner.
- Controlled by access control lists (ACLs), role-based access control (RBAC), and other policy-based controls.

6. Non-Repudiation

- This is the guarantee that an individual cannot contest the legitimacy of their signature on a document or communication that they created.
- This idea is essential when it comes to contracts and legal issues. Comprehensive audit trails and digital signatures can offer non-repudiation.

7. Risk Management

- Recognizing, evaluating, and setting priorities for risks, then working together to reduce, track, and manage the likelihood or consequences of unfavorable occurrences.
- Frequent threat modeling, risk assessments, and the installation of security controls that correspond to the hazards that have been discovered.

8. Defense in Depth

- An advanced cybersecurity strategy that employs a variety of security methods to safeguard data. Other layers remain intact even if one fails.
- Involves a blend of administrative, technical, and physical controls examples include personnel training, physical security, and firewalls and antivirus programs.

9. The Least Privilege Principle

- Limiting access or permissions to what is necessary for people or systems to carry out their duties.

- Managing access through stringent controls and recurrent evaluations of user rights and permissions.

10. Incident Response

- Coordinating, handling, and recuperating from a cyberattack. The goal of incident response is to minimize damage while cutting expenses and recovery times.
- Creating and updating an incident response plan on a regular basis, training and practicing, and having a committed response team.

Any successful security strategy is built upon these core cybersecurity principles. Following these guidelines is crucial for defending large-scale enterprise networks as well as personal digital security. They provide a foundation for comprehending the intricate world of cybersecurity and provide direction for putting strong, practical security measures in place.

Role of Data Analytics in Cybersecurity

Data analytics has become an essential tool in the quickly developing field of cybersecurity for safeguarding digital assets. Data analytics plays a broad role in cybersecurity, helping with risk management, threat detection, and strategic decision-making. This is a thorough examination of how data analytics is changing the cybersecurity environment:

Enhanced Threat Detection and Monitoring

- **Real-Time Analysis**: Network traffic, logs, endpoint systems, and other sources of massive volumes of data may all be analyzed in real-time with the help of data analytics. This aids in the early identification of anomalies and possible security risks.
- **Pattern Recognition**: Trends and patterns that point to potential cyber threats, like atypical network traffic or unauthorized access to private information, can be found using sophisticated analytics tools. Even as they change, machine learning algorithms are very good at identifying these kinds of trends.

Improved Incident Response

- **Quick Response**: Data analytics can assist in ascertaining the seriousness and extent of a security problem promptly upon detection. For event response and mitigation to be effective, this quick evaluation is essential.
- **Forensic Analysis**: Data analytics after an incident helps forensic investigators determine the type of attack, the amount of damage, and

the attackers' strategies. To avoid such tragedies in the future, this understanding is essential.

Risk Management and Compliance

- **Danger assessment**: By processing and analyzing past security data, data analytics technologies can pinpoint network danger regions inside an organization. This aids in the application of risk management techniques that are more successful.
- **Compliance Monitoring**: Data analytics might be utilized by organizations to guarantee adherence to diverse regulatory mandates. They can show conformity to standards and pinpoint any non-compliance areas by evaluating security data.

Proactive Threat Intelligence

- **Threat Intelligence Feeds:** Information from several external sources can be integrated and processed using data analytics to create threat intelligence feeds. This gives a more comprehensive picture of the dangerous environment.
- **Predictive Analytics**: Based on present patterns, advanced data analytics, particularly those utilizing machine learning, can forecast potential security risks in the future. Due to this predictive capacity, businesses may proactively fortify their defenses.

Enhancing Security Posture with Strategic Insights

- **Trend Analysis:** Organizations may better grasp the dynamic nature of cyber hazards by utilizing long-term data analysis to identify trends and patterns in cybersecurity threats.
- **Strategic Decision-Making**: Data analytics insights allow for well-informed strategic choices to be made about resource allocation, cybersecurity policy, and technology investments.

Optimizing Security Operations

- **Automation and Efficiency**: By automating security procedures like threat detection and alerting, data analytics can improve the effectiveness of security operations.
- **Resource Allocation**: Data analytics assists organizations in more efficiently allocating their resources, concentrating on areas that require the greatest protection, by identifying the most important risks and weaknesses.

Data analytics is becoming more and more important in cybersecurity. The capacity to swiftly and effectively evaluate massive datasets is becoming increasingly important for effective security as cyber attacks become more complex. In the end, data analytics leads to a more robust and resilient cybersecurity posture by supporting strategic planning and decision-making in addition to improving the detection and response capabilities of cybersecurity teams.

Techniques for Effective use of Splunk in Cybersecurity

In this section, we'll look at how Splunk can help you improve your cybersecurity procedures. We'll delve into the complexities of Splunk's architecture, see how it connects with other security solutions, and find relevant security use cases for maximum protection.

Understanding Splunk's Architecture and Components

A thorough understanding of Splunk's components and architecture is essential for efficient cybersecurity utilization. The main elements of Splunk are as follows:

Core Architecture

- **Modular Structure:** Splunk's design is flexible and scalable because it is modular in nature. It is appropriate for a range of organizational demands because it can manage enormous amounts of data as well as little ones.
- **Data Ingestion and Indexing**: Splunk's primary function is to ingest and index data from a variety of sources, including network events, system metrics, and logs. In order to facilitate effective searching and analysis, this data is processed and saved in indexes.

Key Components of Splunk

1. Splunk Forwarder

- **Function**: In charge of gathering data in real-time. There are two kinds of forwarders: Heavy Forwarder (used for preprocessing and data filtering) and Universal Forwarder (used for data gathering).
- **Deployment**: Data is forwarded to the Splunk Indexers via installation on the data source systems.

2. Splunk Indexer

- **Function:** Converts machine data into searchable events by indexing it. The data storage is also managed by this component.
- **Capabilities:** The Indexer parses and segments data to provide effective search and analysis.

3. Splunk Search Head

- **Function:** Gives the user interface for searching. The Search Head is used by users to do searches, generate alerts, and construct dashboards.
- **Deployment:** For large-scale deployments, it can be either independent or a component of a Search Head cluster.

4. Splunk Deployment Server

- **Function**: Oversees the distributed environment's Splunk components. The deployment and upkeep of Splunk apps and configuration modifications across numerous forwarders and indexers are automated by it.
- **Usage**: Excellent for handling setups and dispersing content changes in large environments.

5. License Master

- **Role**: oversees the Splunk licenses. It keeps track of the amount of data indexed and guarantees adherence to licensing agreements.
- **Function**: Essential for controlling the overhead related to large volumes of data indexing.

6. Knowledge Manager

- **Function**: Enables users to produce knowledge items, such as computed fields, field extractions, and stored searches.
- **Goal:** Improves the data by providing context and intelligence, which makes searches more effective and perceptive.

7. Data Models and Pivot

- **Function**: Offers sophisticated methods for employing data models to organize, understand, and analyze data. Without requiring an extensive understanding of SPL (Search Processing Language), Pivot offers an interface for creating sophisticated reports and dashboards.

8. Splunk Apps and Add-Ons

- **Function:** Add features to Splunk's repertoire that are suited to various applications or data sources.

- **Variety:** Add-ons and apps are available for a range of uses, from industry requirements to technology monitoring.

Because of its flexible and scalable architecture, Splunk is a reliable option for handling and evaluating massive amounts of data. Together, its parts offer a complete platform for complicated data analysis, security monitoring, and operational intelligence. Knowing the functions of each component and how they work together is essential to maximizing Splunk's potential for a given company.

Integrating Splunk with Various Security Tools and Data Sources

To fully utilize Splunk for security monitoring, analysis, and response, it is essential to integrate it with a variety of security tools and data sources. Splunk is a priceless tool in security architecture because of its capacity to aggregate data from many sources and then correlate it. An overview of the several tools and data sources that Splunk can be integrated with is as follows:

Data Source Integration

- **Log Files and System Data:** Splunk is capable of absorbing information from the operating system, server, and application logs. This comprises information from Linux system logs, Windows event logs, and logs from other server apps.
- **Network Data**: To keep an eye on network activities, logs from switches, routers, and firewalls are essential. To get this information, Splunk can interface with a number of network management tools and protocols, including SNMP.
- **Cloud Services**: To gather logs and analytics, Splunk can establish connections with cloud service providers such as AWS, Azure, and Google Cloud Platform. Monitoring cloud-based apps and infrastructure requires this integration.
- **Endpoint Protection Platforms**: Splunk can gather information on antivirus events, file integrity monitoring, and other endpoint security alerts by integrating with endpoint security products.

Integration with Security Tools

- **SIEM Systems**: Splunk is a SIEM (Security Information and Event Management) system in and of itself, but it can also be integrated with other SIEM tools to improve the capabilities of its data gathering and processing.

- **Threat Intelligence Systems:** To enhance data with context and threat information and facilitate more efficient threat detection and response, Splunk may interact with external threat intelligence systems.
- The integration of Splunk with Identity and Access Management (IAM) solutions yields valuable insights into user activity, access patterns, and potential security breaches that may involve compromised user credentials.
- **Incident Response Tools**: Splunk can automate responses to certain security incident types through integration with incident response tools and platforms, resulting in faster and more efficient reaction times.

Advanced Integrations

- **Machine Learning and AI:** Splunk can provide predictive insights, anomaly detection, and advanced threat detection capabilities by utilizing machine learning models and AI-driven analytics tools.
- **Automation and Orchestration Tools:** Automated remediation of detected threats and security incidents is made possible by integrating Splunk with automation frameworks and orchestration tools, such as SOAR platforms.
- **Custom Applications:** By integrating Splunk with custom-built applications and systems, businesses may customize their security monitoring and analysis to meet their specific requirements thanks to the open API.

Best Practices for Integration

- **Data Normalization:** To facilitate precise analysis and correlation, make sure that data from various sources is standardized for consistency.
- **Scalability Considerations**: Make sure your system can grow, particularly if you're integrating with a lot of sources or massive data streams.
- **Security and Compliance:** Especially in regulated businesses, uphold security and compliance standards when combining Splunk with other solutions.

By integrating Splunk with a variety of security tools and data sources, businesses can establish a more comprehensive and successful security posture. Splunk improves its overall capacity to detect, evaluate, and respond to any security incidents by centralizing data gathering and processing, allowing for deeper insights into security threats.

Identifying Security Use Cases and Requirements

Understanding an organization's specific security use cases and requirements is the first step towards effectively safeguarding its digital infrastructure. This procedure entails determining the particular security goals and problems that an organization must meet. These steps then serve as a roadmap for the choice and execution of security policies and solutions. This is a thorough method for determining these important elements:

Understanding the Business Context

- **Business Operations**: Evaluate the organization's main business procedures, data transmission channels, and technological infrastructure. Determining what needs to be protected requires an understanding of the operational situation.
- **Industry-Specific risks**: Cyber risks vary depending on the industry. Customizing the security approach is made easier by recognizing typical risks in your industry, such as financial fraud in banking or ransomware in the healthcare sector.
- **Adherence to Regulations**: Ascertain the regulatory environment that applies to the company. Compliance mandates (like GDPR, HIPAA, or PCI-DSS) frequently specify particular security protocols.

Assessing the Asset and Data Landscape

- **Asset Inventory:** Make a thorough list of all of your digital and physical assets. Hardware, software, network infrastructure, and important data repositories are all included in this.
- **Data Classification**: Group information according to confidentiality and sensitivity. The most sensitive and valuable data should be prioritized when directing security efforts.
- **Risk Assessment**: To find weak points and possible entry points for threats, thoroughly evaluate your risks. Threats from the outside as well as the inside should be taken into account.

Identifying Key Security Objectives

- **Data Protection**: Specify the needs for safeguarding private and sensitive information, such as encryption, access limits and methods, to avoid data loss.
- **Threat Detection and Response:** Determine the objectives for incident response protocols and threat detection capabilities. This includes

determining the appropriate thresholds for alerting, monitoring, and reaction times.

- **User Access and Identity Management:** Establish what multi-factor authentication, role-based access controls, and user behavior monitoring are required for managing user access and identities.
- **Continuity and Resilience**: List the prerequisites for both IT resilience and business continuity. Planning for data backup, disaster recovery, and continuing business as usual in the event of security problems are all part of this.

Developing Use Cases

- **Scenario Planning**: Create detailed use cases or security scenarios that represent potential threats to the enterprise. These hypothetical situations aid in comprehending the real-world uses for security precautions.
- **Stakeholder Input**: Talk to a range of stakeholders, such as IT personnel, business unit managers, and end users, to get a variety of viewpoints on security requirements and expectations.
- **Benchmarking and Best Practices**: To learn how similar companies are handling their security issues, examine benchmarking data and industry best practices.

Documenting and Prioritizing Requirements

- **Documentation**: Draft a thorough document listing all needs and use cases for security that have been discovered. This document ought to be understandable, succinct, and available to the appropriate parties.
- **Prioritization:** Considering the limitations of resources, order the security requirements according to risk profiles, significance of regulations, and effects on business.

By understanding Splunk's architecture and components, integrating it with other security tools and data sources, and identifying the security use cases and requirements of your company, you can use it to effectively boost cybersecurity. By using these techniques, you'll be able to continuously improve your entire security posture, identify and address attacks in real-time, and obtain insightful information.

Best Practices for Data Ingestion and Normalization with Splunk

This section delves into the best practices for Splunk data import and standardization. We cover techniques for selecting the correct data inputs and forwarders, how to use the Common Information Model (CIM) to accomplish data standardization, and how to successfully manage data preservation and storage regulations for a streamlined and efficient cybersecurity operation.

Choosing the Right Data Inputs and Forwarders

Choosing the right data inputs and forwarders is critical for accurate and effective data intake in Splunk. Consider the following excellent practices:

- **Identify essential data sources:** Identify the data sources that are most relevant to your security use cases, such as firewall logs, network device logs, application logs, and endpoint logs.
- **Use Universal Forwarders (UF) for high-performance data forwarding:** Universal Forwarders are lightweight and can forward large volumes of data with low resource utilization. Use UFs for the majority of data collection chores.
- **Use Heavy Forwarders (HF) for data preprocessing:** Use Heavy Forwarders if you need to preprocess or filter data before sending it to the indexer. However, keep in mind that HFs utilize more resources than UFs, so use them sparingly.
- **Monitor files and directories:** Set up forwarders to monitor certain files and directories, ensuring that relevant log data is ingested as it is generated.
- **Assign appropriate sourcetypes to data inputs:** Assign an appropriate sourcetype to each data input to ensure accurate parsing, indexing, and searching of the data in Splunk.

Implementing Data Normalization using the Common Information Model (CIM)

In Splunk, data normalization is critical for effective data analysis and correlation. The Common Information Model (CIM) is a standardized data model that aids in the standardization of data. Use the following best practices while deploying CIM:

- **Use CIM-compatible add-ons and apps:** Whenever possible, use CIM-compatible Splunk add-ons and apps to ensure that data from many sources is normalized according to the CIM schema.

- **Map custom data sources to CIM:** If you have bespoke data sources that aren't supported by existing CIM-compatible add-ons, you'll need to construct custom field extractions and mapping rules to align the data with the CIM schema.
- **Validate data mapping:** Review and validate your data sources' mapping to the CIM schema on a regular basis to ensure data normalization is accurate and up to date.

Managing Data Retention and Storage Policies

Proper data retention and storage management are critical for keeping your Splunk implementation efficient and cost-effective. Consider the following best practices:

- **Establish retention policies based on data value:** Create retention policies for various categories of data depending on their value and relevance to your security use cases. Keep crucial data for extended periods of time while deleting less important info more regularly.
- **Configure index and volume settings:** Create distinct indexes and volumes for different sorts of data, each with its own retention settings. This method gives you more control over data preservation and helps you save money on storage.
- **Track data ingestion rates and storage consumption:** Track the volume of data ingested into Splunk as well as the storage usage of your deployment on a regular basis. This will assist you in identifying potential bottlenecks, optimizing resource utilization, and planning for future capacity needs.

You can ensure that your security data is accurate, consistent, and efficiently stored by following these best practices for data intake and normalization with Splunk. This foundation enables more effective analysis, correlation, and threat detection, ultimately boosting the entire cybersecurity posture of your firm.

Best Practices for Search and Analytics with Splunk

This section will cover best practices for search and analytics with Splunk. We will discuss how to write efficient and optimized search queries, how to create meaningful and actionable visualizations and dashboards, how to apply machine learning and advanced analytics for proactive threat hunting, and how to improve your cybersecurity defenses through strategic Splunk use.

Writing Efficient and Optimized Search Queries

Efficient and optimized search queries are critical for boosting Splunk deployment performance and obtaining accurate results. When creating search queries, keep the following best practices in mind:

- **Begin with a targeted search:** Focus your search on the data you wish to evaluate, using precise terms and filters to reduce the results.
- **Use time ranges:** By restricting your search to only the relevant time period, you can significantly reduce the processing time and resources required.
- **Use search commands wisely:** To boost search performance, use search commands such as stats, dedup, and top. When feasible, use converting commands such as stats and tstats instead of reporting commands such as time charts.
- **Filter data early:** Use filters as early in the search pipeline as possible to limit the amount of data handled in subsequent steps.
- **Use precise filters:** Improve search performance by using precise filters to decrease the amount of events returned, and avoid utilizing subsearches or wildcard searches, which can waste a lot of resources.

Creating Meaningful and Actionable Visualizations and Dashboards

Splunk has strong visualization and dashboard creation tools that help transform complicated data into useful insights. For the purpose of tracking, evaluating, and reporting on many facets of operational intelligence and cybersecurity, these visual aids are indispensable. This is a tutorial on creating dashboards and visualizations in Splunk that are useful and actionable:

Understanding the Data

- **Data Source Analysis**: Start by having a solid grasp of the data sources. Developing good visualizations requires an understanding of the data that is accessible, its format, and its significance.
- **Determine Crucial Metrics:** Choose the important metrics that require constant observation. These could include user behavior, threat occurrences, system performance data, or network traffic patterns.

Designing the Visualization

- **Select the Correct Visualization Type**: Select the right visualization type based on the data and the insights you wish to share. Splunk provides a number of options, including tables, charts, graphs, and maps.
- **Customization for Clarity**: Make your visuals more comprehensible and clear. Selecting appropriate color schemes, labels, and legends is required for this.
- **Contextual Relevance**: Verify that the information shown in each visualization is pertinent to the context. This could entail comparing various data points to present an all-encompassing picture.

Building Dashboards

- **Dashboard Planning**: Arrange the dashboard's design according to the audience's information requirements. Choose how many visualizations there will be and how they will be arranged.
- **Interactive Components**: Use interactive components such as drop-down menus, time-range pickers, and drill-downs. Users can engage with the dashboard and delve further into the data with these capabilities.
- **Real-Time Updating:** To ensure that operational dashboards provide the most recent information, and enable real-time data updating.

Enhancing Actionability

- **Notifications and Thresholds**: Make sure your dashboards include notifications. Establish thresholds for important metrics that, when surpassed, may cause alerts or other actions.
- **Actionable Insights**: Create dashboards that provide suggestions and insights in addition to data display.

Usability and Accessibility

- **User-Friendly Design**: Regardless of the level of technical proficiency of the target users, make sure dashboards are accessible and user-friendly.
- **Mobile Responsiveness**: Make sure dashboards are accessible and responsive across a range of platforms, given the growing use of mobile devices.

Testing and Feedback

- **Iterative Development**: Test and improve dashboards continuously in response to user input and changing information requirements.
- **Performance Optimization**: Even with big data sets, make dashboards run well by optimizing their loading times.

Documentation and Training

- **Provide Documentation**: Provide concise instructions on how to operate and understand the visualizations and dashboards.
- **Training Sessions:** To optimize the dashboards' usefulness and uptake, hold training sessions for users.

With Splunk, producing insightful and useful dashboards and visualizations requires a synthesis of art and science. It necessitates an awareness of design, a comprehension of the data, and a focus on the requirements of the end user. Effective dashboard design not only facilitates decision-making and action, but also offers critical insights that increase the efficacy of an organization's data-driven strategy overall.

Leveraging Machine Learning and Advanced Analytics for Proactive Threat Hunting

Splunk provides machine learning and advanced analytics technologies that can assist enterprises in proactively identifying threats and vulnerabilities. To efficiently use these features:

- **Make use of the Splunk Machine Learning Toolkit (MLTK):** The MLTK contains a number of pre-built algorithms and models for anomaly detection, grouping, and forecasting that can be applied to your security data.
- **Develop custom machine learning models:** Use Splunk's vast data and analytical capabilities to create bespoke models customized to your organization's specific security use cases.
- **Integrate with external analytics tools:** Integrate Splunk with external machine learning and analytics platforms as needed to enhance your analysis and threat detection capabilities.
- **Continuously refine models:** Review and update your machine learning models on a regular basis to ensure their effectiveness and relevance in an ever-changing threat landscape.

You can increase the performance, accuracy, and value of your security data analysis by following these best practices for search and analytics with Splunk. As a result, you will be able to detect and respond to threats more effectively and proactively, boosting your organization's entire cybersecurity posture.

Best Practices for Alerting and Reporting with Splunk

This section will look at the best practices for alerting and reporting with Splunk. Configuring meaningful alerts and notifications, providing comprehensive and actionable security reports, and integrating Splunk with Incident Response and IT Service Management (ITSM) solutions are key points of focus.

Configuring Meaningful Alerts and Notifications

Properly set alerts and notifications are critical for detecting and responding to security problems in a timely manner. Use the following best practices when configuring alerts in Splunk:

- **Provide explicit alert conditions:** Based on important security events, thresholds, and patterns, provide clear and detailed conditions for triggering alerts.
- **Use alert throttling:** Use alert throttling to avoid alert fatigue caused by a high volume of notifications. This can be accomplished by grouping comparable warnings together or by specifying a time range during which only one alert is created for a given circumstance.
- **Prioritize alerts:** Assign severity levels to alerts based on their potential impact, which assists security teams in prioritizing response efforts.
- **Create meaningful alarm messages:** Ensure that alert messages include pertinent information such as the nature of the issue, affected systems, and recommended actions.
- **Direct alerts to suitable teams:** To guarantee a timely response, direct alerts to the appropriate stakeholders, such as security teams, system administrators, or management.

Creating Comprehensive and Actionable Security Reports

Effective security reporting is critical for keeping track of your organization's security posture. When writing security reports in Splunk, keep the following recommended practices in mind:

- **Include security metrics:** Include metrics related to your organization's security goals and objectives, such as the number of detected threats, incident response times, or vulnerability remediation progress.
- **Use clear and concise graphics:** Present data in a clear and easily comprehensible format, highlighting significant patterns and insights through visuals such as charts, tables, and graphs.
- **Include actionable recommendations:** Based on the report's findings, provide specific recommendations for increasing security. This could involve actions to reduce risks, repair vulnerabilities, or improve detection capabilities.
- **Schedule regular reports:** Set Splunk to generate and send reports on a regular basis to keep stakeholders up to date on the organization's security state.

Integrating Splunk with Incident Response and ITSM tools

With its strong machine learning and sophisticated analytics features, Splunk provides a strong platform for proactive threat hunting. Organizations can greatly improve their capacity to identify, evaluate, and counter possible cybersecurity risks by utilizing these elements. Here's how proactive threat hunting in the context of cybersecurity can be done with Splunk:

Integrating Machine Learning with Splunk for Anomaly Detection

- **Splunk Machine Learning Toolkit (MLTK):** Create and implement unique machine learning models with the MLTK. These models are capable of being trained to recognize anomalies and peculiar patterns in data, which is a crucial sign of possible security risks.
- **Behavioral Analysis**: Utilize machine learning techniques in Splunk to examine the behavior of entities and users. These algorithms are able to identify abnormalities in behavior, which may point to hacked accounts or insider threats.
- **Predictive Threat Modeling**: By using Splunk's machine learning capabilities to forecast security events based on past data, you may better prepare for and avert possible threats.

Advanced Analytics for Comprehensive Data Analysis

- **Data Correlation**: To get a comprehensive picture of the security environment, use Splunk's sophisticated analytics to correlate data from a variety of sources, including network traffic, security logs, and endpoint data.

- **Automated Data Processing**: By using Splunk's analytics to handle heavy security data processing, threat hunters can concentrate on high-value analysis and decision-making.
- **Root Cause Identification**: To identify the methods behind attacks and help reinforce security measures, utilize Splunk to conduct root cause analysis of security incidents.

Proactive Threat Hunting Workflows in Splunk

- **Custom Dashboards**: For real-time monitoring of security events, warnings, and indicators of compromise (IoCs), create custom dashboards in Splunk.
- **Integration with Security technologies**: To improve data gathering and analysis, integrate Splunk with currently in-use security technologies including intrusion detection systems, endpoint protection, and SIEMs.
- **Continuous Model Training**: To preserve accuracy and relevance, continuously update and train Splunk's machine learning models using the most recent data and threat intelligence.

Enhancing Threat Intelligence

- **Intelligence Enrichment:** To help with the proactive identification of risks, Splunk can be used to give context and useful insights into threat intelligence data.
- **Community Collaboration**: Use Splunk to share knowledge and information with larger security communities, assisting in the development of group defense tactics and reaping their benefits.

Addressing Challenges and Ensuring Effective Use

- **Data Quality Management:** To provide precise and trustworthy insights, make sure the data utilized for analytics and machine learning in Splunk is relevant and of high quality.
- **Training and Expertise:** Equip the security team with the know-how needed to properly utilize Splunk's analytics and machine learning capabilities.
- **Balancing Automation with Expertise**: For the best outcomes, combine Splunk's automated features with the critical thinking and instincts of seasoned threat hunters.

By utilizing its machine learning and advanced analytics capabilities, Splunk offers a sophisticated platform for proactive threat hunting. Businesses may proactively identify and mitigate cybersecurity threats by using Splunk for anomaly detection, behavioral analysis, data correlation, and threat prediction. This allows them to stay one step ahead of the constantly changing digital threat landscape.

Best Practices for Scalability and Performance with Splunk

In this section, we'll discuss optimal methods for achieving scalability and performance with Splunk. We will look at how to create a scalable Splunk deployment architecture, how to optimize search performance and resource management, and how to monitor and maintain the health of your Splunk environment to ensure a resilient and high-performing cybersecurity platform.

Designing a Scalable Splunk Deployment Architecture

A scalable Splunk deployment architecture is critical for dealing with increasing data volumes and user demands. When creating your architecture, keep the following recommended practices in mind:

- **Use a distributed deployment:** Distribute Splunk components like forwarders, indexers, and search heads across numerous nodes to spread the burden and increase performance.
- **Enable indexer clustering:** Enable indexer clustering to improve data redundancy and availability, ensuring that your system can continue to operate even if a node fails.
- **Use search head clustering:** Search head clustering is used to disperse search workloads and improve fault tolerance. This aids in maintaining search performance as the number of users and queries increases.
- **Plan for future growth:** Create your deployment architecture with future growth in mind, making it easy to scale out by adding more nodes or resources as needed.

Optimizing Search Performance and Resource Management

Optimizing search performance and resource management is critical for keeping Splunk responsive and efficient. Remember the following best practices:

- **Use summary indexing:** Use summary indexing to precompute commonly used search results, lowering indexer workload, and improving search performance.
- **Put search scheduling and workload management in place:** Schedule resource-intensive searches during low-system utilization periods to reduce their influence on overall performance. To allocate resources depending on search priority, use workload management features.
- **Monitor search performance:** Examine search performance indicators, including execution time, resource utilization, and query complexity on a regular basis to discover and address any bottlenecks.
- **Optimize hardware resources:** Ensure that your Splunk deployment has enough hardware resources to handle the workload, such as CPU, memory, and storage. For increased indexing and search performance, consider adopting solid-state drives (SSDs).

Monitoring and Maintaining the Health of your Splunk environment

Monitoring and maintaining the health of your Splunk environment on a regular basis is crucial for guaranteeing optimal performance and reliability. Use the following best practices:

- **Monitor key performance metrics:** Review important performance measures such as indexing rate, search concurrency, and resource utilization on a regular basis to discover potential issues and guarantee smooth operation.
- **Use the Monitoring Console:** Use Splunk's built-in Monitoring Console to acquire insights into the health and performance of your deployment, discovering issues like resource bottlenecks, configuration errors, and hardware failures.
- **Implement regular maintenance routines:** To keep your Splunk environment working well, perform routine maintenance chores such as cleaning up old data, optimizing search artifacts, and updating configurations.
- **Test and verify changes:** Before making any changes to your Splunk environment, properly test and validate them in a staging or development environment to ensure they do not have a detrimental impact on performance or stability.

You can guarantee that your Splunk deployment remains responsive, dependable, and capable of handling expanding data volumes and user demands by following these best practices for scalability and performance. As a result, your organization's cybersecurity operations and overall security posture remain effective.

Conclusion

It has become clear from our extensive exploration of the nuances of using Splunk in the field of cybersecurity that its capabilities are both extensive and crucial for the current cyber landscape. The guidelines presented in this chapter serve as a starting point for anyone wishing to use Splunk to its fullest capacity in cybersecurity operations.

After providing a general outline of cybersecurity best practices, we underlined the significance of an all-encompassing strategy. Each session gave us a detailed look at how Splunk may be used to its fullest in various cybersecurity tasks as we went along. Cybersecurity professionals can improve their threat detection and response capabilities by learning ways for efficient use. The debate on data input and normalization shed light on how important it is to make sure that the system is fed with consistent and useful data. As with search, analytics, alerting, reporting, scalability, and performance, our investigation into these areas highlighted the importance of each component in turning Splunk into a force multiplier for cybersecurity operations.

However, it's imperative to keep in mind that the best practices described here are not merely standalone actions, but rather integral aspects of a comprehensive approach. Making sure that data is ingested effectively is useless if we can't search or analyze it effectively. Similar to reports, alerts are only as good as the data and analytics used to create them.

Tools like Splunk in the quickly changing field of cybersecurity are only as effective as the rules and procedures that govern their use. Therefore, it is essential to continually review, improve, and modify these best practices in order to stay one step ahead of cyber threats.

Let's solidify our understanding as we move on to the final chapter, *Conclusion and Summary*, and think about the bigger-picture implications of cybersecurity in the modern world. We will achieve this by using the knowledge we've gained throughout the book, making sure readers are not only informed but also motivated to take action, invent, and take the lead in the field of cybersecurity.

CHAPTER 15

Conclusion and Summary

Introduction

This chapter includes a detailed synopsis of the book's important subjects, including an overview of Splunk and its role in cybersecurity, data input and normalization, advanced cybersecurity applications, best practices for Splunk in cybersecurity, and more.

The chapter provides readers with a clear knowledge of how Splunk may be used to handle cybersecurity concerns by giving a recap of the essential concepts and best practices given in each part and chapter. It also provides insights into new cybersecurity issues and how Splunk is evolving to meet these concerns.

Overall, this chapter concludes the book by summarizing the important subjects and presenting insights into how Splunk might be utilized to handle today's cybersecurity concerns.

Structure

In this chapter, we will cover the following topics:

- Recap of key concepts
- Future of Splunk and cybersecurity
- Next steps for further learning and practice
- Final thoughts and recommendations
- Importance of continuous learning

Recap of Key Concepts

We have covered the fundamentals of utilizing Splunk in the context of cybersecurity throughout this book. We began by introducing Splunk and its architecture before moving on to learn how to configure inputs, ingest and normalize data, and use Splunk Enterprise Security (ES) for Security Information and Event Management (SIEM). In addition, we talked about security intelligence, forensic investigations, Splunk connectors, compliance, Security Orchestration, Automation, and Response (SOAR), cloud security, DevOps, and best practices for utilizing Splunk in cybersecurity.

- **Splunk and Cybersecurity:** We discussed the importance of cybersecurity in today's digital landscape, as well as the role of Splunk in assisting enterprises in improving their security posture. Splunk's capacity to collect, analyze, and visualize data from a variety of sources makes it a valuable tool for threat detection and incident response.
- **Splunk Architecture Overview:** We gave an overview of Splunk's components, such as forwarders, indexers, and search heads, and discussed how they operate together in a distributed deployment to manage data intake, indexing, searching, and visualization.
- **Configuring Inputs and Data Sources:** We talked about how to set up data inputs and forwarders to allow Splunk to collect and process data from a variety of sources, including log files, network devices, and security tools.
- **Data Ingestion and Normalization:** We discussed the process of ingesting data into Splunk and normalizing it using the Common Information Model (CIM), which enables more effective search, analysis, and reporting across disparate data sources.
- **Understanding SIEM:** We looked at the notion of Security Information and Event Management (SIEM) and how Splunk Enterprise Security (ES) can be used as a full-fledged SIEM solution, offering real-time monitoring, correlation, and analysis of security events.
- **Splunk Enterprise Security (ES):** We investigated the features and capabilities of Splunk ES, such as its correlation engine, risk scoring methodology, and security dashboards, which assist security teams in more quickly detecting, investigating, and responding to threats.
- **Security Intelligence:** We discussed how Splunk can be used to develop security intelligence by analyzing data trends, detecting abnormalities, and identifying indicators of compromise (IOCs) that can assist organizations in responding to threats proactively.

- **Security Domain Forensic Investigation:** We looked at how Splunk may be used for forensic investigations by offering deep insights into security incidents, assisting analysts in uncovering fundamental causes, and reconstructing attack timelines.
- **Splunk Integration with Other Security Products:** To develop a cohesive security ecosystem, we stressed the significance of integrating Splunk with other security products and platforms, such as firewalls, intrusion detection systems, and endpoint protection solutions.
- **Splunk for Compliance and Regulatory Standards:** We discussed how Splunk may assist organizations in meeting compliance and regulatory standards by monitoring sensitive data access, establishing audit trails, and providing pre-built compliance reports.
- **Security Orchestration, Automation, and Response (SOAR) with Splunk:** We addressed how Splunk can be used to develop SOAR capabilities, automate and streamline incident response procedures, and improve security team collaboration.
- **Splunk for Cloud Security:** We looked at how Splunk can be used to monitor and secure cloud-based infrastructure and applications, offering visibility and insights into potential security issues in cloud environments.
- **DevOps and Security Operations:** We discussed Splunk's role in bridging the gap between DevOps and Security Operations, allowing enterprises to adopt a DevSecOps approach and improve application and infrastructure security.
- **Best Practices for Splunk in Cybersecurity:** We discussed different best practices for efficiently using Splunk in cybersecurity, including data input and standardization, search and analytics, alerting and reporting, and ensuring scalability and performance.

Future of Splunk and Cybersecurity

As cybersecurity threats diversify and become more complex, the demand for advanced security solutions such as Splunk will only increase. Here are some areas where we may anticipate Splunk's and cybersecurity's future development:

- **Enhanced Artificial Intelligence and Machine Learning:** Splunk will continue to invest in and integrate AI and machine learning technologies for better threat detection, anomaly identification, and automated response. These technologies will allow security teams to identify and respond to attacks proactively, lowering the time it takes to notice and remediate security issues.

- **Greater Integration and Interoperability:** As the security landscape gets more complicated, there will be a greater need for a unified security ecosystem. Splunk's integration capabilities with other security products, platforms, and APIs will most certainly be expanded in order to deliver a more smooth and complete security management solution. Organizations will find it easier to manage their security posture across numerous tools and environments as a result of this.
- **Advanced Analytics and Visualization:** Splunk will continue to improve its analytics and visualization capabilities, making it easier for security professionals to detect patterns, trends, and correlations in security data. New visualization techniques and enhanced dashboard capabilities will assist firms in making more informed decisions and effectively responding to threats.
- **Cloud and Multi-Cloud Security:** As enterprises progressively adopt cloud and multi-cloud settings, there will be a greater need for effective cloud security solutions. Splunk will concentrate on improving its ability to deliver visibility and insights into potential security issues in cloud environments. This includes improved support for monitoring cloud-based infrastructure, applications, and services, as well as integration with other cloud-native security tools and platforms.
- **Zero Trust Security:** The Zero Trust security approach, which is based on the philosophy of "never trust, always verify," is gaining popularity as a means to enhance the protection of enterprises against cyber threats. Splunk will certainly include new features and capabilities to help with the adoption of Zero Trust security solutions, including continuous authentication, least privilege access control, and micro-segmentation.
- **Managed Security Services:** As enterprises face growing cybersecurity issues and skills shortages, managed security services will gain popularity. Splunk may increase its capabilities in this area, offering firms outsourced security management and monitoring solutions to assist them in maintaining their security posture without the need to hire and train additional in-house staff.
- **IoT and Edge Computing Security:** As IoT devices and edge computing proliferate, companies face new security challenges. Splunk will almost certainly develop additional capabilities and integrations to assist enterprises in monitoring, analyzing, and securing IoT and edge computing environments, as well as providing visibility into device behavior and detecting possible security concerns.
- **Continuous Security Monitoring and Adaptive Response:** Organizations will need more flexible and dynamic security systems in the future that can adapt to ever-changing threats. Splunk will keep improving its capabilities

for continuous security monitoring and adaptive response, assisting organizations in maintaining a strong security posture in the face of evolving threats. This could incorporate features such as automated threat hunting, real-time risk assessment, and dynamic policy enforcement that can adapt to new information and changing circumstances.

- **Privacy and Data Protection:** As data privacy standards become more stringent, enterprises will need to guarantee that sensitive information is protected and that regulatory obligations are met. Splunk will almost certainly bring additional features and capabilities to assist enterprises in monitoring and managing data privacy, such as improved data classification, data loss prevention, and compliance reporting.
- **Workforce Training and Skills Development:** To address the growing cybersecurity skills gap, Splunk may invest in workforce training and skills development initiatives such as online courses, workshops, and certifications designed to keep security professionals up to date on the latest cybersecurity trends, technologies, and best practices.

Finally, the future of Splunk and cybersecurity will most certainly witness continuing innovation and growth in areas such as AI and machine learning, integration, cloud security, and advanced analytics, among others. Splunk will play a critical role in assisting enterprises to stay ahead of emerging threats and maintain a strong security posture as the cybersecurity landscape evolves.

Next Steps for Further Learning and Practice

Consider the following steps to expand your study and practical experience with Splunk and its applications in cybersecurity:

Splunk Training and Certifications

In order to provide people with the abilities and information required to utilize and administer Splunk's products and solutions, the company offers an extensive array of training programs and certifications. A wide range of positions, including administrators, developers, architects, and security specialists, are catered to by these training courses and certifications. This is a summary of the certification and training programs offered by Splunk:

- **Splunk Training Programs**
    - **Splunk Fundamentals**: For individuals who are unfamiliar with the platform, these courses, such as **Splunk Fundamentals 1** and **Splunk**

Fundamentals 2, address the fundamentals of Splunk's core software. Subjects covered include dashboards, searching, reporting, and fundamental data analysis.

- **Advanced Courses**: Splunk provides advanced courses that explore sophisticated searching, reporting, and alerting for those with more experience. These consist of classes on large data analysis, sophisticated dashboards, and leveraging Splunk's machine learning toolkit.
- **Role-Based Training**: Splunk offers tailored instruction for various positions. For instance, **Splunk for Developers** prioritizes creating apps and custom solutions, whereas **Splunk for Administrators** concentrates on installation, configuration, and management.
- **Splunk Security Courses**: Designed with security experts in mind, these courses cover how to use Splunk for incident investigations, enterprise security, and security information and event management (SIEM).
- **Custom and On-Site Training**: To meet the unique demands of a company, Splunk also provides customized training solutions that can be given digitally or on-site.

- **Splunk Certifications**
    - **Splunk Core Certified User**: For individuals who are unfamiliar with Splunk, this is an entry-level certification. This certification attests to a person's fundamental knowledge of Splunk's main software.
    - **Splunk Core Certified Power User**: This credential indicates a more thorough comprehension of the knowledge object generation process as well as Splunk's search and reporting functions.
    - **Splunk Enterprise Certified Admin**: This certification covers the management facets of the Splunk Enterprise environment and is targeted at system administrators.
    - **Splunk Enterprise Certified Architect**: Those in charge of intricate Splunk Enterprise setups need to possess a thorough grasp of Splunk best practices and scalability.
    - **Splunk Certified Developer**: This certification is intended for experts who use the Splunk Web Framework to create applications.
    - **Splunk Security Certificates**: These include the **Splunk IT Service Intelligence Certified Admin** and **Splunk Enterprise Security Certified Admin** certificates, which concentrate on certain operational intelligence and security applications.

- **Benefits of Splunk Training and Certification**
  - **Skill Enhancement**: Individuals can use training programs to improve their knowledge and abilities, which makes it possible for them to use Splunk more successfully in their jobs.
  - **Professional Development**: Certifications in Splunk are widely accepted in the field and can greatly enhance a professional's qualifications and employment prospects.
  - **Organizational Efficiency**: Having trained Splunk professionals on staff can help businesses use Splunk more effectively and efficiently, making the most of their platform investment.

  For those wishing to become more proficient with Splunk, both individuals and businesses can benefit from Splunk's training and certification programs. Splunk's educational programs support a wide range of demands and skill levels, whether one is starting from zero or wants to specialize in a particular area. This helps to cultivate a trained workforce capable of utilizing Splunk's suite of tools to the fullest.

- **Practical Experience:** Create a Splunk lab environment to explore utilizing the platform in real-world circumstances, such as test data ingestion, search and analytics, alerting, and dashboard generation. Hands-on experience will help you become more adept with Splunk and better understand how to apply it to the security demands of your organization.
- **Participate in Splunk Community Forums:** Connect with the Splunk community by participating in forums, discussion groups, and online platforms. These communities can give you valuable insights, tips, and advice from other Splunk users, helping you to benefit from their experiences and better understand the platform.
- **Attend Industry Conferences and Events:** Attend cybersecurity conferences, webinars, and events featuring Splunk. These events frequently highlight new features, best practices, and use cases that can help you remain up to date on the latest Splunk and cybersecurity advances.
- **Read Industry Blogs and Publications:** Follow industry blogs and publications to stay up to date on the latest Splunk releases, features, and use cases. Splunk's official blog and other credible sources can assist you in staying current on new trends, technologies, and best practices.
- **Investigate Splunk applications and Add-ons:** Splunk offers a large ecosystem of applications and add-ons created by Splunk and third-party developers. Examine these resources to discover how to

combine Splunk with other security products and platforms and to improve the functionality of your Splunk deployment.

- **Participate in Professional Networking:** Reach out to other security professionals, Splunk users, and experts to share knowledge, experiences, and best practices. Networking can help you learn more about Splunk and its applications in cybersecurity while also providing possibilities for collaboration and professional development.
- **Participate in Open-Source initiatives:** There are numerous open-source initiatives linked to Splunk and cybersecurity that you may contribute to and learn from. Participating in these initiatives allows you to hone your skills while giving back to the community. One prominent open-source initiative linked to Splunk and cybersecurity that you can contribute to and learn from is the Open Cybersecurity Schema Framework (OCSF). This project was initiated by AWS and Splunk, along with contributions from other cybersecurity companies. It focuses on creating a common vendor-agnostic taxonomy to simplify and accelerate the ingestion and analysis of security data, thereby facilitating improved detection, investigation, and mitigation of cyberattacks.
- **Stay Informed on Cybersecurity Trends:** Follow industry news, research reports, and expert analysis to stay up to current on the latest cybersecurity trends, threats, and technology. This will assist you in better understanding the changing threat landscape and how to use Splunk to handle emerging security concerns.
- **Continual Learning and Skill Growth:** As the cybersecurity landscape evolves, always strive for continual learning and skill growth. Update your knowledge and abilities on a regular basis to keep ahead of emerging dangers and ensure that you can utilize Splunk successfully to defend your organization's digital assets.

Final Thoughts and Recommendations

We recommend investigating the following sites as you continue to extend your understanding of Splunk and cybersecurity to keep informed and up to date on the newest innovations, best practices, and use cases:

- **Official Splunk Documentation:** The official Splunk documentation is a great place to start learning about the platform, its features, and use cases. Installation, configuration, data ingestion, and app development are among the subjects covered in the documentation. Splunk Docs can be found on the web: https://docs.splunk.com/

- **Splunk Blogs:** The official Splunk blog contains articles produced by Splunk professionals on a variety of topics such as cybersecurity, data analytics, and product updates. Visit the Splunk Blogs website: https://www.splunk.com/en_us/blog
- **YouTube Channels:**

  Splunk: Splunk's official YouTube channel features product demos, training, use cases, and customer success stories. Join the Splunk YouTube channel: https://www.youtube.com/@Splunkofficial

  Splunk .conf: Splunk's annual conference event includes talks and seminars on a variety of Splunk and cybersecurity subjects. Many prior conferences' sessions are available on YouTube. Subscribe to YouTube channel: https://www.youtube.com/@Splunkofficial
- **Books:**

  Splunk 7.x Quick Start Guide by James H. Baxter

  Splunk Operational Intelligence Cookbook by Bill Mathews, Derek Mock, and Josh Diakun

  Splunk Developer's Guide by Kyle Smith
- **Online Training and Courses:**

  Splunk Education: Splunk provides a number of training courses, workshops, and certifications to assist you in learning and mastering the platform. Investigate Splunk Education's offerings:
  https://www.splunk.com/en_us/training

  Coursera: Coursera offers a wide range of cybersecurity-related courses and specializations to help you advance your expertise in the industry. Visit the cybersecurity courses on Coursera:
  https://www.coursera.org/courses?query=cybersecurity
- **Forums and Communities:**

  Splunk Answers: Splunk Answers is a community-driven platform where users may ask questions, share information, and cooperate on Splunk and cybersecurity solutions. Visit Splunk Answers:
  https://answers.splunk.com/

  Splunk User Groups: Splunk User Groups (SplunkTrust) are regional communities where Splunk enthusiasts can interact, share experiences, and learn from one another. Look for a Splunk User Group in your region:
  https://usergroups.splunk.com/

- **Podcasts:**

  SplunkTalk: SplunkTalk is a podcast that provides interviews, news, and insights about Splunk and its different uses. Listen to SplunkTalk podcasts: https://www.splunk.com/en_us/blog/tag/podcast.html

  Cybersecurity Podcasts: There are many podcasts that address cybersecurity news and developments. Some examples are *The CyberWire*, *Darknet Diaries*, and *Security Now*.

- **Social Media:**

  Splunk can be found on Twitter (@splunk) for updates, news, and insights about Splunk and cybersecurity.

  Join relevant LinkedIn groups, such as *Splunk Users* and *Cybersecurity Professionals*, to meet like-minded people and stay current on industry news.

You may enhance your awareness of the platform and its applications while staying up to date on the latest trends and best practices by exploring these resources and connecting with the Splunk and cybersecurity communities. Keep in mind that the cybersecurity landscape is continuously changing, and ongoing learning is required to keep ahead of emerging threats.

Conclusion

We started by dissecting Splunk's complex architecture in order to conduct a thorough investigation of its function in contemporary cybersecurity. Our discussions on configuring inputs, data sources, and the complexities of data ingestion were all supported by this foundation. In order to keep Splunk a formidable tool in any security professional's toolbox, the focus throughout was on the crucial need to properly feed and format data.

As the investigation progressed, the inclusion of SIEM demonstrated Splunk's vast range of capabilities, particularly when focusing on Splunk Enterprise Security (ES) and security intelligence. Splunk's vital function in retrospective analysis and threat hunting was made clear in the portions on forensic investigation. However, its adaptability in the quickly changing field of cloud security, as well as its resilience in assuring compliance with regulatory requirements, made clear just how versatile it is.

The chapters on SOAR, DevOps, and security operations, which marked the end of our voyage, demonstrated the range of Splunk's capabilities, ranging from real-time threat detection and response to bridging the developmental and security gaps for secure application delivery. Our final best practices guide provided a road map for using Splunk effectively in the field of cybersecurity. As we get to a conclusion, it is abundantly evident that Splunk can serve as an ever-evolving defense against contemporary cyber threats.

Index

B

C

D

M

N

P

Q

R

S